SHAME

SERIES IN AFFECTIVE SCIENCE

Series Editors
Richard J. Davidson
Paul Ekman
Klaus Scherer

SHAME

Interpersonal Behavior,

Psychopathology,

and Culture

Edited by
Paul Gilbert
Bernice Andrews

New York   Oxford

Oxford University Press

1998

Oxford University Press

Oxford   New York

Athens   Auckland   Bangkok   Bogotá   Buenos Aires   Calcutta
Cape Town   Chennai   Dar es Salaam   Delhi   Florence   Hong Kong   Istanbul
Karachi   Kuala Lumpur   Madrid   Melbourne   Mexico City   Mumbai
Nairobi   Paris   São Paulo   Singapore   Taipei   Toyko   Toronto   Warsaw

and associated companies in
Berlin   Ibadan

Copyright © 1998 by Oxford University Press, Inc.

Published by Oxford University Press, Inc.
198 Madison Avenue, New York, New York 10016

Oxford is a registered trademark of Oxford University Press

Library of Congress Cataloging-in-Publication Data
Shame : interpersonal behavior, psychopathology, and culture /
edited by Paul Gilbert, Bernice Andrews.
p. cm.—(Series in affective science)
Includes bibliographical references and index.
ISBN 0-19-511479-5; 0-19-511480-9 (pbk)
1. Shame. 2. Shame—Social aspects. I. Gilbert, Paul.
II. Andrews, Bernice. III. Series.
BF575.S45S53 1998
152.4—DC21   97-44735

3 5 7 9 8 6 4 2

Printed in the United States of America
on acid-free paper

Preface

Shame has been recognized since antiquity. A strong theme of shame exists in the early stories of Adam and Eve. However, it has only been in the last 20 years or so that shame has been subject to systematic research and theory development. In this volume we have brought together key individuals who are active in research, theory, and therapy. We hope to offer a book that covers the variety of approaches to shame, as well as ways of conceptualizing shame.

The two introductory chapters in Part I attempt to cover some of the core issues and current controversies concerning shame. Many of the issues covered in the first of these chapters—such as the relationship of shame to negative internal and external evaluation, the linkage with anxiety and anger, and the way in which shame acts as a modulator of interpersonal and social relationships—are taken up as key themes by other authors throughout the book. The second chapter explores methodological and definitional issues related to the study of shame, with a focus on research, since it is only by empirical investigation that a number of the controversies will ultimately be answered. The point is made that, as yet, there remain a large number of obstacles to be overcome in regard to research methodology and shame.

In Part II, on interpersonal behavior, Alan Schore continues his well-regarded explorations into the role of shame on the development of the infant brain. As he points out, by the time the child has become mobile, the primary caregiver has moved from being purely a provider to also being a socializer. As the child enters the domains of prohibitions, shame and the use of shaming play a significant role in the control of the child's behavior. This in turn has major impacts on brain maturation. In chapter 4, Dacher Keltner and Lee Anne Harker explore the fascinating concept of shame in relation to appeasement behavior. The nonverbal communication signals of shame have been recognized for some time (e.g., eye gaze avoidance, slumped posture). The authors, however, explore recent research to present an important hypothesis regarding the appeasement function of shame. In chapter 5, Paul Gilbert and Michael McGuire continue with this theme, exploring the way shame has evolved from submissive appeasement signals, particularly following conflicts between conspecifics. However, they point out that human status and submission tend to be related to specific roles. One can feel inferior in a particular role, for instance, as a leader, as a parent, or as a sexual partner. Gilbert and McGuire explore how humans are motivated to obtain status by being seen as attractive and how shame is often linked to "unattractiveness." Chapter 6, by Michael Lewis, explores the important relationship between shame as a personal and interpersonal construct and stigma as a social label. In chapter 7, James Macdonald considers the notion that shame often involves fear of disclosure. The normal characteristic of a shamed individual is to conceal and hide from view that which is shameful. Macdonald, however, shows that there is far more disclosure of shameful information, particularly in psychotherapeutic contexts, than current research might suggest.

Part III explores the linkage between shame and psychopathology. Again, this is a domain that has a fairly long history in psychoanalysis, although guilt and shame have often been treated as the same phenomenon. In chapter 8, Digby Tantam explores the idea that shame can be understood as a sentiment. He outlines the way in which sentiments may differ from emotions and how sentiments are rather long-lived dispositions which may increase proneness to certain kinds of emotional disorders. In chapter 9, Bernice Andrews explores the link of trauma-induced shame to early physical and sexual abuse and psychopathology. She reviews much of her recent research in the area, noting the important link between abuse, shame, and chronic depression. In chapter 10, Thomas Scheff explores shame via content analysis within the framework of labeling theory. This chapter exposes the way shame often operates in certain kinds of interpersonal conflicts and the manner in which these can be understood by careful content analysis of discourses. In chapter 11, Suzanne Retzinger considers the role of shame in therapeutic countertransference. She makes it clear that shame can disrupt the social bond in both the therapist and the patient. She provides fascinating case material showing how this actually happens and how it is detrimental to the therapy process.

All of these chapters address the important role that shame can play in psychopathology. The authors are concerned with outlining how shame can play a role not only in the formation of pathology and its manifestation but also in efforts to treat pathology.

Part IV raises the important notion that shame is not just related to internal experiences but that notions of shame act as socially shared information about one's status and standing in the community. In chapter 12, Deborah Greenwald and David Harder explore the evolutionary and cultural aspects of shame. They point out that shame seems to be closely associated with some specific domains of social behavior, such as conformity, prosocial, and sexual behavior. Nearly all cultures have some means by which they shame individuals who step out of line in these areas. In chapter 13, Nancy Lindisfarne explores the important notion that the honor and shame systems of males and females can be intimately linked within a socially constructed view of honor. She explores how female virginity and control over female virginity can be a matter of honor, prestige, and shame for males in certain cultures. In chapter 14, Dov Cohen, Joseph Vandello, and Adrian Rantilla take us further into the cultural dynamics of shame by exploring the way social discourses about honor can shape behavioral and emotional responses to insults. They combine a complex and informative experimental methodology within a socially articulate model of shame and honor.

Shame can mean different things to different people. This is both a challenge and a danger. The challenge is not necessarily to homogenize all views of shame but to try to clarify how the different domains operate and how researchers, theorists, and therapists define the concept of shame. The fact that shame can operate at the level of the individual, the interpersonal relationship, the group, and even the culture suggests that, unlike other phenomena such as social anxiety, shame has implicit meanings that go beyond the personal. Shame cannot therefore be seen purely as a self-conscious experience but as one which encapsulates a multitude of domains that relate to social interaction. Indeed, to be unaware of what is shameful within one's social group is to risk both serious damage to one's social identity and ostracism.

Derby   P.G.
Surrey   B.A.
August 1997

Acknowledgments

The idea for this book grew out of a small working group that first met in 1994. James Macdonald organized a "Shame Group" at the University of Warwick, which provided the opportunity for people interested in the topic to exchange many ideas and develop new concepts. The Shame Group has now moved to the University of Derby and meets about twice a year. Another key factor was the encouragement and support of Dr. Paul Ekman. After a very enjoyable breakfast at a Cambridge conference in 1995, Dr. Ekman thought the idea for a book on shame, which focuses on social behavior, might fit in with Oxford University Press's Series on Affective Science. He has been extremely helpful in facilitating this process. We also thank Joan Bossert at Oxford University Press, who was able to take our fledgling ideas for a book and help us develop them into a more robust project. Elaine Kehoe's hard work as copyeditor for the manuscripts brought significant improvements in style and comprehensibilty. Last, but not least, we thank all the authors for their efforts in making our job both a pleasure and a learning experience.

Contents

Contributors

Bernice Andrews
Department of Psychology
Royal Holloway
University of London
Egham
Surrey, United Kingdom TW20 OEX

Dov Cohen
Department of Psychology
University of Illinois
Champaign, Illinois 61820

Paul Gilbert
Department of Clinical Psychology
Mental Health Research Unit
Kingsway Hospital
Derby, United Kingdom DE22 3LZ

Deborah F. Greenwald.
Department of Counseling
Northeastern University
Boston, Massachusetts 02115

David W. Harder
Psychology Department
Tufts University
Medford, Massachusetts 02155

Lee Anne Harker
Department of Psychology
University of Wisconsin
Madison, Winconsin

Dacher Keltner
Department of Psychology
University of California
Berkeley, California 94720

Michael Lewis
Institute for the Study of
    Child Development
Robert Wood Johnson Medical
    School
97 Paterson Street
New Brunswick, New Jersey 08903

Nancy Lindisfarne
School of Oriental and African
    Studies
Anthropology Department
University of London
Thornhaugh Street,
Russell Square
London, United Kingdom WC1H
    OXG

James Macdonald
The Salomons Centre
David Salomons Estate
Broomhill Road
South Bourough
Tunbridge Wells,
Kent, United Kingdom Tn3 OTG

Michael T. McGuire
Neuropsychiatric Institute
University of California
760 Westwood Plaza
Los Angeles, California 90024

Adrian K. Rantilla
Department of Psychology
University of Illinois
Champaign, Illinois 61820

Suzanne Retzinger
3009 Lomita Road
Santa Barbara, California 93105

Thomas J. Scheff
Department of Sociology
University of California
Santa Barbara, California 93105

Allan N. Schore
Department of Psychiatry and
    Biobehavioral Sciences
School of Medicine
University of California
Los Angeles, California

Digby Tantam
Centre for Psychotherapeutic Studies
University of Sheffield
16, Claremont Crescent
Sheffield, United Kingdom S10 2TA

Joseph Vandello
Department of Psychology
University of Illinois
Champaign, Illinois 61820

PART I

CONCEPTUAL ISSUES

1

What Is Shame?

Some Core Issues and Controversies

Paul Gilbert

Much has changed since Helen Lewis (1987a) wrote of shame as the "hidden emotion" and the "sleeper in psychopathology." Indeed, over the last 10 to 15 years shame has been subject to much research and theory, as Tangney and Fischer's (1995) landmark volume shows. Recently, S. Miller argued that shame is now so commonly seen as "the bedrock of psychopathology" and "the gold to be mined psychotherapeutically" that there has been neglect of other emotions and their interaction with shame (1996, p. 151). But while some researchers believe there is a growing consensus about shame—what it is and how it works—this chapter voices caution. There are still many differences of view, and as Andrews (this volume, chapter 2) points out, we do not yet have the methodologies to explore these differences empirically.

A wide variety of shame theories are rooted in different schools of thought. These include *psychoanalytic* theories such as Jungian (Jacoby, 1994), Kohutian self-psychology (Morrison, 1987; Wurmser, 1987), and various combinations (Lansky, 1992; S. Miller, 1996; Mollon, 1993). Shame has been studied using *affect* (e.g., Kaufman, 1989; Nathanson, 1992; Tomkins 1963, 1987a), *affect-cognitive* (e.g., M. Lewis 1992, 1993, 1995), and *cognitive-behavioral* (e.g., Beck, Emery, & Greenberg, 1985; Klass, 1990) theories. Developmental psychologists have different ideas about the origins of shame (Barrett, 1995); some believe it can occur in the first months of life (Nathanson, 1992; Schore, 1994); others suggest that shame is a social emotion not present until much later, starting around 2 or 3 years of age (M. Lewis, 1993, 1995; Stipek, 1995). There are also sociological and anthropological approaches to shame (e.g., Cohen, Vandello, & Rantilla, this volume, chapter 14; Goffman, 1968; Lindisfarne, this volume, chapter 13; Scheff, 1988).

Not only are there different schools and theoretical approaches to shame, but it can also be conceptualized and studied in terms of its components and mechanisms (Tangney, 1996). It can be examined in terms of *emotion* (e.g., as a primary affect in its own right, as an auxiliary emotion, or as a composite of other emotions such as fear, anger, or self-disgust); *cognitions and beliefs* about the self (e.g., that one is and/or is seen by others to be inferior, flawed, inadequate, etc.); *behaviors and actions* (e.g., such as running away, hiding and concealing, or attacking others to cover one's shame); *evolved mechanisms* (e.g., the expression of shame seems to use similar biobehavioral systems to those of animals expressing submissive behavior); and *interpersonal dynamic interrelationships* (shamed and shamer; Fossum & Mason, 1986; Harper & Hoopes, 1990). Shame can also be used to describe phenomena at many different levels, including internal self-experiences, relational episodes, and cultural practices for maintaining honor and prestige.

This chapter explores some of these components, with a special focus on shame emotions and cognitions, and shame-proneness. It attempts to draw attention to overlapping areas of psychological theory and research; for example, the complexity of the cognition-emotion interface. It is suggested that shame researchers and theorists may be in danger of creating yet another subdivision within psychology, with its own key concepts and literature, and with a risk of becoming detached from closely related fields.

Emotions and Shame

Tangney (1990, 1996) argued that shame experiences are primarily ones of "emotion," occurring at specific points in time. Fischer and Tangney argue that "emotions play a basic, adaptive part in human functioning by organising action tendencies that mould, constrain or structure human activity, and thought" (1995, p. 6). Although people can set out to purposefully induce certain emotions such as excitement and pleasure, or to avoid situations associated with negative emotions, many emotional experiences are involuntary. And this is very much the case with shame. Shame is an unwanted and difficult-to-control experience. Tangney (1996) argues that shame experiences should not be confused with preexisting factors, such as low self-esteem, that can be precursors of shame. Nor should shame be confused with post-shame affect. For example, after an experience of shame and feeling devalued people might become depressed, withdrawn, irritable, and so forth. Shame can change mental states from which other affects and moods can flow. And shame can meld into a sense of one's own identity (e.g, as flawed, a failure, unlovable, etc.).

However, even when we focus on specific episodes of shame, there remains controversy over exactly what kind of emotion shame might be. The sections that follow explore aspects of shame affect. It will not discuss *differences* between shame and embarrassment (R. Miller, 1996; Tangney & Miller, 1996), shyness (Cheek & Melchior, 1990), or guilt (Baumeister, Stillwell, & Heatherton, 1994; Gilbert, 1997a), as these have been explored by others.

Shame and Positive Affect

Tomkins (1963) was one of the first to suggest that shame was an innate affect with its own facial display pattern. Writing at the time of the decline of motivational theories and the rise of the cognitive revolution, Tomkins's affect theory was original and offered a useful counter to the "cold" landscape of affects as purely cognitively driven. Tomkins (1981) argued that affects make things matter. Without them nothing may matter; with them anything can. Affect theorists have played a major role in highlighting the importance of shame. Shame, Tomkins believed, is triggered by situations that result in the interruption of pleasure:

> I posit shame as an innate affect auxiliary response and a specific inhibitor of continuing interest and enjoyment. As disgust operates only after something has been taken in, shame operates only after interest or enjoyment has been activated; it inhibits one, or the other or, both.
> The innate activator of shame is the incomplete reduction of interest or joy. (Tomkins, 1987a, p. 143)

Nathanson (1992), who has done much to develop Tomkins's theory of shame, also argues that shame-humiliation is an affect program designed to be triggered in those situations when there is an impediment to the continuation of positive affect but the person remains interested and desirous of the thing that produces positive affect. Nathanson notes that "shame is an auxiliary to the positive affects, rather than a true innate affect . . . [but] bears all the properties of the other affects" (1992, p. 138). Its evolved function is to interrupt and modulate positive affect. Indeed, Nathanson argues that "Earlier in evolution, before the development of the 'higher centers' of cognition, all that shame affect did was turn off positive affects. But the more complex the brain became, the more functions could be influenced by shame." (1992, p. 141).

Shame will certainly interrupt positive affect, especially in social situations, but the idea that shame is an innate affect system, triggered *by and for* the interruption of positive affect, has been criticized (e.g., see Reimer, 1996). Indeed, some years ago Mandler (1975) developed an important approach to emotions in general based on the fact that interruptions in goals and plans (and positive affect) can have many emotional consequences. For example, you are driving home, singing a song and looking forward to a holiday, when out of the blue, another driver bumps your car; or you are playing with your child in the park when suddenly a dog rushes up and threatens your child; or you are having a very pleasant evening with friends when the phone rings and you hear of a close friend who has just had to go into the hospital for cancer. Shame-based interruptions of positive affect per se seem unlikely in these scenarios; more likely reactions will be anger, fear, and sadness, respectively. Shame is more likely to result from a loss of positive affect associated with devaluations of the self; for example, a man planning a pleasant evening with a lover becomes impotent. Hence, shame may inhibit specific kinds of positive, social relationships (by being associated with negative evaluations of the self).

From an evolutionary point of view *most negative affects* should have some capacity to turn off, interrupt, or dampen positive affect because negative affects usually act to alert animals to dangers and to engage defensive behaviors (Gilbert, 1989). An animal eating or copulating needs to rapidly switch off such positive systems at the sight of a predator. It is unlikely that the disruption to positive affect of predator avoidance has anything to do with shame. Fearful, submissive shamelike behaviors could only have evolved in social situations where submissive responses would (usually) turn off or lessen the "attack-mode" of the attacker; that is, where they will have some protective function (see Gilbert & McGuire, this volume, chapter 5; Keltner & Harker, this volume, chapter 4). So at a very minimum "an interruption of positive affect" requires identification of the source of the interruption to know what defensive behavior is required. The idea that one can define an emotion in the absence of the meaning given to a situation has been well refuted (e.g., Oatley, 1992).

Given the growing evidence that positive and negative affect can be separated into two high-order affect dimensions (MacLeod, Byrne & Valentine, 1996; Watson, Clark, et al, 1995; Watson, Weber, et al., 1995) and the growing interest in anhedonia (Snaith et al., 1995), methodologies are developing to test whether shame is specifically designed to modulate positive affect or whether it loads more significantly on negative affect. In the following discussion, we will explore the latter question.

Shame and Negative Affect

Anxiety   Anxiety appears central to the shame experience, and it is difficult to consider shame without it. Could one have a nonanxious shame experience? H. Lewis (1986) argued that episodes of shame have an almost paniclike quality to them, where the capacity for rational thinking steps aside. We are not only aware of the scrutiny of the other but also become intensely and rapidly aroused. With this affect shift we can experience intense anxiety, feel our minds going blank, feel rooted to the spot, wish the ground would open and we could slip out of sight or flee. These seem like involuntary (primitive) defensive reactions, evolved for rapid defense in potentially dangerous situations (Gilbert, 1993).

Shame is also often defined as acute arousal or fear of being exposed, scrutinized, and judged negatively by others (Fischer & Tangney, 1995; Gilbert & Trower, 1990). The description of a "shame-attack" or a shame episode (e.g, H. Lewis, 1986; Reimer, 1996) is, however, almost identical to that of a shy response in social situations. Cheek and Melchior describe shyness reactions as "global feelings of tension, specific physiological symptoms, painful self-consciousness, worry about being evaluated negatively by others, awkwardness, inhibition and reticence" (1990, p. 48). And both shyness and shame episodes are described similarly to social anxiety attacks. Leary and Kowalski (1995) note, "The defining characteristic of social anxiety is that unlike other anxieties, social anxiety arises from *the prospect or presence of interpersonal evaluation in real or imagined social settings. . . .* In fact, social anxiety could just as easily be called "evaluation anxiety" (1995, p. 6). Beck et al. not only regarded social anxiety as evaluation anxiety but also linked it directly to shame: "The experience of shame is important in discussions of social anxiety because the socially anxious person is fearful of being shamed in many situations" (1985, p. 156). However, Tangney and Miller seem to evade a direct equation of social anxiety with shame by noting that:

> Lewis moved beyond the definition of shame as an affective reaction to public disapproval. In shame, the self is both agent and object of observation and disapproval, as shortcomings of the defective self are exposed before an in-

ternalized observing "other." Finally, shame leads to a desire to escape and hide—to sink into the floor and disappear. (1996, p. 1257)

However, again, almost identical descriptions have been written for social phobia (Rapee & Heimberg, 1997) and shyness reactions (Cheek & Melchior, 1990). Clark and Wells (1995) argue that fear of negative evaluation and exposure and social avoidance (hiding) are the hallmarks of social anxiety. Indeed, recent models of social phobia (Rapee & Heimberg, 1997) include (1) evaluations of self by self, and self "as may appear in the eyes of others"; (2) concerns with falling short of standards; (3) attentional and information processing biases; (4) raised sensitivity to internal arousal cues; and (5) clear behavioral dispositions for avoidance and escape. And in some areas, especially in the exploration of biases in information processing, research on social phobia is far ahead of that on shame. The point is that a focus on negative evaluations of self as "object and subject" and escape behavior does not distinguish shame from social anxiety. It would be interesting for shame researchers to look at models like Rapee and Heimberg (1997) or Clark and Wells (1995) and explore how shame experiences and processes might be similar to or different from social phobia models. The same holds true for shyness (Cheek & Melchior, 1990). This raises questions such as: Can some experiences of shame be seen as paniclike social anxiety attacks, so well described in the literature? Gilbert, Pehl, and Allan (1994), for example, found that many of the components of shame (e.g., self-consciousness, inferiority) were as highly correlated with a measure of social anxiety (Fear of Negative Evaluation; FNE) as with shame.

Currently, the literature on social anxiety and on shame share little common ground (Gilbert & Trower, 1990). However, in both bodies of literature there are common key questions about the actual nature of fear in avoidance behavior. For example, social anxiety may be related to the fear of *feeling* ashamed (e.g., the actual aroused emotions and internal feelings), the fear of *being* shamed, or both. The distinction between "being shamed" and "feeling ashamed" is a distinction we will return to throughout the chapter. One may fear being shamed (e.g., because of possible damage to one's career) yet not fear the affects (such as anxiety) of shame. In social anxiety, people may fear the symptoms of anxiety because they believe such symptoms will seriously interfere with their efforts at positive self-presentations.

Anger   H. Lewis (1986) argued that humiliated fury was part of the shame experience. This would appear to differentiate shame from current models of social anxiety. However, there are various hints in the literature that socially anxious (and overcontrolled) people can be subject to brooding resentment. The role of anger in social anxiety has been poorly researched. However, some researchers of shame argue that anger and rage are subsequent responses to shame (anxiety) but that they can be activated so rapidly that a person may lack consciousness awareness of feelings of shame (Retzinger, 1991, 1995; Scheff, 1987). This is often called *by passed shame* (see Scheff, this volume, chapter 10). Tangney, Wagner, Fletcher, and Gramzow (1992) found that shame is associated with increased anger proneness but that guilt is not. Destructive, nonassertive ways of dealing with conflict and anger have also been found to be associated with shame (Tangney, Wagner, Hill-Barlow, Marschall, & Gramzow, 1996).

Kaufman (1989) argues that shame causes ruptures in the "interpersonal bridge," that is, a disconnectedness between persons. Shame-anger is related to such ruptures. However, there are a number of unresolved difficulties here. First, shame theorists have rarely been clear on when anger is shame-related and when it is straight frustration (Berkowitz, 1989).

Second, there are many different types of relationships (e.g., cared for-carer, dominant-subordinate, friend-enemy), and it is not clear if (and how) shame-anger relates to disruptions in all or only some of these. Does an affiliative as opposed to a hostile relationship differ as to its shame potential? Retzinger (1991) and others believe that shame-anger *arises from* threats to a social bond—in particular, attachment bonds. A similar view was held by H. Lewis (1987c), who suggested shame-anger was a kind of protest anger related to the breaking of a bond. Following Bowlby (1973), who named the second volume in his attachment trilogy *Separation, Anxiety and Anger*, H. Lewis focused on the anger aroused by separation. She says, "I suggest this outraged crying and bitter protest are both expressions of humiliated fury" (H. Lewis, 1987c, p. 33). From here it is possible to argue that anger—humiliated fury—is related to breaking bonds and an inability to control attachment objects. In my view this is a problematic line of reasoning. Of course, defining protest as "humiliated fury" sets the scene for later definitions, but we have no reason to assume either that the infant who shows protest at separation is humiliated or that crying is a sign of outrage. It is probably preferable, therefore, to consider protest behavior as a separate and special form of defense, notable in many species and designed to deal with a situation of an absent protector or provider. Protest is part of the "distress call." It has a precise biology and can be turned off by drugs (Insel, 1997; Reite & Field, 1985). Once we start to strip distress calling and protest of their special signaling and behavioral functions, it becomes difficult to see what is related to separation anxiety, what to social and evaluative anxiety, and what to anger over injustice or frustration.

A third concern with the notion of separation-induced shame-humiliation is that if shame itself does not really appear until the individual has a sense both of self and of others as social agents who can approve or disapprove of self (M. Lewis, 1992, 1995; Stipek, 1995), then shame-anger must wait until shame is possible. Before this age, most anger is probably frustration anger. It can also be noted that the self psychologist Kohut (1977) argued that it is not proximity, the separation-closeness dimension, that is the domain of shame (and rage) but mirroring—approval giving and withholding or punishing (see Gilbert, 1992a, for a comparison of Bowlby and Kohut). Undoubtedly, one can feel shamed by a rejection or separation, but much may depend on the attributions and context for it. Is a person shamed by the death of a loved one, even when anger, rage, and protest are part of the normal response to such a loss? This would seem quite different from anger resulting from finding that your lover has had an affair and has left because you were an inadequate lover. The latter situation may well elicit feelings of shame and inadequacy whereas the former would not. In the former case, one is angry about the loss and the unfairness of it, and even angry, with the other for abandoning oneself, but there need be no self-devaluation or sense of having done anything wrong.

Covering or hiding possible shame with anger is often referred to as a "face saving" strategy, known to be a typical source of male violence (Archer, 1994; Daly & Wilson, 1994). In social contexts the relationship between individuals and the image each is trying to create will affect their various "covers" for shame, including anger. Expressions of anger are also related to domains of honor as socially defined (see Cohen, Vandello, & Rantilla, this volume, chapter 14). In gangs of poor males, the experienced of being "dissed" (being shamed) is serious and could be life-threatening if one does not immediately retaliate and show one's strength. Respect and deference are key to survival (Anderson, 1994). So anger and aggression are complex and can be triggered by frustration, negative evaluation, a sense of being cheated, injustice, disappointment, losing face, and so forth. There is also the domain of anger with oneself. There may also be a difference between the anger we feel when another person has spoiled our self-presentation and image, even though we know there is some truth in the accusation (and that we may have overreacted which may be shame-anger), compared to genuine humiliated fury where no amount of reflection will change our belief that it is the other who is at fault.

Humiliation   Anger bears closely on humiliation. Although many researchers (e.g. H. Lewis, 1987a,b,c; Nathanson, 1992) tend to bracket shame and humiliation together, there may be important differences between them. For those who do distinguish between shame and humiliation, there are again differences of view. W. Miller (1993), a lawyer with an interest in the Norse sagas, wrote one of the few specific books on humiliation. He purposely avoided beginning his exploration of humiliation with the domain of torture or sadism, preferring the everyday manifestations. Miller sees humiliation as related to pretensions, or, more accurately, an emotion of pretension deflation. Humiliation strikes when we are revealed to have had aspirations and beliefs that are beyond us; being "too big for our boots":

> Unlike shame, humiliation can run across boundaries of the honour group. If fact, humiliation is the emotional experience of being caught inappropriately crossing group boundaries into territory one has no business being in. *If shame is the consequence of not living up to what one ought to, then humiliation is the consequence of trying to live up to what one has no right to.* . . . (p. 145, italics in the original)

The word *humiliation*, coming from the Latin root *humilis*, meaning *low*, literally means being "brought down" in some way (W. Miller, 1993). However, although the domain of pretension, as well as the control of pretension via social sanction, is obviously important for social life (and Miller offers a fascinating coverage of these themes), it is unclear why this should be related to humiliation and not shame or embarrassment. Indeed, self psychologists, following the ideas of Kohut (1977), see grandiosity as central in human development and shame acting as a modifier of it. Moreover, people can be humiliated without having any reputation or aspiration to be superior to others. A woman walking home at night, dragged into an alley, raped, and urinated on would by most definitions fit the experience of "being humiliated," but it is difficult to see how this is related to her pretensions.

Other views on humiliation focus on issues of social power (Klein, 1991; S. Miller, 1988). Humiliation has long been linked to the aggressive rather than the anxious emotions. Just as we can distinguish "being shamed" and "feeling ashamed," we can do the same with humiliation (Silver, Conte, Miceli, & Poggi, 1986). Specifically, humiliation is what can be done to one person by another person purely for their own pleasure or purpose. S. Miller writes.

There are important phenomenological differences between shame and humiliation that relate the states to distinct self and other interactions and to distinct levels of self-definition. Humiliation implies an activity occurring between oneself and another person. "Humiliated" has a double meaning. It is a state or status, a feeling about where the self is positioned in relation to others; but it is also an interpersonal interaction. Someone has *done something* to the person. More specially humiliation involves being put into a lowly, debased, and powerless position by someone who has, at that moment greater power than oneself. Humiliation often involves rage over one's position, but not always. It may also involve shame over one's position or depression. But the key to humiliation is not the secondary reflections upon the significance of one's state (i.e., it is enraging; it is shameful) but the direct experience of feeling put into that state by another person with more power.

In contrast to humiliation, shame involves primarily a reflection upon the self by the self. . . . Ashamed persons are looking at themselves and judging themselves to be inferior, inadequate or pathetic (1988, p. 44–45).

Stamm suggested that:

Invariably, in contrast to shame, an individual may suffer a humiliating episode without being responsible for it. He may not have behaved, for example, in a reprehensible or ludicrous manner.

And yet, external powers for reasons of their own may elect to castigate him, dishonour him or expose him to untold abasement to further their own ends (1978, p. 425–426).

And Klein argued that "*people believe they deserve their shame; they do not believe they deserve their humiliation*" (1991, p. 117, italics in the original). Elsewhere, Gilbert (1997a, in press) outlined various domains where feelings of shame and humiliation may differ. While both shame and humiliation focus on harm to the self, humiliation may be a less self-conscious and self-focused experience than shame. Humiliation involves: (1) a focus on the other as bad rather than the self; (2) external rather than internal attributions for harmful events; (3) a sense of injustice and unfairness; and (4) a burning desire for revenge. Indeed, vengeance (Frijda, 1994; Scheff, 1994) and (in)justice (Solomon, 1994) seem so intimately linked to humiliation that it is difficult to imagine it without them. Humiliation does not require any change in self-evaluations because one does not locate the source of external attack as arising from some flaw in the self. Indeed, in therapeutic work with some aggressive individuals, it would be helpful if they *could* actually feel and tolerate some shame and guilt rather than perceive every conflict as one of being humiliated.

Nonetheless, Tangney, Hill-Barlow, et al. (1996) developed a new anger scale. One component was labeled "malevolent intentions," which is a measure of desire to get one's own back and to hurt the other—hence, presumably, revenge. These authors found that this aspect of anger was one of the strongest related to shame and inversely to guilt, as measured by Tangney and colleagues' Test of Self-Conscious Affect (TOSCA; see Tangney, Wagner, & Gramzow, 1992, and Andrews, this volume, chapter 2, for a description of this scale). The TOSCA is focused on self-evaluations and actions. However, one can be humiliated without violating any standards and norms, as in the preceding example of a woman raped in an alley. The woman might, however, experience shame when she tries to tell others (e.g., the police or her friends) of what has happened to her.

This raises the intriguing possibility that we can also feel shame (not just humiliation) when we have done nothing wrong; we do not blame ourselves but feel shame simply because we know or believe that we have created a negative, unattractive image of ourselves in the eyes of others. In an actual case of a rape a woman reported, "my husband has been very understanding, but I feel degraded. I don't want him to touch me because I feel dirty." One of her affects was of self-disgust even though she herself had done nothing wrong. This is an example of the idea that one can be scarred, damaged, or contaminated by others (humiliated) but then feel ashamed of having this scar or damage revealed or seen (Gilbert, 1997a). There is not the space here to explore these differences fully, but one can question the assumption that humiliation and shame can be seen as so similar they don't require separate study and conceptual differentiation.

If the psychotherapy of shame can be difficult (Harper & Hoopes, 1990), then so too can that of humiliation (Gilbert, in press). It is possible that one aspect of therapy will involve letting go of intense desires for revenge and developing forgiveness (Enright, 1991; McCullough, Worthington, & Rachal, 1997). However, the use of forgiveness in the therapy of humiliation is unclear.

Disgust   Anger and anxiety are not the only emotions linked to shame. Some researchers argue that shame is derived from (self-)disgust (Power & Dalgleish, 1997). According to Rozin and Fallon's review, the word *disgust* comes from *dis-gust*, meaning *bad taste*. It is primarily an affect of "revulsion at the prospect of oral incorporation of offensive objects" (1987, p. 23). The facial expression involves closing the nose and mouth (to stop ingression). Rozin and Fallon argue therefore that disgust in an affect related to what goes into and comes out of bodies. It is not there at birth (e.g., babies are not disgusted by their own feces), it is subject to cultural practices (e.g., foods that might in the West be stomach-turning, such as rotten fish or grasshoppers, are eaten quite happily in some cultures), and some people can desensitize to disgust objects (e.g., those who have to clean toilets or gut animals and fish for a living). Disgust is an affect that warns of contamination and triggers movement away and, in the extreme, a vomiting reflex, which presumably evolved for the quick expulsion of possible noxious substances.

Gilbert (1992a) suggested that anxiety and disgust may give rise to different forms of shame. The social context may help determine the nature of the other affects associated with shame. For example, behaviors associated with sexual activity (e.g., certain "kinky" sexual practices) or bodily functions and appearances may gain the judgment of "dirty and disgusting." Shame associated with betrayal and breaking loyalties, or shame associated with cowardice, are less likely to be labeled as "disgust." Disgust is not an affect particularly associated with social anxiety or depression as far as we know, although shame is associated with both (Tangney, Wagner, & Gramzow, 1992). However, disgust is an affect people could obviously fear triggering in others. To be seen as an object of disgust is to be seen as very unattractive and undesirable. But there is no data as to how much or in what contexts disgust is key to felt shame.

While some see disgust as the root of shame (Power & Dalgleish, 1997), others see disgust (and dissmell) as a separate affect system all together (Tomkins, 1987a).

M. Lewis (1992) observed that parents often use a "disgust face" when disciplining their children or showing their displeasure. This opens important questions on the facial expressions associated with disapproval: How many are there? In what contexts are they displayed? How are they received? and so forth. And the relationships between (self-)disgust, (self-)contempt, and (self-)hatred are poorly researched, although each may play a salient role in problems associated with (for example) sexual abuse.

The question of indignity   Pride is seen as the contrasting affect to shame (Mascolo & Fischer, 1995). However, this often leaves out the question of dignity. Dignity seems more about being in control of oneself, not necessarily about achieving things others will admire, as in pride. Some writers (e.g., Fossum & Mason, 1986; Tomkins, 1963) see loss of dignity as a major part of shame. However, dignity's relation to shame is quite unclear. One can feel an acute loss of dignity with no personal blame attached either by self or observer. When it comes to suffering from a disease, the fear of "loss of one's dignity" can be a major source of concealment and even avoidance of potential help. Lazare argues that suffering a disease can become an issue of both shame and dignity:

> When patients discuss the importance of "dying with dignity" the indignities they refer to are the altered appearance (edema, emaciation, deformities, etc.), diminished awareness, incontinence, the need to be washed and fed, the need to ask or beg for medicine to relieve pain, the need to use a bed pan, and the perceived loss of meaningful social roles and social value (1987, p. 1654).

An awareness of one's body becoming misshapen, odd or unpleasant in texture and smell, with bodily emissions, and of being a possible source of contagion to others (not to mention the source of the disease itself, such as HIV) are some of the emotional experiences that can operate in or near shame in unique ways. As Lazare (1987) argues, however, much shame in this area is caused by the reactions of others to the ill as much as by internalized values of the ill themselves.

The loss of dignity, like humiliation, is one of those experiences that look, on the surface, to be so similar to shame that there are few efforts to explore more deeply its subtle distinctions from shame. But dignity seems to be specifically about displays of self-control, poise, and respect. I doubt we would think of "shame" as a description of a dying person who has lost control over bodily functions. And most of us would have no wish to be in such a position because of the loss of control—the loss of dignity. However, again I doubt we would see ourselves in a state of shame if such a fate were to befall us. The loss of dignity through disease would not seem to fit Fischer and Tangney's (1995) model of shame that requires a deplorable action, statement, or characteristic with a very strong overtone of wrongdoing.

Psychoanalyst S. Miller (1996) suggests that personality itself—particularly obsession and narcissism—can be built around scripts about what is and what is not shaming and defending against shame. Interestingly, obsession (but not narcissism) is related to maintaining dignity by controlling internal feelings and impulses (whether dependence needs, sexuality, or enthusiasms)—keeping things in order and in place. Success in these efforts is a source of dignified pride. Such are "guarded" persons. Shame is in losing control, letting something out. Narcissism, however, involves constantly attempting to ensure a positive image in the eyes of the other by special feats (of beauty, talent, etc.). The narcissist fears ordinariness and lives in fear of (being revealed as) never being good enough. The narcissist may fly into rages to get what he or she wants (Kinston, 1987). Dignity is not the key issue for them that it is for obsessionals.

Affect combinations   The focus so far has been on single affects (anxiety, anger, etc.), with the argument that some of the emotional bedfellows of shame actually require more research attention and differentiation from shame. However, it is now recognized that in adults it is extremely difficult to study "pure" affects because they undergo radical transformation with maturation. Lane and Schwartz (1987) suggest that emotional development goes through a set of stages that may parallel Piaget's cognitive stages. The stages are awareness of (1) bodily sensations, (2) the body in action, (3) individual feelings, (4) blends of feelings, and (5) blends of blends of feelings. At the lowest level, the baby is only aware of experiences in body sensations, and these are generally crudely differentiated in some pleasure-pain dimension. Subsequently comes the awareness of feelings derived from actions. Later come the more differentiated affects of sadness, anger, anxiety, joy, and so forth. Later the capacity to experience blends of these feelings and the capacity to cope with ambivalence develops. Finally comes more complex blends of blends of feelings. Shame, in this approach, would not occur until at least stage 3 and possibly later. Moreover, any emotion can blend with any other.

Kaufman (1989) argued that shame can *bind* with other emotions and affects (e.g., one can have shame-disgust or shame-excitement). This is a similar idea to blends of affects. In Kaufman's view, affect "binds" arise from the association of shame with certain "scripts" in which these other affects were present (Tomkins, 1987b). For example, consider shame associated with approval-seeking behavior. Imagine Sue, a 3-year-old, drawing a picture. When finished, she proudly holds it up for Mom's approval and admiration. Mom responds by kneeling down and saying, "Wow—that's wonderful. What a clever girl." Now in this encounter Sue not only experiences her mother as proud of her, she also has emotions *in herself about herself*—she feels good about herself. Positive affects become associated with display (in this case drawing). Psychoanalysts would call this a "good self-object" experience (Kohut, 1977), affect theorists a "positive script" (Tomkins, 1987b). But suppose Mom responds with, "Oh, no, not another of those drawings. They're all over the house making a mess." Clearly, Sue is unlikely to have good feelings about herself. Her head may drop, and she moves away in a possible state of disappointment and shame. Shame (internalized emotions elicited by parental disapproval) will be associated with display of abilities (drawing), and thus become a shame script.

We could substitute "anxiety" in the story for "drawing" and imagine Sue being shamed for showing anxiety or crying. Indeed, any potential affect-behavior is open to possible shame via the disapproval of others. Using Ferster's (1973) learning model, Gilbert (1992a) suggested that these kinds of experiences could be understood as classically conditioned emotional responses. Where Kaufman (1989) talks of "binds" or Tomkins (1987a) and Nathanson (1992) of "scripts," it seems as appropriate to suggest a conditioning model of affect, where any affect can be associated with any other. For example, Ferster (1973) relates the case of a child punished for expressing anger. The internal cues of anger (which have been associated with parental punishment) come to elicit intense anxiety. Eventually, a child may only be fully aware of the anxiety in situations that could arouse anger. Thus one can learn to defend against the conscious arousal of affects that have been punished. However, there is nothing special about shame in its ability to be linked or conditioned to other affects.

Affect combinations are important to another concept, that of bypassed shame— a concept favored by some shame researchers, especially as an explanation for some cases of violence (e.g., Retzinger, 1991, 1995). An issue here is not whether people can bypass shame feelings (because they find them intolerable or have never learned to process shame affect) but rather that there is nothing special about bypassed shame. For instance, in Ferster's (1973) example given previously we might wish to talk of bypassed anger. In therapy we might seek to help the person tolerate angry feelings without overwhelming anxiety or sadness. If a conditioning and learning approach is taken, we could have bypassed anger, sadness, guilt, anxiety, and so forth. What level of processing these "affects" progress to before being bypassed is unknown, but some authors do believe that shame can be unconscious (e.g., M. Lewis, 1992).

The next two sections explore facial expression and physiology. These are not affects as such but are normally regarded as part of our affect systems. As in the previous discussion, it will be noted that shame has been difficult to pin down and isolate as a separate system.

Facial expression   Tomkins (e.g., 1963, 1987a, b) believed that affects map directly onto facial expression and systems, with specific emotions related to specific expressions. This has been hard to study and is certainly not as simple as Tomkins believed. For example, in a major review of the research data, Russell found that "emotions can occur without facial expression and facial expression can occur without emotions" (1995, p. 379). Facial expressions can differ according to whether emotions are experienced in private or public. There are sociocultural display rules which affect public expression of emotions (Argyle, 1988). Affect combinations have also plagued researchers who have looked for facial expressions associated with specific affects. In the case of depression, for example, there are differences in nonverbal patterns of communication according to whether the depression is an anxious, angry, or endogenous type (Ellgring, 1989). In everyday experiences of shame, the same is likely to be true, with anger, anxiety, and/or disgust being part of the shame experience and thus part of nonverbal behavior. One way around this problem is to ask people to pose facial expressions, in the absence of any felt affect; but there is increasing concern that asking people to make a face of an affect (e.g., anger, sadness, shame) may use different facial component systems (Carroll & Russell, 1997) and even different brain areas from those of spontaneously elicited emotions (Argyle, 1988). Thus other methodologies are required (Dixon, Gilbert, Huber, Gilbert, & Van der Hoek, 1996; Keltner, 1995). Although caution is needed, there is some general agreement that shame does involve eye-gaze avoidance and head-down movements (see Keltner & Harker, this volume, chapter 4). But as yet it is not clear how these might differ from or be similar to shyness reactions, social anxiety expressions, or efforts to conceal anger.

And so studies of facial expression and emotion remain full of their own complexities and controversies (Russell, 1995).

Physiology   There remains considerable dispute over the physiology of shame, a physiology which may turn out to be quite heterogenous—like depression, perhaps (Thase & Howland, 1995). Some theorists argue that the parasympathetic-demobilization response of very young infants, elicited (for example) when the mother fails to mirror facial expression (e.g., see Tronick & Cohn, 1989), is the prototype of shame affect. Some theorists come close to suggesting that the parasympathetic response associated with reduced sympathetic arousal is what shame is. This is a view taken by Schore (1994 and chapter 3 in this volume) who has attempted to delineate the psychobiology of shame in great detail. However, as he recognizes, shame may well be *associated* with parasympathetic arousal in many but not all situations. R. Miller (1996) reviews some limited data that suggests that social anxiety is associated with sympathetic arousal, whereas embarrassment (especially if it is passive) and shame are associated with parasympathetic arousal (see also Leary & Kowalski, 1995). However, different phobias are also associated with different patterns of parasympathetic and sympathetic arousal; for example, blood phobias, especially those associated with fainting, are linked to parasympathetic arousal (Marks, 1987). If we link shame too closely with parasympathetic activity, then where would this leave anger? Linking physiology and emotion is notoriously difficult (Cacioppo, Klein, Berntson, & Hatfield, 1993). Undoubtedly, many shame experiences are associated with anxiety, self-disgust, and/or anger (and their combination). It is likely that these emotions will affect sympathetic and parasympathetic systems in different ways that are difficult to disentangle.

From an evolutionary point of view, parasympathetic-demobilisation responses are part of an ancient, basic defense repertoire that signals "stop" (Gilbert, 1989) and may, in some species, be expressed to predators ("freeze"). The defensive reaction of turning away and becoming demobilized may well be available in the first days of life, for it is a very ancient and primitive defensive option; but it is probably unwise to call this "shame" at this point because it is a basic defense that can be activated in various situations, both social and nonsocial.

Shame-arousability and reactivity are almost certainly mood-related. To date there is no data on how shame arousal in specific situations changes with mood, but many clinical anedotes suggest shame sensitivity is highly mood-related (and maybe 5-HT related; Gilbert & McGuire, this volume, chapter 5). This has implications for those who wish to argue that shame is a cause of psychopathology. It could equally well be argued that depression and anxiety change shame-arousability. As researchers explore more fully the way mood altering drugs affect emotions, these questions will become more urgent.

Cognitions and Beliefs in Shame

Complex Cognitive Processes

Most shame theorists fall into the category of cognitive-affect theorists; that is to say, they see shame as associated with particular types of appraisals, mostly of the self. However, the relationship between cognition and affect is not straightforward (Izard, 1993). The appraisal theory of emotions (Lazarus, 1991; Smith & Lazarus, 1993) suggests that emotions, including shame, are associated with particular appraisal themes. However, Frijda (1993) pointed out that there are a number of ways appraisals can relate to emotion. First, they can be part of the emotional experience itself, neither antecedent nor consequent to it. Second, appraisals can follow the early instigation of emotions—we start to realize that we will need to cope with an emotion as it is being aroused. Third, we can appraise our own reactions to things some time later (I should not have felt like that). Fourth, preexisting beliefs (e.g., I am not lovable) may predispose a person to both the affect and the evaluation of situations. Shame-based information processing can presumably operate at each level.

Space allows for consideration only of the first level—that of shame affect aroused as part of an emotional experience. Over the last decade there has been increasing recognition that the relationship between appraisal and emotions operates at various levels (Power & Dalgleish, 1997) and that humans have at least two partially independent ways of reaching decisions about important (often social) events. The first, called an experiential system (Epstein, 1994; Epstein, Lipson, Holstein, & Huh, 1992), seems to use heuristics, takes short cuts to reach conclusions quickly, uses crudely integrated information, is reliant on affect and how something feels, is preconscious, and possibly relies on earlier experience and conditioned emotional responses. *Fast-track* modes of functioning may be reliant on more primitive, earlier evolved appraisal-response systems, encoded in limbic and sublimbic areas (Bailey, 1987; MacLean, 1985). The rational system, however, evolved more recently, is able to use logical deductive and symbolic forms of reasoning in a more conscious way, and is less influenced by past events and affects (Power & Brewin, 1991). In fact, there is increasing recognition that information can be processed in many different ways (e.g., fast-slow; emotional-rational; parallel-serial; conscious-unconscious; rigid-flexible; social-nonsocial; defensive-safe). In general, acute experiences of shame would seem to use fast-track, emotional, and involuntary processing that a person finds difficult to control.

Another distinction that has gained credibility has been the distinction between propositional and implicational cognitive systems (Power & Dalgleish, 1997; Teasdale & Barnard, 1993)—which (at the risk of oversimplification) we can relate to intellectual versus emotional reasoning, respectively. As Teasdale (1997) notes, at the propositional level thoughts such as "I am worthless" are simply statements of belief—propositions about properties of self as an object. At the implicational level, however, such a statement represents a rich activation of affect and memories associated with experiences of being rejected or shamed. Clearly, shame theorists are concerned with implicational, not propositional, reasoning, although as yet they do not make this distinction. One major issue, however, is that implicational processing may be difficult to verbalize or even consciously access (Power & Brewin, 1991; Power & Dalgleish, 1997). Thus, insofar as shame-affect(s) may rely on implicational processing, which is difficult to consciously reflect on, then this may limit the value of self-report measures. At best self-report can only reflect conscious products.

Fast-track and implicational forms of reasoning are likely to use evolutionarily meaningful algorithms (Gilbert, 1989, 1995). There is now increasing evidence that social intelligence is not simply general intelligence directed to social problems. Rather, there are probably specific information processing routines for dealing with social information (Cosmides & Tooby, 1992). As noted elsewhere (Gilbert, 1997a; Gilbert & McGuire, this volume, chapter 5), those routines most likely adapted for shame, are concerned with processing socially threatening information—particularly in the domains of social rank/status and social exclusions/rejections.

Shame Contents: The Self-Other Evaluative Domain of Shame

Ideas about the content of shame processing originate in ideas first put forward by Charles Cooley at the turn of the century. He coined the term the "looking-glass self." This refers to the way we judge and feel about ourselves according to how we think others judge and feel about us. The looking-glass self has three cognitive aspects:

> The imagination of our appearance to the other person; the imagination of his judgement of that appearance; and some sort of self feeling, such as pride or mortification. (As quoted in Scheff, 1988, p. 398)

Theories of shame (and social anxiety) have tended to follow a similar focus without clearly separating these domains. Generally, shame seems to focus on either the social world (beliefs about how others see the self), the internal world (how one sees oneself), or both (how one sees oneself as a consequence of how one thinks others see the self).

Being judged negatively by others involves negative judgments that others have made (or will make) about the self. Generally, people try to present themselves in a positive light (Leary, 1995; Trower, Gilbert, & Sherling, 1990); that is, to be seen as attractive to others. It matters little what type of relationship one considers, be it being chosen for the football team, as lover, or to head up a therapy unit; people like to feel they have been chosen by others because others see them as good, able, and talented. Shame is related to the belief that we cannot create positive images in the eyes of others; we will not be chosen, will be found lacking in talent, ability, appearance, and so forth; we will be passed over, ignored, or actively rejected (Gilbert, 1997a). More negatively, we may even be an *object* of scorn, contempt, or ridicule to others. We have been disgraced; judged and found wanting in some way. Gilbert (1997a) suggested the term *external shame* for this domain because the focus is on the outside world: how one is seen by others or how one lives in the eyes of others (Allan, Gilbert, & Goss, 1994; Goss, Gilbert, & Allan, 1994; Mollon, 1984; Retzinger, 1991; Scheff, 1988). M. Lewis (1992) has argued that it is in becoming an object for others that our potential to feel shame begins in earnest. These ideas are similar to an older concept in psychology, that of Fear of Negative Evaluation (FNE; Friend & Gilbert, 1973; Watson & Friend, 1969). Gilbert et al. (1994) found that in students FNE was highly correlated with shame but not with guilt. FNE has also been seen as core to social anxiety. FNE in turn relates to a large literature on self-presentation and image management (Leary and Kowalski, 1990; Leary, 1995; Trower et al., 1990), little of which has impinged on the shame literature.

Negative self-evaluation relates to the subjective sense of self (M. Lewis, 1992). This is normally referred to as *internal or internalized shame* (Cook, 1996; Gilbert

1997a, b; H. Lewis, 1987a) because it is derived from how the self judges the self. Thus, one sees oneself as bad, flawed, worthless, and unattractive. Many theorists have posited inferiority as a central self-evaluation (Tomkins, 1987a); indeed, Kaufman (1989) called shame the "affect of inferiority." In factor analytic studies that measure shame this way, inferiority emerges as a salient factor (e.g., Cook, 1993, 1996; Goss et al., 1994).

Harder (1995) found high correlations of various self-report measures of shame (including Tangney's scenario-based measure, TOSCA) with self-derogation. Karen (1991) gives an example of a man who likes to look at young women in public places. As long as he sees his behavior as "typically male," he does not feel shame. But one day a new image of himself enters his mind: that of an unhappy loner who cannot make secure loving attachments and who few women may actually want. At this point he feels devalued in his own eyes and shamed.

Both the emotions and negative self-cognitions of shame are unwanted and involuntarily aroused. Indeed, as noted elsewhere (Gilbert, 1992a,b, 1997a,b), the central aspect of inferiority of shame is that it is *involuntary*. If we voluntarily accept an inferior position and/or believe our superiors will be helpful to us, there need be no shame. In fact, it can be a pleasurable state to be in—free of responsibility, low expectations, and so forth. Shame cannot, therefore, consist of inferiority alone but, first, must include some notion of a place or position that one does not want to be in or an image one does not wish to create and, second, this place or image must be associated with negative aversive attributes from which one struggles to escape.

Attention   The idea that attention can be focused internally on the self (private self-consciousness) and/or externally on what others might think of the self (public self-consciousness) is now well established in social psychology (see Gibbons, 1990, for a review) and social anxiety (Rapee & Heimberg, 1997) research. Many researchers see the attention focus of shame (and social anxiety) to be inwardly directed, involving a heightened self-consciousness as one becomes acutely aware of failings, flaws, and deficits in the self. Fischer and Tangney (1995) see shame as essentially a self-conscious affect. However, a personal awareness of one's flaws may lead to little anxiety unless one believes that these will be exposed (M. Lewis, 1992). Studies using the private and public self-consciousness scale with various shame scales have found no association between private self-consciousness and shame and only small significant correlations with public self-consciousness (Harder, 1995). This is slightly surprising given that self-consciousness is stressed as such a major component of shame (e.g., M. Lewis, 1995; Tangney & Fischer, 1995), but it probably relates to measurement issues. For example, Gilbert et al. (1994) found self-consciousness to be highly correlated with shame.

Falling short of standards   Over the years shame has been consistently linked to failing to meet ideals and falling short of standards (e.g., S. Miller, 1996; Reimer, 1996). Hence, Mascolo and Fischer, in agreement with many other researchers, suggest that shame is generated by appraisals of having failed to live up to personal and other people's standards of worth and operates to "highlight behaviors that threaten honour and self worth" (1995, p. 68). However, caution should be exercised here, because research suggests there are different types of "self ideals" (Higgins, 1987), and not all such failures need be associated with shame. In fact, there is no direct evidence that shame (rather than disappointment) is associated with falling short as such. Rather, one could make a case that it is not so much distance from the ideal self but closeness to the "undesired self" that is crucial to shame (Ogilvie, 1987). Exploring the idea that shame is about failure to live up to ideals and using qualitative methods, Lindsay-Hartz, de Rivera, and Mascolo found that:

> To our surprise we found that most of the participants rejected this formulation. Rather, when ashamed, participants talked about being who they did *not* want to be. That is, they experienced themselves as embodying an anti-ideal, rather than simply not being who they wanted to be. The participants said things like, "I am fat and ugly," not "I failed to be pretty"; or "I am bad and evil," not "I am not as good as I want to be." This difference in emphasis is not simply semantic. Participants insisted that the distinction was important. (1995, p. 277)

It would appear then that shame requires that there has to be something actually "unattractive" about the person—not just a failure to reach a standard (Gilbert, 1992a, 1997a,b). It remains an open question whether some aspects of the negative self-evaluation of shame are secondary to anticipation of being unattractive to a desired other(s). It is likely that what is undesirable about the self is as much open to social and cultural constructions as what is desirable.

Self-Blame   A number of writers have argued that shame relates to blaming the self, whereas guilt relates to blaming one's actions (see Tangney, 1996). Here again this is a yet to be settled issue (Frijda, 1993; Gilbert, 1997a). Tangney, Wagner, and Gramzow (1992) did find a significant correlation between shame and internal and stable attributions in students. However, this style is not specific to shame and is commonly associated with neuroticism and depression (see Andrews, this volume, chapter 2). As self-blame is discussed at length by Andrews in the chapter 2, it is not explored in detail here. However, it is worth noting that self-blame is somewhat paradoxical when it comes to cognitions about responsibility. Shaver and Drown (1986) make clear distinctions between self-blame, responsibility, and causality. For example, a person may know perfectly well that they did not cause a personal negative attribute (e.g., a birth defect) but can feel shamed by it nonetheless. As noted above for the woman who was raped, she may have a sense of "a bad self" without attributions of personal causality. Indeed, the word *bad* can have different meanings, for instance, a moral/evil sense or a disgust/undesirable sense. Such distinctions are crucially important when working with patients but have yet to impact on shame research.

Self-blame is a close ally of self-criticism, but it is clear that some forms of self-criticism are not related to shame (Driscoll, 1988). Also a large literature on depression suggests that vulnerability to depression is related to two (supposedly orthogonal) dimensions, dependency and self-criticism (Blatt, 1991; Blatt & Zuroff, 1992), but there is little data on how each might relate to shame. According to current theory, self-critical types should be highly shame-prone. But are dependent people, who need not be self-critical, also shame-prone? Clinical experience suggests they often are. Harper and Hoopes (1990) argued that dependency needs can be a salient potential shame script. Are self-critics and dependent individuals shame-prone in different ways (Nietzel & Harris, 1990)? Again, these are areas of study which have developed similar ideas (e.g., on self-blame) but exist in separate literatures.

Social comparison Our standards and ideals are often taken from other people (Suls & Wills, 1991), making social comparison a possible salient cognition in shame. Two central dimensions are "inferior-superior" and "same-different" (Allan & Gilbert, 1995; Gilbert, Price, & Allan, 1995). Ongoing work in our department suggests that measures of (unfavorable) social comparison are highly correlated with various shame measures. Using the Other as Shamer Scale (OAS, Goss et al., 1994), which asks people the degree to which they believe others see them negatively, as a measure of shame-proneness, social comparison correlated at .57 with the OAS in a student population. Both measures had independent negative effects on confidence estimates (Gilbert, Allan, Ball, & Bradshaw, 1996).

As noted above, self-evaluations of being inferior to others have long been associated with shame. Brewin and Furnham (1986) measured what they called preattributional variables in depression and found that depressives often failed to reveal negative experiences to others because of a fear of being seen as different and scorned. In the well-known experiments of Asch (1956), individuals could be made to change their (accurate) judgment of the relative length of a line in the face of others who gave a different judgment. Scheff argues that this is the result of fear of being seen as different, invoking scorn, and being shamed. He notes:

> A reaction that occurred both in independent and yielding subjects was the fear that they were suffering from a defect and that the study would disclose this defect: "I felt like a silly *fool*. . . . A question of being a *misfit*. . . . they'd think I was queer. It made me seem weak eyed or weak headed, like a black sheep." (1988, p. 403, italics added)

Social comparison and the anticipation of how others will evaluate and respond to negative information about the self also plays a crucial role in acts of revelation. It is now known that keeping secrets (e.g., about previous abuse) can be psychologically costly, but revelation is not without its risks—especially if it results in rejection (Kelly & McKillop, 1996; Macdonald, this volume, chapter 7). One of the advantages of group therapy may be providing opportunities for helpful social comparisons and sharing of negative information about the self (Yalom, 1985).

The Relation between Internal and External Shame

Having explored some of the cognitive domains of shame (self-other evaluations, standards, and social comparison), we can now reconsider the internal versus external nature of shame. Although internal and external shame are often highly correlated, they need not always be so. For example, there is clear evidence that having socially stigmatized traits (e.g., being obese) does not necessarily lead to low self-esteem or a sense of internal personal shame (Crocker & Major, 1989). One can be shamed for appearing to lack feelings of shame—being shameless—without a sense of internal shame. And recognizing that others find a person's behavior shameful when the person him-or herself does not find it so can arise in antisocial behavior. A pedophile acknowledged that others see the use of children as sexual objects as bad, yet he had little internal shame for it, although he gave many justifications. Efforts to shame him in prison seemed to have done little except convince him to be more careful not to be caught (conceal his activities). He could acknowledge that his behavior brought him severe social sanctions but not that he was internally shamed by the abuse itself. External shame requires an ability to anticipate how others might judge a behavior or personal attribute. When behavior is controlled purely by external shame, people who think they can avoid discovery may engage in a socially shamed behavior, such as visiting prostitutes. If caught, the person might appear and even feel ashamed by the scrutiny of others (being caught); but it cannot be said that the shame is internal because the person may have the view that prostitution should be legalized and that he has done nothing bad or wrong.

The controversy here is whether shame can occur in the absence of negative self-evaluations for the actions that are shamed. Is the pedophile really shamed but bypassing it (Retzinger, 1991), or is there really no shame at all? Mollon (1984) captures the essence of how shame involves an awareness of living negatively in the minds of others with a quote from the existential writer, Jean-Paul Sartre:

> To see oneself blushing and to feel oneself sweating, etc., are inaccurate expressions which the shy person uses to describe his state; what he really means is that he is physically and constantly conscious of his body, not as it is for him but as it is for the Other. This constant uneasiness which the apprehension of my body's alienation as irredeemable can determine . . . a pathological fear of blushing; these are nothing but a horrified metaphysical apprehension of the existence of my body for the Other. We often say that the shy man is embarrassed by his own body. Actually, this is incorrect; I cannot be embarrassed by my own body as I exist in it. It is my body as it is for the Other which embarrasses me. (As quoted in Mollon, 1984, p. 212)

The difference between "being shamed" and "feeling ashamed" is what is at issue here. But what turns acts of being shamed into feelings of being ashamed? There is actually a long history to these debates (Mollon, 1993), especially within French psychoanalysis (Wilson, 1987). As Wilson makes clear, in this tradition shame only operates at the level of how "self exists for the other," be this in imagination, in memory, or in actuality. Similarly, Mollon (1993) emphasizes the "look of the other" as central to shame. Importantly, then, it is interesting to consider how shame measures assess this. The OAS (Goss et al., 1994), for example, is purely a measure of how one thinks others see oneself, but it is not situationally focused. The Internalized Shame Scale (Cook, 1996), however, is purely of self-evaluation, while the TOSCA is self-focused and situational (Tangney, 1996).

Apart from the OAS (Goss et al., 1994; Allan et al., 1994), most shame measures, be they situation-focused or not, tap only internal self-judgments or actions, with no measure of how the person thinks others see the self or will act. This is not a small issue because there are many examples of prejudice and abuse where people are treated contemptuously, become anxious of their social presentations, and may engage in hiding and submissive behavior. Are they feeling shame? Suppose a person is homosexual or bisexual but does not wish colleagues at work to know for fear that it will change the relationship between them. The person him-or herself does not feel negatively at all about his or her sexuality but may hide it at work because it is easier; if someone asks them directly, they avoid eye gaze and hedge. Are they feeling shame? Or a person is falsely accused of a crime and may see in the eyes of the accuser a belief in their guilt; even though they know they have done nothing wrong, would they feel shame? If Sartre's position is held to, then the answer would be yes; but if shame requires negative self-evaluation, then one might "be shamed" without feeling ashamed by a false accusation.

Finally, people can have a sense of shame for actions that they were not involved in or responsible for. For example, there is some evidence that children of Nazi war criminals have felt a great sense of shame, even though they were only infants when their fathers were convicted (Serney, 1990). We might feel shame because of the actions of another family or group member if we are known as "one of them" or as "cut from the same cloth." Such examples suggest a source of shame not rooted in personal wrongdoing or blame. In a different but related way, in some societies shame by association can be so acute that honor might only be restored by murdering the one who has brought shame on the family (e.g., killing a wife or daughter for illicit sex).

In summary, I am inclined to the view that shame can be purely internal (for example, depressed people may feel intense shame even though others assure them that such perceptions are distortions and that they are their own accusers. However, shame can also be purely external (à la Sartre), as when a person is falsely accused or seen as "cut from the same cloth." Perhaps self-blame, self-consciousness, failing to meet standards, and negative social comparisons, although common correlates of shame, are not central to it. Rather, it is an inner experience of self as an unattractive social agent, under pressure to limit possible damage to self via escape or appeasement, that captures shame most closely. It does not matter if one is rendered unattractive by one's own or other people's actions; what matters in the sense of personal unattractiveness—being in the social world as an undesired self, a self one does not wish to be. Shame is an involuntary response to an awareness that one has lost status and is devalued. Again, however, this is only speculation and requires support from empirical data.

Behaviors of Shame

The behaviors associated with shame can be divided into four aspects: (1) behaviors aroused as part of the shame response—the hot response; (2) behaviors that are triggered to cope with, or conceal, shame as it occurs; (3) behaviors instigated to avoid being shamed (safety behaviors) or shame being discovered; (4) behaviors designed to repair shame. These behaviors can be self-focused to soothe the self, or socially focused to soothe others—for example, making apologies.

Behaviors as Part of Shame

One of the most common beliefs about shame is that it motivates hiding and desires to "sink into the ground" (Lindsay-Hartz et al., 1995; Reimer, 1996; Tangney, 1995). Hiding behavior is, of course, a common response to many threats (including predator threat). If something can hurt you, trying to make yourself as inconspicuous as possible is helpful. Shame researchers have not distinguished shame-based hiding from other forms of camouflage and hiding. For example, an abused woman told me how, when her father came to her room, she would wish for the bed to swallow her so he could not find her. And when he lay on her, she would "try to melt into the bed and just not be there." I think this was a terror feeling and not shame as such. Shame-based hiding may include the immediate "hide" reaction to a shame event and a continuing desire to keep hidden what is seen to be shameful. As Macdonald (this volume, chapter 7) points out, some patients may be far less concealing of their shame than current research would suggest.

The nonverbal communication of shame seems to act as a form of appeasement. These behaviors include a hunched posture and eye gaze avoidance (see Keltner & Harker, this volume, chapter 4). Such behaviors seem to serve the function of damage limitation (see Gilbert & McGuire, this volume, chapter 5), and in mild cases may arouse sympathy and forgiveness (Keltner & Harker this volume, chapter 4).

Coping with or Hiding Shame Affect as It Is Aroused

Gilbert and McGuire (this volume, chapter 5) note a case of how a monkey called Luit, in a dominance fight, used a hand to cover his fear grin (a submissive signal) following a tense encounter. In humans also there can be many situations when one wishes to hide pangs of shame (and its appeasement presentation), for a display of shame might signal to the other a recognition that one sees oneself as in the wrong, in inferior position, fearful, or emotionally disturbed. Such an admission may be contrary to one's conscious desires, just as Luit sought to hide a submissive signal which might have increased the confidence of his opponent.

The desire to conceal a display of shame is well recognized in the literature (Retzinger, 1991), although outside qualitative research on interactional discourses (see Scheff, this volume, chapter 10) has been poorly researched. Various authors (e.g., Nathanson, 1992; Retzinger, 1991) suggest that anger and even aggression can substitute for shame—one becomes angry at having one's flaws and mistakes noted or commented upon. More research is needed here, though, because "ordinary" interpersonal conflicts, which may elicit anger and frustration, have not been clearly separated from "shame defenses" or humiliation. Social rank is also important because dominant individuals can hide their shame in anger far easier than can subordinates.

Avoiding Shame

To engage in tactics of shame avoidance, one must have some sense that investing in avoidance strategies is worthwhile—that shame is so painful or deleterious to the self that it must be avoided. All of us will have some threshold for this; there are (naughty) things that we might like to do, but our desire to avoid shame stops us. At this level, shame avoidance is a safety behavior no different in kind from that associated with any threat; for example, social anxiety (Clark & Wells, 1995; Wells et al., 1995). Shame can also be avoided by withdrawing from those situations where it could be experienced. Avoiding help-seeking, socializing, sex, or competition are examples where shame is dealt with by never putting oneself in situations where shame could arise.

Nathanson (1992) argues that some people attempt to avoid shame not by avoiding situations but by compensating for potential sources of inferiority and aiming to reach high standards. They may do this by working hard or developing perfectionistic standards that put them beyond criticism. Hewitt and Flett (1991a,b) have shown that perfectionist standards can be aimed at oneself or demanded of others and can arise from beliefs that others demand and expect high standards of the self—called *socially prescribed perfectionism*. Given what has been said about shame and standards, perfectionism would seem a disposition rich in potential shame. However, Wyatt and Gilbert (1998) found that it was primarily socially prescribed perfectionism which was especially associated with shame. Such work needs to be replicated with other measures, but it hints again at the importance of "image in the eyes of others"; what one thinks others think about the self is a key variable of shame.

At the level of theory, but still to be researched, are Nathanson's (1992, 1994) ideas that competitiveness, or the constant need to draw attention to one's positive aspects, is also symptomatic of shame. It is unclear, though, whether all competitiveness is shame-related. A recent patient told me that her intense competitiveness served to prove life was meaningful; that there was a sense of emptiness in the absence of achievement. She denied shame and did not appear shame-prone in therapy but was frightened of death (Yalom, 1980). Nathanson (1992) makes the important observation that shame can be avoided through hypersexuality, drinking, and taking illegal drugs; but the same has been posited for death anxiety. As Nathanson notes, however, the choice of coping with shame significantly influences the manifestation and form of any psychopathology.

Secrecy

One way of dealing with shame after the event is keeping it secret, and such secrecy can be personal (Kelly & McKillop, 1996) or at the level of families (Fossum & Mason, 1986) and even societies (Robins, 1993). Such bypassed shame is dealt with by silence or threats to possible revealers or exposers—whistle-blowers. Examples may include Jewish gold hidden in Swiss banks, the way a society treats its minorities, or even gender issues. It can be shameful to acknowledge social shame. When social shame is never discussed, it cannot be worked through or repaired.

Reparations

W. Miller (1993) notes that some cultures have various rituals for the repair of shame. They may even distinguish between reparable and nonreparable shame. Usually, the shamed person has to make an apology or in some way humble him-or herself (show submission) by acknowledging his or her wrongdoing. One must not be seen as too proud to acknowledge one's shame (to quote an old saying: "Pride comes before a fall"). Public demonstrations of one's shame, however, can serve bot   tributive and a reparative function. As Massaro (1991) notes, in America, demands of public naming of wrongdoers (e.g., drunk drivers) mostly concerns retribution.

We actually know rather little about how people try to repair themselves and their relationships where shame has been involved (see Zahn-Waxler & Robinson, 1995, for a discussion of reparations in child-child and child-parent interactions). Although there is some evidence for the current idea that guilt involves reparations in a way shame does not, Gilbert (1997a) noted other evidence to suggest that people will try to repair their self-and social images by making reparations. Even helping behavior can be performed for reasons to do with maintaining a positive self-image and reputation. For example, Steele (1975) found that being criticized led to an increased willingness to help a good cause. He explained this in terms of repair of self-esteem. Once shame is in the open, it may be maladaptive not to try to repair one's self-image; but again there may be differences in the type of shame one tries to repair and the type one feels is irreparable.

Historically, shame and sin have often been linked, and there have been various religious means for repair (e.g., confession, penance). Jung (1954/1993) argued that offering redemption was not only a salient function of priests in confession but also of therapists. Repair of shame may involve forgiveness of self and belief in the forgiveness of others. Repair is partly based on the idea that one can restore one's social image (as attractive, desirable, and trustworthy) and that the other will not harbor secret grudges or distrust. This bears closely on issues of reconciliation. Gilbert (1992a) suggested that one of the problems in depressed and shame-prone people is that they may lack reconciliation skills, as well as opportunities. In clinical practice, one finds that some individuals with shame problems believe that others will never forgive or forget even if they act forgiving. Perhaps humiliated people want revenge while shamed people want reconciliation and forgiveness. As there is so little research in this area, such ideas must await further work, but a deeper understanding of how people forgive themselves and accept and trust the forgiveness (and reconciliations) of others could prove useful in understanding the links of shame to psychopathology. In the growing literature on forgiveness (Enright, 1991; Fitzgibbons, 1986; McCullough et al., 1997), forgiveness is mostly directed to others who have harmed the self. Psychological therapies, however, are often about self-forgiveness, reducing harsh, internal self-attacks and focusing on beliefs that one is forgiven (Gilbert, 1997b).

Shame-Proneness

While shame relates to actual emotional experiences at a point in time (Tangney, 1996), shame-proneness relates to those factors in place before shame is aroused. However, M. D. Lewis notes that this may be an artificial distinction:

> The background states from which appraisals emerge may never be devoid of organised cognitive-emotion activity, and this activity would necessarily influence the character of emerging interpretations. From this point of view, the appraisal process constitutes an ongoing trajectory of cognitive-emotional activity that surges and recedes, moves in and out of attractor states, but has no beginning or end. (1996, p. 21)

Andrews (this volume, chapter 2) points out that shame-proneness or shame vulnerability has been conceptualized in many ways. Affect theorists relate shame-proneness to: (1) the ease or *readiness* to experience certain types of emotion and engage in certain types of behavior in certain situations and (2) the *severity* of negative affects and behaviors triggered in potentially shameful situations. Also, although psychiatric classifications of social phobia make distinctions between specific and generalized forms, shame researchers rarely make this distinction. However, when shame is linked to personality pathology, therapists are usually implying a generalized form of shame, or what Tantam (this volume, chapter 8) has called a "sentiment of shame." Generalized and specific forms of shame are likely to have very different origins and therapies and are likely to be related to self-identity and constructs in different ways.

Normal Origins

There is little argument that shame is an innate potential—that at some point most children will show the capacity for it. Shame itself is not an abnormal affect. However, the exact childhood origins of shame have been subject to much speculation (Barrett, 1995; Reimer, 1996). Affect theorists (Nathanson, 1992; Schore, 1994 and chapter 3 in this volume) tend to see shame as of early origin while others place it later (M. Lewis, 1995). As noted above, much depends on one's definition of shame. In a series of studies exploring self-evaluations and attentiveness to the approval of others, Stipek and her colleagues found that social referencing was especially marked after 2 ½ years. On being asked to play a game, for example, rolling a ball to knock over a tower, "toddlers aged 22–39 months were more likely to look up at the experimenter after they had produced the outcome" than were younger children. In later childhood, children seem to respond to themselves as others have done. Stipek says:

> We are suggesting a curvilinear pattern in development of self-evaluative emotions. Initially, the children experience immediate and autonomous pleasure from having some effect on the environment; they are not particularly interested in or concerned about others' reactions to their behaviors or outcomes. Before they reach the age of 2 years they become concerned about others' reaction, and their own emotional experiences are, to a considerable degree, linked to the anticipation of others' reactions. As they internalize standards and increase in their ability to judge their own performance according to standards, self-evaluative emotions again become independent of the anticipation of others' approval or disapproval. (1995, p. 249)

Self psychologists (Kohut, 1977; S. Miller, 1996) argued that shame-proneness begins when the child needs but is not mirrored (approved of). The example of "Sue" given previously depicts this. Stipek offers evidence for this view that lack of internalized positive mirroring experiences might sensitize a child to later shame and affect social confidence.

Stipek (1995) also reports fascinating data that children below the age of 33 months are not emotionally affected by social competition. For example, in one study children were told that a tower-building game was competitive (to see who could build the fastest). Those below the age of 33 months, who were slower and lost, carried on building their tower quite happily. After 33 months, however, losing the contest tended to make children lose interest in their own tower. If shame is related to social comparisons (feeling inadequate and inferior compared with others), then such data again suggests that shame is a later rather than a very early experience. One twist to this view is that if shame responses are derived from submissive behavioral responses, then clearly animals need only be aware that they are socially threatened and do not require self-awareness.

Innate Shame-Proneness

A key question concerns whether shame-proneness has an genetic dimension. Personality theorist Jerome Kagan (1994) points to the increasing evidence of temperament differences in children. About 15% show traits of behavioral inhibition (BI) associated with fear of the unfamiliar and novel. Such children may be more prone to anxiety and timidness from the first days of life. Although these traits can be modified by certain parenting styles, they may remain as predisposers to later social shyness and anxiety. However, the evidence is far from clear on this. For example, in a major review of BI and anxiety, Turner, Beidel, and Wolff outlined many methodological problems in various studies linking BI to anxiety disorder. They conclude, for example, that "it would appear that the data indicate that BI is more closely associated with disorders characterized by social-evaluative anxiety" (1996, p. 169). But this conclusion is tempered by the finding that "the critical factor seems to be a familial pattern of anxiety that is the key rather than the presence of BI" (p. 169). And as Turner et al. note, there are a number of hypotheses that can link BI to anxiety disorders.

At present we know little about familial patterns of social anxiety and shame-proneness, including possible genetic factors that affect sensitivity to shame (but see Zahn-Waxler & Robinson, 1995). It has, however, been suggested that shyness is linked to possible inherited traits and that shyness might be a particular sensitivity and fear of shame (Zimbardo, 1997). At present, however, the shyness literature and shame literature remain (like that on social anxiety and shame) separate, and more research is needed.

Trauma-Shame-Proneness

At the other extreme are theories that are essentially trauma (environment)-based theories of shame. For example, sexual and physical abuse are commonly traumatizing and produce long-lived symptoms. It is now recognized that such adverse rearing experiences (including emotional neglect, affectionless control, physical and sexual abuse) can significantly affect psychobiological maturation and functioning (Hart, Gunnar, & Cicchetti, 1996; Parker, 1979; Rohner, 1986). Abuse sensitizes people to various forms of interpersonal conflict (shame-proneness) and pathology (Andrews, 1995 and chapter in this volume). Early, intense shaming has been identified as a major source of later interpersonal relationship difficulties, including violence (Dutton, van Ginkel, & Starzomski, 1995). Indeed, many theorists and therapists in the field locate the origins of shame in family systems (Fossum & Mason, 1986; Harper & Hoopes, 1990; Lansky, 1992). And Bradshaw (1988) has developed a self-help approach to shame originating in early shaming experiences. Many therapists (Kaufman, 1989; Nathanson, 1992) suggest that early traumatizing shame (sometimes referred to as "toxic shame" to differentiate it from shame that is mild and helpful in socialization) is at the root of many psychopathologies.

Intense traumatic experiences do require special therapeutic interventions, which Bergner (1987) has called "undoing degradation." The psychotherapy of shame, rooted in abusive experiences, is likely to be very different from that of straightforward social anxiety or even shyness-mediated problems (Harper & Hoopes, 1990). And there are key questions as to how far the individual, the family (Fossum & Mason, 1986; Harper & Hoopes, 1990), or, even, in some cases, institutions should be targets for interventions (Nathanson, 1987).

The role of trauma in igniting serious shame may present problems for certain measures of shame. For example, some shame measures, such as Tangney's TOSCA, were deliberately designed to tap everyday experiences of shame so that people could easily identify with them. Although such measures are often associated with measures of psychopathology (Tangney, Burggraf, & Wagner, 1995), we may require more specialized measures for assessing pathological shame problems, such as those rooted in early trauma. And most work linking situation shame measures to psychopathology has used students. In the same way that the mild dysphoria of some students may be problematic when it comes to extrapolating to serious depression (Costello, 1993), so using students may be problematic for gaining insight into trauma-shame-based psychopathological states. Also, scales like the TOSCA are tapping (assumed) dispositions in certain situations. The kind of shame-humiliation life events associated with psychopathology might be quite different (Brown, Harris, & Hepworth, 1995).

A problem with trauma-derived shame is that trauma is both a categorical concept (e.g., one is or is not sexually abused) and a dimensional concept (one may experience different levels of, say, emotional abuse and neglect). Thus, there are various types of social interactions that might fall short of abuse but are still capable of affecting the maturing central nervous system and subsequent shame-proneness. Schore (1994; this volume, chapter 3, for example, emphasizes the stage at which a child develops mobility and the parent becomes a socializing agent. At this time the child experiences the parent as full of "do's" and "don'ts," rewards and prohibitions. The clash of interests sets the stage for conflict and shame. An atmosphere might not be abusive but nonetheless be harsh and austere. In a study specifically designed to explore recall of mother and father shaming, Gilbert, Allan, & Goss (1996) found that early shaming was associated with increased psychopathology and interpersonal problems in female students.

Cognitive Vulnerability Models

The cognitive-behavioral view of shame suggests that emotions are only elicited after some "meaning" has been given to situations. No matter how crude a schema or how rapid the analysis, some kind of cognitive operation is needed to activate affect (Beck et al., 1985). In cognitive theory, shame-proneness would arise from the formation of early negative schema of self and others (e.g., I am unlovable, I am bad, etc.). However, there is increasing complexity to this idea. For example, the exact nature of a schema and the memory systems involved when it is activated suggest more than one kind of system (Brewin, 1996). And as noted above, for those who advocate script theory (Tomkins, 1987b) and internalized self-objects (Kohut, 1977), there is no separating the cognitive from the affect aspect of a schema. It is likely then that vulnerability is more at the level of emotive script or internalized emotionally conditioned experiences than a purely cognitive, propositional domain.

Self-Esteem and Shame-Proneness

The relationship of low self-esteem to shame-proneness has never been resolved (Cook, 1993). An unpublished study, which utilized Cook's Internal Shame Scale (ISS), the Other as Shamer scale (OAS; Goss et al., 1994) and a situational shame scale (Gilbert et al., 1994) found that in students a number of self-esteem measures and the ISS and OAS were very highly correlated (above $r=.7$ in most cases). Both had lower but significant correlations with situational shame-proneness (Cowdrey, 1995). Some authors view shame-proneness (rooted in various early experiences) as the source of low or poor self-esteem (Jacoby, 1994). In the self-esteem literature itself, definitions and descriptions of self-esteem seem increasingly close to concepts such as shame-proneness. Leary, Tambor, Terdal, & Downs (1995) have eloquently argued that self-esteem is a "sociometer" that is sensitive to social interactions, especially one's standing in relationship to others. Self-esteem, in their view, monitors social interactions and sets the person in a state of mind to be vigilant to certain kinds of social threat. In their model, the main threat is social exclusion. Low self-esteem primes submissive behavior and displays and is a damage-limitation state of mind. Hence, low self-esteem could increase sensitivity to many social emotions such as shame, social anxiety, and shyness.

Conclusion

Shame, neglected for so long, is fast moving up the rankings of socially important affects. However, it is difficult to be clear what kind of affect shame is. Nonetheless, concepts of bypassed shame and 'shame as the affect that interrupts positive affect' has meant that shame can be seen everywhere. In many forms of psychopathology, from violence, depression, and anxiety through to the loneliness of shyness, shame has been seem to play a role. Shame can be a phenomenon suffered by individuals or groups, and shame can act as a moderator of behavior when associated with honor systems. So shame has attracted the attention of researchers from many different backgrounds. This broadness offers considerable excitement and depth to its study, but also brings problems. If it does not matter whether you are shy or a narcissistic extravert, aggressive, violent, or withdrawn, depressed or anxious, or suffering a disease or handicap, because each can be rooted in shame, then shame may be in danger of becoming so all-embracing a concept that it loses its usefulness. So this chapter has tried to show that there are many yet-to-be-resolved issues, including definitional ones.

Attention has been given to three distinctions: shame and social anxiety, shame and dignity, and shame and humiliation. In regard to the latter, it was argued that shame and humiliation have different affect, cognitive structure, and power dynamics. Humiliation is often hidden as shame once was, or neatly subsumed under shame. Humiliation can lead to shame, as when a person becomes known as someone who has been damaged or degraded. One may feel shame when telling friends or helpers of humiliating experiences (e.g., rape, sexual abuse). A person may be psychologically scarred by others and then feel that this scar is demeaning and the source of shame (Gilbert, 1997a). There are, of course, other emotions that might be associated with shame. The relationship of shame to contempt, and even envy, has still to receive research interest.

Shame researchers will find value, I believe, in the new developments in cognitive science, especially in self-processing (Brewin, 1996; Power & Dalgleish, 1996). Most aroused shame is via fast-track, involuntary processes that are difficult to control. As yet shame researchers have been hesitant to explore this domain of work. But one suspects it won't be long before processing biases become a focus of research, as they are in depression and anxiety.

In regard to treatment, there are probably important differences in the conceptualization and treatment of shame that is rooted in personality dispositions compared to that rooted in serious early trauma. Various therapists have made important efforts to explore the many presentations of shame, to talk of different types of shame and indicate different therapies (Harper & Hoopes, 1990; Nathanson, 1992); but we are still in the early stages of this work, and most researchers still treat shame as a single entity measurable with single scales.

As yet there is little research exploring when people are fearful of "being shamed" and when of "feeling ashamed." This is important because if it is the internal affects of shame that are feared, then people may avoid situations associated with certain affects. Treatment for this type of shame problem might be to help the person tolerate shame affect, in much the same way that anxiety reduction methods involve learning to tolerate anxiety (Wells et al., 1995). And working with shame affect can proceed with learning to recognize and gradually tolerate shame affect and cognitive restructuring in vivo (Gilbert, 1992b). Fear of "being shamed" may require a more cognitive approach that focuses on testing negative beliefs about how others see the self. These in turn may be different from deshaming trauma-based specific memories or beliefs about the self (Bergner, 1987). Again, this research is still in its infancy.

I have also offered my own (not original) view on shame as a social but inner experience of self as an unattractive social agent, under pressure to limit possible damage via escape or appeasement. Shame is about being in the world as an undesirable self, a self one does not wish to be. Shame is an involuntary response to an awareness that one has lost status and is devalued. Shame is certainly no longer the "sleeper," as Helen Lewis (1987a) thought. Through her work, and that of people like Silvan Tomkins, Gerald Kaufman, Donald Nathanson, Thomas Scheff, and many others, the sleeper has woken over the last decade or so—but it is still struggling to find its identity and boundaries.

References

Allan, S., & Gilbert, P. (1995). A social comparison scale: Psychometric properties and relationship to psychopathology. *Personality and Individual Differences, 19*, 293–299.

Allan, S., Gilbert, P., & Goss, K. (1994). An exploration of shame measures: 20 Psychopathology. *Personality and Individual Differences, 17*, 719–722.

Anderson, E. (1994, May). The code of the streets. *The Atlantic Monthly, 5*, 81–94.

Andrews, B. (1995). Bodily shame as a mediator between abusive experiences and depression. *Journal of Abnormal Psychology, 104* (2), 277–285.

Archer, J. (1994). Power and male violence. In J. Archer (Ed.), *Male violence* (pp. 310–331). London: Routledge.

Argyle, M. (1988). *Bodily communication* (2nd ed.). London: Routledge.

Asch, S. E. (1956). Studies of independence and submission to group pressure: 1. A minority of one against a unanimous majority. *Psychological Monographs, 70* (8, Whole No. 416).

Bailey, K. G. (1987). *Human paleopsychology. Applications to aggression and pathological processes*. Hillsdale, NJ: Erlbaum.

Barrett, K. C. (1995). A functionalist approach to shame and guilt. In J. P. Tangney & K. W. Fischer (Eds.), *Self-Conscious emotions: The psychology of shame, guilt, embarrassment and pride* (pp. 25–63). New York: Guilford Press.

Baumeister, R. F., Stillwell, A. M., & Heatherton, T. F. (1994). Guilt: An interpersonal approach. *Psychological Bulletin, 115*, 243–267.

Beck, A. T., Emery, G, & Greenberg, R. L. (1985). *Anxiety disorders and phobias: A cognitive approach*. New York: Basic Books.

Bergner, R. M. (1987). Undoing degradation. *Psychotherapy, 24*, 25–30.

Berkowitz, L. (1989). Frustration-aggression hypothesis: Examination and reformulation. *Psychological Bulletin, 106*, 59–73.

Blatt, S. J. (1991). A cognitive model morphology of psychopathology. *Journal of Nervous and Mental Diseases, 179*, 449–458.

Blatt, S. J., & Zuroff, D. C. (1992). Interpersonal relatedness and self-definition: Two prototypes for depression. *Clinical Psychology Review, 12*, 527–562.

Bowlby, J. (1973). *Attachment and loss: Vol. 2. Separation, anxiety and anger*. London: Hogarth Press.

Bradshaw, J. (1988). *Healing the shame that binds you*. Deerfield Beach, Florida: Health Communications.

Brewin, C. R. (1996). Theoretical foundations of cognitive-behavior therapy for anxiety and depression. *Annual Review of Psychology, 47*, 33–57.

Brewin, C. R., & Furnham, A. (1986). Attributional and pre-attributional variables in self-esteem and depression: A comparison and test of learned helplessness theory. *Journal of Personality and Social Psychology, 50*, 1013–1020.

Brown, G. W., Harris, T. O., & Hepworth, C. (1995). Loss, humiliation and entrapment among women developing depression: A patient and non-patient comparison. *Psychological Medicine, 25*, 7–21.

Cacioppo, J. T., Klein, D. J., Berntson, G. C., & Hatfield, E. (1993). The psychophysiology of emotion. In M. Lewis & J. M. Haviland (Eds.), *Handbook of emotions* (pp. 119–142). New York: Guilford Press.

Carrol, J. M., & Russell, J. A. (1997). Facial expressions in Hollywood's portrayal of emotion. *Journal of Personality and Social Psychology, 72*, 164–176.

Cheek, J. M., & Melchior, L. A. (1990). Shyness, self-esteem and self-consciousness. In H. Leitenberg (Ed.), *Handbook of social and evaluation anxiety* (pp. 47–82). New York: Plenum.

Clark, D. M., & Wells, A. (1995). A cognitive model of social phobia. In R. G. Heimberg, M. R. Liebowitz, D. A. Hope, & R. R. Schneier (Eds.), *Social phobia: Diagnosis, assessment and treatment* (pp. 69–93). New York: Guilford Press.

Cook, D. R. (1993). *The Internalized Shame Scale manual*. Menomonie, WI. Channel Press. (Available from the author, Rt. 7, Box 270A, Menomonie, WI 54751)

Cook, D. R. (1996). Empirical studies of shame and guilt: The Internalized Shame Scale. In D. L. Nathanson (Ed.), *Knowing feeling: Affect, script and psychotherapy* (pp. 132–165). New York: Norton.

Cosmides, L., & Tooby. J. (1992). Cognitive adaptations for social exchange. In J. H. Barkow, L. Cosmides, & J. Tooby, (Eds.), *The adapted mind: Evolutionary psychology and the generation of culture* (pp. 163–228). New York: Oxford University Press.

Costello, C. (1993). *Symptoms of depression*. New York: Wiley.

Cowdrey, S. (1995). *Shame and self-esteem*. Unpublished master's thesis, University of Leicester, United Kingdom.

Crocker, J., & Major, B. (1989). Social stigma and self-esteem: The self-protective qualities of stigma. *Psychological Review, 96*, 608–630.

Daly, M., & Wilson, M. (1994). Evolutionary psychology of male violence. In J. Archer (Ed.), *Male violence* (pp. 253–288). London: Routledge.

Dixon, A. K., Gilbert, P., Huber, C., Gilbert, J., & Van der Hoek, G. (1996). Changes in nonverbal behaviour in a neutral and "shame" interview. Unpublished manuscript, University of Derby, United Kingdom.

Driscoll, R. (1988). Self-condemnation: A conceptual framework for assessment and treatment. *Psychotherapy, 26*, 104–111.

Dutton, G. D., van Ginkel, C., & Starzomski, A. (1995). The role of shame and guilt in the intergeneration transmission of abusiveness. *Violence and Victims, 10*, 121–131.

Ellgring, H. (1989). *Nonverbal communication in depression*. Cambridge: Cambridge University Press.

Enright, P. D. (1991). The moral development of forgiveness. In W. M. Kurtines and J. L. Gewirtz, (Eds.), *Handbook of moral behaviour and development: Vol. 1. Theory*. (pp. 123–152). Hillsdale, NJ: Erlbaum.

Epstein, S. (1994). Integration of the cognitive and the psychodynamic unconscious. *American Psychologist, 49*, 709–724.

Epstein, S., Lipson, A., Holstein, C., and Huh, E. (1992). Irrational reactions to negative outcomes: Evidence for two conceptual systems. *Journal of Personality and Social Psychology, 62*, 328–339.

Ferster, C. B. (1973). A functional analysis of depression. *American Psychologist, 28*, 857–870.

Fischer, K. W., & Tangney, J. P. (1995). Self-Conscious emotions and the affect revolution: Framework and overview. In J. P. Tangney & K. W. Fischer (Eds.), *Self-Conscious emotions: The psychology of shame, guilt, embarrassment and pride* (pp. 3–22). New York: Guilford Press.

Fitzgibbons, R. B. (1986). The cognitive and emotive uses of forgiveness in the treatment of anger. *Psychotherapy, 23*, 629–633.

Fossum, M. A., & Mason, M. J. (1986). *Facing shame: Families in recovery*. New York: Norton.

Friend, R., & Gilbert, J. (1973). Threat and fear of negative evaluation as determinants of locus of social comparison. *Journal of Personality, 41*, 328–340.

Frijda, N. H. (1993). The place of appraisal in emotion. [Special issue: Appraisal and Beyond: The Issue of Cognitive Determinants of Emotion]. *Cognition and Emotion, 3/4*, 357–387.

Frijda, N. H. (1994). The lex talioni: On vengeance. In S. H. M. Van Goozen, N. E. Van de Poll, & J. A. Sergeant (Eds.), *Emotions: Essays on emotion theory* (pp. 263–289). Hillsdale, NJ: Erlbaum.

Gibbons, F. X. (1990). The impact of focus of attention and affect on social behaviour. In W. R. Crozier (Ed.), *Shyness and embarrassment: Perspectives from social psychology* (pp. 119–143). Cambridge: Cambridge University Press.

Gilbert, P. (1989). *Human nature and suffering*. Hove, UK: Erlbaum.

Gilbert, P. (1992a). *Depression: The evolution of powerlessness*. New York: Guilford Press.

Gilbert, P. (1992b). *Counselling for depression*. London: Sage.

Gilbert, P. (1993). Defense and safety: Their function in social behavior and psychopathology. *British Journal of Clinical Psychology, 32*, 131–154.

Gilbert, P. (1995). Biopsychosocial approaches and evolutionary theory as aids to integration in clinical psychology and psychotherapy. *Clinical Psychology and Psychotherapy, 2*, 135–156.

Gilbert, P. (1997a). The evolution of social attractiveness and its role in shame, humiliation, guilt and therapy. *British Journal of Medical Psychology, 70*, 113–147.

Gilbert, P. (1997b). *Overcoming depression: a self-help guide using cognitive behavioral techniques*. London: Robinson. New York: Oxford University Press.

Gilbert, P. (in press). Shame and humiliation in the treatment of complex cases. In N. Tarrier, G. Haddock, and A. Wells (Eds.), *Complex cases: Clinical challenges for cognitive behavior therapy*. Chichester, UK: Wiley.

Gilbert, P., Allan, S., Ball, L., & Bradshaw, Z. (1996). Overconfidence and personal evaluations of social rank. *British Journal of Medical Psychology, 69*, 59–68.

Gilbert, P., Allan, S., & Goss, K. (1996). Parental representations, shame, interpersonal problems and vulnerability to psychopathology. *Clinical Psychology and Psychotherapy, 3*, 23–34.

Gilbert, P., Pehl, J., & Allan, S. (1994). The phenomenology of shame and guilt: An empirical investigation. *British Journal of Medical Psychology, 67*, 23–36.

Gilbert, P., Price, J. S., & Allan, S. (1995). Social comparison, social attractiveness and evolution: How might they be related? *New Ideas in Psychology, 13*, 149–165.

Gilbert, P., & Trower, P. (1990). The evolution and manifestation of social anxiety. In W. R. Crozier (Ed.), *Shyness and embarrassment: Perspectives from social psychology* (pp. 144–177). Cambridge: Cambridge University Press.

Goffman, E. (1968). *Stigma: Notes on the management of a spoiled identity*. Harmondsworth, UK: Penguin.

Goss, K., Gilbert, P., & Allan, S. (1994). An exploration of shame measures: 1. The "Other as Shamer Scale." *Personality and Individual Differences, 17*, 713–717.

Harder, D. W. (1995). Shame and guilt assessment, and relationships of shame-and guilt-proneness to psychopathology. In J. P. Tangney & K. W. Fischer (Eds.). *Self-Conscious emotions: The psychology of shame, guilt, embarrassment and pride* (pp. 368–392). New York: Guilford Press.

Harper, J. C., & Hoopes, M. H. (1990). *Uncovering shame: An approach integrating individuals and their family systems*. New York: Norton.

Hart, J., Gunnar, M., & Cicchetti, D. (1996). Altered neuroendocrine activity in maltreated children related to symptoms of depression. *Development and Psychopathology, 8*, 201–214.

Hewitt, P. L., & Flett, G. L. (1991a). Dimensions of perfectionism in unipolar depression. *Journal of Abnormal Psychology, 100*, 98–101.

Hewitt, P. L., & Flett, G. L. (1991b). Perfectionism in the self and social contexts: Conceptualization, assessment, and association with psychopathology. *Journal of Personality and Social Psychology, 60*, 456–470.

Higgins, E. T. (1987). Self-discrepancy: A theory relating self and affect. *Psychological Review, 94*, 319–340.

Insel, T. R. (1997). A neurobiological basis of social attachment. *American Journal of Psychiatry, 154*, 726–735.

Izard, C. (1993). Four systems for emotional activation: Cognitive and noncognitive processes. *Psychological Review, 100*, 68–90.

Jacoby, M. (1994). *Shame and the origins of self-esteem: A Jungian approach*. London: Routledge.

Jung, C. G. (1993). *The Practice of psychotherapy* (2nd ed.). London: Routledge. (Original work published 1954)

Kagan, J. (1994). *Galen's prophecy*. New York: Free Association Books.

Karen, R. (1991, February). Shame. *The Atlantic Monthly*, 40–70.

Kaufman, G. (1989). *The psychology of shame: Theory and treatment of shame-based syndromes*. New York: Springer.

Kelly, A. E., & McKillop, K. J. (1996). Consequences of revealing personal secrets. *Psychological Bulletin, 120* (3), 450–465.

Keltner, D. (1995). Signs of appeasement: Evidence for the distinct displays of embarrassment, amusement and shame. *Journal of Personality and Social psychology, 68*, 441–454.

Kinston, W. (1987). The shame of narcissism. In D. L. Nathanson (Ed.), *The many faces of shame* (pp. 214–245). New York: Guilford Press.

Klass, E. T. (1990). Guilt, shame and embarrassment: Cognitive-behavioral approaches. In H. Leitenberg (Ed.), *Handbook of social and evaluative anxiety* (pp. 385–414). New York: Plenum.

Klein, D. C. (1991). The humiliation dynamic: An overview. *The Journal of Primary Prevention, 12*, 93–121.

Kohut, H. (1977). *The restoration of the self*. New York: International Universities Press.

Lane, R. D., & Schwartz, G. E. (1987). Levels of emotional awareness: A cognitive-developmental theory and its application to psychopathology. *American Journal of Psychiatry, 144*, 133–143.

Lansky, M. R. (1992). *Fathers who fail: Shame and psychopathology in the family system*. New York: Analytic Press.

Lazare, A. (1987). Shame and humiliation in the medical encounter. *Archives of International Medicine, 147*, 1653–1658.

Lazarus, R. S. (1991). *Emotion and adaptation*. New York: Oxford University Press.

Leary, M. R. (1995). *Self-Presentation: Impression management and interpersonal behavior*. Madison, WI: Brown & Benchmark.

Leary, M. R. & Kowalski, R. M. (1990) Impression management: A literature review and two-component model. *Psychological Bulletin, 107*, 34–47.

Leary, M. R., & Kowalski, R. M. (1995). *Social anxiety*. New York: Guilford Press.

Leary, M. R., Tambor, E. S., Terdal, S. K., & Downs, D. L. (1995). Self-esteem as an interpersonal monitor: The sociometer hypothesis. *Journal of Personality and Social Psychology, 68*, 519–530.

Lewis, H. B. (1986). The role of shame in depression. In M. Rutter, C. E. Izard, & P. B. Read (Eds.), *Depression in young people: Developmental and clinical perspectives* (pp. 325–339). New York: Guilford Press.

Lewis, H. B. (1987a). Shame—the "sleeper" in psychopathology. In H. B. Lewis (Ed.), *The role of shame in symptom formation* (pp. 1–28). Hillsdale, NJ: Erlbaum.

Lewis, H. B. (1987b). Shame and the narcissistic personality. In D. L. Nathanson (Ed.), *The many faces of shame* (pp. 93–132). New York: Guilford Press.

Lewis, H. B. (1987c). The role of shame in depression over the life span. In H. B. Lewis (Ed.), *The role of shame in symptom formation* (pp. 29–50). Hillsdale, NJ: Erlbaum.

Lewis, M. (1992). *Shame: The exposed self*. New York: The Free Press.

Lewis, M. (1993). The emergence of human emotions. In M. Lewis & J. M. Haviland (Eds.), *Handbook of emotions* (pp. 223–235). New York: Guilford Press.

Lewis, M. (1995). Self-Conscious emotions. *American Scientist, 83*, 68–78.

Lewis, M. D. (1996). Self-Organising cognitive appraisals. *Cognition and Emotion, 10*, 1–25.

Lindsay-Hartz, J., de Rivera, J., & Mascolo, M. F. (1995). Differentiating guilt and shame and their effects on motivation. In J. P. Tangney & K. W. Fischer (Eds.), *Self-Conscious emotions: The psychology of shame, guilt, embarrassment and pride* (pp. 274–300). New York: Guilford Press.

MacLean, P. (1985). Brain evolution relating to family, play and the separation call. *Archives of General Psychiatry, 42*, 405–417.

MacLeod, A. K., Byrne, A., & Valentine, J. D. (1996). Affect, emotional disorder and future directed thinking. *Cognition and Emotion, 10*, 69–86.

Mandler, G. (1975). *Mind and emotion.* New York: Wiley.

Marks, I. M. (1987). *Fears, phobias, and rituals: Panic, anxiety and their disorders.* Oxford: Oxford University Press.

Mascolo, M. F., & Fischer, K. W. (1995). Developmental transformations in appraisals of pride, shame and guilt. In J. P. Tangney & K. W. Fischer (Eds.). *Self-Conscious emotions: The psychology of shame, guilt, embarrassment and pride* (pp. 64–113). New York: Guilford Press.

Massaro, T. M. (1991). Shame, culture and American criminal law. *Michigan Law Review, 89* (7), 1880–1944.

McCullough, M. E., Worthington, E. L, & Rachal, K. C. (1997). Interpersonal forgiveness in close relationships. *Journal of Personality and Social Psychology, 73*, 321–336.

Miller, R. S. (1996). *Embarrassment: Poise and peril in everyday life.* New York: Guilford Press.

Miller, S. B. (1988). Humiliation and shame: Comparing two affect states as indicators of narcissistic stress. *Bulletin of the Menninger Clinic, 52*, 40–51.

Miller, S. B. (1996). *Shame in context.* Hillsdale, NJ: Analytic Press.

Miller, W. I. (1993). *Humiliation.* Ithaca, NY: Cornell University Press.

Mollon, P. (1984). Shame in relation to narcissistic disturbance. *British Journal of Medical Psychology, 57*, 207–214.

Mollon, P. (1993). *The fragile self: The structure of narcissistic disturbance.* London: Whurr.

Morrison, A. P. (1987). The eye turned inward: Shame and the self. In D. L. Nathanson (Ed.), *The many faces of shame* (pp. 271–291). New York: Guilford Press.

Nathanson, D. L. (1987). Shaming systems in couples, families and institutions. In D. L. Nathanson (Ed.), *The many faces of shame* (pp. 246–270). New York: Guilford Press.

Nathanson, D. L. (1992). *Shame and pride: Affect, sex and the birth of the self.* New York: Norton.

Nathanson, D. L. (1994). Shame, compassion, and the "borderline" personality. *Psychiatric Clinics of North America, 17*, 785–810.

Nietzel, M. T., & Harris, M. J. (1990). Relationship of dependency and achievement/autonomy to depression. *Clinical Psychology Review, 10*, 279–297.

Oatley, K. (1992). *Best laid schemes: The psychology of emotions.* Cambridge: Cambridge University Press.

Ogilvie, D. M. (1987). The undesired self: A neglected variable in personality research. *Journal of Personality and Social Psychology, 52*, 379–388.

Parker, G. (1979). Parental characteristics in relation to depressive disorders. *British Journal of Psychiatry, 134*, 138–147.

Power, M., & Brewin, C. R. (1991). From Freud to cognitive science: A contemporary account of the unconscious. *British Journal of Clinical Psychology, 30*, 289–310.

Power, M., & Dalgleish, T. (1997). *Cognition and emotions: From order to disorder.* Hove, UK: The Psychology Press.

Rapee, R. M., & Heimberg, R. G. (1997). A cognitive behavioral model of anxiety in social phobia. *Behavior Therapy and Research, 35*, 741–756.

Reimer, M. S. (1996). "Sinking into the ground": The development consequences of shame in adolescence. *Developmental Review, 16*, 321–363.

Reite, M., and Field, T. (Eds.). (1985). *The psychobiology of attachment and separation.* New York: Academic Press.

Retzinger, S. (1991). *Violent emotions: Shame and rage in marital quarrels.* Newbury Park, CA: Sage.

Retzinger, S. M. (1995). Identifying shame and anger in discourse. *American Behavioral Scientist, 38* (8), 1104–1113.

Robins, K. (1993). The politics of silence: The meaning of community and the uses of the media in the new Europe. *New Formations, 21,* 80–101.

Rohner, R. P. (1986). *The warmth dimension: Foundations of parental acceptance-rejection theory.* Beverly Hills, CA: Sage.

Rozin, P., & Fallon, A. E. (1987). A perspective on disgust. *Psychological Review, 94,* 23–41.

Russell, J. A. (1995). Facial expressions of emotion: What lies beyond minimal universality? *Psychological Bulletin, 118,* 379–391.

Shaver, K. G., & Drown, D. (1986). On causality, responsibility and self blame: A theoretical note. *Journal of Personality and Social Psychology, 50,* 697–702.

Scheff, T. J. (1987). The shame-rage spiral: A case study of an interminable quarrel. In H. B. Lewis (Ed.), *The role of shame in symptom formation* (pp. 109–149). Hillsdale, NJ: Erlbaum.

Scheff, T. J. (1988). Shame and conformity: The deference-emotion system. *American Review of Sociology, 53,* 395–406.

Scheff, T. J. (1994). *Bloody revenge: Emotions, nationalism and war.* Boulder, CO: Westview Press.

Schore, A. N. (1994). *Affect regulation and the origin of the self: The neurobiology of emotional development.* Hillsdale, NJ: Erlbaum.

Serney, G. (1990, September 23). The sins of the fathers. *The Sunday Times Colour Magazine,* 22–36.

Silver, M., Conte, R., Miceli, M., & Poggi, I. (1986). Humiliation: Feeling, self control and the construction of identity. *Journal of the Theory of Social Behavior, 16,* 269–283.

Smith, C., & Lazarus, R. S. (1993). Appraisal components, core relational themes, and the emotions. *Cognition and Emotion, 7,* 233–269.

Snaith, R. P., Hamilton, M., Morley, S., Humayan, D., & Trigwell, P. (1995). A scale for the assessment of hedonic tone: The Snaith-Hamilton pleasure scale. *British Journal of Psychiatry, 167,* 99–103.

Solomon, R. C. (1994). Sympathy and vengeance: The role of the emotions in justice. In S. H. M. Van Goozen, N. E. Van de Poll, & J. A. Sergeant (eds). *Emotions: Essays on emotion theory* (pp. 291–311). Hillsdale, NJ: Erlbaum.

Stam, J. L. (1978). The meaning of humiliation and its relationship to fluctuations in self-esteem. *International Review of Psychoanalysis, 5,* 425–433.

Steele, C. M. (1975). Name calling and compliance. *Journal of Personality and Social Psychology, 31,* 361–369.

Stipek, D. (1995). The development of pride and shame in toddlers. In J. P. Tangney & K. W. Fischer (Eds.). *Self-Conscious emotions: The psychology of shame, guilt, embarrassment and pride* (pp. 237–252). New York: Guilford Press.

Suls, J., & Wills, T. A. (Eds.). (1991). *Social comparison: Contemporary theory and research.* Hillsdale, NJ: Erlbaum.

Tangney, J. P. (1990). Assessing individual differences in proneness to shame and guilt: Development of the Self-Conscious Affect and Attribution Inventory. *Journal of Personality and Social Psychology, 59,* 102–111.

Tangney, J. P. (1995). Shame and guilt in interpersonal relationships. In J. P. Tangney & K. W. Fischer (Eds.). *Self-Conscious emotions: The psychology of shame, guilt, embarrassment and pride* (pp. 114–139). New York: Guilford Press.

Tangney, J. P. (1996). Conceptual and methodological issues in the assessment of shame and guilt. *Behaviour Therapy and Research, 34,* 741–754.

Tangney, J. P., Burggraf, S. A., & Wagner, P. E. (1995). Shame-proneness, guilt-proneness, and psychological symptoms. In J. P. Tangney & K. W. Fischer (Eds.), *Self-Conscious emotions: The psychology of shame, guilt, embarrassment and pride* (pp. 343–367). New York: Guilford Press.

Tangney, J. P., & Fischer, K. W. (Eds.) (1995). *Self-Conscious emotions: The psychology of shame, guilt, embarrassment and pride*. New York: Guilford Press.

Tangney, J. P., Hill-Barlow, D., Wagner, P. E., Marschall, D. E., Borenstein, J. K., Sanftner, J., Mor, T., & Gramzow, R. (1996). Assessing individual differences in constructive versus destructive responses to anger across the lifespan. *Journal of Personality and Social Psychology 70*, 780–796.

Tangney, J. P., & Miller, R. S. (1996). Are shame, guilt and embarrassment distinct emotions? *Journal of Personality and Social Psychology, 70*, 1256–1269.

Tangney, J. P., Wagner, P., Fletcher, C., & Gramzow, R. (1992) Shamed into anger? The relation of shame and guilt to anger and self-reported aggression. *Journal of Personality and Social Psychology, 62*, 669–675.

Tangney, J. P., Wagner, P., & Gramzow, R. (1992) Proneness to shame, proneness to guilt, and psychopathology. *Journal of Abnormal Psychology, 101*, 469–478.

Tangney, J. P., Wagner, P. E., Hill arlow, D., Marschall, D. E., & Gramzow, R. (1996). Relation of shame and guilt to constructive versus destructive responses to anger across the lifespan. *Journal of Personality and Social Psychology, 70*, 797–809.

Teasdale, J. D. (1997). The transformation of meaning: The interacting cognitive subsystems approach. In M. Power & C. R. Brewin (Eds.), *The transformation of meaning in psychological therapies: Integrating theory and practice*. Chichester, UK: Wiley.

Teasdale, J. D., & Barnard, P. J. (1993). *Affect, cognition and change: Remodelling depressive affect*. Hove, UK: Erlbaum.

Thase, M. E., & Howland, R. H. (1995). Biological processes in depression: An update and integration. In E. E. Beckham & W. R. Leber (Eds.), *Handbook of depression* (2nd ed., pp. 213–279). New York: Guilford Press.

Tomkins, S. S. (1963). *Affect, imagery, consciousness: 2. The negative affects*. New York: Springer.

Tomkins, S. S. (1981). The quest for primary motives: Biography and autobiography. *Journal of Personality and Social Psychology, 41*, 306–329.

Tomkins, S. S. (1987a). Shame. In D. L. Nathanson (Ed.), *The many faces of shame* (pp. 133–161.) New York: Guilford Press.

Tomkins, S. S. (1987b). Script theory. In J. Arnoff, A. I. Rabin, & R. A. Zucker (Eds.), *The emergence of personality* (pp. 147–216). New York: Springer.

Tronick, E. Z., & Cohn, J. F. (1989). Infant-mother face-to-face interaction: Age and gender differences in coordination and the occurrence of miscoordination. *Child Development, 60*, 85–92.

Trower, P., Gilbert, P., & Sherling, G. (1990). Social anxiety, evolution and self-presentation. In H. Leitenberg (Ed.), *Handbook of social and evaluation anxiety* (pp. 11–45). New York: Plenum.

Turner, S. M., Beidel, D. C., & Wolff, P. L. (1996). Is behavioral inhibition related to the anxiety disorders? *Clinical Psychology Review, 16*, 157–172.

Watson, D., & Friend, R. (1969). Measurement of social-evaluation anxiety. *Journal of Consulting and Clinical Psychology, 33*, 448–457.

Watson, D., Clark, L. A., Weber, K., Assenheimer, J. S., Strauss, M. E., & McMormick, R. A. (1995). Testing a tripartite model: 2. Exploring the symptom structure of anxiety and depression in student adult and patient samples. *Journal of Abnormal Psychology, 104*, 15–25.

Watson, D., Weber, K., Assenheimer, J. S., Clark, L. A., Strauss, M. E., & McMormick, R. A. (1995). Testing a tripartite model: 1. Evaluating the convergent and discriminant validity of anxiety and depression symptom scales. *Journal of Abnormal Psychology, 104*, 3–14.

Wells, A., Clarke, D. M., Salkovskis, P., Ludgate, J., Hackman, A., & Gelder, M. (1995). Social phobia: The role of in-situation safety behaviours in maintaining anxiety and negative beliefs. *Behaviour Therapy, 26*, 153–161.

Wilson, E. (1987). Shame and the other: Reflections on the theme of shame in French psychoanalysis. In D. L. Nathanson (Ed.), *The many faces of shame* (pp. 162–193). New York: Guilford Press.

Wurmser, L. (1987). Shame: The veiled companion of narcissism. In D. L. Nathanson (Ed.), *The many faces of shame* (pp. 64–92). New York: Guilford Press.

Wyatt, R. & Gilbert, P. (1998). Dimensions of perfectionism: A study exploring their relationship with perceived social rank and status. *Personality and Individual Differences, 24,* 71–79.

Yalom, I. (1985). *The theory and practice of group psychotherapy* (3rd ed.). New York: Basic Books.

Yalom, I. D. (1980). *Existential psychotherapy.* New York: Basic Books.

Zahn-Waxler, C., & Robinson, J. (1995). Empathy and guilt: Early origins of feelings of responsibility In J. P. Tangney & K. W. Fischer (Eds.), *Self-Conscious emotions: The psychology of shame, guilt, embarrassment and pride* (pp. 143–173). New York: Guilford Press.

Zimbardo, P. G. (1997, July). *The personal and social dynamics of shyness.* Keynote address presented at the International Conference on Shyness and Self-Consciousness, University of Cardiff, Cardiff, Wales, UK.

2

Methodological and Definitional Issues in Shame Research

Bernice Andrews

The measurement of shame cannot be discussed without consideration of the ways in which it has been defined or the purpose for which it is being measured. The shame measures on which this chapter focuses are those that have been used to assess the extent to which individuals are inclined to feel shame. The task has been to measure shame as a trait or a disposition that may be manifested in repeated reactions to particular events. Repetitive patterns of emotional response, whether caused by endogenous or situational processes, can become dysfunctional (Oatley & Jenkins, 1992), and the main purpose of using these measures has been to investigate associations between shame and psychopathology or other maladaptive cognitions and behavior (e.g., Allan, Gilbert, & Goss, 1994; Andrews, 1995, 1997; Andrews & Hunter, 1997; Cook, 1988; Gilbert, Pehl, & Allan, 1994; Harder, Cutler, & Rockart, 1992; Hoblitzelle, 1987; Tangney, Wagner, & Gramzow, 1992, 1992). Very often the aim has been to compare the relation of shame and guilt to psychopathology. Investigations of dispositional shame have also included explorations of etiological factors (e.g., Andrews, 1995; 1997; Andrews & Hunter, 1997; Gilbert, Allan, & Goss, 1996; Hoglund & Nicholas, 1995), and cross-cultural differences (Johnson et al., 1987).

While the focus of this chapter is on self-report measures of dispositional shame, there are other methods of defining and measuring it. Both observational methods and narrative analyses have been used to identify expressions of shame as they occur. For example, nonverbal expressions of shame have been measured in relation to expressions of other emotions (Keltner, 1995) and to social and developmental factors (e.g., Alessandri & Lewis, 1993), and both manifest and latent verbal shame expressions have been assessed in relation to interactions in therapy (e.g., Lewis, 1971; Retzinger, this volume, chapter 11; Scheff, this volume, chapter 10). In the main, studies assessing the expression of current shame do not explicitly focus on shame as a disposition. One exception is the series of experimental observational studies of children carried out by Lewis and colleagues (e.g., Alessandri & Lewis, 1993).

While many have emphasized the role of shame as an adaptive emotion, a viewpoint sometimes apparent in studies that assess current expressions of shame (see Keltner & Harker, this volume, chapter 4), dispositional shame has been viewed as maladaptive and likely to be associated with negative outcomes. A number of dispositional shame measures have been used in published research, and the question arises as to whether all are equally effective in reflecting it. In the main, questionnaire measures have assessed the construct indirectly, using items that are thought to reflect different components of the shame experience. But to what extent do shame scales actually reflect dispositional shame? And what sense can we make of associations between these scales and other measures of psychopathology? The broad aim of this chapter is to address these questions.

There are two strands to the first question, and both have implications for the overall design of scales. One concerns how researchers have conceptualized the characteristics of high-shame individuals in their measures and the extent to which this might truly describe such individuals. The other concerns whether shame scales are actually measuring shame or other related emotions, cognitions, or behaviors. Although there is undoubted overlap in the issues covered, I shall address these two strands separately.

Conceptualization of the Characteristics of High-shame Individuals

The main thrust of investigations of shame in relation to psychopathology is to identify individuals for whom shame is an abiding problem. However, in existing measures, there is some variation in the underlying notion of the characteristics high-shame individuals might have. Examination of the content and construction of existing scales suggests that they have been designed to assess the degree to which people conform to the following types:

1) Individuals who are especially sensitive to feeling shame in potentially shame-eliciting situations, that is, people we might call *shame-prone*.
2) Individuals who frequently or continuously feel generalized or global shame.
3) Individuals who are chronically ashamed of their behavior or particular personal characteristics.

On common-sense grounds the categories are obviously not mutually exclusive, and it would be expected that measures reflecting different shame aspects would be reasonably correlated. Indeed, there is evidence of associations between measures that reflect the first two categories (e.g., Harder, 1995), although the overlap is by no means great, with correlations in the range of .42 to .54. Whether people who are chronically ashamed of specific aspects of self (category 3) usually only have such feelings triggered in particular situations (category 1) and the extent to which shame about specific aspects of self manifests as global shame (category 2) are open to further investigation. In the following discussion, measures that reflect the three different categories are described and evaluated in terms of the assumptions made by researchers regarding the characteristics of the high-shame individuals they are seeking to assess.

Shame-Proneness

Scales that have been most commonly used in published research to assess shame-proneness are the Dimensions of Consciousness Questionnaire (DCQ; Johnson et al., 1987), the well-known Test of Self-Conscious Affect (TOSCA; Tangney, Wagner, & Gramzow, 1989) and its predecessor, the Self-Conscious Affect and Attribution Inventory (SCAAI; Tangney 1990). These questionnaire measures present a series of hypothetical potentially shame-inducing situations or scenarios. In the DCQ, respondents are asked to imagine themselves in shame and guilt-inducing situations and to indicate how badly they would feel on a 7-point scale. An example of a shame situation is "making a scene at a corner of a busy business district," and an example of a guilt situation is "secretly making huge profits at the expense of others." In the SCAAI and the TOSCA, respondents are presented with hypothetical scenarios, followed by four "common reactions" to these situations (including shame and guilt reactions as defined by the researchers). Respondents indicate on a 5-point scale how likely they would be to react in each of the ways described. Examples of TOSCA scenarios are "You break something at work and then hide it" and "you are driving down the road and you hit a small animal." For both measures, scores are summed to assess shame, guilt, and other emotions.

Situations in the DCQ and scenarios and responses in the TOSCA were selected from real-life shame and guilt experiences generated by previous respondents during the development of the instruments. However, the problem remains that scales using hypothetical situations or scenarios may lack ecological validity. There is still the question of whether subjects' responses reflect what they actually do or feel in real-life situations (Brewin & Andrews, 1992; Coyne, 1992; Segal & Dobson, 1992).

On a more specific level there has been criticism of instruments such as the DCQ that are based on situations previously defined as reflecting shame or guilt (see Tangney, 1996). The assumption is that feeling bad about hypothetical "shame" situations specifically reflects shame-proneness, whereas feeling bad about hypothetical "guilt" situations specifically reflects guilt-proneness. However, this does not take into account the complex relationship between shame and guilt and the likelihood that many situations have the potential to elicit either emotion (Tangney, 1992).

One final measurement issue concerns the degree to which high-shame individuals can be solely characterized by a propensity to feel shame in potentially shame-inducing situations. The scenarios included in the SCAAI and the TOSCA measures describe some kind of behavior or (occasionally) an intention about which the respondent might feel more or less ashamed (or guilty). The conceptualization of a shame-prone individual rests on the notion that shame usually occurs in the context of evaluating personal behavior in particular situations. The traditional framework in which shame issues have been researched has been the same one that has been used in relation to guilt. Because guilt is only experienced as a consequence of deeds, intentions, or thoughts about others, it is not surprising that the assessment of high-shame individuals vis-à-vis high-guilt individuals should focus on responses to personal behavior.

However, this does not take account of the fact that personal behavior is not the only focus for shame (Andrews & Hunter, 1997). It is likely that important characteristics of high-shame individuals may be lost if no account is taken of abiding shame about particular personal characteristics that may be independent of shame felt as a consequence of personal behavior. There is evidence that a propensity to feel shame about personal characteristics is to some extent independent of a propensity to feel shame in response to personal behavior: in a recent enquiry carried out with Elaine Hunter involving a sample of depressed patients, we found that correlations between interview measures of behavioral, bodily, and characterological shame did not exceed .40 (Andrews & Hunter, 1997). Furthermore, groundbreaking work by Tangney and colleagues on the structural and phenomenological dimensions of shame, guilt, and embarrassment in students showed that, contrary to received opinion, a surprisingly high proportion of shame experiences involve private events (Tangney, Miller, Flicker, & Barlow, 1996). It seems possible that these private events may involve ruminations about personal shortcomings.

Generalized or Global Shame

In scales measuring global shame, high-shame individuals are conceptualized as frequently or continuously feeling generalized or global shame. Scales most commonly used in published research to assess generalized shame include the Adapted Shame and Guilt Scale (ASGS; Hoblitzelle, 1987), the Internalized Shame Scale (ISS; Cook, 1988, 1996), and the Personal Feelings Questionnaire-2 (PFQ2; Harder & Zalma, 1990). The ASGS and the PFQ2 contain items defined as reflecting both guilt and shame, whereas the ISS contains only items defined as reflecting shame. Items on these scales are brief self-referent statements or adjectives.

In the ASGS respondents are instructed to indicate how well a list of self-referent adjectives describes them on a 7-point scale. Examples of shame adjectives are *bashful* and *mortified*, and examples of guilt items are *liable* and *indecorous*. In the PFQ2, subjects are asked how common the feelings listed are for them on a 5-point scale ranging from *never* to *continuously*. Examples of shame feelings include *embarrassment* and *feeling ridiculous*, and examples of guilt feelings are *mild guilt* and *remorse*. In the ISS, subjects indicate on a 5-point scale the frequency (from *never* to *almost always*) with which they find themselves experiencing feelings described in statements such as "I feel like I am never quite good enough" and "sometimes I feel no bigger than a pea." The assumption is that these scales are reflecting dispositional shame, or shame-proneness (Harder, Cutler, & Rockart, 1992). However, the scales do not assess the length of time over which feelings have been experienced. As global negative self-referent questionnaires tend to be highly mood-dependent (Andrews & Brown, 1993; Barnett & Gotlib, 1988; Brewin, 1985), it is unclear whether the measures are assessing an enduring characteristic that is present even in the absence of negative affective states such as depression. Although the test-retest reliabilities of global (and scenario-based) shame measures has been high, the testing has been carried out over periods of time not exceeding one or two months. I will return to this issue when we consider the meaning of the observed relationship between measures of shame and psychopathology.

Chronic Shame of Personal Attributes and Behaviors

My own studies have employed a semistructured interview with investigator-based ratings to assess shame of personal characteristics and behavior. As the body provides a common and salient real-life focus and is a central concern in shame (Gilbert, 1989; Mollon, 1984; Sartre, 1956), the measure was originally developed to assess bodily shame alone (Andrews, 1995; Andrews, 1997). The measure was later developed to probe for additional sources of shame (Andrews & Hunter, 1997), drawing on Janoff-Bulman's influential distinction between negative judgements directed at one's behavior and at one's character (Janoff-Bulman, 1979). A direct question is asked about whether the respondent has felt ashamed about the particular aspect under investigation (body, character, or behavior) and the duration of the feelings, where relevant. So, for example, the initial question on bodily shame is: "Have you felt ashamed about your body or any part of it?." If the respondent's answer is in the affirmative, he or she is then requested to describe their feelings in greater detail, with probes, where necessary, to cover different aspects of appearance. The investigator then rates their responses on 4-point scales (from *little or none* to *marked*) for the three aspects (bodily shame, characterological shame, and behavioral shame) with reference to a series of examples, according to the intensity, frequency, and specificity of the comments.

In the separate studies using this measure, we have achieved high interrater reliability. The measure does not rest on the assumption that high-shame individuals will have generalized shame but questions specific areas where respondents might feel shame. So, for example, an individual may report feeling intensely ashamed about his behavior, but not about his body or other nonphysical characteristics. Because of this, the measure may be less vulnerable to mood-state effects than questionnaire measures, which rely on more global self-judgments. In the design of the measure, there was also no underlying assumption that what was being measured reflected a disposition. However, we have found that such feelings, where they exist, are usually of long duration, often going back many years (e.g. Andrews, 1995).

Concluding Comments on the Conceptualization of High-shame Individuals

This exploration of the different ways in which high-shame individuals have been conceptualized by the designers of shame measures suggests the possibility that, to a greater or lesser extent, dispositional shame may not be completely captured by existing measures. Scenario-based measures rest on the assumption that dispositional shame reflects a tendency to feel shame in response to behavior in particular situations. However, there is evidence to suggest that dispositional shame can be manifested in other ways, involving a specific focus on physical and nonphysical personal characteristics that may or may not be reflected in everyday behavior. That we may feel ashamed of what we are as well as what we do is inherent in Goffman's seminal work on stigma (Goffman, 1963). As Goffman points out, there is only a very small section of the population that is potentially exempt from experiencing stigma (white, upper-class, well-educated, well-employed, physically adept, married males of good height and physique with pleasing facial features). Those of us who do not measure up to this identity norm manage our "shameful differentness" as best we can. And the extent to which we are unsuccessful in doing so is a likely sign of a tendency to feel shame.

Global shame measures, based on self-referent statements, are not subject to the problem of focusing exclusively on behavior, but there is a real danger that they may simply be reflecting negative affective mood states.

The perspective adopted in the design of the interview measure is that there may not be one distinct type of high-shame individual. However, different types might all be characterized by feeling chronic shame, albeit about different aspects of themselves or their behavior. In this respect, the measure is at odds with notions of dispositional shame, which have driven questionnaire measures. It is possible that high-shame individuals may focus on different aspects of self and behavior at different times in their lives, depending on their circumstances. Distinctions between different aspects may therefore be arbitrary and artificial. However, this issue can only be resolved by further investigation.

Do Shame Scales Measure Shame?

The Operationalization of Shame in Questionnaire Measures

The difficulty that researchers face in general in attempting to devise scales to measure emotion has been well captured by Ken Strongman:

> Many different states may share one expressive pattern, and many different expressions may characterize one emotion. Analysis and conceptualization become difficult. (1973, pp. 156–157)

Regarding shame in particular, it may be instructive to note the words of Donald Nathanson, writing over a decade ago:

> Try as I might, I was unable to understand shame from the excellent writings already available. So many authors described shame from such highly individual points of view that sometimes it seems as if they were describing different emotions. (1987, p. ix)

Although much has been written about shame since that time, the question of whether it is possible to operationalize the unique individual phenomenological experience of shame is as relevant as ever. Recently there have been lively discussions in the literature concerning the definition of dispositional shame, discussions which have mainly centered on the difference between shame-and guilt-proneness (see Harder, 1995; Tangney, Burggraf, & Wagner, 1995). Differences in definitions have implications for the design of shame scales, although much of the controversy appears to have arisen after, rather than before, the most commonly used scales were designed.

Shame scales vary in the way they are derived. They may be based on theory or informed by empirical investigation or statistical analysis, sometimes in varying combinations. Given that theories differ in their descriptions of shame, before evaluating the content of existing measures we should first consider empirical investigations of the shame experience. Two studies have contrasted experiences of different emotions in student samples. Wicker, Payne, and Morgan (1983) asked 152 students to recall situations where they felt shame and guilt and then to rate these experiences on 34 predetermined dimensions. This procedure was repeated for 121 of the students, generating ratings for three shame and three guilt situations. In a more recent study, Tangney et al. (1996) used a similar (but nonrepeated) procedure with 182 students, who were asked to recall experiences of shame, guilt, and embarrassment and to rate them on 31 dimensions. Dimensions in the two studies covered broadly the same ground, although there was not complete overlap.

Overall, the findings in the two studies were quite similar. Both suggested more similarities than differences between shame and guilt, but shame was the more intense, incapacitating emotion and more often involved physiological accompaniments such as blushing, feelings of inferiority, powerlessness, and self-consciousness, and the desire to hide and conceal transgressions. In addition, others were more often seen as angry or rejecting in shame. In Wicker et al.'s (1983) study, shame also more often involved feeling inhibited and passive; in Tangney et al.'s (1996) study, shame was also uniquely associated with feelings of isolation and a wish to have acted differently. Surprisingly, Tangney et al. found far more differences between shame and embarrassment than between shame and guilt.

Items included in the most commonly used shame scales all contain at least some of the elements found to be specific to shame in the empirical research, along with other items derived from theory. However, the weight given to different shame aspects and the emphasis on what is considered to be the most salient and central aspects of shame differ depending on the measure. Examination of items included in the TOSCA, ISS, ASGS, and PFQ2 illustrates the point.

Scenarios in the TOSCA were selected from accounts provided by several hundred college students, whereas the items representing the different emotional responses were drawn from a larger pool of responses provided by noncollege adults. There appears to be no published account of the selection procedure for the shame responses included in the measure, so it is difficult to tell the extent to which they are truly representative of all responses. Ten of the 15 shame-response items involve attributions of characterological self-blame (Janoff-Bulman, 1979) for the hypothesized behavior described in the scenario. For example, items include thinking or feeling that one is inconsiderate, incompetent, and inadequate. Four of the other shame-response items involve hiding or concealment, and one involves feeling isolated.

A number of authors have likened the distinction between shame and guilt to that between characterological (CSB) and behavioral self-blame (BSB) (Hoblitzelle, 1987; Lewis, 1987; Weiner, 1986). It has been suggested that shame, with its focus on stable negative characteristics of the self (implicated in CSB), is in direct contrast to guilt, where the focus is thought to be on the negative judgment of the self's behavior (implicated in BSB). However, the question arises of whether CSB is synonymous with or exclusive to shame. Although there is evidence that statements "undoing" or changing aspects of self more often follow descriptions of shame than of guilt (Niedenthal, Tangney, & Gavanski, 1994), other research has shown no differences between guilt and shame experiences in the degree to which participants blame either their actions and behavior or their personality and self (Tangney et al., 1996).

Emphasis on aspects of shame in the scales representing global shame varies quite considerably. According to Cook (1988), who designed the measure, the development of items in the ISS was informed by theoretical conceptions of shame by authors such as G. Kaufman, H. B. Lewis, and S. Tomkins. The ISS comprises 24 items (with 6 additional filler items from the Rosenberg Self-Esteem Scale), nearly half involving global negative self-esteem or global self-criticism. Other items can be loosely classified as involving other-focused self-evaluation (3 items), fear of exposure (3 items), feelings of emptiness (5 items), bodily fragility (2 items), and rumination (1 item). This classification is similar to factors identified by Cook using statistical analysis: he labeled the first factor "inadequate and deficient" and states that internalized shame is best described as "a deep sense of inferiority, inadequacy or deficiency" (cited in Tangney, 1996, p. 745).

In terms of their specificity to shame, many ISS items may have more theoretical than empirical support. The scale has already been criticized by Tangney (1996) on the grounds that it has more to do with low self-esteem than shame and that the two are distinct constructs. Tangney's objection is based in part on her particular conceptualization of dispositional shame as a tendency to experience shame as an emotion in response to specific aversive events. Because global negative self-esteem is for the most part independent of specific situations, it is viewed by Tangney as essentially a self-evaluative construct with little affective component.

However, emotions and moods may be elicited via endogenous processes (Oatley, 1992), and individuals can feel shame about personal shortcomings in the absence of specific events (e.g., Andrews, 1995). Nevertheless, while negative self-evaluation may be a *necessary* element of shame, it is unlikely that it is *sufficient* as a definition of shame. In other words, the two are not synonymous. As I have argued elsewhere, negative self-evaluation does not necessarily involve concealment of supposed deficiencies nor an inordinate concern about how one appears to others (Andrews, 1995).

Unlike the TOSCA and the ISS, the two other measures of global shame (and guilt), the ASGS and the PFQ2, both include sizable proportions of items with high face validity. That is, there are items directly recognizable as pertaining to shame and guilt, respectively. The 10 items on the ASGS shame scale were derived from a factor analysis, and shame items include self-referent adjectives such as *mortified, humiliated,* and *ashamed.* However, one item (*depressed*) had a high loading on the shame factor and was included in the scale. Given the fact that the scale has been used to explore the relative contributions of shame and guilt to psychopathology, particularly depression, its inclusion is questionable.

It has been argued that items on the shame and guilt scales of the ASGS may require a level of verbal understanding beyond the reach of large sections of the population (e.g., Tangney, 1996). The PFQ2 is more accessible, and the 10 shame items reflect aspects that have been shown to be specific to shame in empirical research, including feelings of helplessness, being disgusting to others, and blushing, along with more direct expressions of shame, such as feeling humiliated. However, when Harder and Zalma (1990) factor analyzed the PFQ2, they found anomalies. Shame items such as feeling humiliated and self-conscious did not load on the factor labeled as shame but unexpectedly loaded on the guilt factor.

The Operationalization of Shame in an Interview Measure

My own shame measure (Andrews, 1995; Andrews & Hunter, 1997) employs interview methodology, where respondents are questioned directly about the degree of behavioral, characterological, and bodily shame they feel currently and have felt at any other time in their lives. Unlike the questionnaire measures, shame ratings are based on the respondent's own interpretation of shame. The measure is not without disadvantages. On a practical level, in common with all interview assessments, a larger investment of time and effort is required than with questionnaire assessments. The measure involves investigator-based ratings, and a certain amount of instruction is necessary to achieve satisfactory interrater reliability.

On a methodological level, there are some possible problems. One is that face-to-face interviews might induce shame in already shame-prone individuals and thereby decrease the likelihood that aspects of shame will be divulged. There is some evidence that respondents might feel uneasy when answering questions about shame. In a recent videotaped study of nonverbal behavior (Dixon et al., 1997), 10 psychology students were questioned about their professional ambitions (neutral interview) before the Body, Character, and Behavior Shame Interview was administered. The students showed increased gaze avoidance and more frequent and longer hesitations before answering questions in the shame interview, although there was no difference between the two interviews in the amount they spoke. It is possible, however, that the constraints posed by the experimental setup (the students' facial expressions were videotaped at close proximity) may have increased these effects.

There is other evidence that respondents express more difficulties in talking about shame experiences than about guilt experiences when interviewed, although this does not appear to prevent them from doing so (Lindsay-Hartz, 1984). A related problem inherent in all assessments of dispositional shame is the possibility that much shame may not be experienced at a conscious level (*bypassed shame*; Lewis, 1971). The type of indirect statements that represent shame manifestations in self-report questionnaires may be more effective in tapping unconscious feelings than is direct face-to-face questioning. However, it is doubtful whether this issue could ever be resolved by empirical test (see Harder, 1995).

Our own experience in interviewing adult and teenage women and depressed male and female patients is that most are willing to talk in detail about shame experiences. Talking to trained, sensitive interviewers, around 40% of the older women and just under half of the younger women in our studies have admitted to feeling at least some bodily shame at the time, while over half the depressed patients talked about current feelings of bodily, characterological, and behavioral shame. Furthermore, these proportions increase when mention of past shame feelings is included. It is, of course, possible that larger proportions of our respondents may have divulged shame in response to a questionnaire where anonymity was preserved. A task for the future will be to compare responses to questionnaire and interview shame measures with similar content. We are in the process of developing a questionnaire based on our interview, that will enable us to explore this issue.

Another objection to measures using direct questioning about shame may be that individuals cannot be expected to know the difference between shame and guilt in the abstract, and that definitions of shame and guilt are best left to the researcher (Tangney, 1996). The issue is not directly relevant to shame of physical and nonphysical personal characteristics, as we cannot feel guilty about who we are, only about what we do. The relationship between behavioral shame and guilt, however, is more problematic. While there is evidence for the discriminant validity of the TOSCA shame and guilt scales (depression is related to shame, but not to guilt), the definition of guilt apparent in the scale is not universally accepted (see Harder, 1995). As already outlined, studies comparing structural and phenome-nological dimensions of shame and guilt have confirmed that there are more sim-ilarities than differences in people's accounts of their experiences of the two emo-tions (Tangney et al., 1996; Wicker et al., 1983).

This problem of discrimination is apparent in a pilot study we carried out with 31 college employees and 7 psychiatric patients using our shame interview (An-drews & Hunter, 1996). After respondents were asked whether they had felt ashamed of their behavior, where relevant they were further asked whether the feelings were more about shame or about guilt. Of the 20 respondents who initially indicated at least some behavioral shame, 12 said they had both feelings, 4 said their feelings were purely shame, and, on reflection, 4 said it was guilt, not shame, that they felt. Typical responses were that it was hard to separate the two emotions. One respondent said, "As far as I am concerned, the two are intertwined; if I'm feeling guilty it leads to a sense of shame."

However, this problem is not resolved when definitions of shame and guilt are left to the investigator. There are still substantial correlations between question-naire measures of the two emotions. In fact, discriminant correlations between measures of shame and guilt are sometimes higher than convergent correlations between different measures of shame. For example, correlations between guilt and shame using the same method (TOSCA: .47; PFQ2: .52) are higher than the corre-lation between TOSCA and PFQ2 shame measures (.42) (Harder, 1995).

Concluding Comments on the Operationalization of Shame in Shame Measures

It appears that the content of the most commonly used questionnaire scales does not always conform to phenomenological experiences specific to shame that are identified in empirical enquiries. The majority of items in the TOSCA refer to characterological self-blame. CSB does not appear to be specific to shame, accord-ing to one study (Tangney et al., 1996), although there is support for its association with shame on theoretical grounds, and it has been shown to correlate with shame in empirical studies (Hoblitzelle, 1987; Weiner, 1986). Similarly, the largest group of items in the ISS refers to global low self-esteem and self-criticism, a self-evaluative construct related to shame but, unlike shame, judged as having little affective component (Tangney, 1996). On theoretical grounds, negative self-attitudes such as characterological self-blame, low self-esteem, and self-criticism all have a long tradition of being implicated in the causation or maintenance of psychological problems, such as depression, without reference to shame. It would seem therefore that these negative self-attitudes are related to shame and are likely manifestations of shame, but they are not exclusive to shame and may be experienced independently of shame.

As with the measurement of many other trait variables, the general approach taken in the measurement of dispositional shame is to include a number of different but related manifestations of the construct in one scale. The alternative assumptions underlying this approach have been outlined by Carver (1989) in the context of evaluating research strategies of theorists who use measures based on multifaceted constructs. Carver points out that the adoption of a multifaceted construct appears to reflect one of two assumptions, although the assumption is rarely made explicit by the theorist. One is that the underlying construct is assessed directly by means of its various components (the latent variable approach). The second is that a construct is more than the sum of its component parts, inasmuch as each part gains something from its association with the other parts (the synergistic approach). The latent variable approach appears to reflect the assumptions of authors of shame scales, as items are summed to produce an overall score. However, in scales such as the TOSCA and the ISS, where separate components are readily identifiable and large proportions of items represent constructs identified as being independent of shame, the use of a synergistic approach to test predictions may be more appropriate. So, for example, the statistical interaction between negative self-attitudes and shame-specific components such as hiding or concealment may provide a more accurate reflection of shame than a simple summing of the responses. A high shame score obtained by summing the responses is in danger of simply reflecting the largest component in the measure, that is, negative self-attitudes. At the very least, where there are identifiable components in a measure, Carver suggests they should be tested separately in relation to the dependent variables under investigation.

However, these different approaches may not solve all the problems, as manifestations of shame are numerous, and not all are represented in shame scales. There is also the problem of discriminating shame items from guilt items in existing scales (Harder & Zalma, 1990). According to the present review, shame appears to be an elusive concept that, like other emotions, does not lend itself easily to being operationalized (Polivy, 1981; Strongman, 1973). Given the inherent problems of definition in existing shame questionnaires, one solution is to pilot new questionnaire measures that incorporate direct questions about shame felt with reference to both self and behavior. Respondents would rate the degree of shame felt from their own personal understanding of the term. This approach is likely to be no more problematic than relying on researchers' definitions of shame and may offer some advantages in the long run.

The Relationship between Shame Measures and Measures of Psychopathology

All the commonly used questionnaire shame scales so far reviewed have shown significant and usually substantial correlations with indices of psychopathology measured on dimensional scales in student samples. Indices associated with shame measures include somatization, obsessive compulsivity, psychoticism, anxiety, and depression. But are these correlations reflecting genuine associations between shame and disorder, and, if so, what do they tell us about the nature of these associations?

In general, there has been increasing disillusion over the widespread use of cross-sectional questionnaire studies with student samples to investigate the role of cognitive, personality, and other psychosocial factors in disorders such as depression (e.g. Barnett & Gotlib, 1988; Coyne & Downey, 1991; Tennen, Hall, & Affleck, 1995). Particular objections raised involve the use of nonclinical student samples and dimensional measures of psychopathology to investigate clinical phenomena, the inadequacy of cross-sectional designs to distinguish factors as antecedents, concomitants, or consequences of the disorder under investigation, and the lack of consideration of social context. These objections are all relevant to questions regarding associations between questionnaire measures of shame and psychopathology.

To begin with, there is a danger that measures of psychopathology and shame are actually representing the same thing. If measures cannot be sufficiently differentiated, it is difficult to interpret what the correlations are representing. This might be especially cogent in the case of the ISS, where particularly high correlations in the region of .71–72 have been shown with different measures of depression (Allan et al., 1994; Cook, 1996). Dimensional measures of different types of psychopathology are usually highly correlated (e.g., Gotlib, 1984; Tambs & Moum, 1993), and in student samples scales are likely to be measuring no more than mild and transient general negative affectivity (Coyne, 1994; Gotlib, 1984). Because of the high reliance on negative and global self-referent items in current questionnaire shame scales, correlations between measures of shame and particular disorders may be solely a consequence of a diffuse negative affectivity reflected in both measures.

Although there has been much theoretical discussion of the role of shame in psychopathology, its functional role in particular disorders does not appear to be perceived as a central issue. Most theorists consider shame as a key component in a variety of disorders (e.g. Kaufman, 1989; Lewis, 1987; Nathanson, 1987), with the occasional mention of its etiological role (e.g., Lewis, 1987). Similarly, in correlational studies, there has been little discussion of what associations might represent. Of course, this may not present a problem for researchers who take the view that shame is a key component of particular disorders (e.g., Cook, 1996). However, this view does little to increase understanding of the role of shame in psychopathology, as it leaves a number of important questions unanswered. For example: Does shame affect the course of disorder? Is shame a concomitant of certain disorders which disappears with remission? (If so, should it be conceptualized as a trait or disposition?) Or does it persist beyond symptomatic recovery? Can shame be a consequence of having had a particular disorder? Does shame precede the onset of symptoms and thereby confer vulnerability to particular disorders?

In our own research, we have started to address some of these issues. For example, in our investigations, we have assessed depressive and other disorders, such as bulimia, in nonstudent samples of teenage and adult women in the community using clinical interviews (Andrews, 1995, 1997). In one prospective study, women were followed over an 8-year period with clinical assessments at 4 time points. There was a strong relationship between our interview measure of bodily shame and chronic or recurrent depressive disorder in the study period when current symptoms were controlled. A lifetime history of depression had also been taken, and, with one exception, feelings of bodily shame predated first episode in women who had experienced depression. This suggests that shame in its bodily form might confer vulnerability to depression in women and affect its course.

To pursue the issue of the role of shame on depression course, we have recently carried out a small-scale study of 35 depressed male and female patients (Andrews & Hunter, 1997). Patients whose depression had taken a chronic or recurrent course were distinguished from those who had experienced just one acute episode. After controlling for age, we found significantly higher levels of bodily, characterological, and behavioral shame in the chronic or recurrently depressed patients than in patients with one acute depressive episode. This suggests that shame may affect the course of depression. However, in a few cases it was apparent that shame may very well have been a consequence of persistent depressive and other symptomatology. For example, one woman patient was ashamed that for a long time she had been unable to function as she had previously and was unable to look after herself and her family.

These observations also suggest the importance of considering the social context to better understand the nature of the relationship between shame and psychopathology. Interview assessments of shame are an obvious way to pursue this issue because of the flexibility they afford in investigating shame in real-life situations. However, this does not rule out the possibility of collecting such information, albeit in cruder form, with the use of appropriately designed questionnaires.

Conclusion

It is apparent that to understand more fully the nature of dispositional shame and its relation to factors such as psychopathology and other maladaptive behaviors and cognitions, we must move beyond current questionnaire measures and cross-sectional correlational research. Longitudinal research in clinical and nonclinical samples is necessary to understand the extent to which shame functions as an antecedent, concomitant, and consequence of psychopathology. Current questionnaires that purport to assess dispositional shame may not be adequate for this task. There is a danger that they may be reflecting diffuse negative affectivity and may not be sufficiently specific to capture enduring shame feelings that involve self and behavior. In scenario-based measures in particular, where only behavioral shame is assessed, there is also the danger that shame and guilt may be confounded. It may well be that a "pure" assessment of dispositional shame can only be achieved by assessing shame of personal characteristics through direct questioning. Designing a new generation of questionnaire shame measures is a challenge for the future.

References

Alessandri, S. M., & Lewis, M. (1993). Parental evaluation and its relation to shame and pride in young children. *Sex Roles, 29*, 335–343.

Allan, S., Gilbert, P., & Goss, K. (1994). An exploration of shame measures: 2. Psychopathology. *Personality and Individual Differences, 17,* 719–722.

Andrews, B. (1995). Bodily shame as a mediator between abusive experiences and depression. *Journal of Abnormal Psychology, 104* (2), 277–285.

Andrews, B. (1997). Bodily shame in relation to abuse in childhood and bulimia: A preliminary investigation. *British Journal of Clinical Psychology, 36,* 41–50.

Andrews, B., & Brown, G. W. (1993). Self-esteem and vulnerability to depression: The concurrent validity of interview and questionnaire measures. *Journal of Abnormal Psychology, 102,* 565–572.

Andrews, B., & Hunter, E. (1996). *An investigation into the nature of bodily, characterological and behavioral shame.* Unpublished manuscript, Royal Holloway University of London.

Andrews, B., & Hunter, E. (1997). Shame, early abuse and course of depression in a clinical sample: A preliminary study. *Cognition and Emotion, 11,* 373–381.

Barnett, P. A., & Gotlib, I. H. (1988). Psychosocial functioning and depression: Distinguishing among antecedents, concomitants and consequences. *Psychological Bulletin, 104,* 97–126.

Brewin, C. R. (1985). Depression and causal attributions: What is their relation? *Psychological Bulletin, 98,* 297–309.

Brewin, C. R., & Andrews, B. (1992). The role of context and autobiography in cognitive assessment. *Psychological Inquiry, 3,* 229–231.

Carver, C. S. (1989). How should multifaceted personality constructs be tested? Issues illustrated by self-monitoring, attributional style, and hardiness. *Journal of Personality and Social Psychology, 56,* 577–585.

Cook, D. (1988). Measuring shame: The internalized shame scale. *Alcoholism Treatment Quarterly, 4,* 197–215.

Cook, D. (1996). Empirical studies of shame and guilt: The Internalized Shame Scale. In D. L. Nathanson (Ed.), *Knowing feeling: Affect, script and psychotherapy* (pp. 132–165). New York: Norton.

Coyne, J. C. (1992). Cognition in depression: A paradigm in crisis. *Psychological Inquiry, 3,* 232–235.

Coyne, J. C. (1994). Self-reported distress: Analog or ersatz depression? *Psychological Bulletin, 116,* 29–45.

Coyne, J. C., & Downey, G. (1991). Social factors in psychopathology. *Annual Review of Psychology, 42,* 401–425.

Dixon, A. K., Gilbert, P., Huber, C., Gilbert, J. G., & Van der Hoek, G. (1996). *Changes in nonverbal behaviour in a neutral and "shame" interview.* Unpublished manuscript, University of Derby, UK.

Gilbert, P. (1989). *Human nature and suffering.* Hover, UK: Erlbaum.

Gilbert, P., Allan, S., & Goss, K. (1996). Parental representations, shame, interpersonal problems, and vulnerability to psychopathology. *Clinical Psychology and Psychotherapy, 3,* 23–34.

Gilbert, P., Pehl, J., & Allan, S. (1994). The phenomenology of shame and guilt: An empirical investigation. *British Journal of Medical Psychology, 67,* 23–36.

Goffman, E. (1963). *Stigma: Notes on the management of a spoiled identity.* Englewood Cliffs, Prentice-Hall.

Gotlib, I. H. (1984). Depression and general psychopathology in university students. *Journal of Abnormal Psychology, 93,* 19–30.

Harder, D. W. (1995). Shame and guilt assessment, and relationships of shame-and guilt-proneness to psychopathology. In J. P. Tangney & K. W. Fischer (Eds.), *Self-Conscious emotions: The psychology of shame, guilt, embarrassment and pride* (pp. 368–392). New York: Guilford Press.

Harder, D. W., Cutler, L., & Rockart, L. (1992). Assessment of shame and guilt and their relationships to psychopathology. *Journal of Personality Assessment, 59,* 584–604.

Harder, D. W., & Zalma, A. (1990). Two promising shame and guilt scales: A construct validity comparison. *Journal of Personality Assessment, 55,* 729–745.

Hoblitzelle, W. (1987). Differentiating and measuring shame and guilt: The relation between shame and depression. In H. B. Lewis (Ed.), *The role of shame in symptom formation* (pp. 207–236). Hillsdale, NJ: Erlbaum.

Hoglund, C. L., & Nicholas, K. B. (1995). Shame, guilt, and anger in college students exposed to abusive family environments. *Journal of Family Violence, 10,* 141–157.

Janoff-Bulman, R. (1979). Characterological versus behavioral self-blame: Inquiries into depression and rape. *Journal of Personality and Social Psychology, 37,* 1798–1809.

Johnson, R. D., Danko, G. P., Huang, Y. H., Park, J. Y., Johnson, S. B., & Nagoshi, C. T. (1987). Guilt, shame and adjustment in three cultures. *Personality and Individual Differences, 8,* 357–364.

Kaufman, G. (1989). *The psychology of shame: Theory and treatment of shame-based syndromes.* New York: Springer.

Keltner, D. (1995). Signs of appeasement: Evidence for the distinct displays of embarrassment, amusement and shame. *Journal of Personality and Social Psychology, 68,* 441–454.

Lewis, H. B. (1971). *Shame and guilt in neurosis.* New York: International Universities Press.

Lewis, H. B. (1987). The role of shame in depression over the life span. In H. B. Lewis (Ed.), *The role of shame in symptom formation* (pp. 29–50). Hillsdale, NJ: Erlbaum.

Lindsay-Hartz, J. (1984). Contrasting experiences of shame and guilt. *American Behavioral Scientist, 27* (6), 689–704.

Mollon, P. (1984). Shame in relation to narcissistic disturbance. *British Journal of Medical Psychology, 57,* 207–214.

Nathanson, D. L. (1987). A timetable for shame. In D. L. Nathanson (Ed.), *The many faces of shame* (pp. 1–63). New York: Guilford Press.

Niedenthal, P. M., Tangney, J. P., & Gavanski, I. (1994). "If only I weren't" versus "if only I hadn't": Distinguishing shame and guilt in counterfactual thinking. *Journal of Personality and Social Psychology, 67,* 585–595.

Oatley, K. (1992). *Best laid schemes: The psychology of emotions.* Cambridge: Cambridge University Press.

Oatley, K., & Jenkins, J. M. (1992). Human emotions: Function and dysfunction. *Annual Review of Psychology, 43,* 55–85.

Polivy, J. (1981). On the induction of emotions in the laboratory: Discrete moods or multiple affect states? *Journal of Personality and Social Psychology, 41,* 803–817.

Sartre, J. P. (1956). *Being and nothingness.* New York: Philosophical Library.

Segal, Z. V., & Dobson, K. S. (1992). Cognitive models of depression: Report from a consensus development conference. *Psychological Inquiry, 3,* 219–225.

Strongman, K. (1973). *The psychology of emotion.* London: Wiley.

Tambs, K., & Moum, T. (1993). How well can a few questionnaire items indicate anxiety and depression? *Acta Psychiatrica Scandinavica, 87,* 364–367.

Tangney, J. P. (1990). Assessing individual differences in proneness to shame and guilt: Development of the Self-Conscious Affect and Attribution Inventory. *Journal of Personality and Social Psychology, 59,* 102–111.

Tangney, J. P. (1992). Situational determinants of shame and guilt in young adulthood. *Personality and Social Psychology Bulletin, 18,* 199–206.

Tangney, J. P. (1996). Conceptual and methodological issues in the assessment of shame and guilt. *Behavioral Research and Therapy, 34,* 741–754.

Tangney, J. P., Burggraf, S. A., & Wagner, P. E. (1995). Shame-proneness, guilt-proneness, and psychological symptoms. In J. P. Tangney & K. W. Fischer (Eds.), *Self-Conscious emotions: The psychology of shame, guilt, embarrassment and pride* (pp. 343–367). New York: Guilford Press.

Tangney, J. P., Miller, R. S., Flicker, L., & Barlow, D. H. (1996). Are shame, guilt, and embarrassment distinct emotions? *Journal of Personality and Social Psychology, 70*, 1256–1269.

Tangney, J. P., Wagner, P., & Gramzow, R. (1989). *The Test of Self-Conscious Affect.* Fairfax, VA: George Mason University.

Tangney, J. P., Wagner, P., & Gramzow, R. (1992). Proneness to shame, proneness to guilt, and psychopathology. *Journal of Abnormal Psychology, 101*, 469–478.

Tangney, J. P., Wagner, P. E., Fletcher, C., & Gramzow, R. (1992). Shamed into anger? The relation of shame and guilt to anger and self-reported aggression. *Journal of Personality and Social Psychology, 62*, 669–675.

Tennen, H., Hall, J. A., & Affleck, G. (1995). Depression research methodologies in the *Journal of Personality and Social Psychology*: A review and critique. *Journal of Personality and Social Psychology, 68*, 870–884.

Weiner, B. (1986). *An attributional theory of motivation and emotion.* New York: Springer.

Wicker, F. W., Payne, G. C., & Morgan, R. D. (1983). Participant descriptions of guilt and shame. *Motivation and Emotion, 7*, 25–39.

PART II

INTERPERSONAL BEHAVIOR

3

Early Shame Experiences
and Infant Brain Development

Allan N. Schore

The scientific study of emotion, begun by Charles Darwin, Sigmund Freud, and William James in the last century, has been neglected for much of this one. Overshadowed by behavior and cognition, the formal study of internal emotional states, events that are central to the understanding of the human condition, is only recently receiving the attention of a growing number of experimental researchers and clinical authors. Within the entire spectrum of emotional states, perhaps the last to become a focus of observation of scientific scrutiny has been the "hidden" emotion of shame. A rapid expansion of knowledge about this emotion has occurred only within the last ten years, as contributions from a variety of disciplines are now actively attempting to understand more deeply the unique psychological and biological properties of shame.

A primary purpose of this chapter is to place shame within the context of very recent developmental psychological studies that describe the emergence of emotional states over the course of infancy, as well as of developmental neurobiological research which suggests that these early emotional experiences are required for maturation of the brain in the first two years of life. In pioneering work, H. B. Lewis (1980) referred to shame as "attachment emotion," a theme I will elaborate on by offering a developmental model of shame that integrates current attachment research. In light of the long-established principle that attachment is more than overt behavior and is "built into the nervous system, in the course and as a result of the infant's experience of his transactions with the mother" (Ainsworth, 1967, p. 429) and the recently demonstrated finding that parenting directly influences the developing patterns of neuronal connectivity in the infant's brain (Dawson, 1994), I shall present multidisciplinary evidence which suggests that primordial shame experiences play a central role in not only psychological but in neurobiological human development.

To this end I will focus on emotional development in early and then late infancy to demonstrate the tight coupling between the psychobiological processes that underlie attachment and shame dynamics. Attachment transactions in the first year occur within attuned face-to-face interactions that generate increasingly higher levels of positive affects, whereas socialization transactions in the second year involve misattuned face-to-face interactions that generate shame and inhibit these same positive states. I will also outline how, at the end of the first year, dyadic nonverbal communications of internal, positive affective states directly influence the experience-dependent development of a corticolimbic structure involved in attachment functions that begins a critical period of growth at this time. Socialization experiences in the second year that generate stressful levels of shame allow for the further maturation of this frontal system, which is expanded in the early maturing right brain. The right hemisphere plays a dominant role in the processing of socioemotional information, autonomic activities, and the expression and regulation of primitive emotions, including shame. In the final section, I will discuss the adaptive psychobiological role of cortically regulated shame states.

The developmental models presented are not fixed statements or established principles but heuristic proposals that can be evaluated by experimental and clinical research. A more complete referencing of the interdisciplinary studies presented here can be found in Schore (1991, 1994, 1997a,b,c). For conveniences, the terms *primary caregiver* and *mother* are used interchangeably throughout this chapter.

Emotional Development in Early Infancy

The last decade has seen a rapid, indeed an explosive, expansion of knowledge about emotional development in the first year of human life. Over the course of this year, the primary caregiver-infant relationship co-constructs an increasingly complex dynamic system of mutual reciprocal influences that mediates the formation of an attachment bond within the dyad. This interactive mechanism regulates the infant's psychobiological states, thereby allowing the child to tolerate more intense and longer lasting levels of heightened, yet modulated, arousal. This ontogenetic achievement, central to human development, enables the infant to experience very high levels of the positive affects of interest-excitement and enjoyment-joy by the end of the first year.

Dyadic Visuoaffective Transactions and the Development of Attachment Dynamics

Early socioemotional development is closely tied into the maturation of sensory systems, and it now appears that, in particular, visual experiences play a paramount role in social and emotional development (Hobson 1993; Preisler, 1995; Wright, 1991). In fact, the mother's emotionally expressive face is, by far, the most potent visual stimulus in the infant's environment, and the child's intense interest in her face, especially in her eyes, leads him or her to track it in space, and to engage in periods of intense mutual gaze. The infant's gaze, in turn, reliably evokes

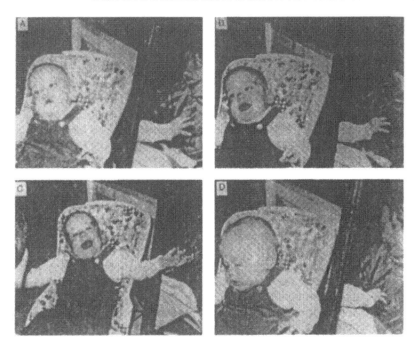

Figure 3.1. A typical sequence observed during "attuned" interactions of normal infants and their mothers, here shown split-screen but seated face to face and looking at each other: (a) the infant looks at the mother and the mother shows an exaggerated facial expression (mock surprise); (b) the infant and mother smile; (c) the infant laughs, the mother "relaxes" her smile; and (d) the infant looks away, the mother ceases smiling and watches her infant. From Field, 1982. Copyright 1982 by Lawrence Erlbaum Associates. Reprinted by permission.

the mother's gaze, thereby acting as a potent interpersonal channel for the transmission of reciprocal mutual influences. These face-to-face transactions are quite common and can be of very long duration, and they mediate the dialogue between mother and child.

With the onset of increasing myelination of the visual areas of the infant's occipital cortex over the second and third quarter of the first year, mutual gaze interactions increase significantly. These interactions occur within the context of social play between mother and infant, and they are expressed in synchronous rapid movements and fast changes in affective expressions within the dyad. An organized dialogue occurs within milliseconds, and it acts as an interactive matrix in which both partners match states and then simultaneously adjust their social attention, stimulation, and accelerating arousal in response to the partner's signals. This microregulation continues, as soon after the "heightened affective moment" of an intensely joyful full-gape smile the baby will gaze avert in order to regulate the potentially disorganizing effect of this intensifying emotion (see figure 3.1).

In order to maintain the infant's positive emotion, the psychobiologically attuned mother takes her cue, backs off to reduce her stimulation, and waits for the baby's signals for reengagement. In this way, not only the tempo of their engagement but also of their disengagement and reengagement is coordinated. In this process of contingent responsivity, the more the mother tunes her activity level to the infant during periods of social engagement, the more she allows him or her to recover quietly in periods of disengagement; and the more she attends to his or her reinitiating cues for reengagement, the more synchronized their interaction. In this manner, the caregiver facilitates the infant's information processing by adjusting the mode, amount, variability, and timing of stimulation to the infant's actual integrative capacities. These early experiences of "interaffectivity" (Stern, 1985) are thus organized by ongoing regulations, and the development of such mutually attuned synchronized interactions is fundamental to the ongoing affective development of the infant (Feldman & Greenbaum, 1997; Schore, 1994).

But facial mirroring exchanges generate much more than overt facial changes in the dyad; they represent a transformation of inner events. To enter into this communication, the mother must be psychobiologically attuned not so much to the child's overt behavior as to the reflections of his or her internal state. The human face is a unique stimulus whose features display biologically significant information, and as the mother and infant synchronize with each other's temporal and affective patterns, each recreates an inner psychophysiological state similar to the partner's. In this dynamic system, the crescendos and decrescendos of the infant's psychobiological state are in resonance with similar states of crescendos and decrescendos, cross-modally, of the mother. In physics, a property of resonance is sympathetic vibration, the tendency of one resonance system to enlarge and augment through matching the resonance frequency pattern of another resonance system. Stern (1985) refers to the delight the infant displays in reacting to the augmenting effects of his or her mother's playful, empathically attuned behavior. The caregiver's attuned resonance with the child's affect thereby allows for a multimodal sensory amplification of the child's state. Consequently, both experience a state transition as they move together from a state of neural affect and arousal to one of heightened positive emotion and high arousal (see figure 3.1). It is now thought that the attachment relationship is essentially a regulator of arousal (van der Kolk & Fisler, 1994), that regulatory processes are the precursors of psychological attachment and its associated emotions (Hofer, 1994), and that psychobiological attunement is the mechanism that mediates attachment bond formation (Field, 1985).

According to Bowlby (1969), vision is central to the establishment of a primary attachment to the mother, and imprinting is the learning mechanism that underlies attachment bond formation. Imprinting involves a state of mutually entrained central nervous system (CNS) propensities and a synchrony between sequential infant-maternal stimuli and behavior (Petrovich & Gewirtz, 1985). Emde (1988) suggests that the infant is biologically prepared to engage in visual stimulation *to stimulate its brain*. This brings us to another level of analysis—the neurobiological level. In this "transfer of affect between mother and infant," how are developing systems of the organizing brain influenced by these interactions with the social environment?

This question is directly addressed by Trevarthen's (1993) studies of maternal-infant "protoconversations," which he describes as an interactive mechanism by which older brains engage with mental states of awareness, emotion, and interest

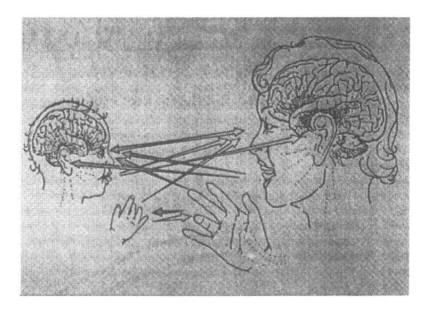

Figure 3.2. Channels of face-to-face communication in protoconversation. Proto-conversation is mediated by eye-to-eye orientations, vocalizations, hand gestures, and movements of the arms and head, all acting in coordination to express inter-personal awareness and emotions. From Trevarthen (1993). Copyright 1993 by Cambridge University Press. Reprinted by permission.

in younger brains (figure 3.2). Coordinated with eye-to-eye messages as channels of communication are auditory vocalizations and tactile and body gestures. A traffic of visual and prosodic (variations in pitch, rhythm, and auditory stress that convey affect) signals induce instant emotional effects; excitement and pleasure are amplified within the dyad. Indeed, the resonance of the dyad ultimately permits the intercoordination of positive affective brain states. Trevarthen's studies underscore the fundamental principle that the baby's brain is not only affected by these transactions, but also that its growth literally requires brain-brain interaction and occurs in the context of a positive affective relationship between mother and infant. Trevarthen concludes that "the affective regulations of brain growth" are embedded in the context of an intimate relationship and that they promote the development of cerebral circuits.

The psychoneurobiological mechanism underlying these events is revealed in Hofer's (1990) research, which demonstrates that the mother influences the neural substrates for emotion by directly regulating the levels of the catecholamines dopamine and noradrenaline in the infant's brain. Dopamine is centrally involved in arousal, elation (joy), and the anticipation of reward. Amplified levels of interest-excitement in the mother's face are also accompanied by elevated levels of corticotropin-releasing factor, a neuropeptide produced in paraventricular hypothalamic centers that activates the energy-mobilizing sympathetic division of the autonomic nervous system (ANS) and increases in plasma concentrations of noradrenaline (Brown et al., 1982), thereby intensifying levels of ergotropic (sympathetic-dominant) arousal (Gellhorn, 1970) associated with heightened infant activity levels. The mother's face also triggers high levels of endogenous opiates (endorphins) in the child's growing brain (Hoffman, 1987; Kalin, Shelton, Lynn, 1997) that biochemically mediate the pleasurable qualities of social interaction, social affect, and attachment via activation of the ventral tegmental dopamine system (Bozarth, 1986). Both catecholamines and opioids act as trophic regulators of neural development.

Infant studies thus reveal that the primary function of early synchronized gaze interactions is the generation of pleasurable states and that the baby becomes attached to the modulating caregiver, who expands opportunities for positive affect and minimizes negative affect. In other words, the affective state underlies and motivates attachment, and the central adaptive function of dyadic attachment dynamics is to interactively amplify and maintain optimal levels of the pleasurable states of what Tomkins (1962) referred to as enjoyment-joy and interest-excitement.

The Onset of a Critical Period for the Maturation of the Orbitofrontal Cortex at the End of the First Year

Attachment functions involve highly visual mechanisms and generate positive affect, and they mature near the end of the first year of life. Mary Main, perhaps the most influential attachment researcher, now concludes that "The formation of an attachment to a specified individual signals a quantitative change in infant behavioral (*and no doubt also brain*) organization" (1995, p. 214; italics added). Gilbert (1989) proposes that the mother-child relationship has important and very specific effects on the maturation of the infant's limbic system. So the question is: What specific limbic areas of the brain are beginning a critical period of growth at 10 to 12 months and are involved in attachment functions?

In earlier work (see Schore, 1994, 1996), I proposed that dyadic communications which generate intense positive affective states and high levels of dopamine and endogenous opiates represent a growth-promoting environment for the prefrontal cortex, an area that undergoes a major maturational change at 10 to 12 months (Diamond & Doar, 1989). The maturation of the prefrontal areas, which represent 30% of the total surface of the human cortex, is completely postnatal, and the limbic orbital prefrontal areas are known to mature before the nonlimbic dorsolateral prefrontal areas (figure 3.3). Attachment experiences, face-to-face transactions between caregiver and infant, directly influence imprinting, the final circuit wiring of this system. Indeed, there is now evidence to show that activity of the orbitofrontal cortex, an area which contains neurons that specifically respond to the emotional expressions of faces (Scalaidhe, Wilson & Goldman-Rakic, 1997), is directly associated with attachment functions (Steklis & Kling, 1985). This cortical region plays an essential role in the processing of social signals necessary for the initiation of affiliative behaviors and in the pleasurable qualities of social interaction.

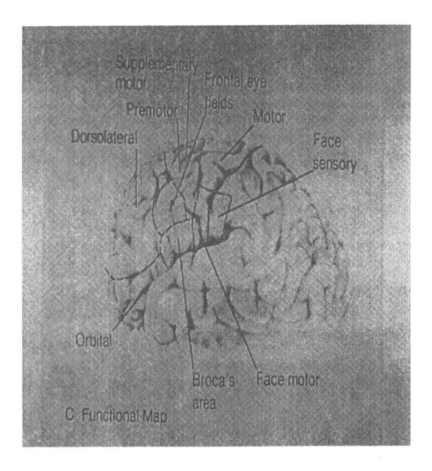

Figure 3.3. Boundaries of functional zones of the human cerebral cortex, showing the dorsolateral and orbital prefrontal areas. From Kolb & Whishaw (1990). Copyright 1990 by W. H. Freeman. Reprinted by permission.

The orbital area of the prefrontal cortex (so called because of its relation to the orbit of the eye) is "hidden" in the ventral and medial surfaces of the prefrontal lobe. This unique cerebral region is so intimately interconnected limbic areas that it has been conceived of as an "association cortex" for the limbic forebrain. In addition to receiving multimodal input from all sensory association areas of the posterior cortex, it uniquely projects extensive pathways to limbic areas in the temporal pole and the amygdala, to dopamine neurons in reward centers of the ventral tegmental areas of the anterior reticular formation, and to drive centers in the paraventricular hypothalamus that are associated with the sympathetic branch of the autonomic nervous system. This excitatory limbic circuit, the ventral tegmental limbic forebrain-midbrain circuit (Nauta & Domesick, 1982), is involved with the generation of positively valenced states associated with motivational reward, approach behavior, and active coping strategies.

This area is especially expanded in the right cortex (Falk et al., 1990), which matures before the left (Chiron et al., 1997), is known to be specifically affected by early social experiences, and is centrally involved in attachment experiences (Schore, 1994). Indeed, it is now thought that "The emotional experience of the infant develops through the sounds, images, and pictures that constitute much of an infant's early learning experience, and are disproportionately stored or processed in the 'visuospatial' right hemisphere during the formative stages of brain ontogeny" (Semrud-Clikeman & Hynd, 1990, p. 198). As the first year draws to a close, the initial phases of the anatomical maturation of the orbitofrontal cortex, a system that subserves cognitive-emotional interactions (Barbas, 1995), allows for developmental advances. This system can now generate interactive representations that encode expectations of being matched by, and being able to match, the partner, as well as "participating in the state of the other" (Beebe & Lachmann, 1988). By the end of the first year, a period when the infant begins to toddle and explore the world, the child can access internal working models of the infant's transactions with the primary attachment figure in order to appraise self and other in encounters with the social and physical environments.

Emotional Development in Late Infancy

In optimal growth-promoting environments, the interactive mechanism for generating positive affect becomes so efficient that by the time the infant begins to toddle he or she is experiencing very high levels of elation and excitement. The socioemotional environment of the caregiver-infant dyad, however, changes dramatically from early to late infancy. At 10 months, 90% of maternal behavior consists of affection, play, and caregiving. In sharp contrast, the mother of the 13–17-month-old toddler expresses a prohibition on the average of every 9 minutes. In the second year, the mother's role now changes from primarily a caregiver to a socializing agent, as she must now persuade the child to inhibit unrestricted exploration, tantrums, bladder and bowel functions; that is, activities that he or she enjoys.

Socialization Experiences and the Emergence of the Attachment Emotion of Shame

In other words, to socialize the child, the mother must now engage in affect regulation to reduce the heightened levels of positive affect associated with the pleasure of these activities. How does she inhibit and restrict the behaviors that the child finds pleasurable? In fact, there is one very specific inhibitor of accelerating pleasurable emotional states. Shame, "the primary social emotion" (Scheff, 1988), acts as a specific inhibitor of the activated ongoing affects of interest-excitement and enjoyment-joy and uniquely reduces self-exposure or exploration powered by these positive affects (Tomkins, 1963). In earlier work (Schore, 1991, 1994), I presented multidisciplinary developmental data which suggests that shame makes its initial appearance at 14 to 16 months.

In the second year, the ambulatory infant, now able to physically separate him- or herself from the mother for longer periods of time, is able to explore realms of the physical and social environment that are beyond her watchful eye. Upon return from these forays, the toddler brings the things he or she is exploring and attempting to master to the mother, but now, more than any time previously, these reunions can engender interactive stress. Excitedly expecting her "sparkling-eyed pleasure" (Emde, 1988), the toddler is suddenly and unpreparedly confronted with the "unexpected noncooperation of the mirroring object" (Kohut, 1978). Face-to-face encounters that at one time elicited only joy become the principal context for stressful shame experiences.

The experience of shame is associated with unfulfilled expectations and is triggered by an appraisal of a disturbance in facial recognition, the most salient channel of nonverbal communication. The toddler's attentive focus on the mother's eyes and the frustration of the child's expectation of her participation in eye-to-eye contact and visuoaffective communication may be the key visual cue that triggers the visual, nonverbal affect of shame. Reciprocal gaze behavior, the most intense form of interpersonal communication, acts as a powerful mediator of affect attunement, but it can also transmit misattunement, because "this visual feedback system carries within it the potential of mutual gratification as well as frustration" (Riess, 1978, p. 382). The impediment to anticipated positive affect is specifically a perception of a facial display which conveys not mirroring but, rather, disgust. M. Lewis (1992) points out that a disgusted face is widely used in the socialization of children, though parents are often unaware that they are producing it.

These developmental data describe the rapid state-transforming events that underlie the primordial shame transaction. As a result of earlier dyadic mirroring experiences, when the senior toddler approaches the caregiver in a state of accelerating positive affect, he or she expects this state of rising positive arousal to be amplified. Recall that the child now has access to presymbolic representations that encode the expectation of being matched by, and being able to match, the partner, as well as "participating in the state of the other" (Beebe & Lachmann, 1988). Despite an excited expectation of a psychobiologically attuned shared positive affect state with the mother and a dyadic amplification of the positive affects of excitement and joy, the infant unexpectedly encounters a facially expressed affective misattunement. The ensuing break in an anticipated visual-affective communication triggers a sudden shock-induced deflation of positive affect, and the infant is thus propelled into a state which he or she cannot yet autoregulate. Shame represents this rapid state transition from a preexisting positive state to a negative state.

Psychobiological attunement drives the attachment process by acting as a mechanism that maximizes and expands positive affect and minimizes and diminishes negative affect. The negative affect of shame is thus the infant's immediate physiological-emotional response to a perceived interruption in the flow of an anticipated maternal regulatory function—psychobiological attunement which generates positive affect—and to the mother's use of misattunement to mediate the socialization process. In other words, shame, which has been called an "attachment emotion" (Lewis, 1980), is the reaction to an important other's unexpected refusal to cocreate an attachment bond that allows for the dyadic regulation of emotion (Sroufe, 1996). Thus, in the prototypical object relation of shame, a separation response is triggered in the presence of and by the mother, who spontaneously and unconsciously blockades the child's initial attempt to emotionally reconnect with her in a positive affective state. It is well established that attachment bond disruptions precipitate an imbalance in the regulation of affect. In the shame transaction, instead of encountering the synchronizing function of the significant other who regulates the child's homeostatic equilibrium, the individual experiences a traumatic interruption of interpersonal synchronizing processes (Maunder, 1996). The misattunement in shame, as in other negative affects, represents a regulatory failure and is phenomenologically experienced as a discontinuity in what Winnicott (1958) calls the child's "going-on-being."

In direct contrast to the psychobiologically energized state, shame, an acutely painful stress-associated affect, triggers a rapid de-energizing state in the infant in which the deflated self, depleted of energy, withdraws, recoils, and attempts to disappear from the view of significant objects. As opposed to processes that promote and prolong contact and facilitate "merging with sources of satisfaction" in order to generate euphoric emotions and pleasurable activity, shame induces "ending contact and halting arousal" (Knapp, 1967). The conscious subjective experience of shame, a sharp gradient of change in emotion, represents a rapid, unexpected, uncontrollable transition from a "crescendo" to a "decrescendo," an "animate" to an "inanimate" feeling state (Stern, 1985), a switch from an attachment-affiliation or exploratory-assertive to an aversive motivational functional system. Shame stress thus precipitates a rapid and unexpected contraction of the self.

This state is mediated by a different psychobiological pattern than positive states—corticosteroids are produced in a stress response, and these reduce opioid and corticotropin-releasing factor in the brain. Even short-lived elevations of corticosteroids induce inhibition and withdrawal (Stansbury & Gunnar, 1994). The psychobiological components of the shame response involve an influx of autonomic proprioceptive and kinesthetic feedback into awareness, reflecting a neurobiological activation of medullary reticular formation activity in the brain stem. In contrast to the attuned state, shame elicits a painful infant distress state, manifested in a sudden decrement in mounting pleasure, a rapid inhibition of excitement, and cardiac deceleration by means of vagal impulses in the medulla oblongata (Knapp, 1967). This shift reflects the reduced activation of the excitatory ventral tegmental limbic forebrain-midbrain circuit and increased activation of the inhibitory lateral tegmental limbic forebrain-midbrain circuit.

The onset of the interactively triggered shame state thus represents a sudden shift from energy-mobilizing sympathetic to energy-conserving parasympathetic dominant ANS activity, a rapid transition from a hyperaroused to a hypoaroused state, and a sudden switch from ergotropic (sympathetically driven) to trophotropic (parasympathetically driven) arousal. Indeed, Buss (1979) has demonstrated that shame represents parasympathetic arousal. In such a psychobiological state transition, sympathetically powered elation, heightened arousal, and elevated activity level instantly evaporate. This represents a shift into a low-keyed inhibitory state of parasympathetic conservation-withdrawal that occurs in helpless and hopeless stressful situations (Engel & Schmale, 1972). How long the child remains in this stress state is an important factor.

In fact, active parental participation in regulating the child's shame state is critical to enabling the child to shift from the negative affective state of deflation and distress to a reestablished state of positive affect. In early development, parents provide much of the necessary modulation of states, especially after a state disruption and across a transition between states, and this allows for the development of self-regulation. This transition involves and highlights the central role of stress recovery mechanisms in affect regulation. Stress has been defined as the occurrence of an asynchrony in an interactional sequence; further, "a period of synchrony, following the period of stress, provides a 'recovery' period" (Chapple, 1970 p. 631). The child's facial display, postural collapse, and gaze aversion act as nonverbal signals of his or her internal distress state. If the caregiver is sensitive, responsive, and emotionally approachable, especially if she reinitiates and reenters into mutual gaze visual affect regulating transaction, the dyad is psychobiologically reattuned, shame is metabolized and regulated, and the attachment bond is reestablished. The key to this is the caregiver's capacity to monitor and regulate her own affect.

In this essential pattern of what Beebe and Lachmann (1994) call "disruption and repair," the "good-enough" caregiver who induces a stress response in her infant through a misattunement reinvokes in a timely fashion her psychobiologically attuned regulation of the infant's negative affect state that she has triggered. This reattunement is mediated by the mother's reengagement in dyadic visuoaffective transactions that regenerate positive affect in the child. Her shame-stress-regulating interventions allow for a state transition in the infant—the parasympathetic-dominant trophotropic arousal of the shame state is supplanted by the reignition of sympathetic-dominant ergotropic arousal that supports increased activity and positive affect. Shame transactions are carried out continually throughout the early period of socialization, and a characteristic pattern of regulating and thereby coping (or not coping) with misattuned states and distressing affects develops within the dyad. These events are stored within an internal working model of a secure attachment.

If, on the other hand, an attachment figure frequently humiliates, ridicules, and rejects the child's requests for comfort in stressful situations, the child develops not only an internal working model of the parent as rejecting but also one of him-or herself as unworthy of help and comfort. I suggest that, as opposed to the elevated parasympathetic autonomic component which always accompanies shame, humiliation, a common accompaniment of early physical trauma, involves an extremely dysregulated state of elevated parasympathetic plus heightened sympathetic reactivity. Psychophysiologically this may represent, respectively, a state of activated trophotropic arousal versus an intensely stressful state of trophotropic combined with ergotropic arousal, a state of "shame-rage" (H. B. Lewis, 1987). Clinical observers note that failures of early attachment invariably become sources of shame (Kaufman, 1989), that impairments in the parent-child relationship lead to pathology through an enduring disposition to shame (M. Lewis, 1992), and that early abuse engenders intense bodily shame (Andrews, 1995). These data imply that it is not shame itself but rather an early developing inefficient capacity to autoregulate or interactively regulate this potent affect that is psychopathogenic.

Specific emotions are now understood to involve a distinctive "core relational theme" which describes an essential person-environment relationship (Lazarus, 1991) and to be elicited by an appraisal of actual or expected changes that are important to the individual (Frijda, 1988). In light of the fact that shame is directly related to visual phenomena, the core relational shame transaction becomes internalized in implicit, procedural memory as a visual stored image. Nathanson describes shame as "a biological system by which the organism controls its affective output so that it will not remain interested or content when it may not be safe to do so, or so that it will not remain in affective resonance with an organism that fails to match its patterns stored in memory" (1992, p. 140). Although the origin of shame is dyadic and external, "the experience of being looked at by the Other" (Wright, 1991), it eventually becomes internalized as "the eye of the self gazing inward" (Morrison, 1987). By the end of late infancy, the elicitation of this affect does not require the presence of an external person—it can be activated by an internal image. Morrison (1989) asserts that turning the potential control of shame inward is an important developmental step. Most important, because shame generally inhibits the expression of emotion *per se*, the capacity to internally regulate shame allows for an ability to experience a broad range of positive and negative affects.

The Maturation of the Orbitofrontal Cortex

These advances in emotional functions reflect structural progressions in the limbic system, specifically a reorganization and maturation of the orbitofrontal cortex, a corticolimbic area that is centrally involved in affect regulation (Schore, 1994, in 1996; 1997a, b; in press). A period of structural development in this cortex occurs in the first year of infancy, and a second period marked by further anatomical changes occurs in the second year of human life. This reorganization of the prefrontal region is "open to interactions with the external world" (Kostovic, 1990). In the second year, such interactions are expressed in dyadic shame and interactive repair transactions that are part of the socialization process. These experiences trigger specific psychobiological patterns of hormones and neurotransmitters, and the resultant biochemical alterations of brain biochemistry influence the experience-dependent maturation of the orbitofrontal cortex.

Specifically, the interactive misattunements generated in socialization transactions induce shame, an interruption of interpersonal synchronizing processes. Developmental psychobiological research indicates that interruptions of the attachment bond are correlated with increased cortisol and decreased endogenous opioid levels (Trad, 1986). The sudden triggering of shame reflects an alteration of the infant's psychobiological state and the onset of a stress reaction, manifested in elevated levels of corticosteroids in the infant's brain. Corticosteroids suppress production of corticotropin-releasing factor and thereby reduce endorphin levels. But during critical periods of cortical maturation these neurohormones do more than just transiently perturb states—in fact, they directly influence brain growth (Meyer, 1985). Developmental shame experiences thus induce a neurobiological reorganization of evolving brain circuitries.

In optimal socialization experiences in the second year, the child is exposed not only to interpersonal transactions that induce negatively valenced shame and inhibition and withdrawal behaviors but also to interactive regulations that repair this state and resume positively valanced excitatory activities and approach behaviors. These distinct types of socioemotional experiences allow for the critical-period experience-dependent structural maturation of the orbitofrontal cortex. (In contrast, misattuned relational environments that generate high and long-enduring levels of negative affect act as growth-inhibiting environments for developing fron-tolimbic systems; Schore, 1996). This organization includes the fine-tuning of de-scending projections from the prefrontal cortex to subcortical structures that are known to mature during infancy. Of particular importance is the growth of pre-frontal axons back down to subcortical targets on noradrenergic neurons in the nucleus of the solitary tract of the brain stem caudal reticular formation and the vagal complex in the medulla (Yasui, Itoh, Kaneko, Shigemoto, & Mizuno, 1991) and in parasympathetic autonomic areas of the hypothalamus (Kita & Oomura, 1981). By this process the organization of the lateral tegmental forebrain-midbrain limbic circuit that brakes arousal and activates the onset of an inhibitory state is completed. Along with the earlier developing ventral tegmental limbic forebrain-midbrain circuit, the orbitofrontal system now connects into both the excitatory and the inhibitory limbic circuits. Its direct connections with the hypothalamus enable it to act as a major center of central nervous system control over the energy-mobilizing sympathetic and energy-conversing parasympathetic branches of the autonomic nervous system (Neafsey, 1990).

Because of the organization of its dense connections, with sites in both the cortex and subcortex, this corticolimbic system plays an essential adaptive regu-latory role. At the orbitofrontal level cortically processed exteroceptive informa-tion concerning the external environment (such as visual and prosodic information emanating from an emotional face) is integrated with subcortically processed ex-teroceptive information regarding the internal visceral environment (such as con-current changes in the emotional or bodily state). This adaptive function allows for incoming social information to be associated with emotional and motivated states. Orbitofrontal areas are involved in the generation of high-level psycholog-ical representations of other individuals (Brothers & Ring, 1992) and in the self-regulation of bodily states (Luria, 1980). According to Hofer (1984), internal rep-resentations of external human relationships serve an important intrapsychic role as "biological regulators" that control physiological processes. The essential activ-ity of this ventromedial system in emotional behavior (Damasio, 1994; Price, Car-michael, & Drevets, 1996) and in mediating processes relevant to the organism's participation in social groups (Zald & Kim, 1996) is thus the adaptive switching of internal bodily states in response to changes in the external social environment that are appraised to be personally meaningful (Schore, in press, c). This includes the onset of a parasympathetically driven inhibitory shame state in response to the appraisal of a facially (visually and prosodically) expressed stressful alteration of the interpersonal environment.

Over 60 years ago, MacCurdy (1930) proposed that the immobility seen in shame is due to a shift in balance in the autonomic nervous system, with an offset of sympathetic activity and an onset of vagal activity, leading to cardiac deceler-ation and a fall in blood pressure. The shame state is manifested in a rapid inhi-bition of excitement, a sudden decrement in mounting pleasure, and cardiac de-celeration by means of vagal impulses (Knapp, 1967). Activation of the orbitofrontal cortex, a cortical area that receives direct vagal inputs (Hardstaff, Jagadeesh, & Newman, 1973) and acts as a "nonspecific system governing internal inhibition" (Velasco & Lindsley, 1965), psychobiologically mediates the onset of socially-induced stressful shame states, since direct projections from frontal corticolimbic areas down to subcortical autonomic sites allows for an orbital role in "vagal restraint" and in the energy-conserving inhibition of autonomic function (Kaada, Pribram, & Epstein, 1949). Stimulation of particular orbitofrontal sites triggers an almost instantaneous inhibition of gastrointestinal motility, respiratory movements of inspiration, and somatic locomotor activity and a dramatic precipitous fall in blood pressure, thereby accounting for the influx of autonomic feedback into awareness that accompanies shame. The involvement of orbitofrontal-vagal connections in shame is suggested by the "active restraining quality" of this affect, which brakes arousal and triggers a "partial paralysis of outer activity" (Knapp, 1967), since orbital activity inhibits muscle tone and brain-stem-regulated somatic reflexes (Sauerland, Knauss, Nakamura, & Clemente, 1967). The central role played by frontolimbic areas in shame states is also expressed in its neurohormonal regulatory operations—orbitofrontal activation triggers increases of hypothalamico-pituitary-adrenocortical corticosteroid levels (Hall & Marr, 1975), a function mediated by the parasympathetic branch of the ANS (Henry & Stephens, 1977).

Indeed, this prefrontolimbic region comes to act in the capacity of an executive control function for the entire right cortex (see figure 3.4). The right hemisphere is particularly well connected reciprocally with limbic (Tucker, 1992) and autonomic (Spence, Shapiro, & Zaidel, 1996) areas, and is therefore dominant in controlling fundamental physiological and endocrinological functions whose primary control centers are located in subcortical regions of the brain (Wittling & Pfluger, 1990). These authors point out that the right cortex is also centrally involved in regulating corticosteroid activity. Furthermore, a right hemispheric vagal circuit of emotion regulation, hierarchically dominated by the right orbitofrontal cortex, has been recently described by Porges, Doussard-Roosevelt, and Maiti (1994). I suggest that the activity of this right brain cortical-subcortical circuit, identical to the arousal-braking, inhibitory lateral tegmental forebrain-midbrain limbic circuit, mediates all forms of shame-related emotional behaviors. Neurobiological studies show that the orbitofrontal system plays a major role in the adjustment or correction of emotional responses (Rolls, 1986; Schore, 1994), that is, affect regulation. It acts as a recovery mechanism that efficiently monitors and autoregulates the duration, frequency, and intensity of not only positive but also negative affect states, including stressful shame states.

The Adaptive Psychobiological Role of Cortically Regulated Shame States

The emergent capacity of experiencing and autoregulating the intensely negative affect of shame thus reflects the experience-dependent maturation of a right frontlimbic system that can access cortically processed social information in order to modulate subcortical autonomic functions that underlie various emotional states. There is now a large body of evidence which indicates that negative emotions activate and are modulated by the right (not left) hemisphere (e.g., Davidson, Ekman, Saron, Senulis, & Friesen, 1990; Heilman & Bowers, 1990; Heller, 1993, Schore, 1997b). This hemisphere, which contains a "primitive affect system" (Gazzaniga, 1985) and a "nonverbal affect lexicon" of facial expressions (Bowers,

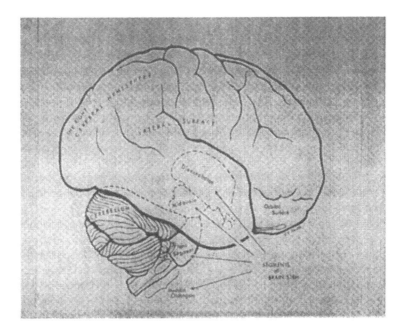

Figure 3.4. Relationships of brain stem structures to the orbital surface of the right hemisphere. From Smith (1981). Copyright 1981 by Urban & Schwarzenberg. Reprinted by permission.

Bauer, & Heilman, 1993), is dominant for the regulation of the autonomic correlates of emotional arousal (Heilman, Schwartz, & Watson, 1977). These data strongly suggest that "primitive, biologically based" shame (Broucek, 1982), perhaps the most painful and least tolerable negative affect, is a right-brain phemonenon. Indeed, a neuropsychological study shows that the words "shame" and "humiliation," when presented tachistoscopically, specifically activate and prime the right hemisphere (Van Strien & Morpugo, 1992).

Almost 50 years ago, Erikson (1950) offered the classical conception of shame as a feeling of being visible and exposed to the eyes of an Other, which leads to an urge to hide and cover one's face. The importance of regulating and thereby being able to tolerate shame from toddlerhood through adulthood lies in the adaptive capacity of conservation-withdrawal. Powles characterizes this state, in which the inhibited organism passively disengages in order to attempt to become "unseen," as the organismic strategy "to conserve energies and strive to avoid attention, to foster survival by the risky posture of feigning death, to allow healing of wounds and restitution of depleted resources by immobility" (1992, p. 213). This primary regulatory process for organismic homeostasis allows for a passive coping mechanism that improves survival efficiency through inactive disengagement and unresponsiveness to environmental input in order to conserve resources and to assure organismic autonomy until environmental conditions are once again more compatible (Engel & Schmale, 1972). As opposed to sympathetically driven "fight-flight" active coping strategies, parasympathetically mediated passive coping mechanisms expressed in immobility and withdrawal associated with "giving up" (Benus, Bohus, Koolhaas, & Van Oortmersen, 1991) and submission (Gilbert, 1992) and in seeking a physical environment of "refuge," a place to hide without being seen (Mealey & Theis, 1995), represent an alternative but equivalent strategy for effectively regulating social interactional stress. In contrast to "problem focused coping," which entails direct action on the self or on the environment to remove the source of stress, this "emotion focused coping" is directed toward the reduction of the emotional impact of stress through psychological processes (Folkman & Lazarus, 1980).

The physiological expression of emotion is dependent upon the coordinated responses of both the sympathetic and parasympathetic components of the ANS, and this allows for parasympathetically dominant shame states to combine with sympathetically driven states of, for example, fear, anger, and joy. It is known that parasympathetic inhibitory systems, such as in the frontal lobes, develop more slowly than sympathetic excitatory processes (Thompson, 1990), that emotion expression changes developmentally as a function of the experience-dependent maturation of neural inhibitory mechanisms (Izard, Hembree, & Huebner, 1987), and that the maturation of the frontal region in the second year is responsible for affect regulation and the development of complex emotions such as shame (Fox, 1991). In light of the fact that affects in general serve the critical adaptive function of informing the individual who is tracking biologically relevant goals (Gilbert, 1992) and that specific emotions help to prepare for and sustain the person-environment relationship (Lazarus, 1991), successful emotional adaptation requires the capacity to tolerate both positive and negative affects of formidable intensity. Internal working models are now thought to essentially encode coping stategies of affect regulation which are unconsciously used to regulate distress in situations that normally elicit attachment behaviors. The attachment dynamic continues in adult life, and the ability to cope with the stressful ruptures of attachment that elicit shame is essential to ongoing development, because this affect, which is generated by virtually constant monitoring of the self in relationship to others, comes to play a central role in the regulation of all emotional expression and therefore all human interaction.

References

Ainsworth, M. D. S. (1967). *Infancy in Uganda: Infant care and the growth of love.* Baltimore: Johns Hopkins University Press.

Andrews, B. (1995). Bodily shame as a mediator between abusive experiences and depression. *Journal of Abnormal Psychology, 104* (2), 277–285.

Barbas, H. (1995). Anatomic basis of cognitive-emotional interactions in the primate prefrontal cortex. *Neuroscience and Biobehavioral Reviews, 19,* 499–510.

Beebe, B., & Lachmann, F. M. (1988). The contribution of mother-infant mutual influence to the origins of self-and object relationships. *Psychoanalytic Psychology, 5,* 305–337.

Beebe, B., & Lachmann, F. M. (1994). Representations and internalization in infancy: Three principles of salience. *Psychoanalytic Psychology, 11,* 127–165.

Benus, R. F., Bohus, B., Koolhaas, J. M., & van Oortmerssen, G. A. (1991). Heritable variation for aggression as a reflection of individual coping strategies. *Experientia*, *47*, 1008–1019.

Bowers, D., Bauer, R. M., & Heilman, K. M. (1993). The nonverbal affect lexicon: Theoretical perspectives from neuropsychological studies of affect perception. *Neuropsychology, 7*, 433–444.

Bowlby, J. (1969). *Attachment and loss: Vol 1. Attachment*. New York: Basic Books.

Bozarth, M. A. (1986). Neural basis of psychomotor stimulant and opiate reward: Evidence suggesting the involvement of a common dopaminergic system. *Behavioral Brain Research, 22*, 107–116.

Brothers, L., & Ring, B. (1992). A neuroethological framework for the representations of minds. *Journal of Cognitive Neuroscience, 4*, 107–118.

Broucek, F. J. (1982). Shame and its relationship to early narcissistic developments. *International Journal of Psycho-Analysis, 63*, 369–378.

Brown, M. R., Fisher, L. A., Spiess, J., Rivier, C., Rivier, J., & Vale, W. (1982). Corticotropin-releasing factor: Actions on the sympathetic nervous system and metabolism. *Endocrinology, 111*, 928–931.

Buss, A. H. (1979). *Self consciousness and anxiety*. San Francisco: Freeman.

Chapple, E. D. (1970). Experimental production of transients in human interaction. *Nature, 228*, 630–633.

Chiron, C., Jambaque, I., Nabbout, R., Lounes, R., Syrota, A., & Dulac, O. (1997). The right brain hemisphere is dominant in human infants. *Brain, 120*, 1057–1065.

Damasio, A. R. (1994). *Descartes' error*. New York: Grosset/Putnam.

Davidson, R., Ekman, P., Saron, C., Senulis, J., & Friesen, W. (1990). Approach-withdrawal and cerebral asymmetry: Emotion expression and brain physiology: 1. *Journal of Personality and Social Psychology, 58*, 330–341.

Dawson, G. (1994). Development of emotional expression and emotion regulation in infancy. In G. Dawson & K. W. Fischer (Eds.), *Human behavior and the developing brain* (pp. 346–379). New York: Guilford Press.

Diamond, A., & Doar, B. (1989). The performance of human infants on a measure of frontal cortex function, the delayed response task. *Developmental Psychobiology, 22*, 271–294.

Emde, R. N. (1988). Development terminable and interminable: 1. Innate and motivational factors from infancy. *International Journal of Psycho-Analysis, 69*, 23–42.

Engel, G. L., & Schmale, A. H. (1972). Conservation-withdrawal: A primary regulatory process for organismic homeostasis. In *Physiology, emotion, and psychosomatic illness* (pp. 57–85). CIBA Foundation Symposium 8. Amsterdam: Elsevier.

Erikson, E. (1950). *Childhood and society*. New York: Norton.

Falk, D., Hildebolt, C., Cheverud, J., Vannier, M., Helmkamp, R. C., & Konigsberg, L. (1990). Cortical asymmetries in frontal lobes of Rhesus monkeys *(Macaca mulatta)*. *Brain Research, 512*, 40–45.

Feldman, R., & Greenbaum, C. W. (1997). Affect regulation and synchrony in mother-infant play as precursors to the development of symbolic competence. *Infant Mental Health Journal, 18*, 4–23.

Field, T. (1982). Affective displays of high-risk infants during early interactions. In T. Field & A. Fogel (Eds.), *Emotion and early interaction* (pp. 101–125). Hillsdale, NJ: Erlbaum.

Field, T. (1985). Attachment as psychobiological attunement: Being on the same wavelength. In M. Reite & T. Field (Eds.), *The psychobiology of attachment and separation* (pp. 415–454). Orlando, FL: Academic Press.

Folkman, S., & Lazarus, R. S. (1980). An analysis of coping in a middle-aged community sample. *Journal of Health and Social Behavior, 21*, 219–239.

Fox, N. A. (1991). If it's not left, it's right: Electroencephalography asymmetry and the development of emotion. *American Psychologist, 46*, 863–872.

Frijda, N. H. (1988). The laws of emotion. *American Psychologist, 43*, 349–358.

Gazzaniga, M. S. (1985). *The social brain: Discovering the networks of the mind.* New York: Basic Books.

Gellhorn, E. (1970). The emotions and the ergotropic and trophotropic systems. *Psychologische Forschung, 34,* 48–94.

Gilbert, P. (1989). *Human nature and suffering.* Hove, UK: Erlbaum.

Gilbert, P. (1992). *Depression: The evolution of powerlessness.* New York: Guilford Press.

Hall, R. E., & Marr, H. B. (1975). Influence of electrical stimulation of posterior orbital cortex upon plasma cortisol levels in unanesthetized sub-human primate. *Brain Research, 93,* 367–371.

Hardstaff, V. H., Jagadeesh, P., & Newman, P. P. (1973). Activity evoked in the orbital cortex from splanchic, vagal and cutaneous afferents. *Journal of Neurophysiology, 231,* 16P.

Heilman, K., & Bowers, D. (1990). Neuropsychological studies of emotional changes induced by right and left hemisphere studies. In N. Stein, B. Leventhal, & T. Trabasso (Eds.), *Psychological and biological approaches to emotion.* Hillsdale, NJ: Erlbaum.

Heilman, K. M., Schwartz, H., & Watson, R. T. (1977). Hypoarousal in patients with the neglect syndrome and emotional indifference. *Neurology, 38,* 229–232.

Heller, W. (1993). Neuropsychological mechanisms of individual differences in emotion, personality, and arousal. *Neuropsychology, 7,* 476–489.

Henry, J. P., & Stephens, P. M. (1977). *Stress, health and the social environment.* New York: Springer-Verlag.

Hobson, R. P. (1993). Through feeling and site through self and symbol. In U. Neisser (Ed.), *The perceived self: Ecological and interpersonal sources of self-knowledge* (pp. 254–279). New York: Cambridge University Press.

Hofer, M. A. (1984). Relationships as regulators: A psychobiologic perspective on bereavement. *Psychosomatic Medicine, 46,* 183–197.

Hofer, M. A. (1990). Early symbiotic processes: Hard evidence from a soft place. In R. A. Glick & S. Bone (Eds.), *Pleasure beyond the pleasure principle* (pp. 55–78). New Haven: Yale University Press.

Hofer, M. A. (1994). Hidden regulators in attachment, separation, and loss. *Monographs of the Society for Research in Child Development, 59,* 192–207.

Hoffman, H. S. (1987). Imprinting and the critical period for social attachments: Some laboratory investigations. In M. H. Bornstein (Ed.), *Sensitive periods in development, interdisciplinary studies* (pp. 99–121). Hillsdale, NJ: Erlbaum.

Izard, C. E., Hembree, E. A., & Huebner, R. R. (1987). Infants' emotion expressions to acute pain: Developmental change and stability of individual differences. *Developmental Psychology, 23,* 105–113.

Kaada, B. R., Pribram, K. H., & Epstein, J. (1949). Respiratory and vascular responses in monkeys from temporal pole, insular orbital surface, and cingulate gyrus. A preliminary report. *Journal of Neurophysiology, 12,* 347–356.

Kalin, N. H., Shelton, S. E., & Lynn, D. E. (1995). Opiate systems in mother and infant primates coordinate intimate contact during reunion. *Psychoneuroendocrinology, 20,* 735–742.

Kaufman, G. (1989). *The psychology of shame: Theory and treatment of shame-based syndromes.* New York: Springer.

Kita, H., & Oomura, Y. (1981). Reciprocal connections between the lateral hypothalamus and the frontal cortex in the rat. *Brain Research, 213,* 1–16.

Knapp, P. H. (1967). Purging and curbing: An inquiry into disgust, satiety and shame. *Journal of Nervous and Mental Disease, 144,* 514–544.

Kohut, H. (1978). Thoughts on narcissism and narcissistic rage. In P. Ornstein (Ed.), *The search for the self.* New York: International Universities Press.

Kolb, B., & Whishaw, I. Q. (1990). *Fundamentals of human neuropsychology (3rd ed.).* New York: Freeman.

Kostovic, I. (1990). Structural and histochemical reorganization of the human prefrontal cortex during perinatal and postnatal life. *Progress in Brain Research, 85,* 223–239.

Lazarus, R. S. (1991). Progress on a cognitive-motivational-relational theory of emotion. *American Psychologist, 46,* 819–834.

Lewis, H. B. (1980). "Narcissistic personality" or "Shame-prone superego mode". *Comparative Psychotherapy, 1,* 59–80.

Lewis, H. B. (1987). Shame and the narcissistic personality. In D. L. Nathanson (Ed.), *The many faces of shame* (pp. 93–132). New York: Guilford Press.

Lewis, M. (1992). *Shame: The exposed self.* New York: The Free Press.

Luria, A. R. (1980). *Higher cortical functions in man (2nd ed.).* New York: Basic Books.

MacCurdy, J. T. (1930). The biological significance of blushing and shame. *British Journal of Psychology, 21,* 174–182.

Main, M. (1995). Discourse, prediction, and recent studies in attachment: Implications for psychoanalysis. In T. Shapiro & R. N. Emde (Eds.), *Research in psychoanalysis: Process, development, outcome.* Madison, CT: International Universities Press.

Maunder, R. (1996). System as metaphor in the psychology and biology of shame. *Psychiatry, 59,* 196–205.

Mealey, L., & Theis, P. (1995). The relationship between mood and preferences among natural landscapes: An evolutionary perspective. *Ethology and Sociobiology, 16,* 247–256.

Meyer, J. S. (1985). Biochemical effects of corticosteroids on neural tissues. *Physiological Reviews, 65,* 946–1020.

Morrison, A. P. (1987). The eye turned inward: Shame and the self. In D. L. Nathanson (Ed.), *The many faces of shame* (pp. 271–291). New York: Guilford Press.

Morrison, A. P. (1989). *Shame: The underside of narcissism.* Hillsdale, NJ: Analytic Press.

Nathanson, D. L. (1992). *Shame and pride: Affect, sex, and the birth of the self.* New York: Norton.

Nauta, W. J. H., & Domesick, V. B. (1982). Neural associations of the limbic system. In A. L. Beckman (Ed.), *The neural basis of behavior* (pp. 175–206). New York: SP Medical and Scientific Books.

Neafsey, E. J. (1990). Prefrontal cortical control of the autonomic nervous system: Anatomical and physiological observations. *Progress in Brain Research, 85,* 147–166.

Petrovich, S. B., & Gewirtz, J. L. (1985). The attachment learning process and its relation to cultural and biological evolution: Proximate and ultimate considerations. In M. Reite & T. Field (Eds.), *The psychobiology of attachment and separation* (pp. 259–291). Orlando, FL: Academic Press.

Porges, S. W., Doussard-Roosevelt, J. A., & Maiti, A. K. (1994). Vagal tone and the physiological regulation of emotion. *Monographs of the Society for Research in Child Development, 59,* 167–186.

Powles, W. E. (1992). *Human development and homeostasis.* Madison, CT: International Universities Press.

Preisler, G. M. (1995). The development of communication in blind and in deaf infants—similarities and differences. *Child: Care, Health and Development, 21,* 79–110.

Price, J. L., Carmichael, S. T., & Drevets, W. C. (1996). Networks related to the orbital and medial prefrontal cortex; a substrate for emotional behavior? *Progress in Brain Research, 107,* 523–536.

Riess, A. (1978). The mother's eye: For better and for worse. *Psychoanalytic Study of the Child, 33,* 381–409.

Rolls, E. T. (1986). Neural systems involved in emotion in primates. In R. Plutchik & H. Kellerman (Eds.), *Emotion: Theory, research, and practice* (*Vol. 3,* pp. 125–143). Orlando, FL: Academic Press.

Sauerland, E. K., Knauss, Y., Nakamura, Y., & Clemente, C. D. (1967). Inhibition of monosynaptic and polysynaptic reflexes and muscle tone by electrical stimulation of the cerebral cortex. *Experimental Neurology, 17,* 159–171.

Scalaidhe, S. P. O., Wilson, F. A. W., & Goldman-Rakic, P. S. (1997). Areal segregation of face-processing neurons in prefrontal cortex. *Science, 278,* 1135–1138.

Scheff, T. J. (1988). Shame and conformity: The deference-emotion system. *American Review of Sociology, 53,* 395–406.

Schore, A. N. (1991). Early superego development: The emergence of shame and narcissistic affect regulation in the practicing period. *Psychoanalysis and Contemporary Thought, 14,* 187–250.

Schore, A. N. (1994). *Affect regulation and the origin of the self: The neurobiology of emotional development.* Hillsdale, NJ: Erlbaum.

Schore, A. N. (1996). The experience-dependent maturation of a regulatory system in the orbital prefrontal cortex and the origin of developmental psychopathology. *Development and Psychopathology, 8,* 59–87.

Schore, A. N. (1997a). Interdisciplinary developmental research as a source of clinical models. In M. Moskowitz, C. Monk, C. Kaye, &. S. Ellman (Eds.), *The Neurobiological and developmental basis for psychotherapeutic intervention* (pp. 1–77). Northvale, NJ: Aronson.

Schore, A. N. (1997b). The early organization of the nonlinear right brain and the development of a predisposition to psychiatric disorders. *Development and Psychopathology, 9,* 595–631.

Schore, A. N. (1997c). A century after Freud's Project: Is a rapprochement between psychoanalysis and neurobiology at hand? *Journal of the American Psychoanalytic Association, 45,* 808–838.

Schore, A. N. (in press). The experience-dependent maturation of an evaluative system in the cortex. In K. H. Pribram & J. King (Eds.), *Fifth Appalachian Conferences on Behavioral Neurodynamics, "Brain and Values."* Hillsdale, NJ: Erlbaum.

Semrud-Clikeman, M., & Hynd, G. W. (1990). Right hemisphere dysfunction in nonverbal learning disabilities: Social, academic, and adaptive functioning in adults and children. *Psychological Bulletin, 107,* 196–209.

Smith, C. G. (1981). *Serial dissection of the human brain.* Baltimore and Munich: Urban & Schwarzenberg.

Spence, S., Shapiro, D., & Zaidel, E. (1997). The role of the right hemisphere in the physiological and cognitive components of emotional processing. *Psychophysiology, 33,* 112–122.

Sroufe, L. A. (1996). *Emotional development: The organization of emotional life in the early years.* New York: Cambridge University Press.

Stansbury, K., & Gunnar, M. R. (1994). Adrenocortical activity and emotion regulation. *Monographs of the Society for Research in Child Development, 59,* 108–134.

Steklis, H. D., & Kling, A. (1985). Neurobiology of affiliative behavior in nonhuman primates. In M. Reite & T. Field (Ed.), *The psychobiology of attachment and separation* (pp. 93–134). Orlando, FL: Academic Press.

Stern, D. N. (1985). *The interpersonal world of the infant.* New York: Basic Books.

Thompson, R. A. (1990). Emotion and self-regulation. *Nebraska Symposium on Motivation* (pp. 367–467). Lincoln: University of Nebraska Press.

Tomkins, S. (1962). *Affect, imagery, consciousness: Vol. 1. The positive affects.* New York: Springer.

Tomkins, S. (1963). *Affect, imagery, consciousness: Vol. 2. The negative affects.* New York: Springer.

Trad, P. V. (1986). *Infant depression.* New York: Springer-Verlag.

Trevarthen, C. (1993). The self born in intersubjectivity: The psychology of an infant communicating. In U. Neisser (Ed.), *The perceived self: Ecological and interpersonal sources of self-knowledge* (pp. 121–173). New York: Cambridge University Press.

Tucker, D. M. (1992). Developing emotions and cortical networks. In M. R. Gunnar &

C. A. Nelson (Eds.), *Minnesota symposium on child psychology.* Vol. 24, *Developmental behavioral neuroscience* (pp. 75–128). Hillsdale, NJ: Erlbaum.

van der Kolk, B. A., & Fisler, R. E. (1994). Childhood abuse and neglect and loss of self-regulation. *Bulletin of the Menninger Clinic, 58,* 145–168.

Van Strien, J. W., & Morpugo, M. (1992). Opposite hemisphere activations as a result of emotionally threatening and non-threatening words. *Neuropsychologia, 9,* 845–848.

Velasco, M., & Lindsley, D. B. (1965). Role of orbital cortex in regulation of thalamo-cortical electrical activity. *Science, 149,* 1375–1377.

Winnicott, D. W. (1958). The capacity to be alone. *International Journal of Psycho-Analysis, 39,* 416–420.

Wittling, W., & Pfluger, M. (1990). Neuroendocrine hemisphere asymmetries: Salivary cortisol secretion during lateralized viewing of emotion-related and neutral films. *Brain and Cognition, 14,* 243–265.

Wright, K. (1991). *Vision and separation: Between mother and baby.* Northvale, NJ: Aronson.

Yasui, Y., Itoh, K., Kaneko, T., Shigemoto, R., & Mizuno, N. (1991). Topographical projections from the cerebral cortex to the nucleus of the solitary tract in the cat. *Experimental Brain Research, 85,* 75–84.

Zald, D. H., & Kim, S. W. (1996). Anatomy and function of the orbital frontal cortex: 2. Function and relevance to obsessive-compulsive disorder. *Journal of Neuropsychiatry and Clinical Neurosciences, 8,* 249–261.

4

The Forms and Functions of the Nonverbal Signal of Shame

Dacher Keltner
LeeAnne Harker

Shame is perhaps the most negative and disturbing emotional experience. Shame follows events in which the individual violates rules of a moral nature that apply to core aspects of the self (Darwin, 1872; Keltner & Buswell, 1996; Miller & Tangney, 1994; Tangney, 1992). Shame is characterized by devastating and paralyzing feelings of self-condemnation, disgust, anger, and inferiority and the pronounced desire to withdraw and disappear (Tangney, Miller, Flicker, & Barlow, 1996). The frequent and prolonged experience of shame relates to several psychological disorders, including chronic depression (Andrews, 1995; Kaufman, 1989) and antisocial behavior and hostility (Tangney, Wagner, Fletcher, & Gramzow, 1992). It is hard to argue against the claim that life would be better without shame.

Does shame benefit humans in any way? In this chapter, we will argue that shame serves the important function of appeasing observers of social transgressions, a function which reestablishes social harmony following the rule violations that inevitably disrupt social interaction. In characterizing the appeasement functions of shame, we will review studies that have examined the nonverbal display of shame, which should play a critical role in appeasement-related processes. Our review of the evidence will focus on whether shame is marked by (1) distinct nonverbal behavior that (2) is accurately identified by observers, (3) resembles the appeasement behaviors of other species, and (4) evokes responses in observers that lead to forgiveness and reconciliation.

Our review is relevant to several questions and concerns. First, we will assess whether the empirical evidence indicates that the nonverbal display of shame is distinct from that of related emotions, such as embarrassment. Theorists have not spoken with a consistent voice regarding this issue: most typically, the display of shame has been equated to that of embarrassment (e.g., Izard, 1971; Tomkins, 1963,

1984). Evidence regarding whether shame has a distinct nonverbal display is relevant to the more general claim that shame is a distinct emotion that belongs in a taxonomy of universal emotions (e.g., Ekman, 1992; Tangney et al., 1996). Such a taxonomy informs theories that explicate emotion, the functions of emotion-related responses (Roseman, Wiest, & Swartz, 1994), and cross-cultural variation in emotion (Haidt & Keltner, 1997).

Second, what are the functions of the nonverbal display of shame? Does the display have any regular, beneficial consequences that might account for its role in the evolved repertoire of human emotion displays? Does the display of shame have consistent effects upon others that benefit social relations? Although the experience of shame is marked by the pronounced tendency to escape, hide, and not be seen, which would suggest that shame would not be marked by a distinct, identifiable display, we will argue that the display of shame appeases observers of social transgressions.

Third, we believe our review is relevant to clinical studies of shame (e.g., Andrews, 1995; Kaufman, 1989; Tangney et al., 1992). To the extent that shame does indeed signal disturbing feelings and events, clinicians would be well served by a knowledge of the valid behavioral indicators of shame to aid in the identification of shame in ongoing therapeutic interactions. Our review will attempt to specify these behaviors. Additionally, other people's responses to the ashamed individual may enable that person to reintegrate into social relations (Moore, 1993). Our review of the appeasement functions of shame will identify the specific emotional processes by which shame leads to social reconciliation, processes which may also play a critical role in the social adjustment of ashamed individuals.

The Communicative Functions of Emotion Displays

Like other theorists (e.g., Darwin, 1872; Ekman, 1984; Izard, 1971), we believe that emotion displays, including that of shame, have been refined in the course of human evolution to serve informative, instrumental, and evocative functions that coordinate adaptive social behavior. Emotion displays provide quick, reliable, and easily identified signals of current emotions (Ekman, 1984; Izard, 1971) appraisals of objects in the social environment (Klinnert, Campos, Sorce, Emde, & Svejda, 1983), and the nature of social relations; for example, whether either the individual or the recipient of the display is submissive or dominant, intimate friend or foe (Keltner, 1995; Keltner, Young, Oemig, Heerey, & Monarch, 1996). Emotion displays serve instrumental functions, rewarding ongoing social activity, as in the case of laughter (Provine, 1992), or deterring or punishing undesirable behavior. Finally, emotion displays serve evocative functions, evoking specific emotions in others which may themselves be universal (Darwin, 1872). The responses emotion displays evoke in others (for example, displays of distress evoke sympathy) facilitate adaptive responses to the problems of survival and contribute significantly to the bonds between parents and children, romantic partners, and group members (Bowlby, 1969; Barrett & Campos, 1987; Levenson & Gottman, 1983). The informative, instrumental, and evocative functions of the shame display play a critical role in appeasement processes.

Shame as an Appeasement-related Process

Human social life is governed by myriad rules, which individuals inevitably violate, thereby threatening the harmony of social relationships and, according to some, the very foundations of the social order (Goffman, 1967). To remedy social relations following transgressions of social rules, humans rely on apologies and appeasement gestures, which, like similar displays in other species (see, e.g., de Waal, 1988), involve submissive and affiliative displays that lead to forgiveness, social approach, and reconciled relations (e.g., Keltner, Young, & Buswell, 1997, Tavuchis, 1991).

It has recently been proposed that shame and related states, such as humiliation and embarrassment, serve appeasement functions (Castelfranchi & Poggi, 1990; Gilbert, Pehl, & Allan, 1994; Keltner, 1995; Keltner & Buswell, 1996; Miller & Leary, 1992; Ohman, 1986). An appeasement analysis of shame suggests that the nonverbal display of shame (1) follows transgressions of social and moral rules that govern behavior and experience related to the sense of virtue and character, a claim for which there is substantial evidence (e.g., Keltner & Buswell, 1996; Miller & Tangney, 1994; Tangney, 1992; Tangney et al., 1996); and (2) is expressed in a distinct display that resembles submissive, appeasement-related behavior, which (3) restores social relations by reducing aggression and evoking social approach in observers.

An appeasement analysis of shame therefore makes certain predictions that will guide our review of the evidence related to the nonverbal display of shame. First, this approach suggests that shame will be marked by a distinct nonverbal display (see Keltner, 1995). To address this claim, we will review *encoding component studies* of shame, which have examined the actual behavior that accompanies shame. Second, the appeasement analysis suggests that the nonverbal display of shame will be readily perceived by others. To address this claim, we will review *judgment studies*, which determine whether across cultures observers accurately identify displays of shame. Third, the appeasement analysis suggests that the nonverbal display of shame has the functions of reducing aggression and increasing social approach, which produce social reconciliation. To assess whether the display of shame has these functions, we will briefly examine the *convergent evidence* that indicates whether the display of shame resembles the appeasement behavior of other species and the *evocative studies* that have documented the inferences and emotions that shame displays evoke in others. Across these studies, we will focus our analysis on whether the forms and functions of the shame display are distinct from those of similar emotions, in particular embarrassment and guilt.

Encoding Component Studies of the Nonverbal Behavior of Shame

How do people look and behave when feeling ashamed? The simple answer to this question would be found in an encoding component study that would examine the nonverbal behavior people display when currently experiencing shame. No study, however, has examined the behavioral correlates of the actual experience of shame.

To ascertain what the nonverbal display of shame is, therefore, we will consider a broader array of conceptually relevant studies that have linked shame to nonverbal behaviors, including gaze, posture, and head and facial muscle activity, and, in some instances, to verbal behavior. These studies include observational or experimental studies that have examined individuals' actual responses to shame-inducing situations (although self-reports of the experience of shame were not gathered); self-report studies that have asked individuals to recall and describe their responses, including certain nonverbal behavior, when ashamed; and individual difference studies that have examined the correlations between individuals' self-reported tendency to experience shame in various situations with their self-reported frequency of relevant behaviors. The findings from these studies are summarized in table 4.1. Although each of these types of studies has limitations, when viewed together, a coherent pattern of behaviors involved in the experience of shame emerges.

Behavior Observed during Shame-related Situations

A defining element of shame-inducing situations is failure, and in particular failure at tasks that define the core self (Tangney et al., 1996). Several studies have looked at the behavior of young children (2 to 5 years old) in the contexts of these kinds of failures. Most of these studies experimentally manipulated success and failure and then compared children's behavior following these two different outcomes, which were assumed to produce pride and shame, respectively. Success typically results in direct eye contact with the competitor or experimenter, smiles, and a triumphant, open body posture. Failure, in contrast, generally leads to gaze aversion, frowns, body collapse, and a closed and avoidant body posture (Geppert & Gartmann, 1983; Halisch & Halisch, 1980; Heckhausen, 1984; Lewis, Alessandri, & Sullivan, 1992; Lutekenhaus, Grossmann, & Grossmann, 1985; Stipek, Recchia, & McClintic, 1992). Failure is also sometimes accompanied by verbal statements of failure (Halisch & Halisch, 1980; Stipek et al., 1992), negative self-evaluative statements (Lewis et al., 1992), reduced effort (Lutekenhaus et al., 1985), and withdrawal from the task situation (Lewis et al., 1992). Thus, the results of these studies indicate that the behavioral display of shame, as revealed in failure situations, involves a shrinking and folding in of the body, gaze aversion, and motor avoidance, which may signal inferiority and withdrawal. These behaviors are likely to occur in other situations, but they do seem to occur during shame-related situations.

These studies of shame-related behavior suffer from one general limitation. Since no self-report measures were gathered, one cannot be certain that shame was the only or even primary emotion shown by these children in the failure conditions. Sadness, frustration, and embarrassment, for instance, are equally plausible emotional responses to public failure. Lewis and colleagues (1992) recognized this problem and made an attempt to distinguish sadness from shame by taking into account task difficulty. They found that children exhibited shame-related behaviors (e.g., gaze aversion, frowns, body collapse) when they failed at easy tasks but not when they failed at difficult tasks, a situation less likely to have negative implications for the self. As the authors stress, this differential responding to tasks that vary in difficulty suggests that an evaluative process occurred. Children only

Table 4.1 Behaviors Reported in Encoding Studies of Shame

Type of Study	Gaze	Face	Posture	Behavior	Action Tendencies	Physical Sensations
Children's Behavior following Failure						
Geppert & Gartmann (1983)	Directed down and/or around	Mouth corners lowered	Head down and chin in, trunk forward and down			
Halisch & Halisch (1980)	No eye contact	Embarrassed smile	Body bent down, high tension	Verbal statement of failure		
Heckhausen (1984)	Directed at own work		Body collapsed and bent down, head tilted to side, hands stay on own work			
Lewis, Alessandri, & Sullivan (1992)	Eyes lowered, gaze directed downward or askance	Corners of mouth down, lower lip tucked between teeth	Body collapsed	Negative self-evaluative statement, withdrawal from task situation		
Lutekenhaus, Grossman, & Grossmann (1985)	Reduced glances toward experimenter	Frown		Reduced speed during task completion		
Stipek, Recchia, & McClintic (1992)	Gaze aversion	Lips pursed, lip corners lowered	Avoidant posture (e.g., head and chin down, body to side or squirm, back to experimenter);	Says "I can't"		

(continued)

			Closed posture (e.g., Shoulders hunched, hands down, hands touching, arms crossed or close to body, arms/hands in front of face)			
Children's Behavior after Breaking Doll						
Barrett, Zahn-Waxler, & Cole (1993)	Gaze aversion	Smile followed by gaze aversion		Backed up or moved away from experimenter		
Self-report: Recalled Experiences of Shame						
Ablamowicz (1992)	Avoidance of eye contact	Blushing	Shoulders slumped, head down	Fell silent, halting speech, withdrawal from people	Desire to escape, become invisible	Reduced in size, weak and achy, sick to stomach
Lindsay-Hartz (1984)				Silence	Desire to hide or escape	Shrinking, feels small
Miller & Tangney (1994)		Did not smile		Apologized, tried to make things better	Wish to redo situation	
Scherer & Wallbott (1994)				Withdrawal behaviors, attempts to hide/control emotion, low expressivity, silence		High felt temperature, heart beating faster

Table 4.1 *(continued)*

Type of Study	Gaze	Face	Posture	Behavior	Action Tendencies	Physical Sensations
Tangney, Miller, Flicker, & Barlow (1996)		Blushing			Desire to make amends; desire to hide, did not want to confess, wished they had acted differently	Physiological changes (e.g., increased heart rate), feels smaller
Wicker, Payne, & Morgan (1983)		Blushing			Desire to hide (vs. make restitution), inhibited	
Children's Responses to Hypothetical Shame-Inducing Situations						
Ferguson, Stegge, & Damhuis (1991)					Desire to avoid (vs. approach) others	
Behavioral Correlates of Shame-Proneness						
Gilbert, Pehl, & Allan (1994)				Submissive behavior		
Tangney, Wagner, Burggraf, Gramzow, & Fletcher (1991)				Teacher reports of aggression		
Tangney, Wagner, Fletcher, & Gramzow (1992)				Indirect hostility		

84

displayed shame when they failed to meet a standard which they believed they actually could or should have met. This interpretation is further supported by the fact that shame behaviors in this study often included negative self-evaluative statements such as "I'm no good at this."

Other research suggests that the behavior associated with shame may differ from that associated with guilt (Barrett, Zahn-Waxler, & Cole, 1993). In this study, toddlers' behavior was observed as they played with a doll that was rigged to break during play, an emotionally charged transgression during early childhood. Children were classified into two different groups according to their emotional responses to breaking the doll—avoiders and amenders. Amenders tried to repair the toy quickly and readily confessed to the experimenter. Avoiders exhibited gaze aversion, embarrassed smiles, and/or backed up or moved away from the experimenter. These different response patterns suggest that amenders may have primarily felt guilt in response to breaking the toy, whereas the avoiders may have primarily felt shame. Certainly this speculation is consistent with studies of adults' recalled experiences of shame and guilt, which find that shame is associated with avoidant behavior (see the following discussion), whereas guilt is associated with attempts to repair the situation, confess, and apologize (see, e.g., Baumeister, Stillwell, & Heatherton, 1994; Tangney et al., 1996). This speculation was additionally supported by the finding that membership in the amenders' group versus the avoiders' group correlated with parental reports of the tendency to exhibit guilt as opposed to shame behavior in the home.

In the only encoding study of adult displays of shame, Dixon, Gilbert, and their colleagues compared the nonverbal behavior adults displayed when asked questions unrelated to shame (such as why they were studying psychology) with the behavior they displayed in response to shame-inducing questions (such as whether they feel ashamed of any part of their body) (Dixon, Huber, Gilbert, Gilbert, & Van der Hoek, 1996). Consistent with the studies reviewed so far, the shame-inducing questions produced increased gaze aversion compared to the more neutral questions.

In sum, these encoding component studies of both children and adults find certain behaviors that appear to occur during shame-inducing situations, including gaze aversion, body collapse, and motor avoidance, that are distinct from the behaviors associated with sadness (e.g., Lewis et al., 1992), embarrassment (e.g., Keltner, 1995), and perhaps even guilt (Barrett et al., 1993). Other behaviors associated with shame, however, such as the embarrassed smile and the frown, are also observed in the displays of other emotions.

Recollections of Shame and Concomitant Behavior

A second approach to the study of the shame display has been to ask people to recall and describe personal experiences of shame. The obvious limitation of this research is that it relies on self-reports of behavior, which may not capture the responses that occur during the actual experience of the emotion. The benefits of self-report studies are several: researchers can generalize the findings from laboratory studies to real-life situations, directly compare the behaviors associated with shame with those of other emotions, and gather information about the physical sensations and action tendencies that accompany shame.

Although most of these studies do not inquire about facial or postural expression, Ablamowicz (1992) found that some participants mentioned avoiding eye contact, slumping their shoulders, and keeping their heads down when feeling ashamed. Miller and Tangney (1994) asked participants to specifically contrast the experiences of shame and embarrassment and found that people associated smiling and laughing with embarrassment and not smiling with shame. This suggests that the smiles found in the encoding studies described previously may be more a product of embarrassment than of shame (see also Keltner, 1995).

Individuals in several studies reported that the experience of shame involved blushing (e.g., Ablamowicz, 1992; Tangney et al., 1996; Wicker, Payne, & Morgan, 1983) or the related sensation of rapid increases in temperature (Scherer & Wallbott, 1994) which accompanies the blush (Shearn, Bergman, Hill, Abel, & Hinds, 1990). Some participants also noted increased heart rate (Scherer & Wallbott, 1994; Tangney et al., 1996), although in general participants report that shame is characterized by sensations of reduced physiological arousal (Scherer & Wallbott, 1994). Interestingly, whereas in one study individuals recalled feeling sick to their stomachs during shame (Ablamowicz, 1992), only 11% of participants in Scherer and Wallbott's (1994) study reported that shame was characterized by stomach problems. Other physical sensations or feelings that participants commonly report in their recollections of shame include feeling small and reduced in size (Ablamowicz, 1992; Lindsay-Hartz, 1984; Tangney et al., 1996) and feeling weak and achy (Ablamowicz, 1992).

In terms of actual behavior, people report that shame is accompanied by low levels of expressive behavior in general (Scherer & Wallbott, 1994), becoming or remaining silent (Ablamowicz, 1992; Lindsay-Hartz, 1984; Scherer & Wallbott, 1994), and attempting to hide or control their shame (Scherer & Wallbott, 1994). Additionally, whereas some participants report withdrawing from people (Ablamowicz, 1992; Scherer & Wallbott, 1994), participants in another study reported apologizing and trying to make things better (Miller & Tangney, 1994). In addition to these actual behaviors, many studies find that participants express certain action tendencies. For example, most studies find that participants desire to hide or escape from the situation rather than confess or make amends (Ablamowicz, 1992; Ferguson, Stegge, & Damhuis, 1991; Lindsay-Hartz, 1984; Tangney et al., 1996; Wicker, Payne, & Morgan, 1983). However, other studies have found that participants wanted to make amends (Tangney et al., 1996) or wished they had acted differently or could redo the situation (Miller & Tangney, 1994; Tangney et al., 1996). In summary, self-report studies find behavioral expressions of shame to entail avoidance of eye contact, slumped shoulders, head down, blushing, little or no verbal behavior, and the inclination to apologize and withdraw from others. Additionally, participants reported an increase in heart rate, a feeling of shrinking in size, feeling small and weak, and wishing to hide or escape from the situation. These behaviors, physical sensations, and action tendencies all seem consistent with the view that shame displays signal submission and withdrawal.

Behavioral Correlates of Shame-Proneness

The last type of encoding study examines the relationship between shame-proneness and certain types of behavior. These studies typically measure shame-proneness by asking subjects to imagine themselves in a number of potentially shame-eliciting situations and then rate how they would feel in these situations. The tendency to report feeling shame in these hypothetical situations is then correlated with the tendency to engage in behaviors conceptually related to shame. Using this method, Gilbert and colleagues (Gilbert et al., 1994) found shame-proneness to correlate with the self-reported frequency of prototypical submissive behavior. This finding supports the notion that submission organizes the display of shame.

Other studies of shame-proneness, however, raise questions about the association between submissive behavior and shame. For example, the tendency for fifth-grade boys to report being prone to shame was correlated with self-reported anger and teacher reports of aggression (Tangney, Wagner, Burggraf, Gramzow, & Fletcher, 1991). Consistent with these findings, another study found that shame-proneness in adults correlated with self-reports of anger arousability and indirect hostility but was largely unrelated to assault or verbal hostility (Tangney et al., 1992). Still other studies by Tangney (1995) and her colleagues found that shame-proneness correlated with the self-reported tendency to engage in direct, indirect, and displaced aggression when feeling angry.

Taken together, these findings seem incongruent with findings of most other studies that link shame to submissive and/or avoidant facial and body expressions and behaviors. Because these studies are correlational, however, the exact nature of the relationship between shame and aggression cannot be determined. Aggressive behavior may follow rather than accompany shame. As Tangney et al. (1992) speculate, the painful, ego-threatening feelings of shame may lead some individuals to lash out at others involved in the shaming situation as a means of defending or reempowering the self. Alternatively, the expression of aggressive behavior may lead people to feel ashamed. Another possibility is that shame-proneness, anger arousability, and the tendency to act aggressively in difficult situations all relate to a broader dimension of psychopathology or maladjustment. Finally, the anger associated with shame may also be a response to the loss of status (Gilbert, 1997).

In conclusion, the findings from observational, self-report, and shame-proneness studies reveal a consistent portrait of the behaviors involved in shame. First, the nonverbal signal of shame entails downward, averted eye gaze, lowered lip corners, blushing, body collapse, and avoidant and closed posture. The self-report studies confirm many of these findings and further indicate that shame is associated with increased bodily temperature and the physical sensations of feeling weak, small, and inhibited. Although people sometimes make negative statements about the self or apologize when feeling ashamed, there appears to be little verbal expression of shame in general. Motor behaviors typically involve moving away from others or withdrawing from the situation. Many people also report trying to hide or control their shame. In describing action tendencies, people commonly report a desire to hide or escape from the situation, yet some also express a desire to make amends. Generally speaking, these facial and gestural expressions, physical sensations, behaviors, and action tendencies all seem consistent with the view that the behavioral display of shame signals submission and withdrawal. With their face, body, words, and actions, ashamed individuals make themselves appear smaller and nonthreatening and communicate retreat, surrender, and appeasement (see, e.g., Darwin, 1872).

Judgment Studies of the Nonverbal Display of Shame

Our review indicates that shame is marked by a pattern of nonverbal behavior that includes gaze aversion, head movements down, and constricted and collapsed posture. We next address the question of whether observers can reliably identify the nonverbal display of shame. An appeasement analysis suggests that observers' identification of the ashamed individual's shame, regret, and remorse is critical to appeasement processes. That is, in certain contexts, observers are likely to forgive an individual who has committed shameful acts to the extent that they perceive that the ashamed individual is clearly expressing personal shame, regret, and pain, implying his or her understanding of the moral and social significance of the act (see, e.g., Castelfranchi & Poggi, 1990; Goffman, 1956, 1967). On the other hand, the recognized experience of shame has costs, such as the loss of esteem and acknowledgment of wrongdoing, and is associated with the acute desire not to be seen, suggesting that people may engage in behaviors that hide their shame.

Judgment studies have examined whether observers can reliably identify as shame either still photographs of the nonverbal displays of shame, represented in slightly different ways across studies, or videotapes of spontaneous shame-related behavior, as depicted in dynamic gaze and head movements down. The first judgment study of shame was carried out by Izard in his influential cross-cultural studies of the judgment of emotion (reported in Izard, 1971). Target individuals were photographed as they posed shame, along with eight other emotions (anger, contempt, disgust, fear, interest, happiness, sadness, surprise). Lowered gaze, head movements down, lips drawn in and tightened in the corners, and protruding or tucked between teeth, were listed as the defining behaviors of shame (Izard, 1971), although examples of the photographs that represented shame (Izard, 1971) indicate that certain photos differed from this theoretically derived prototype. Pretested photographs of four individuals displaying the nine emotions were presented to university students in nine different cultures, including individuals from Europe, Africa, Japan, and, in subsequent research, India and Turkey. Participants were asked to select from nine emotion clusters the cluster of terms that best matched the emotion displayed in the photo. Each of the nine emotions represented in the photographs had a correspondent cluster of four synonymous terms, preselected for their coherence as an emotion concept (for example, the four words for the shame cluster were *shy, embarrassed, ashamed,* and *guilty*).

Across these dramatically different cultures, the mean level of accuracy in identifying the shame display was 64.8%; chance level would be 11.1%. Levels of accuracy in identifying the shame display were significantly lower for the Japanese (41.2%) and African participants (43.2%), although this was true in judgments of other emotions as well. Subsequent research also found that participants from India and Turkey identified shame displays with above-chance accuracy (reported in Izard, 1971).

This first judgment study of shame did not determine whether observers could accurately differentiate displays of shame from those of embarrassment, which certain authors assume shares the nonverbal display of shame (e.g., Darwin, 1872; Izard, 1971; Tomkins, 1984). Relevant research, however, has shown that embarrassment is marked by a pattern of behavior, namely, gaze aversion (typically to the side), head movements down and away, controlled smiles, and face touching, that appears to be distinct from the downward gaze aversion and head movements of shame (Keltner, 1995). Four more recent studies have examined whether the shame display, represented as downward gaze aversion and head movements down, was accurately discriminated from other displays, including those of embarrassment (Haidt & Keltner, 1997; Keltner, 1995; Keltner & Buswell, 1996).

In a first study, photographic slides of 14 facial expressions displayed by four Caucasian adults (two females and two males) were presented to observers, who were asked to select the emotion term, from 13 possible terms, that best matched the emotion shown in the photograph or to choose "no emotion" if they believed the display did not communicate emotion (Keltner & Buswell, 1996). These photos included emotions with well-established displays (anger, contempt, disgust, fear, happiness, sadness, and surprise), potential displays of emotion (amusement, awe, and sympathy), and likely displays of embarrassment (gaze down, controlled smile, head movements down and away, and face touching) and shame (gaze and head movements down). Also included were theoretically derived candidate displays of guilt, including self-contempt and pain, which sometimes follows mistakes.

Again, results indicated that observers could accurately identify the displays of shame. Observers identified shame (51.2%) and embarrassment (53.6%) with above-chance accuracy, although with less accuracy than the well-studied emotions, such as anger or disgust, which were judged with accuracy rates above 80%. Contrary to previous suppositions (e.g., Izard, 1971; Tomkins, 1984), observers did not confuse the displays of shame and embarrassment with each other. Observers rarely judged displays of embarrassment as shame (7%) or the displays of shame as embarrassment (3.4%). The second most common label for the display of shame was guilt (21.9%).

In a second study, participants in rural India and the United States were given photographs of 14 facial displays of emotion, again posed by Caucasian adults, including those of embarrassment and shame, and, after providing their own interpretation of the display, selected the emotion term from 15 provided that best matched the emotion displayed in the photo (Haidt & Keltner, 1997). In the United States, participants labeled the shame display with above-chance accuracy (57.5%), whereas in India participants were more inclined to label the shame display as sadness (42.9%) and guilt (22.5%) than *lajya* (15.0%), the Oriyan word most closely synonymous with shame.

Three other findings from this study are relevant to our discussion of the nonverbal display of shame. First, we found that the voluntary, emblematic action of covering the eyes with a hand was frequently identified as shame, both in the United States (45%) and India (35%). Second, the tongue bite, a display thought to signal shame and embarrassment in Southeast Asia (La Barre, 1947), was identified as *lajya* and guilt in India (47.5% combined) but not in the United States (10% combined), suggesting that the culturally specific displays of shame may be those that can be voluntarily produced. Third, analyses of participants' free responses to the shame displays found that participants across the two cultures were more likely to spontaneously label shame displays as sadness than as shame, consistent with previous findings demonstrating that the accuracy of identifying shame drops when free-response methods are used (Izard, 1971). This evidence indicates that the spontaneous interpretation of shame displays, as portrayed by gaze and head movements down, may be more open than the interpretations of the displays of such emotions as anger and disgust. That is, simple gaze and head movements down have multiple interpretations (e.g., the person is looking down at the ground, is reading, is sad, etc.) and lead to inferences of shame when contextual factors, provided experimentally by forced-choice methodologies or the nature of the social interaction, justify such an inference.

A third study has addressed whether observers could reliably identify the videotaped displays of shame displayed by African American and Caucasian adolescent males during the administration of an interactive IQ test (Keltner, 1995, Study 5). Observers were presented with videotapes of spontaneous displays of amusement (laughter), enjoyment, anger, disgust, embarrassment, and shame. Observers viewed each spontaneous display only once, for 3 to 4 seconds on average, much as they would in ordinary interactions. Following the presentation of each display, participants were asked to select the term, from six possible emotion terms, that best matched the emotion displayed in the video. Following their categorical judgment of the display, participants then rated the intensity of emotion displayed by each target.

In this study, observers achieved an accuracy rate of 67%; whereas chance level would be 16.7%. In fact, observers judged the shame displays more accurately than the displays of the other emotions, suggesting that shame may be more reliably identified than other emotions when observers are judging dynamic displays of emotion. The second most common label for the shame displays was disgust (12.9%). Observers rarely labeled the shame displays as embarrassment, although they did label the embarrassment displays as shame with above-chance levels (12.8%). Shame was judged to be the most intense emotional display.

In a fourth study relevant to our discussion (Keltner, 1995, Study 3), observers rated the extent to which 34 different individuals, whose displays of embarrassment or amusement were presented on videotape in 5-second segments, appeared to be experiencing nine different emotions, including shame and embarrassment. The primary aim of this study was to determine whether displays of amusement and embarrassment evoked different emotion attributions in observers. This proved to be the case. More specific analyses looked at the correlations between distinct nonverbal behaviors, including gaze down, head movements down, smiles, smile controls, and face touching, and the attributions of specific emotions. These correlations are relevant to the question of whether observers rely on different behavioral cues in making attributions of shame and embarrassment. The findings indicated that to a certain extent they did. Across observers' judgments of the videotaped targets, observers' attributions of shame, compared to their attributions of embarrassment, correlated more strongly with targets' gaze movements down, head movements down, head movements to the side, and smiling intensity (negatively correlated). In contrast, observers' attributions of embarrassment correlated with smile controls, such as lip presses, whereas their attributions of shame did not.

In sum, the judgment studies yielded two kinds of evidence indicating that observers reliably identify the displays of shame, represented most typically as gaze and head movements down. First, in categorical judgment studies of both posed and spontaneous displays, observers accurately identified the nonverbal display of shame and reliably differentiated it from the displays of related emotions, such as embarrassment. Second, observers' specific attributions of the levels of shame correlated with theoretically relevant behavior, including gaze and head movements down. We now turn to the evidence relevant to whether the rather simple display of shame shares the form of appeasement behaviors of other species and the evocative functions that bring about social reconciliation.

Similarity between the Display of Shame and Nonhuman Appeasement Displays

Beginning with Darwin, evolutionary theorists have proposed that human displays of emotion, for example, displays of fear or smiling, evolved from the displays of other species (Darwin, 1872; Ekman, 1992; Izard, 1971; van Hooff, 1972). Comparisons of the expressive behavior of humans with that of other species provide convergent evidence that indicates that across species certain adaptations have evolved in the face of similar selection pressures. When the comparisons involve humans and related species, such analysis also potentially illuminates the origins of human expressive behavior in related species' response systems. For example, several theorists have drawn connections between the human laugh and the open-mouthed play face of other species (e.g., van Hooff, 1972). This kind of evidence is germane to speculations regarding the evolutionary history and functions of emotion displays (Darwin, 1872; Ekman, 1972; Keltner & Gross, 1997).

This sort of cross-species comparison of expressive behavior was a centerpiece of Darwin's influential analysis of emotion in humans and other species (Darwin, 1872). Darwin did not identify the origins of the human shame display in the behaviors of other species, however, in large part because he focused on the association between shame and the blush, which he regarded as a signal unique to humans (for discussion, see Castelfranchi & Poggi, 1990; Keltner et al., 1997). More recently, however, researchers have speculated that the displays of shame and embarrassment, and possibly even the blush, resemble the appeasement displays of other species (Dixon, 1983; Keltner & Buswell, 1997; Leary & Meadows, 1991; Miller & Leary, 1992; de Waal, 1986).

To address whether the human displays of shame and embarrassment resemble appeasement behaviors of other species, we have reviewed forty studies of the behavior displayed by other species when appeasing a likely aggressor (Keltner & Buswell, 1997). The species included different kinds of primates, rodents, and birds. Certain appeasement-related behaviors that are common in other species are not ordinarily seen during human shame, including smiling, lip smacking, lying on the back, and high-pitched vocalizations. Many of the most common behaviors observed in other species' appeasement displays, however, define the display of shame, including gaze aversion, head movements down, postural constriction and reduced physical size, and even self-touching or grooming, which was found to signal shame in the judgment studies described above. Both shame and embarrassment seem to have their origins in the appeasement systems of related species. In the section that follows, we speculate as to why humans may have two appeasement-related displays of emotion.

Evidence of the Evocative Nature of Shame Displays

An appeasement analysis suggests that shame displays, much like the appeasement gestures of other species (see, e.g., de Waal, 1988), lead to reconciliation following social transgressions. Appeasement and reconciliation involve certain processes, therefore, that should characterize shame displays. First, submissiveness is an organizing feature of appeasement gestures (see, e.g., Eibl-Eibesfeldt, 1989; de Waal, 1988) and should therefore be a salient attribute of shame displays. Second, appeasement gestures reduce aggressive and punitive tendencies (de Waal, 1988), as should human shame displays. Third, shame displays, like appeasement gestures, should increase affiliative tendencies and emotions. We conclude our review by discussing the evidence related to these three claims about the evocative properties of the shame display.

Relations between Shame Displays and Submissiveness

Submissiveness is a core element of the appeasement displays of humans (e.g., Darwin, 1872; Eibl-Eibesfeldt, 1989; Ginsburg, Pollman, & Wauson, 1977) and other species (de Waal, 1998). Submissiveness likewise organizes the core responses of human shame. Submissiveness defines the experience of shame, which involves the sense of being small and inferior (Kaufman, 1989; Tangney et al., 1996). As we reported in the preceding discussion, one study found that the self-reported tendency to experience shame was highly correlated with a sense of personal inferiority, helplessness, and submissive behavior (Gilbert et al., 1994).

The nonverbal display of shame involves several submissive behaviors, including gaze and head movements down, face covering, and postural shrinkage, which reduces body size (Darwin, 1872; Ellyson & Dovidio, 1985; Keltner, 1995). Observers perceive shame displays as highly submissive. Specifically, when asked to attribute levels of affiliation and submissiveness to individuals displaying different emotions, observers attributed extremely high levels of submissiveness to displays of shame (Algoe & Keltner, 1996). Other studies have shown that observers are more likely to attribute shame to individuals from stereotypically low-status groups, demonstrating linkages between people's concepts of shame and their stereotypes of individuals of low-status groups. Specifically, when presented with objectively comparable displays, observers attributed greater shame to women and African Americans than to men and Caucasians (Keltner, 1995, Studies 3 and 5). Finally, one study found that low-status fraternity members were more likely to display shame, coded as gaze down and head movements down, than high-status members during group teasing interactions (Keltner et al., 1997). In sum, these studies indicate that shame is closely associated with submissiveness.

Shame Displays and Reduced Aggression

Appeasement gestures in other species reduce aggressive tendencies (de Waal, 1988). Similarly, appeasement gestures in humans, such as offers of food or greeting rituals, reduce aggression (Eibl-Eibesfeldt, 1989). Several studies indicate that timely displays of shame or related behavior reduce aggression and punitive tendencies in humans. In a first study, mock jurors rendered legal judgments of a hypothetical defendant convicted of selling drugs who displayed either anger, shame, or no emotion at the moment of sentencing (Young, Keltner, & Lingswieler, 1996, Study 1). As expected, participants sentenced the hypothetical defendant who displayed shame to shorter sentences under less severe conditions than they did the defendants who displayed anger or no emotion. This finding is consistent with studies of mock juries and actual trials that document that defendants who show signs of sadness and remorse are less likely to be convicted (reviewed in Young et al., 1996). In a similar study, political partisans were less likely to punish their favored political candidate who was charged with illegal campaign fundraising when he displayed shame than when he showed other emotions (Young et al., 1996, Study 3). Parents have also been shown to punish children less who display shame and embarrassment following transgressions (Semin & Papadopoulou, 1990).

Shame Displays and Increased Affiliation

Finally, an appeasement analysis suggests that shame evokes affiliative responses in others that bring about social reconciliation. A variety of studies indicate that shameful and embarrassed behavior, most notably gaze aversion and head movements down, produce affiliative behavior in others. Across studies, participants who either watched an individual knock over a supermarket display (Semin & Manstead, 1982), informed a confederate of bad news (Edelmann, 1982), or judged political candidates (Masters, 1988), were more inclined to like and to forgive, when relevant, an individual who displayed shameful, embarrassed behavior than they were a comparison individual who displayed other nonverbal behavior or no emotion. We have also recently found that men who tease their romantic partners by delivering their teasing with submissive posture and head movements down evoke more positive emotions in their partners (Keltner et al., 1996). These sorts of affiliative responses that shame evokes in others may account for why delinquency treatment techniques that bring together the defendant and victim and their respective families and allow the defendant to express remorse significantly reduce the rates of criminal recidivism (Moore, 1993).

We have conducted several studies to explore the mechanisms that might account for why observers like participants who display shame (Keltner et al., 1997). In these studies, participants were presented with a series of photos of individuals who displayed different emotions and whom they were asked to imagine had committed a social transgression. After viewing each photo, participants rated the emotions they felt in response to the individual. As expected, shame displays elicited noticeably higher levels of sympathy than did the embarrassment display. Sympathy motivates altruistic helping behavior (Eisenberg et al., 1989) and would be appropriate for rectifying the more serious transgressions associated with shame.

Embarrassment displays, in contrast, elicited higher levels of amusement, an emotion that leads observers to make light of transgressions (Cupach & Metts, 1990) and increases social approach (Keltner & Bonanno, 1997).

Summary and Conclusions

We have proposed that shame appeases observers of transgressions of a moral nature. Consistent with this perspective, our review found that shame is marked by a distinct nonverbal display that involves gaze down, head movements down, and constricted posture and that is reliably identified by observers as a signal of shame. Consistent with the hypothesis that shame shares the functions of appeasement gestures, we further found that the shame display resembles the appeasement displays of other species and reduces aggression and increases affiliation in ways that can promote social reconciliation. Although the experience of shame is painful and debilitating, the nonverbal display of shame can promote more favorable social relations.

Several questions await further empirical attention. To begin with, there are numerous contexts in which shame displays fail to reduce aggression. Bullying interactions on the playground, certain aggressive encounters between men, spousal abuse, and other diverse examples of victim derogation amply illustrate the myriad contexts in which appeasement displays do not reduce aggression. There are several possible reasons for the failure of shame displays to appease others. Shame displays may only lead to reconciliation in certain interactions, for example, those between members of the same group. Shame displays may not lead to reconciliation when the recipient of the display is insensitive to the apologetic nature of the display or lacks the capacity to forgive. The shame display itself may be mixed with other emotions, such as anger, that reduce the likelihood that the display will reduce aggression and evoke forgiveness.

In addition, recent research (see, e.g., Tangney & Fischer, 1995), some of which we have referred to in this review, has focused on the similarities and differences between three self-conscious emotions, namely, shame, embarrassment, and guilt, which all relate to reconciled relations following social transgressions. We believe that an important next step in research and theory is to ascertain why three emotions seem to serve similar functions. In other contexts, we have argued that both shame and embarrassment are appeasement-related emotions, but they appease through qualitatively different processes depending on the transgressions involved (see Keltner et al., 1997). Shame follows serious moral transgressions of the core self (Tangney et al., 1996) and appeases observers by eliciting sympathy (Keltner et al., 1997), which leads observers to express forgiveness and offer help (Eisenberg et al., 1989), thereby serving to elevate the ashamed individual's negative sense of self. Embarrassment follows transgressions of less important rules (i.e., social conventions), involves a nonverbal display that includes affiliative smiling behavior, and appeases others by eliciting more lighthearted emotions in observers, such as amusement, which incline observers to discount the importance of the transgression (Cupach & Metts, 1990; Keltner et al., 1997; Sharkey, 1991; Tangney et al., 1996).

It has also been claimed that guilt is a remedial emotion (e.g., Baumeister et al.,

1994; Tangney et al., 1996), suggesting that guilt, like shame, repairs social relations following transgressions. Our review and other relevant studies indicate, however, that although the two self-conscious emotions follow transgressions of a serious moral nature (e.g., Keltner & Buswell, 1996; Tangney et al., 1996), they restore social relations through different social processes. Shame does so largely through the nonverbal display of submissiveness; guilt does so through remedial behavior, such as apologies, confessions, and tending to others' pain (e.g., Baumeister et al., 1994; Tangney et al., 1996). Shame and guilt may involve different appeasement or remedial processes for several reasons. The nature of the transgression often differs for the two emotions (e.g., Tangney, 1992), which may require different actions. For example, shame often involves the individual's failure at a task, whereas guilt often involves harming others. The social context also seems to differ for the two emotions. Shame is more likely to occur in the presence of higher status individuals; thus the likelihood of nonverbal behavior that requires others to reestablish the social relation may be increased. The study of these sorts of issues will further reveal the social benefits of the self-conscious emotions.

References

Ablamowicz, H. (1992). Shame as an interpersonal dimension of communication among doctoral students: An empirical phenomenological study. *Journal of Phenomenological Psychology, 23*, 30–49.

Algoe, S. B., & Keltner, D. (1996). *Perceptions of dominance, submissiveness, coldheartedness, and affiliation in facial expressions of emotion.* Manuscript in preparation.

Andrews, B. (1995). Bodily shame as a mediator between abusive experiences and depression. *Journal of Abnormal Psychology, 104 (2)*, 277–285.

Barrett, K. C., & Campos, J. J. (1987). Perspectives on emotional development: 2. A functionalist approach to emotions. In J. D. Osofsky (Ed.), *Handbook of infant development* (2nd ed., pp. 555–578). New York: Wiley.

Barrett, K. C., Zahn-Waxler, C., & Cole, P. M. (1993). Avoiders vs. amenders: Implications for the investigation of guilt and shame during toddlerhood? *Cognition and Emotion, 7*, 481–505.

Baumeister, R. F., Stillwell, A. M., & Heatherton, T. F. (1994). Guilt: An interpersonal approach. *Psychological Bulletin, 115*, 243–267.

Bowlby, J. (1969). Attachment and loss: Vol. 1. *Attachment*. New York: Basic Books.

Castelfranchi, C., & Poggi, I. (1990). Blushing as discourse: Was Darwin wrong? In W. R. Crozier (Ed.), *Shyness and embarrassment: Perspectives from social psychology* (pp. 230–254). Cambridge: Cambridge University Press.

Cupach, W. R., & Metts, S. (1990). Remedial processes in embarrassing predicaments. In J. Anderson (Ed.), *Communication yearbook* (Vol. 13, pp. 323–352). Newbury Park, CA: Sage.

Darwin, C. (1872). *The expression of emotions in man and animals.* New York: Philosophical Library.

Dixon, A. F. (1983). Observations on the evolution and behavioral significance of "sexual skin" in female primates. *Advances in the Study of Behavior, 13*, 63–106.

Dixon, A. K., Gilbert, P., Huber, C., Gilbert, J., & Van der Hoek, G. (1996). Changes in nonverbal behaviour in a neutral and "shame" interview. Unpublished manuscript, University of Derby, UK.

Edelmann, R. J. (1982). The effect of embarrassed reactions upon others. *Australian Journal of Psychology, 34*, 359–367.

Eibl-Eibesfeldt, I. (1989). *Human ethology.* New York: Aldine de Gruyter Press.

Ekman, P. (1972). Universals and cultural differences in facial expressions of emotion. In J. Cole (Ed.), *Nebraska Symposium on Motivation 1971* (pp. 207–283). Lincoln: University of Nebraska Press.

Ekman, P. (1984). Expression and the nature of emotion. In K. Scherer & P. Ekman (Eds.), *Approaches to emotion.* (pp. 319–344). Hillsdale NJ: Erlbaum.

Ekman, P. (1992). An argument for basic emotions. *Cognition and Emotion, 6,* 169–200.

Ellyson, S. L., & Dovidio, J. F. (Ed.). (1985). *Power, dominance, and nonverbal behavior.* New York: Springer-Verlag.

Ferguson, T. J., Stegge, H., & Damhuis, I. (1991). Children's understanding of guilt and shame. *Child Development, 62,* 827–839.

Geppert, U., & Gartmann, D. (1983, August). *The emergence of self-evaluative emotions as consequences of achievement actions.* Paper presented at the biennial meeting of the International Society for the Study of Behavioral Development, Munich, Germany.

Gilbert, P. (1997). The evolution of social attractiveness and its role in shame, humiliation, guilt and therapy. *British Journal of Medical Psychology, 70,* 113–147.

Gilbert, P., Pehl, J., & Allan, S. (1994). The phenomenology of shame and guilt: An empirical investigation. *British Journal of Medical Psychology, 67,* 23–36.

Ginsburg, J. J., Pollman, V. A., & Wauson, M. S. (1977). An ethological analysis of nonverbal inhibitors of aggressive behavior in male elementary school children. *Developmental Psychology, 13,* 417–418.

Goffman, E. (1956). Embarrassment and social organization. *American Journal of Sociology, 62,* 264–271.

Goffman, E. (1967). *Interaction ritual: Essays on face-to-face behavior.* Garden City, NY: Anchor.

Haidt, J., & Keltner, D. (1997). Culture and emotion: New methods and new emotions. Manuscript in preparation.

Halisch, C., & Halisch, F. (1980). Kognitive Voraussetzungen Fruhkindlicher Selbstewertungsreaktionen nach Erfolg und Mißerfolg. *Zeitschrift fur Entwicklungspsychologie und Padagogische Psychologie, 12,* 193–212.

Heckhausen, H. (1984) Emergent achievement behavior: Some early developments. *Advances in Motivation and Achievement, 3,* 1–32.

Izard, C. E. (1971). *The face of emotion.* New York: Appleton-Century-Crofts.

Kaufman, G. (1989). *The psychology of shame: Theory and treatment of shame-based syndromes.* New York: Springer.

Keltner, D. (1995). Signs of appeasement: Evidence for the distinct displays of embarrassment, amusement and shame. *Journal of Personality and Social Psychology, 68,* 441–454.

Keltner, D., & Bonanno, G. A. (1997). A study of laughter and dissociation: The distinct correlates of laughter and smiling during bereavement. *Journal of Personality and Social Psychology, 73,* 687–702.

Keltner, D., & Buswell, B. (1996). Evidence for the distinctness of embarrassment, shame, and guilt: A study of recalled antecedents and facial expressions of emotion. *Cognition and Emotion, 10* (2), 155–172.

Keltner, D., & Buswell, B. (1997). Embarrassment: Its distinct form and appeasement functions. *Psychological Bulletin, 122,* 250–270.

Keltner, D., & Gross, J. (1997). The functions of emotion. Manuscript in preparation.

Keltner, D., Young, R., & Buswell, B. N. (in press). Social-emotional processes in human appeasement. *Aggressive Behavior.*

Keltner, D., Young, R. C., Oemig, C., Heerey, E., & Monarch, N. D. (1996). The social and emotional functions of teasing: Threat, appeasement, and reconciliation in groups and romantic couples. Manuscript submitted for publication.

Klinnert, M., Campos, J., Sorce, J., Emde, R., & Svejda, M. (1983). Social referencing in infancy. In R. Plutchik & P. Kellerman (Eds.), *Emotion theory, research, and methods,* Vol. 2: *Emotions in early development* (pp. 57–68).

La Barre, W. (1947). The cultural basis of emotions and gestures. *Journal of Personality*, *16*, 49–69.

Leary, M. R., & Meadows, S. (1991). Predictors, elicitors, and concomitants of social blushing. *Journal of Personality and Social Psychology, 60*, 254–262.

Levenson, R. W., & Gottman, J. M. (1983). Marital interaction: Physiological linkage and affective exchange. *Journal of Personality and Social Psychology, 45*, 587–597.

Lewis, M., Alessandri, S. M., & Sullivan, M. W. (1992). Differences in shame and pride as a function of children's gender and task difficulty. *Child Development, 63*, 630–638.

Lindsay-Hartz, J. (1984). Contrasting experiences of shame and guilt. *American Behavioral Scientist, 27* (6) 689–704.

Lutekenhaus, P., Grossmann, K. E., & Grossmann, K. (1985). Transactional influences of infants' orienting ability and maternal cooperation on competition in three-year-old children. *International Journal of Behavioral Development, 8*, 257–272.

Masters, R. D. (1988). Nice guys DON'T finish last: Aggressive and appeasement gestures in media images of politicians. In M. R. A. Chance (Ed.), *Social fabrics of the mind* (pp. 277–295). Hillsdale, NJ: Erlbaum.

Miller, R. S., & Leary, M. R. (1992). Social sources and interactive functions of embarrassment. In M. Clark (Ed.), *Emotion and social behavior* (pp. 202–221). New York: Sage.

Miller, R. S., & Tangney, J. P. (1994). Differentiating embarrassment and shame. *Journal of Social and Clinical Psychology, 13*, (3), 273–287.

Moore, D. B. (1993). Shame, forgiveness, and juvenile justice. *Criminal Justice Ethics, 12*, 3–25.

Ohman, A. (1986). Face the beast and fear the face: Animal and social fears as prototypes for evolutionary analysis of emotion. *Psychophysiology, 23*, 123–145.

Provine, R. R. (1992). Contagious laughter: Laughter is a sufficient stimulus for laughs and smiles. *Bulletin of the Psychonomic Society, 30*, 1–4.

Roseman, I. J., Wiest, C., & Swartz, T. (1994). Phenomenology, behaviors, and goals differentiate discrete emotions. *Journal of Personality and Social Psychology, 67*, 206–221.

Scherer, K. R., & Wallbott, H. G. (1994). Evidence for universality and cultural variation of differential emotion response patterning. *Journal of Personality and Social Psychology, 66*, 310–328.

Semin, G. R., & Manstead, A. S. R. (1982). The social implications of embarrassment displays and restitution behavior. *European Journal of Social Psychology, 12*, 367–377.

Semin, G. R., & Papadopoulou, K. (1990). The acquisition of reflexive social emotions: The transmission and reproduction of social control through joint action. In G. Duveen & B. Lloyd (Eds.), *Social representations and the development of knowledge* (pp. 107–125). Cambridge: Cambridge University Press.

Sharkey, W. F. (1991). Intentional embarrassment: Goals, tactics, and consequences. In W. Cupach & S. Metts (Eds.), *Advances in interpersonal communication research* (pp. 105–128). Normal, IL: Illinois State University.

Shearn, D., Bergman, E., Hill, K., Abel, A., & Hinds, L. (1990). Facial coloration and temperature responses in blushing. *Psychophysiology, 27*, 687–693.

Stipek, D., Recchia, S., & McClintic, S. (1992). Self-evaluation in young children. *Monographs of the Society for Research in Child Development, 57*, 1–84.

Tangney, J. P. (1992). Situational determinants of shame and guilt in young adulthood. *Personality and Social Psychology Bulletin, 18*, 199–206.

Tangney, J. P. (1995). Shame and guilt in interpersonal relationships. In J. P. Tangney & K. W. Fischer (Eds.), *Self-Conscious emotions: The psychology of shame, guilt, embarrassment and pride* (pp. 114–139). New York: Guilford Press.

Tangney, J. P. & Fischer, K. W. (1995). *Self-Conscious emotions: The psychology of shame, guilt, embarrassment and pride.* New York: Guilford Press.

Tangney, J. P., Miller, R. S., Flicker, L., & Barlow, D. H. (1996). Are shame, guilt, and embarrassment distinct emotions? *Journal of Personality and Social Psychology, 70*, 1256–1269.

Tangney, J. P., Wagner, P. E., Burggraf, S. A., Gramzow, R., & Fletcher, C. (1991, June). *Children's shame-proneness, but not guilt-proneness, is related to emotional and behavioral maladjustment*. Poster session presented at the annual meeting of the American Psychological Society, Washington, DC.

Tangney, J. P., Wagner, P., Fletcher, C., & Gramzow, R. (1992). Shamed into anger? The relation of shame and guilt to anger and self-reported aggression. *Journal of Personality and Social Psychology, 62*, 669–675.

Tavuchis, N. (1991). *Mea culpa: A sociology of apology and reconciliation*. Stanford, CA: Stanford University Press.

Tomkins, S. S. (1963). *Affect, imagery, consciousness. Vol. 2. The negative affects*. New York: Springer.

Tomkins, S. S. (1984). Affect theory. In K. Scherer & P. Ekman (Eds.), *Approaches to emotion*. (pp. 163–195). Hillsdale, NJ: Erlbaum.

van Hooff, J. A. R. A. M. (1972). A comparative approach to the phylogeny of laughter and smiling. In R. A. Hinde (Ed.), *Nonverbal communication*. (pp. 209–241). Cambridge: Cambridge University Press.

Waal, F. B. M. de (1986). The integration of dominance and social bonding in primates. *The Quarterly Review of Biology, 61*, 459–479.

Waal, F. B. M. de (1988). The reconciled hierarchy. In M. R. A. Chance (Ed.), *Social fabrics of the mind* (pp. 105–136). Hillsdale, NJ: Erlbaum.

Wicker, F. W., Payne, G. C., & Morgan, R. D. (1983). Participant description of guilt and shame. *Motivation and Emotion, 7*, 25–39.

Young, R. C., Keltner, D., & Lingswieler, R. (1996). *Appeasement in the courtroom, negotiations, and politics*. Unpublished manuscript.

5

Shame, Status, and Social Roles

Psychobiology and Evolution

Paul Gilbert *&* Michael T. McGuire

Shame, Rank, and Social Status

Shame is well understood to be an aversive experience, related to feeling demeaned, reduced, disgraced, or diminished, which people are highly motivated to avoid. One of the intriguing questions about shame is whether its underpinning psychobiological mechanisms are of recent origin, related to human self-consciousness and self-awareness, or whether shame is an elaboration of phylogenetically older mechanisms. In this chapter we suggest the latter, stressing in particular the following points. The psychobiological mediators of human shame evolved from phylogenetically older mechanisms that originally evolved to regulate social rank and status behavior, in particular submissive behavior. (2) The elicitors of both submissive behavior and human shame are associated with hostile and/or rejecting social signals. (3) Such social signals, indicating disruption to social relationships, not only affect emotions but are psychobiological dysregulating; thus shame is an experience of psychobiological dysregulation. (4) Human social status and acceptance in groups and relationships have evolved to be highly reliant on signals of being attractive, valued, wanted and approved of by others, such that losses of these signals can be dysregulating. (5) The self-consciousness dimension of human shame may be observable in nonhuman primates.

To develop this approach, we proceed in a series of steps. First, we explore some basic issues in evolutionary psychology. Second, we outline how social signals provide the external sources of information that regulate psychobiological states and behavioral strategies in the pursuit of biosocial goals. The strategy most closely associated with shame is involuntary submissive behavior. Third, we explore how human shame is often related to role behaviors and being seen as unattractive or inadequate in that domain (e.g., as physically unattractive as a sexual partner, uncaring, exploitive, deceptive). Fourth, we review animal data on various psychobiological mediators of social communication, especially dominant-subordinate interactions, with a special focus on the role of the neurotransmitter 5-HT (serotonin). This allows us to argue that shame relates to the triggering of involuntary submissive behavior. Fifth, we explore how such data can be used to inform theory and research on shame, including self-consciousness.

Evolutionary Continuity

The advantages of utilizing an evolutionary approach to the study of emotions and social behavior has been outlined elsewhere (Buss, 1995; McGuire, Marks, & Troisi, 1997; Nesse, 1990). Evolutionary continuity is related to the conservation of form; that is, evolution does not create new designs but adapts already existing designs (MacLean, 1990). The human brain contains a complex array of potential motivational systems and social strategies which evolved and have been modified over millions of years. Many of the earliest forms of social behavior, such as courting, sexual advertising, mating, threatening, harassing, territorial defense, ritual threat displays, and submission, can be observed in our early ancestors, the reptiles (MacLean, 1990). Behaviors such as caring for young and group cohesiveness are common to many mammals, while play, reassurance giving, care provision and complex communicative languages are of more recent origin and are particularly characteristic of primates.

Biosocial goals   The phylogenetic history of primates, including humans, has given rise to a number of specific biosocial goals which act as motivators for social behavior (Gilbert, 1989, 1995, 1997a). Stated briefly, primates are biologically motivated not only to follow their own sexual and mating strategies but also (1) to need and to utilize care (especially when young, although help, support, and care-seeking behavior continue throughout life in various ways); (2) to provide care for their own offspring (and kin); (3) to form alliances (including sexual liaisons), friendships, and in-group relationships—to get along with others in mutually (reciprocal) helpful ways; and (4) to pursue the various resources associated with status. Indeed, status (the rank position in a group) often affects how well placed an animal will be to pursue other goals. For example, the higher one's status, the more resources one might have to care for offspring, attract and retain mates, and form alliances. As noted in a subsequent discussion, shame commonly matches violations in these kinds of specific domains of social activity (for example, one can be shamed for certain sexual behaviors; for seeking too much care and being too dependent; for being untrustworthy in relationships; for not conforming to social norms, etc; see also Greenwald & Harder, this volume, chapter 12).

Strategies   In the pursuit of biosocial goals, such as seeking a mate, caring for offspring, forming alliances, and gaining status, individuals use many different strategies and tactics. Strategies follow an "if A do B" format. For example, other things being equal, a strategy might be "if stimuli indicate threat *then* take defensive action (e.g., run)." Strategies will be more effective, more "fit," if they are functional. Consider the "distress call," which is a common mammalian strategy to signal a distant parent to return. However, an infant who continues to make distress calls when there is no evidence that a parent is likely to be present in the near future could signal its location to predators. A functional strategy would be flexible and would terminate distress calling after a certain time if the distress signal is not answered. In other words, strategies are context-dependent and entrained to the presence or absence of certain signals. This flexibility and signal dependence of strategies helps animals avoid pursuing goals that cannot be obtained or that would decrease fitness if they were pursued without regard to danger or cost.

Social strategies   Social strategies are complex because it is other conspecifics who provide the salient signals about which strategy to use and whether a strategy is working or not. Thus, the success of a strategy (be it in courting, defending a territory, or trying to form alliances) requires consideration of what others are doing. For example, among many animals, forming cooperative alliances is central to the control of status and access to fitness-enhancing resources. It would, however, be detrimental to fitness to form alliances with those who constantly cheat and who don't repay help given to them. Thus, alliance forming may well have evolved with a capacity to detect and punish or ostracize and defect from cheats (Argyle, 1991; Cosmides & Tooby, 1992). In fact, help giving tends to follow certain rules (strategies), such as giving preferential treatment to kin and those who are likely to reciprocate (Burnstein, Crandall, & Kitayama, 1994).

How might the concept of evolved flexible social strategies, which are sensitive to conspecific signals, relate to shame? First, we think that simply positing shame as an evolved social strategy is relatively novel. Second, contextualizing it this way allows us to note its evolutionary origins, function, and typical triggers. Strategies evolved because they solved problems (Buss 1991, 1995). Now one key social problem that conspecifics face is that in pursuing any biosocial goal—such as gaining access to resources, establishing territories, access to sexual opportunities, or making alliances—there will be others who are pursuing the same goals. This will bring conspecifics into conflict with one another. Before an animal can acquire the resources it seeks, it often has to deal with competitors. In a straightforward contest, where there is likely to be a winner and a loser, the animal who loses requires a strategy that will inhibit (turn off) its challenging behavior. To fight or struggle on regardless will only intensify conflicts (Caryl, 1988; Gilbert, 1992). In fact, losers can run away, hide, and/or become physiologically demobilized (Toates, 1995). At the most basic level, in conflict situations, there are just two basic choices: to escalate or de-escalate. As noted elsewhere (Dixon, Gilbert, Huber, Gilbert, & van der Hoek, 1996; Gilbert, 1997b; Keltner & Harker, this volume chapter 4), the nonverbal communicative patterns of shame appear to be related to de-escalation in potential and actual conflict situations.

Shame and Submissiveness

The inhibitory dimensions of shame suggest that shame functions as a defensive strategy which can be triggered in the presence of interpersonal threat (Gilbert, 1997b). In most domains of social interaction, animals must be able to influence the feelings and behaviors of others (and in humans their thoughts) via the signals they send out and exchange. For example, an infant sending distress signals elicits care and protection from the parent; an animal soliciting sex attempts to arouse the sexual interest of another; an animal warning another to "back off" expresses threat signals to generate fear in the other. Thus, there are a range of social signals that serve as communicative devices. The ability to de-escalate a conflict (or avoid escalating it) and thus avoid serious damage depends on a variety of behaviors. One is flight/escape—one simply runs away. Another strategy, however, is appeasement. This involves sending signals that affect the minds (and strategies) of others. In the case of expressing submissive appeasement signals, the aim is to turn off the "attack" strategies in the attacker, to calm it down and send signals that inhibit it from inflicting serious damage. Indeed, so important is submissive behavior that MacLean points out:

> Ethologists have made it popularly known . . . that a passive response (a submissive display) to an aggressive display may make it possible under most circumstances to avoid unnecessary, and sometimes mortal, conflict. Hence it could be argued that the *submissive display is the most important of all displays* [italics added] because without it numerous individuals might not survive. (1990, p. 235)

Shame signals (e.g., head down, gaze avoidance, and hiding) are generally regarded as submissive and appeasement displays, designed to de-escalate and/or escape from conflicts (Gilbert, 1989; Keltner, and Harker, 1995 and chapter 4 in this volume; Ohman, 1986). Thus, insofar as shame is related to submissiveness and appeasement behavior, then it is a *damage limitation strategy*, adopted when continuing in a shameless, nonsubmissive way might provoke very serious attacks or rejections from others. Thus, an experience of shame affect can be seen as an involuntary submissive response, typically triggered by a social threat, the function of which is to de-escalate conflict.

Submissive behavior is also central to the formation of social hierarchies. For example, it is not only aggression that determines dominance and rank structure but also the subordinate behaviors that are elicited. Bernstein put it this way:

> A dominance relationship between two individuals is inferred not because one or both "assert" their dominance but because one readily submits. If, and only if, the subordinate recognizes the relationship, or "predicts" the outcome of an agonistic encounter by immediately showing submission, can we assume that a dominance relationship exists. . . . It is . . . the timing and sequencing of submissive signals in an interaction that allows us to infer the existence of a dominance relationship between two individuals.
>
> It is only the submission of subordinates that allows us to argue that dominance may function to partition resources or reduce fighting. (1980, pp. 80–81)

One should not underestimate the importance of animals being highly motivated to seek the prizes and rewards of rank, of course, but one can see this "deferential principle" mirrored in human socially constructed dimensions of shame (Scheff, 1988). Although episodes of shame experience are usually rapid, emotional, and involuntary, *what* is shaming can vary. What is shaming at one historical epoch or in one culture may not be in another. What is shaming is affected by the structure of the social group, that is, whether it is competitive or cooperative (e.g., Fiske, 1992). Furthermore, for humans, the social bonds people form (and desire to form) play a salient role in this acceptance of what is shaming (Scheff, personal communication). If one wants to or needs to belong to a particular group or family, then it is important to submit to the social rules and standards of that group. When people are voluntarily submitting, there need be no shame (e.g., submitting to a loved leader or God or even fashion). One might see such submitting as shame avoidant—that is, one might feel shame or anxiety if one did not submit—but that is a researchable point that may vary from case to case. For the moment we wish to emphasize the salience of *involuntary* submissive behavior in shame without detracting from the complexity and variety of triggers in humans.

Social Roles and Interpersonal Attunement

An expression of involuntary submissive behavior is most likely when an animal is under social threat. Such threats are conveyed by social signals and communications with others. In fact, group-dwelling primates, including humans, live under a constant bombardment of social signals of many types (and humans experience imaginations and fantasies of possible social signals as well). Social signals, such as those of sexual interest, acceptance, approval, indifference, rejection, or scorn, are being constantly generated and responded to according to the social goals being pursued.

Pursuing different biosocial goals (e.g., courting a sexual partner, looking after offspring, defeating or "outshining" competitors) requires different social behaviors and enactments (Gilbert, 1989, 1995, 1997a). For example, the way we care for a child is different from the way we act in courting a mate, and these are different from the way we act when working with others in a team. Different social roles are associated with different rules (have different strategies) and social signals. When two or more people are matched in a reciprocal way in their role enactments with each other (e.g., mother offers care and infant is calmed and prospers; a person makes a sexual advance and the other is receptive), social signals operate "according to the rules." Hence each person in that interaction receives appropriate feedback signals to maintain that role relationship. However, if an individual enacts behaviors that are misattuned to the appropriate role, others will signal to that person that their behavior is misattuned or does not fit. Examples of forms of misattunements are seen when people are trying to create different role relationships. For example, a person may assume more authority and rank than others wish to bestow; or whereas deceiving or outsmarting competitors is seen as good, doing the same to one's friends is not. Making sexual advances toward people who come for care (e.g., a doctor who exploits his or her position) will lead to professional rejection. There is nothing wrong with acting with authority, trying to score over others, or making sexual advances, but to avoid shame one must operate in the agreed-upon, appropriate domains and contexts. Not to do so invites attacks.

A variety of responses can serve as signals to denote that one is misattuned with others. These responses vary from polite requests for change to outright attack or rejection, depending on the seriousness and chronicity of the misattunement. The recipient of corrective disapproval signals from others can also experience a variety of feelings, from confusion to anxiety, anger, and, of course, shame. W. Miller (1993) explored the Norse sagas and noted that there was in these cultures a shame that was redeemable and a shame that was not. Redeemable shame usually required some admission of wrongdoing and show of submissive behavior, but nonredeemable shame resulted in exile.

The relative social rank of the actors will play a role in determining who has to attune with whom. As will be noted below, dominant animals have much more power to make subordinates attune to their self-interests than the other way around. The same is true in many human relationships, where down-rank shaming (to force the shamed to attune to the shamer's self-interest) is more powerful than up-rank shaming. This pertains to many relationships, including parent-child, employer-employee, teacher-pupil, gang leader–follower, and so forth. With various degrees of threat for noncompliance, the dominant individual usually has more power than the subordinate to shape the behavior of others in interactions. It is, to our mind, interesting why shame researchers rarely explore or take account of the power relationship when studying shame.

A key theme of this chapter is that social interactions are associated with constant communications among participants regarding their compliance and deviance from accepted social roles. It follows, therefore, that if certain types of deviance can elicit rejection, threat, or attack from conspecifics, animals must be able to recognize when they are about to act, or have acted, outside the norms of acceptable behavior. Recognition that others see one's behavior as deviant, undesirable, and so forth, and that a serious attack or rejection could result shifts arousal and (often) activates defensive responses (Gilbert, 1989, 1993). Contextualized this way, we suggest that in its potentially adaptive role shame functions to alert actors to the fact that certain social signals they are sending, or have sent, will elicit negative (devaluation) signals from others. Hence a loss of status or diminishment in the role is a likely consequence of sending (or having sent) certain inappropriate signals.

If small doses of shame (or fear of being shamed) do not succeed in inducing caution, compliance, and deference, then more serious consequences can follow. The signals of devaluation by others can then include actual attacks and ostracism. Following a "shameful" discovery, allies may break contact, the phone calls and invitations stop, and positive interactions decline; one is rejected by a form of social exclusion. W. Miller (1993) opens his book on humiliation with a story of how a new member to their group failed to obey the rules of deference within the group. He was seen as arrogant and overbearing, and in the end was humiliated and excluded when others planned not to attend a meeting organized in the offender's house. Had he been more attentive to the minor criticisms and cues of social disapproval and acted more submissively (humbly) within the group, such a fate might not have befallen him.

Social Signals Control Physiological States

Individuals are guided to biosocial goals (such as finding sexual partners and forming alliances and friendships) via the detection, evaluation, and meaning of social signals. The idea that social interactions have physiological and psychological consequences undoubtedly extends back beyond antiquity, but it had to await the investigations of Bowlby (1973) and Harlow (Harlow & Harlow, 1962; Harlow &

Mears, 1979) in the middle of this century before becoming a cornerstone of psychology. For these and numerous other investigators, normal and atypical development, as well as daily functioning, are contingent upon the types and frequencies of social interaction (Belsky, 1993; Belsky, Steinberg, & Draper, 1990). Infants require holding, touching, and vocal input (Montagu, 1986). Without such interactions, they become psychologically distraught and physiologically distressed and dysregulated (Hofer, 1984; Schore, 1994, the volume, chapter 3). Infants are motivated to elicit specific types of social signals (to alter and control the frequency and type of others' behavior) and to be calmed or pleasured by the arrival of certain signals and distressed by their absence. For example, infants are highly attentive to the human face and able to discriminate facial expressions. Research has shown that if a baby smiles and the mother smiles back, this attunement of facial expressions is positively rewarding and biologically regulating for the infant. Conversely, if the mother presents a blank, expressionless face, this is experienced as aversive, and the infant may become distressed and fretful and turn away (Schore, 1994; Tronick & Cohn, 1989). The fact that mismatches or misattunements in social signaling are aversive to the infant is evidence for the power of social signals to exert physiological effects (Tronick, 1989). Indeed, the social signals and interactions of early life can have a major impact on the maturing central nervous system (CNS), with long-lasting effects (Schore, 1994, this volume, chapter 3).

In the extreme, extended social deprivation (absence of social signals) can result in the failure to thrive and even death (Spitz, 1945). It is now recognized that adverse rearing experiences (including emotional neglect, affectionless control, physical and sexual abuse) can significantly affect psychobiological maturation and functioning (Hart, Gunnar, & Cicchetti, 1996; Parker, 1979; Rohner, 1986; Rosenblum, et al., 1994; Schore, 1994). Similar points apply to nonhuman primates, where studies have repeatedly documented that specific types of social interactions are essential for the optimal unfolding of maturational programs (Harlow & Harlow, 1962; Harlow & Mears, 1979; Kramer & Clark, 1991; Mineka & Suomi, 1978; Reite, Short, Seiler, & Pauley, 1981; Rosenblum et al., 1994). A review of many of the physiological systems that are affected by social interactions can be found elsewhere (McGuire, 1988).

Regulation-Dysregulation Theory (RDT)

Social signals (e.g., reassurance vs. criticism) normally have powerful effects on the confidence individuals have in performing social roles. In shame, the signals received are ones of misattunement, of being bad and deviant in some way, inadequate, unattractive, and so forth. Such signals are obvious threats to social standing and social acceptance. As such, they will activate various defensive responses and strategies. Be it a subordinate behaving in a way that invites attack from a more dominant animal or a human eliciting criticism or contempt from their fellows, speedy appeasement or escape may be the most adaptive response. Defensive responses have evolved for rapid action rather than rationality, and, when activated, shift information processing towards more "fast track," automatic, stereotypic, and segregated forms of functioning; there is a rush of anxiety, a sudden blush, or a flush of rage (see Gilbert, this volume, chapter 1). These may be against the conscious wishes of a person, who may feel overwhelmed by these highly charged internal experiences (Gilbert, 1989, 1993, 1995). In effect, the person loses the ability to consciously self-regulate his or her emotions and thoughts.

Regulation-dysregulation theory (RDT) was first used by McGuire and Troisi (1987a) to offer insights into the ways that social signals, originating in the external world, impinge on and influence the biological state of the receiver(s). It is an approach that stresses the psychobiological nature of interactions and interactional sequences and is derived from an evolutionary analysis of social behavior (McGuire et al., 1997).

The term *regulation* references a state in which physiological and psychological systems function optimally. The term is synonymous with *homeostasis* as it is used in the medical literature: a state of equilibrium or balance between opposing pressures in the body with respect to functions and to the chemical compositions of fluids and tissues (*Steadman's Medical Dictionary*, 1990). In a regulated state one feels well, has the energy and confidence to do what one wants to do, thinks clearly, feels in control of one's own thoughts and feelings, and is asymptomatic. Individuals differ not only in their physiological and psychological states relative to ideal states but also in their capacities to tolerate physiological and psychological change without experiencing symptoms (McGuire & Troisi, 1987a,b).

The term *dysregulation* refers to atypical physiological and psychological states associated with symptoms (e.g., depression, anxiety, anger, boredom) and reduced capacities to concentrate and act efficiently. Dysregulation may be mild or severe. In moderate-to-severe instances, persons are unable to control their thoughts and feelings. Indeed, people may seek help (therapy or drugs) as ways of stopping themselves from feeling and thinking things they do not wish to feel or think. Generally, given a choice, people will choose positive affect over negative affect. Increasingly, various therapists have come to recognize that affect dysregulation (the experience of powerful, painful, and unwanted emotions) is at the heart of many psychological difficulties (e.g., Greenberg & Safran, 1987; Linehan, 1993). In his writings on self psychology, Kohut (1977) referred to a similar concept in his discussions of "cohesiveness of the self" and the loss of cohesiveness and fragmentation as a source of psychopathology.

Dysregulation and defense system activation are likely in the presence of social signals that indicate role misattunement. Examples can include the demobilized, fretful state of the infant whose mother does not respond to his or her facial signals; the fearful anticipation of the parent waiting for the child to return home when he or she is late; the pining and distress of grief; a quarrel between lovers; and of course, the anxious, withdrawn, ruminative state of the shamed—all these are examples of dysregulation. *Interpersonal sequences* can serve to reregulate biological states and relationships. For example, the mother does mirror facial expressions; the child returns home safely; and the lovers apologize to each other and reconcile. Dysregulation amplification sequences are also common. For example, the child cries, the mother becomes angry (does not offer reassurance), and the child becomes more dysregulated; when the child returns home the parent humiliates him or her for being late and causing worry; the lovers continue in mutual blaming and recriminations. In the case of shame, a person is criticized and may withdraw; but the critic may want compliance, not withdrawal, so he or she criticizes the person for withdrawing, leading to a cycle of intensification in the exchange of dysregulating signals (Retzinger, 1991, this volume, chapter 11). Of course, the withdrawal (or anger) following a criticism may not be a shame affect at all but may be a corrective signal to the shamer: "don't treat me this way or I will withdraw from you." There is, however, no research data that depicts when such withdrawal is genuine shame and when it is a corrective signal to the critic (Andrews, personal communication).

In view of the propositions given above, the following points can be argued. (1) Shame is a form of dysregulation associated with unpleasant feelings and thoughts that increases the probability of various disorders among persons at risk for disorders and involves the emergence of symptoms and signs among individuals with disorders. (2) In such states, people can feel they have little conscious or voluntary control over feelings, thoughts, and behaviors. (3) Misattunements of social signals are commonly dysregulating. (4) Individuals seek out social environments that facilitate regulation (McGuire, 1988; McGuire, Fawzy, Spar, Wiegel, & Troisi, 1994; McGuire & Troisi, 1987a,b) and avoid those that increase dysregulation. However, when dysregulation is severe, excessive defensive behaviors (e.g., aggression, anxious withdrawal, or depressed shutdown) tend to lower further the chances of eliciting those social signals that could help to regulate the internal state, for such behaviors are usually deemed unattractive by others.

As noted in chapter 1, being shamed can be separated from feeling ashamed. Thus, being shamed relates to social signals of misattunement, whereas feeling ashamed relates to the degree of psychobiological dysregulation plus the degree of involuntary submissive behavior aroused and felt. Thus, being shamed can be dysregulating, and recognizing one's own dysregulation (symptoms) can be further shaming.

Serotonin Measures and Social Status

A key issue in *dysregulation from the misattunement of roles* is that it matters greatly whether we look at misattunement from the point of view of a dominant or subordinate. The dominant is able to threaten, coerce, or offer various rewards to ensure that others behave in ways that increase subordinate attunement to the dominant's self-interest. The subordinate has far less ability to do this. In the next sections, we explore the benefits of high status as well as one of its physiological correlates, serotonin (5-HT). We emphasize how sensitive physiological variables (in regard to regulation-dysregulation) are to social signals.

Nonhuman Primate Studies

Experimental data consistent with RDT can be found in reports by a variety of investigators who have studied a variety of species (e.g., Kravitz, 1988; Reite et al., 1981; Rosenblum et al., 1994; Sapolsky, 1989, 1990). Here we will focus on interactions between social status and both peripheral and CNS serotonin (5-HT) measures in adult male vervet monkeys (*Cercopithecus aethiops sabaeus*). This focus has been selected because of the abundance of evidence. Details of studies discussed can be found elsewhere (McGuire, Raleigh, & Johnson, 1983, 1994; Raleigh,

Brammer, McGuire, & Yuwiler, 1985; Raleigh & McGuire, 1993; Raleigh, McGuire, Brammer, Oikkacjrn, & Yuwiler, 1991; Raleigh, McGuire, Brammer, & Yuwiler, 1984).

Among adult male vervets, there are strong positive correlations between peripheral 5-HT levels, measures of CNS 5-HT sensitivity, and social status. High-status or dominant adult males have peripheral 5-HT levels averaging between one and one-half to two times the levels of low-status or subordinate males; and dominant males show proportionally greater behavioral responses to substances, such as tryptophan and fluoxetine, that augment CNS 5-HT concentrations and turnover. The greater the proportional response, the greater the CNS 5-HT sensitivity. When CNS 5-HT sensitivity is high, the frequency of initiated aggressive behavior is low; animals are more relaxed socially, minimally vigilant of other group members, and more tolerant of the behavior of other animals and they more frequently initiate and respond to affiliative gestures. Essentially the opposite findings apply to animals with low CNS 5-HT sensitivity: animals initiate and receive fewer affiliative behaviors; they receive and initiate more threats; and they devote a high percentage of their time to interanimal vigilance.

While adult male vervets no doubt compete for high social status because high status is associated with priority access to females, food, and perches, findings also permit the interpretation that they compete because of the physiological and psychological effects associated with elevated CNS 5-HT sensitivity, such as being more relaxed socially and more often the recipients of affiliative behavior. Such behavior is analogous to humans competing for specific social roles (high status) because such roles are assumed or known to be associated with desired psychological and physiological states.

The levels of 5-HT in dominant males are very sensitive to the submissive signals offered to them by subordinates. Figure 5.1 illustrates the preceding points through an analysis of interactions between dominant and subordinate males and peripheral 5-HT levels among dominant males.

The vertical axis in figure 5.1 depicts peripheral blood 5-HT levels in a socially dominant male; the horizontal axis measures time. At the top of the figure, the downward-pointing arrows depict both the frequency per unit time of dominance displays by a dominant male directed toward a subordinate male and the frequency of submissive displays by a subordinate male that are directed toward the dominant male. There is a near relationship between display and response. Among vervets, dominant males initiate dominance displays towards subordinate males approximately 30 times per day, although this number will vary for reasons given in the following discussion. In the majority of instances (> 80%), subordinate males respond submissively to dominance displays by lowering their hindquarters, backing off, shifting their weight, angling their heads to the side, and positioning themselves to flee. On occasion, subordinate males threaten back. Dominant males are tolerant of such behavior provided it is infrequent and not intense. However, if subordinate males threaten excessively, dominant males will respond aggressively. Physical contact rarely occurs in these interactions. Rather, they are ritualized and reliant on social signals which serve to confirm and perpetuate hierarchical relationships. However, if a dominant male seriously threatens a subordinate male, then the subordinate avoids the dominant for up to an hour after the encounter.

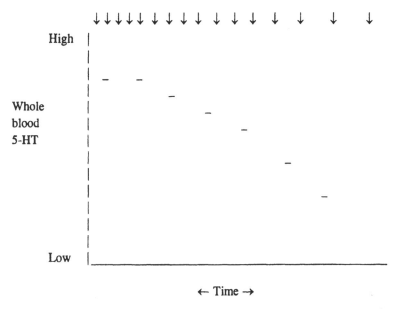

Figure 5.1. The influence of submissive displays by subordinate vervet males on whole blood 5-HT in dominant males. Downward pointing arrows indicate the frequency of submissive displays per unit of time by subordinate males. As the frequency of submissive displays decreases, whole blood 5-HT levels decrease. Conversely, as the frequency of submissive displays increases, whole blood 5-HT levels increase.

If the frequency of submissive displays by subordinate males declines, peripheral 5-HT levels decline among dominant males. This effect is illustrated in the right half of figure 5.1. The effect can be demonstrated experimentally by manipulating the frequency of submissive displays received by dominant males, for example, temporarily separating dominant and subordinate males or placing dominant males behind one-way mirrors where they can observe and threaten subordinate males but where they do not receive submissive displays in return. One-way mirror studies are used to determine if a reduction in dominance displays by dominant males, which occurs when dominant and subordinate males are physically and visually separated yet not when dominant males are behind one-way mirrors, is a factor contributing to the decline in peripheral 5-HT levels. Because one-way mirror studies show the same rate of decline in peripheral 5-HT levels as is seen when dominant animals are socially isolated, the observation of submissive displays by dominant animals appears to be essential for maintaining high peripheral 5-HT levels and elevated CNS 5-HT sensitivity.

In both natural and captive settings, the behavior of high-status males can be characterized in terms of their moving back and forth along the top left half of figure 5.1, where the following behavior-physiological events are postulated to occur: (1) dominant males with high CNS 5-HT sensitivity and high levels of peripheral 5-HT (a regulated state) → (b) increased tolerance toward subordinate males and reduced frequency of dominance displays by dominant males → (c) reduced frequency of submissive displays by subordinate males → (d) decline in CNS 5-HT sensitivity and peripheral 5-HT levels in dominant males (a moderately dysregulated state) → (e) increased frequency of dominance displays by dominant males → (f) increased frequency of submissive displays by subordinate males → (g) increased CNS 5-HT sensitivity and peripheral 5-HT levels among dominant males (a regulated state). In this model, subordinate males are chronically dysregulated, while dominant males move back and forth from regulated to moderately dysregulated states. Should a subordinate male become dominant, or a dominant male become subordinate, their behavior and physiological measures change to those characteristic of their new social status. In the RDT model, physiological and psychological regulation and dysregulation are *not* permanent states but rather contingent states, changing in response to social information type and frequency, of which social behavior, peripheral 5-HT levels, and CNS 5-HT sensitivity can serve as measures.[1]

Changes in 5-HT in subordinates are also powerfully affected by changes in their status. For example, in Raleigh et al.'s (1984) study, removing the dominant male resulted in a significant fall in its 5-HT and a significant rise in blood 5-HT in the subordinate who rose to become the dominant male. Reintroducing the dominant male some weeks later resulted in a reversal of these changes. Interestingly, the return of the old dominant resulted in the blood level of 5-HT in the "new" dominant falling below that of baseline as it became subordinate again. Hence, gaining rank and then losing it seems to produce a major change in blood 5-HT, leaving the subordinate slightly worse off than if no change had occurred.

Studies of Other Species

There is now increasing evidence that subordinates in many species can be subject to high levels of social stress due to the threat from dominants and that such stress affects hormones (Toates, 1995) and 5-HT. McKittrick, Blanchard, Blanchard, McEwen, and Sakai (1995) found that socially stressed subordinate rats had elevated cortisol and reduced 5-HT$_{1A}$ receptor binding in the hippocampus and dentate gyrus. In general, subordinates (compared to dominants) are more restricted in their behavior, more internally vigilant, and more physiologically restricted (lower 5-HT and higher cortisol). Dominants, on the other hand, are more flexible behaviorally, more externally vigilant, and physiologically viable (higher levels of 5-HT, lower cortisol). This may reflect the fact that not only are subordinates fearful of challenging dominants but also dominants are both socially and physiologically buffeted from experiencing serious dysregulation to threats from subordinates.

Human Studies

Social rank dynamics, especially of who can shame or criticize who, remains a powerful variable in human interactions (Gilbert, 1989; Wilkinson, 1996). Positive correlations between social status and peripheral 5-HT levels are known among human males (Madsen, 1985, 1986; Madsen & McGuire, 1984). These and related studies point to at least a four-way relationship between status, personality, genetic information, and 5-HT measures. For example, in male college students, peripheral

5-HT levels and high status correlate positively among socially interactive competitors (sometimes called "Machiavellians"). For more deferent (less socially interactive) high-status individuals (sometimes called "moralists"), the relationship is strongly negative (Madsen, 1986). The ratio of Machiavellians to moralists is 7: 1 among the samples studied thus far (Madsen, personal communication). Studies of personality and personality disorders suggest that different ratios of the neurotransmitters 5-HT, norepinephrine, and dopamine are associated with distinct personality types, and different ratios positively correlate with behavior patterns, such as harm avoidance and sensation seeking (Cloninger, 1986; Cloninger, Svrakic, & Przybeck, 1993). To the degree that personality disorders are genetically influenced, and studies suggest they may be (Guze, Goodwin, & Crane, 1970; Coryell, 1980), different baseline levels of CNS 5-HT sensitivity are likely.

Taken together, the preceding findings suggest that baseline CNS 5-HT availability, sensitivity, and metabolism differ across individuals. Social status, and, more important, the social signals (deference and respect) that go with it, are likely to be important contributing factors that influence CNS 5-HT sensitivity. Further, individuals may be members of several groups and have a different social status in each. How loss of status in one domain is offset by status in another is unknown.

On the Human Nature of Shame

Although making jumps from one species to another is always risky, there is increasing evidence that up-and down-rank social signals are biologically potent in humans (Kemper, 1990; Wilkinson, 1996). Clues to a connection between shame and (perceptions of) social rank and social standing come from recent theory and research. First, shame is nearly always associated with depictions of loss of status, for example, of being devalued, disgraced, demoted, and dishonored. Kaufman (1989) referred to shame as the affect of inferiority, while Scheff (1988) called shame the emotion of deference. Second, using self-report scales, shame-proneness has been found to correlate significantly with inferiority (Cook, 1993, 1996), submissive behavior, and interpersonal constraints to acting assertively (Gilbert, Allan, & Goss, 1996; Keltner & Harker, this volume, chapter 4). Third, studies of nonverbal behavior have found that shame-affect is associated with nonverbal facial displays that are characteristic of submissiveness (e.g., eye gaze avoidance and turning away; Keltner, 1995; Keltner & Harker, this volume, chapter 4). Fourth, many researchers agree that shame motivates desires to escape, conceal, and hide (e.g., H. Lewis, 1986, 1987a,b; M. Lewis, 1992; Tangney & Fischer, 1995). And fifth, shame is associated with a variety of problems related to low self-esteem (Nathanson, 1992; Tangney, Burggraf, & Wagner, 1995).

Attractiveness and Rank

Despite the importance of social rank for both human and nonhuman primates, the last two million years of specifically humanoid evolution has played a large part in human shame. This is because the niche that humans evolved within was of fairly close knit, rather isolated groups (Cosmides & Tooby, 1992; Tooby & Cos-

Table 5.1 Strategies for Gaining and Maintaining Rank and Status

Strategy	Aggression	Attractiveness
Tactics used	Coercive Threatening Authoritarian	Showing talent Showing role competence Affiliative
Outcome desired	To be obeyed To be reckoned with or submitted to	To be valued To be chosen To be freely given to
Purpose of strategy	To inhibit others To stimulate fear	To inspire, attract others To stimulate positive affect

Adapted from Gilbert (1992). Copyright 1992 by Lawrence Erlbaum Associates and The Guilford Press. Reprinted by permission.

mides, 1990). In these social contexts, social acceptance and being liked and included were important social outcomes. Perhaps the greatest social dangers for early humans within a group were probably not so much aggressive fights as being ignored, rejected, or ostracized. In a cooperative environment, one had to impress upon others one's value to them.

One factor that complicates the biological linkage of shame to rank in humans, and thus obscures its evolutionary origins and psychobiological continuities with rank-mediating mechanisms in animals, is that human social rank and status are usually gained and maintained via displays of attractiveness (Gilbert, 1989, 1992, 1997b). The technical term given to this element is *social attention holding power*, or SAHP (Gilbert, 1989, 1997b). Human social status depends greatly on the social signals elicited from others (Barkow, 1989; Kemper, 1990), on our attention eliciting and holding ability. Whether it is being chosen as a lover, friend, or team player; gaining employment; being seen as a valued person; or indeed in most domains of social life, the desire appears to be to elicit and hold other people's attention and interest. We hope that our lover is thinking of us; that we will get invitations to parties; that people are reading our work; that the team selects us; that other people want us around. In this sense, it is others who make judgments of our worth and who allocate, accept, and support (or reject and demean) those roles that we might wish to place ourselves in and to be valued for.

Some people will go to great lengths to be liked and approved of, often inhibiting displays of overt aggression, to maintain SAHP and not to activate conflicts where they might lose it. Strategies of advancing oneself via aggression and use of threats are not redundant but work in different ways from SAHP. In general, aggressive strategies are designed to send signals that stimulate the fear/submit brain areas of conspecifics. Attractiveness strategies are designed to stimulate the reward/approach brain areas of conspecifics. In other words, a person may gain status because others bestow it upon him or her. The person is experienced by others as useful, desirable, and so forth. Table 5.1 lists some of these strategies.

Aggression and attractiveness are dimensions, not mutually exclusive strategies. For example, if one does not obtain the sought-after level of positive attention (approval, recognition, praise, admiration, etc.), then aggression and coerciveness might be used. When charm fails, threats might succeed. Baumeister (1982) has pointed out that the most effective self-presentations show a person to be neither too aggressive, pushy, and self-focused nor too submissive, fearful, or weak-willed. There is likely to be some internal monitoring of the signals of acceptance and attractiveness or desirability being elicited to help balance self-presentation in the way Baumeister notes. Sudden deviations, signals that one is unattractive in some way or has behaved poorly in a role, can trigger affects designed to limit the damage to SAHP.

The importance of the shift to ranking via attractiveness and the need for supportive relationships (Baumeister & Leary, 1995) have very major physiological payoffs. While subordinates of many species are stressed by down-rank harassment, humans need not experience ranked social relationships as stressful, particularly if the higher ranks are supportive of the lower. For example, there is now much evidence that social support carries major physiological benefits (Uchino, Cacioppo, & Kiecolt-Glaser, 1996). Hence, loss of the signals of social support and of being valued by others (as occurs in shame) can be physiologically costly. It is now recognized that stress hormones, neurotransmitters, and immune functions are highly sensitive to social signals and the quality of supportive social environments (Uchino et al, 1996). Given this, then losing support (because of acting shamefully) could be very costly because one loses the ability to elicit social signals (e.g., of support from others) that are physiologically beneficial and regulating.

Hence losses of SAHP signals may be quite dysregulating for humans. Generally, human shame is not focused on a fear of being physically attacked or injured but on having one's SAHP injured. Human shame tends to focus on signals that imply unattractiveness and undesirability. Hence, as argued in chapter 1, shame may be an inner experience of self as an unattractive social agent, under pressure to limit possible damage via escape or appeasement. It does not matter if one is rendered unattractive by one's own or other people's actions; what matters is the sense of personal unattractiveness, of being in the world as an undesired self, a self one does not wish to be. Shame is an involuntary response to an awareness that one's attractiveness is under threat. In such contexts of demotion in the eyes of others, all the inclusive fitness benefits of eliciting support and having high(ish) ranking friends and lovers and access to resources could be damaged too. And although there is no evidence as yet, we suspect that in humans the signal of positive SAHP (being liked and valued) may have 5-HT regulating properties, just as submissive signals affect the 5-HT of dominant animals.

Is a Shame Presentation Attractive?

If a function of shame is to reduce damage to one's social standing, status, and attractiveness in the eyes of self and others, then a key question is, how effective is it? Miller and Tangney (1994) offer some limited evidence that embarrassment might be mildly attractive to others, and certainly more so than an unembarrassed display that could be seen as arrogant. And Keltner and Harker (this volume, chapter 4) note that shame displays can, in some contexts, activate sympathy. However, we have argued that shame is derived from a primitive system of social defense— one that evolved to control aggression. Even though outright physical aggression is not usually the major cause of shame, this social defense is still rooted in primitive involuntary submissive behavioral mechanisms. One of the most primitive and salient defensive signals is eye-gaze avoidance. Confronted on a subway by a large, aggressive-looking man who may have been drinking sitting in an opposite seat, most people would avoid eye gaze. The most common defensive behavior of shame is also eye-gaze avoidance (see Keltner & Harker, this volume, chapter 4). Such automatic defenses (e.g., eye-gaze avoidance) did not originally evolve to cope with losses of attractiveness but with aggression.

In fact, there is now evidence that eye-gaze avoidance is not only related to shame but to personality (e.g., dispositional shyness) and to mental illness. Moreover and crucially, eye-gaze avoidance is seen as a very unattractive trait. Eye-gaze avoiders, especially women, are seen as less trustworthy, less attractive, and even of lower intelligence (Larsen & Shackelford, 1997). Because evolution can only adapt previously evolved systems, we suggest that here is a classic case of a primitive defense system being recruited to solve new problems. The involuntary submissive behavior (anxiety, hiding, and general inhibition) of shame can be highly detrimental to humans who have (recently) evolved to be so dependent on positive social signals. So shame is a two-edged sword. On the one hand, sensitivity to it can help avoid serious breaches in social attractiveness, and mild displays might invoke sympathy or forgiveness; on the other hand, many of the components of shame are unattractive. And if the involuntary submissive system is too sensitive, then even potentially neutral or friendly encounters could lead to overly submissive behavior. Although this may solve problems of aggression or attack, it can lead to rejection by others, because such submissive behavior can be seen as unattractive (Baumeister, 1982). Like depressives, highly shame-prone and inhibited people may not be seen as good bets to make alliances with or as socially rewarding (Argyle, 1991).

Basic Premises

In the preceding discussion, we have tried to contextualize shame within an evolutionary approach by considering how the evolved social strategies utilize social signals (both sent and received) to regulate biological states. This leads to a number of basic premises in regard to human social behavior, social motivations, and shame-proneness.

1. Humans are social animals who are strongly predisposed to live in close proximity to one another (Baumeister & Leary, 1995). Indeed, the evolution of nearly all salient social behaviors (e.g., acquiring mates, forming alliances, and gaining status) took place in the confines of group living. Thus, over the long term, social interactions have shaped the brain and its psychobiological strategic infrastructures.

2. Humans are highly motivated to engage others in specific social roles. These social roles are those which have, over the long term, advanced the fitness of those who carry genes that contribute to such behavior. Hence, social roles focus on specific social domains, for example, caring for offspring, eliciting and seeking care, developing helpful alliances, seeking out and relating to sexual partners, and optimizing status (Buss, 1991; Gilbert, 1989, 1995).

3. Specialized processing systems evolved to facilitate the competent enactment of roles. For example, in caregiving, the capacity for empathy and sympathy may be important. In cooperative relationships, the capabilities for reciprocal altruism and detecting cheats are important, along with covering up one's own cheating and seeking to maximize the benefits and reduce the costs in such relationships (Argyle, 1991; Cosmides & Tooby, 1992). In seeking to optimize status, one needs to ensure that one neither reaches too high and fails (and is heavily "put down" by superiors) nor aims too low and misses opportunities. In humans, status also depends on having socially desired talents or attributes. One may be the greatest Ki-Hi painter in the world, but, if no one else likes or values Ki-Hi painting, this talent is not status-enhancing. (One might, however, gain respect for perseverance).

4. Specialized processing systems are targeted on self-other interactions and coordinate cognition, emotion, and behavior. As noted above, the social signals to which others attend and respond vary according to role. If a person runs away or submits when one is competing with them, this might be experienced as rewarding to the winner; but if someone runs away when one is trying to be caring, this would not be rewarding and might signal a problem with one's caring behavior. If a person wants to be accepted into a group because of talent but others only respond to his or her sexual attractiveness, this could be threatening. These are mismatches and misattunements of roles and goals.[2]

5. Other persons' signals influence receivers' physiological and psychological states. Thus, for example, potent threat signals such as signals of being ignored, rejected, disliked, criticized, excluded, and so forth, will have direct biological effects. Social signals, therefore, cue affective arousal and indicate a need for reparative, defensive, or retaliatory action. Again, however, rank is important. Criticism from a higher rank is likely to have a different biological impact than does criticism from a lower rank.

6. Biological states prime specific roles. The state that pertains when a particular social signal(s) arrives influences cognition, affect, and the responses to the signal. For example, an extroverted man, before becoming depressed, might enjoy going to parties and meeting new people. But when depressed he responds to a social invitation with dread, anxiety, and avoidance. Hence, because of their (pre-)existing states (e.g., low 5-HT), some people may be far more prone to serious dysregulations of shame.

7. Socialization shapes the specific expressions of social roles that relate, for example, to sexual attractiveness, enhanced status, or caring behavior. People learn what is attractive about themselves and what is not, what is acceptable to display and demonstrate and what is not, and what can be shared about the self and what should be hidden. They learn these things through experiences of praise and punishment and through observations of others. Most of the time, our primary concern is to both enhance and avoid damage to our social presentations (Leary & Kowalski, 1990; Leary, 1996).

Rank in Social Roles

In humans, concern with status can be domain specific. For example, authors of chapters in this book might not compete for status as football players, but we might compete in trying to secure research monies. As noted earlier, humans and animals function in specific domains and core social roles. The tasks of life are complex: obtaining status and control over material resources, securing a position within a group supported by allies, securing sexual partners, investing in offspring, and so forth. Each role operates via different rules and signals. The way persons evaluate their sexual attractiveness might be through the (admiring) signals from potential mates. The way persons evaluate their alliance-gaining ability is often by signals of help, support, and liking from conspecifics and/or the degree to which they are chosen to be on a team or members of a group. The way persons evaluate their status within a group is often measured by their success in overcoming other challengers and the deference and respect shown by others. And the way persons evaluate their caregiving abilities is often through signals of gratitude or seeing others prosper and grow. Thus, status and attractiveness to others can arise from various domains. Placed in this context, shame can relate to signals of unattractiveness or ineffectiveness in a role (Greenwald & Harder, this volume, chapter 12). For example:

Sexual and mate value   One might gain status by being seen as desirable and physically attractive, and/or as having access to useful resources such as wealth (Buss, 1989). There is now much data on the nature of physical attractiveness and sexual selection, including posture, hip-to-waist ratio, youthful looks, healthiness, and hardiness (Barber, 1995). In this domain, shame can be related to signals of physical unattractiveness (e.g., being told one is ugly, or not conforming to sexually attractive stereotypes—being too fat or thin, or suffering from acne, or even being poor). Related to this are a variety of physical and psychological foci of the body having to do with disease and disfigurations that are associated with shame (Lazare, 1987) as well as illnesses that connote disreputable behavior (e.g., venereal disease).

Value as a close personal ally   A combination of talents and abilities might increase attractiveness here. Being seen as reliable, caring, empathic, and helpful but also talented and able can increases one's attractiveness. However, a person who is seen as vastly superior might also be seen as likely to defect. Choosing and being attracted to long-term partners, both for sex and child rearing, may be highly influenced by signals of altruism (Jensen-Campbell, Graziano, & West, 1995). Close personal friendships probably also depend on altruism (Argyle, 1991). Shame can result if people receive signals that they are not desirable as close allies or have done something that makes them unattractive in this role, for example, by acting exploitatively or nonaltruistically or being untrustworthy. Efforts to induce guilt and shame are typical ways that partners or friends try to ensure that the other does give enough (e.g., Baumeister, Stillwell, & Heatherton, 1994).

Value as a carer   Selfishness, being seen as hard and uncaring and lacking empathy, can be shaming. The British press saw this as one reason for the defeat of

Margaret Thatcher and subsequently the defeat of the conservative party in 1997. Being placed in the role of carer and being seen to do this well may increase our attractiveness (e.g., being known as a good parent, charity worker, caring nurse or doctor, etc.). We can gain (and lose) much prestige from displays of how caring and altruistic we are (or aren't; Hill, 1984; Greenwald & Harder, chapter 12). Shame may come from signals that suggest we are seen as uncaring, neglectful, too self-focused, and selfish. On the other hand, to be seen as too caring may conflict with gender image (Tice and Baumeister, 1985).

Value as a group or team member   Here status and acceptance depends on being seen to work for the team's good—being reliable or a good conforming party member. Most teams will select from the talented rather than the untalented. If the team prospers, all prosper. Shame may arise from letting the team down, not giving one's best, or being a "free rider." Although demands for conformity vary between groups (Bond & Smith, 1996), shame, disgrace, and rejection (and fear of them) are probably central interpersonal factors that enforce conformity to team values and efforts.

Value as a status seeker   This relates to our efforts to rise in (or hold onto) rank, to increase general status via promotion or gaining prestige. Here attractiveness may depend on displays of confidence, ability, and knowledge, on charisma, and so forth. Again, shame may arise when one is seen to perform badly in a role or to be using one's position for exploitative self-interest. Shame in more mundane status-seeking roles comes from signals that one is seen as not being worthy of the rank sought or held, not being good enough in some way; as making mistakes and being flawed. When we consider competing for high rank, we speak of leadership. In leadership battles in democracies, it is not uncommon for a badly beaten contestant to be seen as suffering a "humiliating defeat." Generally, though, shame in leadership roles is similar to other typical domains of human shame; that is, it arises from sexual (mis)behavior, cheating and exploitation, defecting from in-group values, showing cowardice, or feigning abilities.

Value as a care seeker   Expressing signals of distress (care-eliciting signals) can be shaming, especially for males, who are taught that "big boys don't cry." Groups and individuals constantly evaluate who is worthy of help and who is not. To seek help when one is seen as unworthy of help invites shame (e.g., begging). And there are many shame terms for help seekers who others believe could do more for themselves—scroungers, loafers, dependent, and so forth. Also the act of seeking help in itself can be seen as shameful by those who are in need. For this reason, some people refrain from asking for help, even when it is easily available and could be highly beneficial (Fisher, Nadler, & Whitcher-Alagna, 1982). To be proudly self-sufficient or never show distress can be a key concern (Gilbert, 1995).

To be shamed is to risk demotion in one or more social roles, to become seen as an undesired self (Gilbert, this volume, chapter 1). And shame seems to carry serious implications for the future, unlike, say, momentary embarrassment (Miller & Tangney, 1994). The common contexts of shame are related to evolutionarily meaningful events and include such behaviors as failing to conform to stereotypes, not being able to fulfill expected roles, being exploitative, cheating, defecting, and so forth. Whether it be sexual misbehavior or swindling the company of funds, to be caught pursuing one's own self-interest at the expense of others can be experienced as shaming, as can various forms of failure.

However, importantly, it is not always the case that traits and behaviors that are stigmatized by one group will result in shame (Crocker & Major, 1989; Gilbert, 1997b). And there may be individual differences in the degree to which people can tolerate negative social signals from others. Tolerance might relate to group identification—the judgments of others with whom we are, or desire to be, in close contact may be more powerful than those of people with whom we are not in contact or with whom we do not wish to be associated. Thus, to be shamed by a "distant" group may have much less impact than being shamed in our core social group. The role for which one is seeking status is also important; for example, being seen as fat and unattractive may worry a powerful businessman less than it might a young person seeking his or her first sexual contact. Being seen as a cheat may worry (shame) a con man less than it would persons who pride themselves on their integrity. As noted elsewhere (Gilbert, 1997b), for internalized shame to occur the person has to accept the negative judgments of others as both true in some measure and undesired. And the role or domain related to negative judgments has to be seen as important to that individual.

To summarize, evolution has shaped our desires and typical social forms of relating. It has led to various biosocial goals and strategies (e.g., to find mates, care for offspring, form helpful alliances, etc.). Social signals are the most important sources of information, indicating whether we are successfully pursuing these evolutionarily meaningful goals. Social signals are central to individuals in maintaining states of internal regulation and indicating how attuned each person is in his or her social roles. Shame is a signal that one is misattuned. Such misattunement usually produces some physiological dysregulation and alerts actors to the need for some defensive, reparative, or retaliatory actions. Shame motivates hiding and concealment of that which is believed to be undesirable and unattractive. Once shame has occurred, the affects may be depressive or anxious due to a perception of some diminishment or demotion in social status, respect, and relative attractiveness.

Self-Cognitions and Self-Consciousness

The evolution of self-consciousness offered many advantages in social manipulation and cooperation (Whiten, 1991). However, self-consciousness did not create new motivational systems or biosocial goals—except perhaps the wish to escape death because we became aware of it. The urges to care for one's own offspring, to mate, to have friends, and to be valued by others were as powerful as ever. Self-consciousness, however, has allowed us to know ourselves as if we were relating to another. So, for example, we can be caring of the self, recognizing a need to look after ourselves; we can be aggressive toward the self, which in Freudian terms means having a punitive superego; we can attempt to exclude or reject parts of the self via denial; and we can even have sexual desires and enjoyment of self, as in masturbation. And, of course, we can be ashamed of ourselves. There are then a variety of possible internal relationships that have self-directed voices (Gilbert, 1989; Hermans, 1996).

If the archetypal psychobiology of shame is located in prehuman social defensive behaviors such as submissiveness and appeasement, then what does this say about the role of self-consciousness in shame? The complex, self-conscious experiences of shame are likely to be elaborations of phylogenetically old mechanisms which evolved for the coordination of social behavior. From an evolutionary point of view, behavior—not cognition—is the primary medium for selection. Cognitions (and self-aware cognitions) serve the function of coordinating social behavior, and it is only through their effects on behavior that they can influence fitness. Self-awareness may have evolved because it increased fitness by exerting effects over social behavior (Whiten, 1991).

The evolved function of self-consciousness is presumably to allow a better monitoring of social displays and control over social displays. The capacity for awareness of one's own and others' mental states has become a fundamental part of human cognition, known as "theories of mind" (Baron-Cohen, 1997; Whiten, 1991). To the best of our knowledge, shame has not been explored in relation to the "theory of mind" approach, although shame, with its focus on metacognitions of what others might think about the self, seems well suited for such an approach. Nonetheless, self-awareness may be particularly useful for deception and concealment, although it is not without its problems. Chimpanzees, for example, have a degree of self-awareness and are also able to conceal the display of their social signals. Consider the following from Cheney, Seyfarth, & Smuts:

> In a captive group of chimpanzees two adult males Nicki and Luit were engaged in a prolonged struggle for dominance. During one fight Nicki was driven into a tree. As Luit sat at the bottom of the tree, he nervously "fear grinned". He then turned away from Nicki, put a hand over his mouth and pressed his lips together to hide a sign of submission. Only after the third attempt when Luit succeeded in wiping the grin from his face did he once again turn to face Nicki. (1986, pp. 1364)

Luit seems to have some kind of awareness that he should conceal certain kinds of social signal that he is involuntarily emitting in order to advance his dominance chances. In humans too, controlling one's display of social signals is often paramount. Such behavior is noted in our efforts to inhibit the revelation of negative information about the self, to conceal signals or behaviors that might elicit negative responses from others (Ekman, 1991). Self-consciousness does not create shame de novo. Rather, shame is a complex experience reliant on both old and new brain mechanisms.

Regulation-dysregulation theory suggests that the more dysregulated a person becomes, the more sensitive and responsive they are to negative social signals, and the more difficult it is for them to competently control emitted social signals. This may be because of strong competing affects and behaviors (e.g., fear-retreat vs. angry-attack). Luit, for example, could not inhibit his fear grin but had to hide it. Thus, self-conscious shame can be a postevent response, arising after we blush or after we see the look of disdain in the eyes of others (Frijda, 1993). To put this another way, self-consciousness has to "manage" social presentations in contexts where more primitive visceral responses have been or are likely to be triggered. Thus, highly dysregulated persons might find themselves having to cope with biologically powerful affects (rage and anxiety) that they consciously would prefer not to have to manage.

Self-consciousness may also allow for the ability to imagine how we will look to others in the future (Gilbert, 1989). Anticipation of being seen as flawed and inadequate offers the opportunity to manage our self-presentations to minimize the risk (Leary & Kowalski, 1990). Imagination also allows us to internalize signals. Just as we can be sexually aroused by internally generated fantasies or become anxious by thoughts and images of harm, so (presumably) shame can be aroused by internally generated images, memories, and fantasies.

Conclusions

This chapter has drawn attention to the role of evolved mental mechanisms that serve the function of navigating animals and humans to fitness-enhancing biosocial goals. In this context, social signals are the primary vehicles for directing animals and humans to their goals. Against this background we have argued that shame plays a central role in human psychology because it is linked to status, social standing, and social success; shame is one of the experiences that can be triggered by signals of rejection and social demotion, its function being damage limitation. The experience of shame suggests the triggering of an involuntary submissive response in the context of an actual or potential social threat. We focused on status and rank because a loss of status goes with the loss of other potentially fitness-enhancing opportunities, but also noted loss of status in roles.

We have argued that shame is not purely a self-consciousness emotion, although self-consciousness and "theory of mind" psychology may be central to our human experience of it. Shame, we suggested, also rests upon more primitive psychobiological mechanisms that evolved to enable animals to be sensitive to social threats and to take defensive actions. Self-consciousness, the ability to construct internal models of the self that are open to inspection, evaluation, prediction, and rumination, has undoubtedly complicated the mechanisms by which shame plays a major role in serious psychopathologies; but it is the primitive psychobiological mechanisms that fuel the pain of shame. Shame is an evolved elaboration of defensive behavior in the service of interpersonal interactions.

Notes

1. The 5-HT system is, of course, far more complex than the preceding discussion suggests. For example, there are over a dozen and perhaps as many as two dozen subtypes of 5-HT receptors, many of which have separate functions. And, contrary to the generally held views that 5-HT is primarily a modulator of the actions of other neurotransmitters and that the 5-HT system has diffuse and largely nonspecific projections throughout functionally diverse regions of the forebrain, recent studies show region-specific patterns of 5-HT forebrain axon termination, differential distribution of 5-HT receptor subtypes in forebrain termination fields, and region-specific release of 5-HT in response to specific environmental stressors (Frazer, Kosofsky, & Lucki, 1996).

2. Psychotherapy is replete with these problems. For example, patients attend ther-

apy for help, but for reasons to do with therapist and/or patient styles, their interactions get locked into competitive and conflictual relationships. The therapist feels that his or her caring is rejected and (maybe) inadequate (shame). Patients can feel overpowered or shamed by the therapist; they may think there must be something wrong with them if they do not improve with the therapist's attentions. If they do not improve, they will be rejected. As an example of a different type of misattunement, as noted in the text, a therapist or patient may try to turn this "caring" relationship into a sexual one against the other's wishes, thus producing a role mismatch.

References

Argyle, M. (1991). *Cooperation: The basis of sociability*. London: Routledge.

Barber, N. (1995). The evolutionary psychology of physical attractiveness: Sexual selection and human morphology. *Ethology and Sociobiology, 16*, 395–424.

Barkow, J. H. (1989). *Darwin, sex and status: Biological approaches to mind and culture*. Toronto: University of Toronto Press.

Baron-Cohen, S. (1997) How to build a baby that can read minds: Cognitive mechanisms in mind reading. In S. Baron-Cohen (Ed.), *The maladapted mind: Classic readings in evolutionary psychopathology (pp. 207–239)*. Hove, UK: Psychology Press.

Baumeister, R. F. (1982). A self-presentational view of social phenomena. *Psychological Bulletin, 91*, 3–26.

Baumeister, R. F., & Leary, M. R. (1995). The need to belong: Desire for interpersonal attachments as a fundamental human motivation. *Psychological Bulletin, 117*, 497–529.

Baumeister, R. F., Stillwell, A. M., & Heatherton, T. F. (1994). Guilt: An interpersonal approach. *Psychological Bulletin, 115*, 243–267.

Belsky, J. (1993). Etiology of child maltreatment: A developmental analysis. *Psychological Bulletin, 114*, 414–434.

Belsky, J., Steinberg, L., & Draper, P. (1990). Childhood experiences, interpersonal development, and reproductive strategy: An evolutionary theory of socialization. *Child Development, 62*, 647–670.

Bernstein, I. S. (1980). Dominance: A theoretical perspective for ethologists. In D. R. Omark, F. F. Strayer, & D. G. Freedman (Eds.), *Dominance relations: An ethological view of conflict and social interaction* (pp. 71–84). New York: Garland Press.

Bond, R., & Smith, P. B. (1996). Culture and conformity: A meta-analysis of studies using Asch's (1952b, 1956) line judgement task. *Psychological Bulletin, 119*, 111–137.

Bowlby, J. (1973). *Attachment and Loss*. Vol. 2. *Separation, anxiety and anger*. London: Hogarth Press.

Burnstein, E., Crandall, C., & Kitayama, S. (1994). Some neo-Darwinian rules for altruism: Weighing cues for inclusive fitness as a function of biological importance of the decision. *Journal of Personality and Social Psychology, 67*, 773–807.

Buss, D. M. (1989). Sex differences in human mate preference: Evolutionary hypotheses tested in 37 cultures. *Brain and Behavioral Sciences, 12*, 1–49.

Buss, D. M. (1991). Evolutionary personality psychology. *Annual Review of Psychology*, 459–491.

Buss, D. M. (1995). Evolutionary psychology: A new paradigm for psychological science. *Psychological Inquiry, 6*, 1–87.

Caryl, P. G. (1988). Escalated fighting and the war of nerves: Games theory and animal combat. In P. H. Bateson & P. H. Klopfer (Eds.), *Perspectives in ethology: Vol. 4. Advantages of diversity* (pp. 199–224). New York: Plenum.

Cheney, D., Seyfarth, R., & Smuts, B. (1986). Social relationships and social cognition in nonhuman primates. *Science, 234*, 1361–1365.

Cloninger, C. R. (1986). A unified biosocial theory of personality and its role in the development of anxiety states. *Psychiatric Developments, 3,* 167–226.

Cloninger, C. R., Svrakic, D. M., & Przybeck, T. R. (1993). A psychobiological model of temperament and character. *Archives General Psychiatry, 50,* 975–990.

Cook, D. R. (1993). *The Internalized Shame Scale manual.* Menomonie, WI: Channel Press. (Available from the author, Rt. 7, Box 270A, Menomonie, WI 54751)

Cook, D. R. (1996). Empirical studies of shame and guilt: The Internalized Shame Scale. In D. L. Nathanson (Ed.), *Knowing feeling: Affect, script and psychotherapy* (pp. 132–165). New York: Norton.

Coryell, W. A. (1980). A blind family history study of Briquet's syndrome. Further validation of the diagnosis. *Archives General Psychiatry, 37,* 1266–1269.

Cosmides, L., & Tooby, J. (1992). Cognitive adaptations for social exchange. In J. H. Barkow, L. Cosmides, & J. Tooby (Eds.), *The adapted mind: Evolutionary psychology and the generation of culture* (pp. 163–228). New York: Oxford University Press.

Crocker, J., & Major, B. (1989). Social stigma and self-esteem: The self-protective qualities of stigma. *Psychological Review, 96,* 608–630.

Dixon, A. K., Gilbert, P., Huber, C., Gilbert, J., & Van der Hoek, G. (1996). Changes in nonverbal behavior in a neutral and "shame" interview. Unpublished manuscript, University of Derby, UK.

Ekman, P. (1991). *Telling lies: Clues to deceit in the marketplace, politics and marriage.* New York: Norton.

Fisher, J. D., Nadler, A., & Whitcher-Alagna, S. (1982). Recipient reactions to aid. *Psychological Bulletin, 91,* 27–54.

Fiske, A. P. (1992). The four elementary forms of sociality: Framework for a unified theory of social relations. *Psychological Review, 99,* 689–723.

Frazer, A., Kosofsky, B., & Lucki, I. (1996, January–February). Neurobiology of the dorsal raphe nucleus: New evidence for functional specificity within a broadly projecting brainstem monoaminergic pathway. Paper presented at the Winter Conference on Brain Research, Snowmass Village, CO.

Frijda, N. H. (1993). The place of appraisal in emotion. [Special issue: Appraisal and Beyond: The Issue of Cognitive Determinants of Emotion] *Cognition and Emotion, 3/4,* 357–387.

Gilbert, P. (1989). *Human nature and suffering.* Hove, UK: Lawrence Erlbaum Associates.

Gilbert, P. (1992). *Depression: The evolution of powerlessness.* New York: Guilford Press.

Gilbert, P. (1993). Defense and safety: Their function in social behaviour and psychopathology. *British Journal of Clinical Psychology, 32,* 131–154.

Gilbert, P. (1995). Biopsychosocial approaches and evolutionary theory as aids to integration in clinical psychology and psychotherapy. *Clinical Psychology and Psychotherapy, 2,* 135–156.

Gilbert, P. (1997a). The biopsychosociology of meaning. In M. Power & C. R. Brewin (Eds.), *The transformation of meaning in psychological therapies: Integrating theory and practice* (pp. 33–56.). Chichester, UK: Wiley.

Gilbert, P. (1997b). The evolution of social attractiveness and its role in shame, humiliation, guilt and therapy. *British Journal of Medical Psychology, 70,* 113–147.

Gilbert, P., Allan, S., & Goss, K. (1996). Parental representations, shame, interpersonal problems and vulnerability to psychopathology. *Clinical Psychology and Psychotherapy, 3,* 23–34.

Gilbert, P., Pehl, J., & Allan, S. (1994). The phenomenology of shame and guilt: An empirical investigation. *British Journal of Medical Psychology, 67,* 23–36.

Gilbert, P., Price, J. S., & Allan, S. (1995). Social comparison, social attractiveness and evolution: How might they be related? *New Ideas in Psychology, 13,* 149–165.

Goss, K., Gilbert, P., & Allan, S. (1994). An exploration of shame measures: 1. The "Other as Shamer Scale." *Personality and Individual Differences, 17,* 713–717.

Greenberg, L. S., & Safran, J. D. (1987). *Emotion in psychotherapy*. New York: Guilford Press.

Guze, S. B., Goodwin, D. W., & Crane, J. B. (1970). A psychiatric study of the wives of convicted felons: An example of assortative mating. *American Journal of Psychiatry, 126*, 1773–1776.

Harlow, H. F., & Harlow, M. K. (1962). Social deprivation in monkeys. *Scientific American, 207*, 136–146.

Harlow, H. F., & Mears, C. (1979). *The human model: Primate perspectives*. New York: Winston.

Hart, J., Gunnar, M., & Cicchetti, D. (1996). Altered neuroendocrine activity in maltreated children related to symptoms of depression. *Development and Psychopathology, 8*, 201–214.

Hermans, H. J. M. (1996). Voicing the self: From information processing to Dialogical interchange. *Psychological Bulletin, 119*, 31–50.

Hill, J. (1984). Human altruism and sociocultural fitness. *Journal of Social and Biological Structures, 7*, 17–35.

Hofer, M. A. (1984). Relationships as regulators: A psychobiologic perspective on bereavement. *Psychosomatic Medicine, 46*, 183–197.

Jensen-Campbell, L. A., Graziano, W. G., & West, S. G. (1995). Dominance, prosocial orientation and female preference: Do nice guys really finish last? *Journal of Personality and Social Psychology, 68*, 427–440.

Kaufman, G. (1989). *The psychology of shame*: Theory and treatment of shame-based syndromes. New York: Springer.

Keltner, D. (1995). Signs of appeasement: Evidence for the distinct displays of embarrassment, amusement and shame. *Journal of Personality and Social Psychology, 68*, 441–454.

Kemper, T. D. (1990). *Social structure and testosterone: Explorations of the socio-biosocial chain*. New Brunswick, NJ: Rutgers University Press.

Kohut, H. (1977). *The restoration of the self*. New York: International Universities Press.

Kramer, G. W, & Clarke, S. (1991). The behavioral neurobiology of self-injurious behavior in rhesus monkeys. *Progress Neuropharmacology Biology Psychiatry, 14*, S141–S168.

Kravitz, E. A. (1988). Hormonal control of behavior: Amines and the biasing of behavioral output in lobsters. *Science, 241*, 1775–1781.

Larsen, R. J., & Shakelford, T. K. (1997). Gaze avoidance: Personality and social judgements of people who avoid direct face-to-face contact. *Personality and Individual Differences, 21*, 907–917.

Lazare, A. (1987). Shame and humiliation in the medical encounter. *Archives of International Medicine, 147*, 1653–1658.

Leary, M. R. (1995). *Self-Presentation: Impression management and interpersonal behavior*. Madison, WI: Brown & Benchmark.

Leary, M. R., & Kowalski, R. M. (1990). Impression management: A literature review and two-component model. *Psychological Bulletin, 107*, 34–47.

Lewis, H. B. (1986). The role of shame in depression. In M. Rutter, C. E. Izard, & P. B. Read (Eds.), *Depression in young people: Development and clinical perspectives* (pp. 325–339). New York: Guilford Press.

Lewis, H. B. (1987a). Shame and the narcissistic personality. In D. L. Nathanson (Ed.), *The many faces of shame* (pp. 93–132). New York: Guilford Press.

Lewis, H. B. (1987b). Shame—the "sleeper" in psychopathology. In H. B. Lewis (Ed.), *The role of shame in symptom formation* (pp 1–28). Hillsdale, NJ: Erlbaum.

Lewis, M. (1992). *Shame: The exposed self*. New York: The Free Press.

Linehan, M. M. (1993). *Cognitive-behavioral therapy treatment of borderline personality disorder*. New York: Guilford Press.

MacLean, P. D. (1990). *The triune brian in evolution*. New York: Plenum.

Madsen, D. (1985). A biochemical property relating to power seeking in humans. *American Political Science Review, 79,* 448–457.

Madsen, D. (1986). Power seekers are biochemically different: Further biochemical evidence. *American Political Science Review, 80* 261–269.

Madsen, D., & McGuire, M. T. (1984). Whole blood 5-HT and the Type A behavior pattern. *Psychosomatic Medicine, 46,* 546–548.

McGuire, M. T. (1988). On the possibility of ethological explanations of psychiatric disorders. *Acta Psychiatrica Scandinavica, 77* (Suppl.), 7–22.

McGuire, M. T., Fawzy, F. I., Spar, J. E., Weigel, R. W., & Troisi, A. (1994). Altruism and mental disorders. *Ethology and Sociobiology, 15,* 299–321.

McGuire, M. T., Marks, I., & Troisi, A. (1997). Evolutionary biology: A basic science for psychiatry. In S. Baron-Cohen (Ed.), *The maladapted mind: Classic readings in evolutionary psychopathology* (pp. 23–37). Hove, UK: Psychology Press.

McGuire, M. T., Raleigh, M. J., & Johnson, C. (1983). Social dominance in adult male vervet monkeys: General considerations. *Social Science Information, 22,* 311–328.

McGuire, M. T., & Troisi, A. (1987a). Physiological regulation-disregulation and psychiatric disorders. *Ethology and Sociobiology, 8,* 9S–12S.

McGuire, M. T., & Troisi, A. (1987b). Unrealistic wishes and physiological change. *Psychotherapy Psychosomatics, 47,* 82–94.

McKittrick, C. R., Blanchard, D. C., Blanchard, R. J., McEwen, B. S., & Sakai, R. P. (1995). Serotonin receptor binding in a colony model of chronic stress social stress. *Biological Psychiatry, 37,* 383–397.

Miller, R. S., & Tangney, J. P. (1994). Differentiating embarrassment and shame. *Journal of Social and Clinical Psychology, 13* (3), 273–287.

Miller, W. I. (1993). *Humiliation.* New York: Cornell University Press.

Mineka, S., & Suomi, S. J. (1978). Social separation in monkeys. *Psychological Bulletin, 85,* 1376–1400.

Montagu, A. (1986). *Touching: The human significance of the Skin.* (3rd ed.). New York: Harper & Row.

Nathanson, D. L. (1992). *Shame and pride: Affect, sex and the birth of the self.* New York: Norton.

Nesse, R. M. (1990). Evolutionary explanations of emotions. *Human Nature, 1,* 261–289.

Ohman, A. (1986). Face the beast and fear the face: Animal and social fears as prototypes for evolutionary analyses of emotion. *Psychophysiology, 23,* 123–145.

Parker, G. (1979). Parental characteristics in relation to depressive disorders. *British Journal of Psychiatry, 134,* 138–147.

Raleigh, M. J., Brammer, G. L., McGuire, M. T., & Yuwiler, A. (1985). Dominant social status facilitates the behavioral effects of serotonergic agonists. *Brain Research, 348,* 274–282.

Raleigh, M. J., & McGuire, M. T. (1993). Environmental constraints, serotonin, aggression, and violence in vervet monkeys. In R. Masters & M. McGuire (Eds.), *The neurotransmitter revolution* (pp. 129–145). Carbondale, IL: Southern Illinois University Press.

Raleigh, M. J., McGuire, M. T., Brammer, G. L., Oikkacjm, D. B., & Yuwiler, A. (1991). Serotonergic mechanisms promote dominance acquisition in adult male vervet monkeys. *Brain Research, 559,* 181–190.

Raleigh, M. J., McGuire, M. T., Brammer, G. L., & Yuwiler, A. (1984). Social and environmental influences on blood 5-HT concentrations in monkeys. *Archives of General Psychiatry, 41,* 405–410.

Reite, M., Short, R., Seiler, C., & Pauley, J. D. (1981). Attachment, loss, and depression. *Journal Child Psychology and Psychiatry, 22,* 221–227.

Retzinger, S. (1991). *Violent emotions: Shame and rage in marital quarrels.* Newbury Park, CA: Sage.

Rohner, R. P. (1986). *The warmth dimension: Foundations of parental acceptance-rejection theory.* Beverly Hills, CA: Sage.

Rosenblum, L. A., Coplan, J. D., Friedman, S., Bassoff, T., Gorman, J. M., & Andrews, M. W. (1994). Adverse early experiences affect noradrenergic and serotonergic functioning in adult primates. *Biological Psychiatry, 35,* 221–227.

Sapolsky, R. M. (1989). Hypercortisolism among socially subordinate wild baboons originates at the CNS level. *Archives General Psychiatry, 46,* 1047–1051.

Sapolsky, R. M. (1990). Adrenocortical function, social rank, and personality among wild baboons. *Biological Psychiatry, 28,* 862–878.

Scheff, T. J. (1988). Shame and conformity: The deference-emotion system. *American Review of Sociology, 53,* 395–406.

Schore, A. N. (1994). *Affect regulation and the origin of the self: The neurobiology of emotional development.* Hillsdale, NJ: Erlbaum.

Spitz, R. (1945). *The Psychoanalytic Study of the Child: Vol. 1. Hospitalism.* New York: International Universities Press.

Steadman's Medical Dictionary (25th ed.) (1990). Baltimore, MD: Williams & Wilkins.

Tangney, J. P., Burggraf, S. A., & Wagner, P. E. (1995). Shame-proneness, guilt-proneness, and psychological symptoms. In J. P. Tangney & K. W. Fischer (Eds.), *Self-Conscious emotions: The psychology of shame, guilt, embarrassment and pride* (pp. 343–367). New York: Guilford Press.

Tangney, J. P., & Fischer, K. W. (Eds.). (1995). *Self-Conscious emotions: The psychology of shame, guilt, embarrassment and pride.* New York: Guilford Press.

Tice, D. M., & Baumeister, R. F. (1985). Masculinity inhibits helping in emergencies: Personality does predict the bystander effect. *Journal of Personality and Social Psychology, 49,* 420–428.

Toates, F. (1995). *Stress: Conceptual and biological aspects.* Chichester, UK: Wiley.

Tooby, J., & Cosmides, L. (1990). The past explains the present: Emotional adaptations and the structure of ancestral environments. *Ethology and Sociobiology, 11,* 375–424.

Tronick, E. Z. (1989). Emotions and emotional communication in infants. *American Psychologist, 44,* 112–119.

Tronick, E. Z., & Cohn, J. F. (1989). Infant-mother face-to-face interaction: Age and gender differences in coordination and the occurrence of miscoordination. *Child Development, 60,* 85–92.

Uchino, B. N., Cacioppo, J. T., & Kiecolt-Glaser, J. K. (1996). The relationship between social support and physiological processes: A review with emphasis on underlying mechanisms and implications for health. *Psychological Bulletin, 119,* 488–531.

Whiten, A. (1991). *Natural theories of mind.* London: Basil Blackwell.

Wilkinson, R. G. (1996). *Unhealthy societies: The afflictions of inequality.* London: Routledge.

6

Shame and Stigma

Michael Lewis

In this chapter, I should like first to focus on the general problem of shame and stigma. Before doing this, I need to define both *shame* and *stigma*. In the second half of the chapter, I will apply my theory to work with children known to have been sexually or physically abused. Studying children soon after a known abuse allows us to see developmentally the effect of the abuse better than does studying adults who are recalling their earlier abuse.

Stigma, Attribution, and Shame

Shame is best understood as an intense negative emotion having to do with the self in relation to standards, responsibility, and such attributions as global self-failure (Lewis, 1992). Shame is elicited when one experiences failure relative to a standard (one's own or other people's), feels responsible for the failure, and believes that the failure reflects a damaged self (Lewis, 1995a, b; Tangney, 1990; Weiner, 1993). Stigma, as we shall see, also makes reference to a damaged self (Goffman, 1963). The association between shame and stigma thus appears obvious. Lewis (1992, 1995a), as well as others, has shown how shame, a much misunderstood emotion, affects human life (Borkowski, Weyhing, & Turner, 1986; H. B. Lewis, 1971; Tomkins, 1963). The relation of stigma to shame has been noticed by others, yet the analysis of stigma, at least from Goffman (1963) on, has been plagued by the problem of what stigma might be. Clearly, from Goffman's point of view, it is a public mark, something which can be noticed by others and which involves a "spoiled identity."[1] It has been noticed by social psychologists that the issue of stigma has to be related to social values and social good (Jones et al., 1984). These conflicting ideas about stigma are readily satisfied by our analysis of the attributions related to the self-conscious emotions and, in particular, to those of shame (see Lewis, 1992). Perhaps the single biggest discrepancy between the theory of shame which I have proposed and stigma is related to the issue of public versus private acts. While the issue of public failure is relevant to the emotion of embarrassment, it is not relevant to the emotions of shame, guilt, or even pride. For these self-conscious emotions to occur, one can act either in public or in private (Lewis, 1995b, c). Shame can take place privately as long as the attributions that give rise to it occur. Stigma, for the most part, constitutes a public violation or action. For a person to fear stigma from such a violation, it must be transparent, such as in physical appearance or action. As Goffman points out:

> The immediate presence of normals is likely to reinforce this split between self-demands and self, but, in fact, self-hate and self-degradation only *can occur when he and a mirror are present*. The awareness of inferiority is what the stigmatized person is unable to keep out of consciousness, the formulation of some chronic feeling of the worst sort of insecurity, the anxiety of being shamed. (Goffman, 1963, p. 7; [italics added].

The literature on stigma and its relation with shame supports the idea of stigma as a cause of shame (Borkowski et al., 1986; Cook, 1983; Gibbons, 1985; Turner, 1994; Turner, Dofny, & Dutka, 1994; Wehmeyer, 1994). To begin with, standards, rules, and goals are necessary and need to be incorporated in individuals' cognitive capacities for them to judge whether or not their behavior meets or does not meet these standards. From the point of view of standards, it is quite clear that the stigma that an individual possesses represents a deviation from the accepted standards of the society; this deviation may be in appearance, in behavior, or in conduct. Nonetheless, the person is stigmatized by possessing characteristics which do not match the standard. It is, of course, well recognized that these standards may change with time and with culture, but such standards exist, and individuals whose appearance and behavior deviate from them can be said to suffer from a stigma.

The second critical feature in the elicitation of shame, as well as the other self-conscious emotions, is the issue of responsibility or self-blame. Here, again, stigma and shame analyses lead to the same conclusion: The degree to which stigmatized persons can blame themselves or are blamed by others for their condition reflects their degree of shame. The idea of responsibility and perceived responsibility is central to stigma and shame. Weiner (1993) recently has discussed this topic of perceived responsibility. For example, overweight people are perceived as responsible for their condition, because they have control over their eating and, therefore, being overweight is a stigma. Weiner describes a study in which he examined the relationship between the stigma, perceived responsibility, and emotions. Adults rated the following ten stigmata on personal responsibility: AIDS, Alzheimer's disease, blindness, cancer, drug addiction, heart disease, obesity, paraplegia, child abuse, and Vietnam War syndrome. Adults also were asked to rate their reactions of anger or sympathy to each condition. The results reveal that six of the stigmata, Alzheimer's disease, blindness, cancer, heart disease, paraplegia, and Vietnam War syndrome, were rated low on perceived personal responsibility, whereas AIDS, abusing children, having a drug addiction, and being obese were rated high on personal responsibility. Conditions where people were not held responsible elicited pity, but not anger. Therefore, responsibility and self-blame or the blame of others toward the self are very much related. Thus, social rules involve not only standards and rules but also societal beliefs about controllability. Responsibility can change as a function of new knowledge and information or a change in social values. When illness was regarded as a form of punishment imposed for wrong-doing, then illness could be thought of as something to be blamed on the person with the illness. However, new knowledge revealed that disease was caused by germs; thus, germs were known to originate outside of individuals and were therefore not their responsibility. A changing technology changes beliefs about responsibility. The idea of controllability, therefore, must play a very important part in our attribution theories. Lewis's (1995b,c) and Weiner's (1993) attempts to focus our attention on responsibility is an important addition to our understanding in this regard.

Responsibility is not only personal but also involves the perceptions that others hold about responsibility. For example, a mother who gives birth to a child with mental retardation can blame herself for the condition, claiming she did not eat well or take care of herself during pregnancy, or she can see it as a chance event with no self-blame. However, we not only need to convince ourselves that we are not responsible but also to convince others that it is not our fault. For example, an overweight woman may know full well that her condition is glandular and that there is nothing she can do to control her weight; yet, it still remains a stigma for her because she knows others see her as responsible.

Holding oneself responsible is a critical feature in stigma and in the generation of shame, because violation of standards, rules, and goals is insufficient to elicit shame unless responsibility can be placed on the self. Stigma may differ from other elicitors of shame and guilt, in part because it requires a social appearance factor. The degree to which the stigma is socially apparent is the degree to which one must negotiate the issue of blame, not only for oneself but between oneself and others who witness the stigma. Stigmatization is a much more powerful elicitor of shame and guilt because it requires a negotiation between oneself and one's attri-butions, as well as between oneself and the attributions of others.

The major distinction that I have drawn between shame and guilt or regret rests on the idea that, in shame, the entire self is no good, as captured in the expression "I am a bad person." Goffman's expression of stigma as a "spoiled identity" makes clear that stigma constitutes a global attribution about the self as bad (Goffman, 1963). A spoiled identity reflects a whole self spoiled by some condition or behav-ior. Much of the pathology associated with stigma is that the stigma represents the individual; thus, the whole self becomes defined by the stigma. The expressions "the Down's child," "the mentally retarded person," or "the fat lady" all reflect an inescapable realization that the stigma is the defining feature of the self. In this regard, the attempt to alter others' perceptions of people by altering their language, such as referring to "a person who has a disability" rather than "a disabled person," is an attempt to remove the stigma as the defining element of the person and thus to remove the power of the stigma to reflect upon the total self.

That the stigma reflects the spoiled identity shows its similarity to our concept of shame and allows us to appreciate how the very act of stigmatization is shame-inducing. It is not surprising to find in the descriptions of stigma associated feelings of lack of self-esteem and, with it, depression and acting-out behaviors (Angrosino, 1992; Gibbons, 1985; Reiss & Benson, 1984; Rogers, 1991; Szivos-Bach, 1993; Taylor, Asher, & Williams, 1987; Varni, Setoguchi, Rappaport, & Talbot, 1992.) Stigma reflects the idea of difference and how difference shames us and those we know.

The Nature of Stigma

The list of stigmas in our society is long and varied, and justice cannot be done to all of the things which can be considered stigma. Some stigmata are more obvious than others; for example, sickness, cancer in particular. Betty Ford's announcement of having breast cancer was considered brave for the very reason that she dared reveal her stigma. Historically, the examples of leprosy and epilepsy as stigmas are well known.

Physical appearance can also serve as a stigma, and a very important one, for both women and men. For women, having too much weight is a very powerful social marker, one which bears a stigma. Anorexia and other eating disorders found so prevalent in women may be due to this powerful sense of being marked and stigmatized (Lerner & Brackney, 1978; Lerner & Jovanovic, 1990; Lerner, Karabenick, & Stuart, 1973; Lerner et al., 1991; Markus, Jamill, & Sentis, 1987; Mathes & Kahn, 1975; Rosenblum, 1995).

Although men have not been studied to the same degree as women, evidence shows that the same sort of stigmatization occurs for somewhat different reasons. As a child, I remember reading in comic books about a course given by Charles Atlas. This was a weight-lifting, bodybuilding course, which promised to relieve the stigma of being puny and nonmuscular. In those days, the "97-pound weakling" was a stigmatization which every young man sought to avoid. Today it may still influence some men to build up their bodies and to take steroids.

Physical appearance is public, and our appearance, therefore, constitutes a potential stigma. Being physically ugly can constitute a stigma for both men and women. The stigma of ugliness affects our sense of identity and marks us throughout our lives. While our sense of the attractive and, therefore, the ugly is culturally defined, evidence shows that across cultures particular aspects of appearance are universally considered ugly. Langlois has been able to demonstrate that fineness of facial features and symmetrical proportions are universally considered, even by young infants, to be attractive and that they are more attention-holding than cross-featured and asymmetrical faces (Langlois et al., 1987). Ugliness, without any physical deformity, constitutes a stigma.

If physical unattractiveness is stigmatizing, how much more so is a physical disability of some type? Think about people who have a hunchback, a missing limb, a limp, or facial paralysis. Physical disabilities, because they serve as public markers, cannot help but produce embarrassment and shame in those individuals possessing them (Birenbaum, 1992; Cahill & Eggleston, 1995). Many attempts to cope with such stigmata have been made. Corrective surgery may be recommended not so much to affect ability as to offset the public appearance of the disability— for example, plastic surgery may be performed on children with Down syndrome. In general, corrective surgery has been found to be less effective than one might hope, in part because stigmas are not only associated with physical appearance but also with how people act. Thus, although one might be able to correct some physical stigmas, any underlying conditions such as mental retardation cannot be eliminated with cosmetic surgery. To our list of the stigmatized, then, we must add all those people who have disabilities.

The most extensive literature on stigmata focuses on the effects of mental retardation (Lewis, 1995c). The mentally retarded feel the stigma of their condition. Older children and adults who suffer from mild mental retardation experience their stigma and are shamed by it. Some of us are familiar with the former TV program *L.A. Law*, in which a mildly retarded man was portrayed. At least part of the time that the character Benny, portraying a mentally retarded adult, is shown, the segment deals with his shame, embarrassment, and even anger and rage when he perceives that others are responding to his stigma. It is no television play, but real life, that Benny represents. Consider a UPI report in the *Hartford Courant* from November 1981. The headline of the article reads "Teenager describes how it feels to be retarded":

> Sometimes it makes me want to cry inside because I am retarded. I am retarded, but sometimes, other people may forget about me being retarded. I can't stand it if someone teases me, it makes me feel weird inside. I can't stand it! Nobody likes that, but when they realize that they are hurting my feelings, sometimes they come over and apologize to me.

The stigma associated with mental retardation has a powerful effect and strong impact not only on the person's sense of a spoiled identity and feelings of shame and embarrassment but also on how they go about trying to cope with their everyday lives. Such an intense feeling of a spoiled identity, of a self that is no good, of an unworthy person, must be a public mark almost too hard to bear.

Our list of potential stigmas, since it reflects standards and rules, is open to change as a function of historical time and culture. For example, in our culture today, being old is a stigma and reflects a spoiled self. We try and hide this stigma: we dye our hair, use plastic surgery to remove the wrinkles on our faces, and use cosmetics by the millions to hide the appearance of our age. This is true of men as well as women.

It should be clear that stigmata, and the age stigma in particular, are in large part culturally determined. Although youth is valued in all societies, if for no reason other than that old age reflects the end of one's life, there are strong cultural differences. A Japanese colleague told me of an interesting distinction in insurance payments in the case of an accident. If an elderly person were to die in an airplane accident in the United States, payment for his loss of life would be dependent upon lost income to him and, therefore, to his family. Because an old man is likely to generate little income at this point in life, his family would be poorly compensated for his loss, as compared to a young man who still had much of his earnings ahead of him. Not so in Japan, where age is associated with wisdom. An older person, who presumably has acquired more of this commodity with the years, is valued more than a young person, who has yet not accrued such wisdom through age. Compensation, then, is greater for the old man than for the young one. Such views of value and worth as a function of different societies suggest that the idea of stigma not only resides in the marked individual but also in the societal value system as reflected in its standards, rules, and goals.

The effects of stigmatization and its relation to shame has been known for some time. Goffman (1963) addresses the nature of self-presentation and the role of stigma in interpersonal relations. He states that people with stigmas are thought of as not quite human:

> The standards he (the person with a stigma) has incorporated from the wider society equipped him to be intimately alive to what others see as his failing, inevitably causing him . . . to agree that he does indeed fall short of what he really ought to be. Shame becomes a central possibility. (Goffman, 1963, p. 7)

For Goffman, stigma represents a spoiled identity, the idea that somehow one is imperfect with regard to the standards of the society in which he or she lives. While the concept of stigma is not easily defined, we can say that it is a mark or characteristic that distinguishes a person as being deviant, flawed, limited, spoiled, or generally undesirable. The deviating characteristics of the person are sufficient reason for the occurrence of the stigma. Stigma relates the self to others' views. Although the feelings of being stigmatized may occur in the absence of other people, the associated feelings come about through one's interactions with other people or through one's anticipation of interactions with other people. For example, a woman who has one leg shorter than the other and who limps when she walks notices others looking at her. At home, she anticipates walking in public and being observed by others. Stigmatization is a public mark.

Jones et al. (1984) points to the connection between stigmatization and dysfunction. However, the relationship between stigma and shame has been less articulated. Nevertheless, the stigmatized individual has been characterized as having a disrupted emotional, cognitive, and behavioral response system, likely to be caused in part by their dysfunction and in part by their feelings of shame. Imagine for yourself the effect of stigmatization.

Jones and colleagues (1984) make clear that the stigma felt by the individual is profound, resulting in emotions as diverse as anger, sadness, humiliation, shame, and embarrassment.

Stigma and Shame Contagion

The shame impact of stigma is wide; it not only affects those who are stigmatized but also those associated with the person so marked. Goffman (1963) called it "courtesy stigma." Stigmata are contagious; they affect members of the family or friends of the stigmatized person. Like an infectious disease, the stigma not only appears for the victim of the stigma but for all those who are associated with him or her.

Parents of Stigmatized Children

The parents of children with a stigma are themselves stigmatized and suffer the same fate as the stigmatized child. Because the literature on mental retardation is extensive on this subject, examples from this literature can be used to illustrate. There is no question that the parents of a child who has mental retardation become themselves objects of the stigma. We see the impact of stigmatization in the description of what happens to parents when they are informed that their child has retardation or a disability of some sort. First comes shock and disbelief that the child is in imperfect health. This is followed by anger and rage. Subsequently, sadness replaces the anger, and, finally, comes the coping stage. Whatever stage parents of a child with a stigma are in, they must learn to cope with their shame and embarrassment at having such a child. The shame of having such a child lasts a lifetime and leads to many family difficulties, including a high rate of marital discord and divorce, as each parent seeks to blame the other for the stigmatized child (Childs, 1981; David & Donovan, 1975; Hurley & Hurley, 1987; Margalit & Miron, 1983; Peat, 1991; Rimmerman & Portowicz, 1987). Given the differences between men and women in the acceptance of blame (Dweck & Bush, 1976; Nolen-Hoeksema, Morrow, & Frederickson, 1993), it is not surprising that husbands tend to blame wives for the stigmatized child and that mothers tend to accept that self-blame more than do fathers. This provides fathers with the opportunity to blame the mother and, therefore, to separate themselves from the shame of the stigmatized child (Frey, Greenberg, & Fewell, 1989).

The shame of the parents can be examined by looking at intervention studies designed to reduce stress in parents who have a child with difficulties. The most successful research projects are those that focus on parents' feelings of shame, as well as work with their loss. Frey, Greenberg, and Fewell (1989) intervened to alter the appraisal pattern of parents, which they claim leads to shame and embarrassment. Without dealing with this problem, they could not get parents to function appropriately.

Programs that treat families who are suffering from the stress of having a stigmatized child reveal that focusing on the parents' attributions and, therefore, their shame provides the best chance of altering the family dynamics and helping the child. Nixon and Singer (1993) describe an intervention program to help mothers of children with mental retardation. In the program participants spent ten hours discussing how they thought about their children. The treatment condition focused on the cognitive distortions that contributed to self-blame and guilt and on techniques to deal with these cognitive distortions. Working with the attribution model, the authors changed the cognitive distortions and automatic thoughts of parents. The results, although modest, demonstrated that the emotions of shame, guilt, and depression could be altered by altering the cognitive attributional style of parents. The authors, in discussing their findings, conclude that the treatment was effective

in reducing self-blame and guilt in parents of children with severe disabilities, because there were significant reductions in automatic thoughts, internal negative attributions, and depression. There is evidence that cognitive distortions were effectively restructured. Therefore, there is evidence that cognitive restructuring was an important contributor to the reduction of parental self-blame and guilt. (Nixon & Singer, 1993, p. 670)

The authors discuss guilt and make no distinction between guilt and shame. However, a careful reading of this research project, as well as many others that use the term *guilt*, leaves little doubt that the authors are speaking of shame. Indeed, the very term "spoiled identity" addresses the all-encompassing total-self feature of stigma.

Siblings of Stigmatized Children

Although most attention has been paid to the parents of children with stigma, we should not neglect the impact of stigma on the other children in the family. The problems for the siblings of children who are stigmatized are manifested in many different ways. Gath (1992) and Shulman (1988), in discussing the brothers and sisters of mentally retarded children, point to this difficulty. Clearly, a child with disabilities is a source of shame to his or her family and this includes his or her brothers and sisters. According to Gath (1992), siblings of children with a stigma must bear the emotional distress and disappointment of their parents. Their parents' grieving and stress affects them. Moreover, the parents' energy must be directed toward the stigmatized child, thus leaving less time and energy for the "normal" siblings. In addition, siblings without stigma are required to share more of the load of family life than they might normally have. They have to take care of the sibling when the parents are not available. The issues of fairness and sibling rivalry also are problems. The normal competition between siblings is likely to be settled in favor of the stigmatized child. The sibling who is without stigma is likely not only to be neglected but also to be expected to assume a greater burden and more responsibility within the family. For example, Sarah reported that even when her sister did something wrong, her parents insisted that she, "the normal sister," understand and make allowances for her sister's behavior.

Although no accurate data exist on the effect of the stigma on other members of the family, there can be no question that the stigma associated with having a sibling with difficulties is a burden for the nonaffected siblings, a burden which, given their young age and their lack of coping behavior, may be a serious stress for which they are ill equipped. Moreover, the support system which they might receive from other adults around them is likely to be limited, given the need of the parents to support themselves and the stigmatized child. Thus, the prognosis for the siblings appears to be risky, and the little clinical literature on the topic suggests that siblings of children with disabilities are a group particularly at risk for problems related to high standards, self-blame, and the accompanying emotions of shame, embarrassment, and guilt.

Child Abuse and Shame

Rather than relying on Goffman's (1963) discussion about stigmatization, I should prefer to look at abuse, both physical and sexual, as examples of how events that happen to children without their control or desire cause attributions that in turn lead to shame. Child abuse is an important topic, and one which is taken up by Andrews (this volume, chapter 9) in regard to depression and bulimia.

Initially, Freud did consider sexual abuse as the cause of hysteria; however, he soon changed his view, never returning to the connection again (Masson, 1984). While the connection between sexual abuse, pathology, and shame is now recognized, empirical work remains quite limited (see Andrews, 1995, 1997; Andrews & Hunter, 1997, for exceptions). As I have tried to indicate elsewhere (Lewis, 1992, 1995a), abuse is likely to lead to attributions about the self and to shame in the victim. Attributions about sexual abuse mediate the influence of the abuse on subsequent feelings of shame. Internal, stable, and global attributions for negative events—"This happened because I am a bad person"—are the type of attributions most likely to lead to shame.

Finkelhor and Browne (1986) and Wolfe and Gentile (1992) also regard sexual abuse as leading to negative feelings and thoughts about the self, although these feelings and thoughts are not necessarily described as shame. These thoughts and feelings occur during and following the sexual abuse. In our work with children and adults who were abused as children, both physically and sexually, we found that they denigrate themselves and express the desire to hide and avoid exposure. Self-denigration takes the form of such statements as "I am stupid, awful, a bad person, a blob." In adults, shame can often be inferred by the fact that they continue to keep their childhood molestation a secret. Both sexually abused children and adults have often been observed to avoid eye contact, hide their faces, or hide their bodies behind chairs when talking about the abuse (Feiring, Taska, & Lewis, 1996; Lewis, 1992). Shame is enhanced if the victim is immersed in a social environment where the self is denigrated and humiliated (Finkelhor & Browne, 1986; Friedrich, Berliner, Urquiza, & Beilke, 1988).

Given the association between sexual abuse, stigmatization, and shame, it is possible to explore the processes that connect the abuse to shame. While certain characteristics of the abusive event may be more likely to elicit shame, cognitive evaluation of the event or the attribution style of the victim mediates the extent to which shame will be experienced (Lewis, 1992). Support for this comes from evidence which suggests that how the victim evaluates the abuse is a central component of victimization and mediates the long-lasting effects of the abuse itself (Conte, 1985; Gold, 1986; Janoff-Bulman & Frieze, 1983; Wyatt & Mickey, 1988). The relationship between adults' attribution styles and their reactions to their sexual abuse as children also supports the idea that attribution style and shame mediate the effects of sexual abuse (Andrews & Brewin, 1990; Gold, 1986; Wyatt & Mickey, 1988). For example, Gold (1986) compared the current functioning of women who had been sexually abused as children to women who did not report being abused. Women who were sexually abused in childhood and who currently report psychological distress and low self-esteem are more likely to have an attribution style characterized by internal, stable, global attributes for negative events. Another study of women who reported being sexually abused as children found that a self-blaming attribution style was related to more severe forms of abuse (Wyatt & Mickey, 1988). These findings suggest that self-blame attributions may be related to more shame.

Studies of self-blame in abused subjects find a relationship to depression (Andrews, this volume, chapter 9; German, Habenicht, & Futcher, 1990; Wolfe & Gentile, 1992). Shame over the sexual abuse may mediate the development of behavior problems. The empirical literature on sexual abuse has not examined shame and its relationship to adjustment. Theoretically, the traumagenic dynamics of stigmatization have been linked to shame, but the exact processes have not been explored (Finkelhor & Browne, 1986). It is reasonable to connect shame, sexual abuse, stigmatization, and adjustment, and the literature on shame indicates how the continued experience of this emotion can lead to poor adjustment. Both the clinical and empirical literature suggest that shame-proneness is related to affective disorders, particularly depression (Harder & Lewis, 1986; Hoblitzelle, 1987; H. B. Lewis, 1971, 1987; Lewis, 1992; Tangney, 1990). Problems of dissociation, in particular multiple personality disorders, have been linked to sexual abuse and may be mediated by shame (Lewis, 1992; Ross, 1989). The abuse leads to shame which is too intense. Abused children use dissociation to separate themselves from the abuse: "This is not happening to me but to someone else"; thus the development of multiple personality disorders (Ross, 1989).

To explore the mediation of shame between sexual abuse and its stigmatization and psychopathology, Feiring, Taska, and Lewis (in press) have studied a large number of *known* sexually abused children. We propose that stigmatization can be defined by the emotional experience of shame and by the children's attributional style of self-blame. We argue that the effects of abusive characteristics (e.g., number of events, severity, etc.) on adjustment are mediated by shame and attribution style. More shame and a self-blaming attribution style should be related to more psychological distress and pathology. The effects of shame and attribution style on adjustment may be additive, with each contributing some variance to adjustment.

To explore this possibility, 142 participants, consisting of 82 children, ages 8–11 years, and 60 adolescents, ages 12–15 years, who were known to have been sexually abused, were studied. The study involved examining the patterns of abuse characteristics, feelings of shame, attribution style, and psychological adjustment. Abuse was directly related to psychopathology, with more abuse being associated with more depressive symptoms. More abuse was also related to more shame and negative attribution style while more shame and negative attribution style were related to more depressive symptoms. Thus, abuse directly and abuse through the elicitation of shame and attribution indirectly relate to depressive symptoms. Other measures of psychopathology, such as self-esteem and post traumatic stress disorder measures, also showed the same pattern.

The results from this study strongly support the idea that shame is the result of sexual abuse and is related to increased psychological distress, including more depressive and post traumatic stress disorder symptoms, as well as lower self-esteem. Although previous theoretical work has suggested the importance of negative self-feelings for the process of stigmatization (Feiring, Taska, & Lewis, 1996; Finkelhor & Browne, 1986; Lewis, 1995b, c,), this study provides the first strong empirical evidence of the importance of shame for children's and adolescents' adaptation to sexual abuse.

Alessandri and Lewis (1996) have recently begun to study physical abuse and shame in preschool children reported to protective services because of known maltreatment. In a series of studies that looked at matched groups of maltreated and nonmaltreated preschoolers, we found that maltreated girls showed significantly more shame when they failed a task and significantly less pride when they succeeded than did the matched nonmaltreated girls. Maltreated boys, on the other hand, showed both less shame and less pride than did the matched nonmaltreated boys. These findings suggest that maltreatment is likely to have a somewhat different effect depending on the sex of the child; for girls, maltreatment leads to what appears to be a depressed state (more shame, less pride), while for boys maltreatment may lead to a turning off of emotional responses to either success or failure. This emotional turnoff may, then, be related to the often unexplained and "shameless" acts of violence that are seen in the aggressive behavior of boys.

Thus, studies of both kinds of abuse—sexual and physical—suggest that abuse may be related to pathological attributions, which in turn lead to shame. Shame and negative attributions, in turn, are likely to lead to symptom formation, including rage, violence, and depression (H. B. Lewis, 1987; Lewis, 1992). Because shame is believed to reflect an indictment of the entire self, its consequences for psychological functioning are insidious and pervasive (Lewis, 1992). The experience of such negative self-feelings may result in heightened levels of psychological distress. The continued experience of shame over the abuse may disrupt processes essential to self-development, such as self-agency and self-affectivity, and may engender negative affect in a wide range of self-representations (Alessandri & Lewis, 1996; Tangney, Burggraf, & Wagner, 1995; Westen, 1994).

It has been suggested that, when shamed repeatedly, individuals will act to eradicate this negative state in ways that lead to depression, acting out, and dissociation (Andrews, Valentine, & Valentine, 1995; Harder & Lewis, 1986; H. B. Lewis, 1971, 1987; Lewis, 1992; Tangney et al., 1995). Future research should investigate what factors may intensify or mitigate feelings of shame in stigmatized victims. Of particular importance would be an examination of changes in shame and related symptomatology over time and how these patterns are related to interpersonal processes with family, friends, and service providers. For example, research on families suggests that several family processes are related to the development of shame. These include parenting discipline styles (Ferguson & Stegge, 1995), parental attributions about blame (Alessandri & Lewis, 1996; Dix & Reinhold, 1991; Lewis & Sullivan, in press), and a family environment where the negative emotions of anger and disgust are more frequently expressed (Ferguson & Stegge, 1995; Grych & Fincham, 1993).

Stigmatization

Goffman's (1963) definition of stigmatization, which includes the idea of a spoiled self, something imperfect, leads us quickly to the topic of shame. If shame had not been ignored for so long (Nathanson, 1987), shame rather than stigmatization might have become the central construct in relating sexual abuse and subsequent maladjustment. Lewis (1992) and Masson (1984) have suggested that Freud's earlier observation that his hysterical patients were in fact abused might not have given way to his later idea of fantasy but might have allowed us to explore earlier the relation between sexual and physical abuse, shame, and symptom formation.

It is important to distinguish between types of stigmatization and their relation to shame. While all stigmatized children and adults are likely to be highly shamed, stigmatization originally referred to visible marks, something physical that was public and that resulted in what Goffman (1963) referred to as a "spoiled self." It is clear that other forms of stigmatization are possible that are less visible. For example, the child who is sexually abused and who has revealed the abuse becomes stigmatized to the extent that the revelation results in labeling or in special treatment. Stigmatization also includes contagion. Children and adults who are related to others with certain illnesses or difficulties become themselves marked. For example, children of alcoholic parents are stigmatized by their associations. Thus, stigmatization, the marking of a spoiled self, can occur through the public marking of either the self or others. In all such cases, shame and negative self-attributions are likely.

Shame, however, can be both public and private (Lewis, 1992). That quality is not what distinguishes it as an emotion nor what differs it from guilt (H. B. Lewis, 1971). Shame and stigma are likely to represent the same spoiled self whether or not the stigma is a public or visible mark.

If shame is elicited by failure relative to a standard, our own or another's—a failure which is our own fault and which reflects the spoiled nature of our selves—then there exists a large number of people who are stigmatized and shamed. It must include the young child who is ridiculed and not allowed to play with the big children, the old, the sick, the physically challenged, the unattractive—those who reflect failure that is visible to all. Stigmatization, and therefore shame, also apply to those less visibly but nonetheless psychologically marked, including, for example, the children of sick parents or of parents who have died.

Such a view of stigmatization, a view which considers both surface and inner markings, makes clear that the extent of stigmatization and of the shame felt may be quite large. But, perhaps more important, it points to the fact that if shame and humiliation are the emotional consequences of stigmatization, then shame exists across a large number of people and is likely to underlie, at least in part, the psychopathology which so often occurs with stigmatization. What better way to see this than to listen to the words of a woman who, because of an automobile accident, became a paraplegic: "Suddenly I was one of those people my mother used to tell me not to stare at on the street. I thought if I didn't die in the hospital, I would kill myself when I got out" (Jones et al., 1984). Wishing to hide, disappear, or die is the hallmark of a shamed and spoiled self.

Note

1. Goffman not only considers stigma as a public mark but also discusses individuals whose differences are not immediately apparent. Abused children's experience may not be immediately obvious to others; nevertheless, it is obvious to themselves, thus affecting their attributions and, therefore, their shame.

References

Alessandri, S. A., & Lewis, M. (1996). Differences in pride and shame in maltreated and nonmaltreated preschoolers. *Child Development, 67*, 1857–1869.

Andrews, B. (1995). Bodily shame as a mediator between abusive experiences and depression. *Journal of Abnormal Psychology, 104* (2), 277–285.

Andrews, B. (1997). Bodily shame in relation to abuse in childhood and bulimia: A preliminary investigation. *British Journal of Clinical Psychology, 36*, 41–49.

Andrews, B., & Brewin, C. R. (1990). Attribution of blame for marital violence: A study of antecedents and consequences. *Journal of Marriage and the Family, 52*, 757–767.

Andrews, B., & Hunter, E. (1997). Shame, early abuse, and course of depression in a clinical sample: A preliminary study. *Cognition and Emotion, 11*, 373–381.

Andrews, B., Valentine, E. R., & Valentine, J. D. (1995). Depression and eating disorders following abuse in childhood in two generations of women. *British Journal of Clinical Psychology, 34*, 37–52.

Angrosino, M. V. (1992). Metaphors of stigma: How deinstitutionalized mentally retarded adults see themselves. *Journal of Contemporary Ethnography, 21* (2), 171–199.

Birenbaum, A. (1992). Courtesy stigma revisited. *Journal of Mental Retardation, 30,* 265–268.

Borkowski, J. G., Weyhing, R. S., & Turner, L. A. (1986). Attributional retraining and the teaching of strategies. *Exceptional Children, 53* (2), 130–137.

Cahill, S. E., & Eggleston, R. (1995). Reconsidering the stigma of physical disability: Wheelchair use and public kindness. *Sociological Quarterly, 36,* 681–698.

Childs, R. E. (1981). Maternal psychological conflicts associated with the birth of a retarded child. *Maternal-Child Nursing Journal, 21,* 175–182.

Conte, J. (1985). The effects of sexual abuse on children: A critique and suggestions for future research. *Victimology: An International Journal, 10* (1–4), 110–130.

Cook, R. E. (1983). Why Jimmy doesn't try. *Academic Therapy, 19* (2), 155–162.

David, A. C., & Donovan, E. H. (1975). Initiating group process with parents of multihandicapped children. *Social Work in Health Care, 1* (2), 177–183.

Dix, T., & Reinhold, D. (1991). Chronic and temporary influences on mothers' attributions for children's disobedience. *Merrill-Palmer Quarterly, 37* (2), 251–271.

Dweck, C. S., & Bush, E. S. (1976). Sex differences in learned helplessness: 1. Differential debilitation with peer and adult evaluators. *Developmental Psychology, 12,* 147–156.

Feiring, C., Taska, L., & Lewis, M. (1996). A process model for understanding adaptation to sexual abuse: The role of shame in defining stigmatization. *Child Abuse and Neglect, 20* (8), 767–792.

Feiring, C., Taska, L., & Lewis, M. (in press). The role of shame and attribution style in children's and adolescents' adaptation to sexual abuse. *Maltreatment.*

Ferguson, T. J., & Stegge, H. (1995). Emotional states and traits in children: The case of guilt and shame. In J. P. Tangney & K. D. Fischer (Eds.), *Self-conscious emotions: Shame, guilt, embarrassment and pride.* (pp. 174–197). New York: Guilford Press.

Finkelhor, D., & Browne, A. (1986). Initial and long-term effects: A conceptual framework. In D. Finkelhor (Ed.), *A sourcebook on child sexual abuse* (pp. 180–198). Beverly Hills, CA: Sage.

Frey, K. S., Greenberg, M. T., & Fewell, R. R. (1989). Stress and coping among children: A multidimensional approach. *American Journal on Mental Retardation, 94* (3), 240–249.

Friedrich, W. M., Berliner, L., Urquiza, A. J., & Beilke, R. (1988). Brief diagnostic group treatment of sexually abused boys. *Journal of Interpersonal Violence, 3,* 331–343.

Gath, A. (1992). The brothers and sisters of mentally retarded children. In F. Boer & J. Dunn (Eds.), *Children's sibling relationships: Developmental and clinical issues* (pp. 101–108). Hillsdale, NJ: Erlbaum.

German, D. E., Habenicht, D. J., & Futcher, W. G. (1990). Psychological profile of the female adolescent incest victim. *Child Abuse and Neglect, 14,* 429–438.

Gibbons, F. X. (1985). Stigma perception: Social comparison among mentally retarded persons. *American Journal of Mental Deficiency, 90* (1), 98–106.

Goffman, E. (1963). *Stigma: Notes on the management of a spoiled identity.* Englewood Cliffs, NJ: Prentice-Hall.

Gold, E. R. (1986). Long-term effects of sexual victimization in childhood: An attributional approach. *Journal of Consulting and Clinical Psychology, 54,* 471–475.

Grych, J. H., & Fincham, F. D. (1993). Children's appraisals of marital conflict: Initial investigations of the cognitive-contextual framework. *Child Development, 64,* 215–230.

Harder, D. W., & Lewis, S. J. (1986). The assessment of shame and guilt. In J. N. Butcher & C. D. Spielberger (Eds.), *Advances in personality assessment* (Vol. 6, pp. 89–114). Hillsdale, NJ: Erlbaum.

Hoblitzelle, W. (1987). Differentiating and measuring shame and guilt: The relation between shame and depression. In H. B. Lewis (Ed.), *The role of shame in symptom formation* (pp. 207–236). Hillsdale, NJ: Erlbaum.

Hurley, A. D., & Hurley, F. J. (1987). Working with the parents of handicapped children. *Psychiatric Aspects of Mental Retardation Reviews, 6* (11), 53–57.

Janoff-Bulman, R., & Frieze, I. (1983). A theoretical perspective for understanding reactions to victimization. *Journal of Social Issues, 39*, 1–17.

Jones, E. E., Farina, A., Hastorf, A. H., Markus, H., Miller, D. T., & Scott, R. A. (1984). *Social stigma: The psychology of marked relationships.* New York: Freeman.

Langlois, J. H., Roggman, L. A., Casey, R. J., Ritter, J. M., Rieser-Danner, L. A., & Jenkins, V. Y. (1987). Infant preferences for attractive faces: Rudiments of a stereotype? *Developmental Psychology, 23*, 363–369.

Lerner, R. M., & Brackney, B. E. (1978). The importance of inner and outer body parts: Attitudes in the self-concept of late adolescents. *Sex Roles, 4*, 225–228.

Lerner, R. M., & Jovanovic, J. (1990). The role of body-image in psychosocial development across the lifespan: A developmental perspective. In T. T. Cash & T. Pruzinsky (Eds.), *Body-images: Development, deviance and change* (pp. 110–127). New York: Guilford Press.

Lerner, R. M., Karabenick, S. A., & Stuart, J. L. (1973). Relations among physical attractiveness, body attitudes, and self-concept in male and female college students. *Journal of Psychology, 85*, 119–129.

Lerner, R. M., Lerner, J. V., Hess, L. E., Schwab, J., Jovanovic, J., Talwar, R., & Kucher, J. S. (1991). Physical attractiveness and psychosocial functioning among early adolescents. *Journal of Early Adolescence, 11*, 300–320.

Lewis, H. B. (1971). *Shame and guilt in neurosis.* New York: International Universities Press.

Lewis, H. B. (Ed.). (1987). *The role of shame in symptom formation.* Hillsdale, NJ: Erlbaum.

Lewis, M. (1992). *Shame: The exposed self.* New York: Free Press.

Lewis, M. (1995a). Embarrassment: The emotion of self exposure and embarrassment. In J. P. Tangney & K. W. Fischer (Eds.), *Self-Conscious emotions: The psychology of shame, guilt, embarrassment and pride* (pp. 198–218). New York: Guilford Press.

Lewis, M. (1995b). Self-Conscious emotions. *American Scientist, 83*, 68–78.

Lewis, M. (1995c). *Shame: The exposed self.* New York: The Free Press.

Lewis, M., & Sullivan, M. W. (in press). Three studies of preschoolers' self-conscious emotion and attribution in achievement tasks. *Monographs of the Society for Research in Child Development.*

Margalit, M., & Miron, M. (1983). The attitudes of Israeli adolescents toward handicapped people. *Exceptional Child, 30* (3), 195–200.

Markus, H., Jamill, R., & Sentis, K. P. (1987). Thinking fat: Self schemas for body weight and the processing of weight-relevant information. *Journal of Applied Social Psychology, 17*, 50–71.

Masson, J. M. (1984). *The assault on the truth: Freud's suppression of the seduction theory.* New York: Farrar, Strauss, & Giroux.

Mathes, E. W., & Kahn, A. (1975). Physical attractiveness, happiness, neuroticism and self-esteem. *Journal of Psychology, 90*, 267–275.

Nathanson, D. L. (Ed.) (1987). *The many faces of shame.* New York: Guilford Press.

Nixon, C. D., & Singer, G. H. S. (1993). Group cognitive-behavioral treatment for excessive parental self-blame and guilt. *American Journal on Mental Retardation, 97* (6), 665–672.

Nolen-Hoeksema, S., Morrow, J., & Frederickson, B. L. (1993). Response styles and the duration of episodes of depressed mood. *Journal of Abnormal Psychology, 102*, 20–28.

Peat, M. (1991). Community based rehabilitation-development and structure: 2. *Community Rehabilitation, 5*, 231–239.

Reiss, S., & Benson, B. A. (1984). Awareness of negative social conditions among mentally retarded, emotionally disturbed outpatients. *American Journal of Psychiatry, 141* (1), 88–90.

Rimmerman, A., & Portowicz, D. J. (1987). Analysis of resources and stress among parents of developmentally disabled children. *International Journal of Rehabilitation Research, 19* (4), 439–455.

Rogers, S. J. (1991). Observation of emotional functioning in young handicapped children. *Child Care Health and Development, 17,* 303–312.

Rosenblum, G. A. (1995). Body image, physical attractiveness and psychopathology during adolescence. Unpublished doctoral dissertation, Rutgers University, New Brunswick, New Jersey.

Ross, C. A. (1989). *Multiple personality disorder.* New York: Wiley.

Shulman, S. (1988). The family of the severely handicapped child: The sibling perspective. *Journal of Family Therapy, 10,* 125–134.

Szivos-Bach, S. E. (1993). Social comparisons, stigma and mainstreaming: The self-esteem of young adults with a mild mental handicap. *Mental Handicap Research, 6* (3), 217–236.

Tangney, J. P. (1990). Assessing individual differences in proneness to shame and guilt: Development of the Self-Conscious Affect and Attribution Inventory. *Journal of Personality and Social Psychology, 59,* 102–111.

Tangney, J. P., Burggraf, S. A., & Wagner, P. E. (1995). Shame-proneness, guilt-proneness and psychological symptoms. In J. P. Tangney & K. W. Fischer (Eds.), *Self-Conscious emotions: The psychology of shame, guilt, embarrassment and pride* (pp. 343–367). New York: Guilford Press.

Taylor, A. R., Asher, S. R., & Williams, G. A. (1987). The social adaptation of mainstreamed mildly retarded children. *Child Development, 58,* 1321–1334.

Tomkins, S. S. (1963). *Affect, imagery, consciousness: Vol. 2. The negative affects.* New York: Springer.

Turner, L. A. (1994, May). *Attributional beliefs of students with retardation.* Paper presented at the 4th Annual Conference of the Center for Human Development and Developmental Disabilities, Emotional Development in Atypical Children, New Brunswick, NJ.

Turner, L. A., Dofny, E. M., & Dutka, S. (1994). Effect of strategy and attribution training on strategy maintenance and transfer. *American Journal on Mental Retardation, 98* (4), 445–454.

Varni, J. W., Setoguchi, Y., Rappaport, L. R., & Talbot, D. (1992). Psychological adjustment and perceived social support in children with congenital/acquired limb deficiencies. *Journal of Behavioral Medicine, 15* (1), 31–44.

Wehmeyer, M. L. (1994). Perceptions of self-determination and psychological empowerment of adolescents with mental retardation. *Education and Training in Mental Retardation and Developmental Disabilities, 29* (1), 9–21.

Weiner, B. (1993). On sin versus sickness: A theory of perceived responsibility and social motivation. *American Psychologist, 48* (9), 957–965.

Westen, D. (1994). The impact of sexual abuse on self-structure. *Rochester Symposium on Developmental Psychopathology, 5,* 223–245.

Wolfe, V. V., & Gentile, C. (1992). Psychological assessment of sexually abused children. In W. O'Donohue & J. H. Geer (Eds.), *The sexual abuse of children: Clinical issues* (Vol. 2, pp. 143–187). Hillsdale, NJ: Erlbaum.

Wyatt, G. E., & Mickey, M. R. (1988). The support of parents and others as it mediates the effects of child sexual abuse: An exploratory study. In G. E. Wyatt & G. J. Powell (Eds.), *Lasting effects of child sexual abuse* (pp. 211–225). Newbury Park, CA: Sage.

7

Disclosing Shame

James Macdonald

The first part of this chapter provides an overview of theoretical approaches to the relationship between shame and disclosure. This will include phenomena which may make this relationship more complex, such as experiences of shame that are momentary and possibly minimally conscious, as well as theoretical perspectives which emphasize a relationship between nondisclosure and the need to avoid shame. Following this, an attempt will be made to review the existing empirical evidence on the relationship between shame and disclosure. Although there does seem to be evidence which supports the theoretical argument that the "action tendency" in shame is one of hiding, some of this work suggests that people may subsequently disclose experiences of shame, at least in certain contexts. At the end of the chapter, a small body of work will be reviewed that suggests that the anticipation of shame plays a role in the nondisclosure of emotional experience more generally.

Theoretical Perspectives

Shame and Hiding

"All I can think of is I just wanted to hide myself away."
"I hide it because I didn't tell nobody [inaudible] kept it all to myself."
"I tried my best to hide my whole body. All the time. Wearing huge jumpers and huge skirts constantly."

These remarks were made by people who had just described incidents involving strong feelings of shame and who were then asked by the interviewer, "If you could have done, was there anything about yourself you wanted to hide?" (Macdonald and Tantam, 1994). The word *shame* is in fact thought to derive from an Indo-European word meaning *hide*, and the idea that shame motivates hiding and concealment is a central defining component of shame for most theorists. Fischer and Tangney, in the introduction to their recent edited volume on the "self-conscious emotions," suggest that in shame "The person tries to hide or escape from observation or judgement" and may "turn . . . away from other people" (1995, p. 10). In the same volume, Barrett suggests that the "action tendency" of shame is "Withdrawal; avoidance of others; hiding of the self" (1995, p. 43). In a similar vein, Lazarus says "I propose that the action tendency in *shame* is to hide, to avoid having one's personal failure observed by anyone, especially someone who is personally important" (1991, p. 244). These theoretical perspectives on shame and hiding are congruent with the layperson's understanding of shame. Lindsay-Hartz (1984; Lindsay-Hartz, de Rivera, & Mascolo, 1995) used a method known as "conceptual encounter," in which the interviewer compares his or her *a priori* conceptualization with that of research participants. One of the goals of both studies was to "develop abstract descriptions of guilt and shame that would describe *each and every example* of shame" (p. 276; italics in original). On the basis of this approach and the interviewees' own accounts of their shame, Lindsay-Hartz et al. (1995) arrived at a summary statement of what they called the "instruction" of shame: "we wish *to hide* in order to *get out* of the interpersonal realm and escape our painful exposure before the other" (1995, p. 278; italics in original).

It would appear, then, that there is a reasonable consensus among theorists, researchers, and lay people that the experience of shame involves an impulse to get away from other people, an action tendency of interpersonal avoidance. This link between shame and hiding suggests that, at least at the time of experiencing shame, people are unlikely to disclose or talk about how they are feeling.

Unacknowledged Shame

There is, however, another layer to the issue of concealment and shame. This is that shame may be concealed from conscious acknowledgement. A number of writers have focused on fleeting experiences of shame which may never be labeled or even consciously experienced as such (H. Lewis, 1971; M. Lewis, 1992; Retzinger, this volume, chapter 11; Scheff, this volume, chapter 10). H. Lewis (1971) coined the term *unacknowledged shame* to refer to this phenomenon after analyzing transcripts of a number of psychotherapy sessions using Gottschalk's coding scheme for detecting "shame anxiety" and "guilt anxiety." Lewis was struck by the amount of shame she discovered that remained unacknowledged by both client and therapist. As she puts it, "Difficulties in identifying one's own experience as shame have so often been observed that they suggest some intrinsic connection between shame and the mechanism of denial" (1971, p. 196). According to Lewis, denial operates in two ways. In the first of these ways:

> Shame affect is overt or available to consciousness but the person experiencing it either will not or cannot identify it. At the moment that the person himself says: "I am ashamed," shame affect is likely to be diminishing. An observer may identify that the other person is having a shame reaction, or

the person himself may identify it as it is receding, but while shame is occurring the person himself is unable to communicate. He often says only that he feels "lousy," or "tense," or "blank." (H. Lewis, 1971, p. 197)

This kind of shame is referred to as *overt, unidentified shame*. The second kind of denial-tempered shame is referred to as *bypassed shame*, and, according to Lewis, it involves much cognitive activity focused on "doubt about the self's image from the other's viewpoint" (1971, p. 197), although there appears to be little of the feeling component characteristic of overt, unidentified shame, only a "wince," "blow," or "jolt" that constitutes a "peripheral, nonspecific disturbance in awareness" (p. 197).

Lewis thus raises the issue of how the level of awareness at which shame is experienced influences the degree to which it is communicated or even communicable. Thus, in addition to being unwilling to talk about their experience, people may also lack the verbal schemas needed to articulate that they feel ashamed. Various other descriptors might be used to label internal experiences, such as *awkward* or *hurt*, but not shame (Retzinger, 1991).

According to Lewis, another reason that these fleeting experiences of shame remain unacknowledged, both to others and to the self, is that people are ashamed of their own shame reactions. Scheff (1988; 1990; 1995), drawing on Lewis' notion of unacknowledged shame and Cooley's notion that we constantly "live in the minds of others without knowing it" (Cooley, 1922, quoted in Scheff, 1988, p. 398), suggested that shame "is the most frequent and possibly the most important of emotions [because of its role in maintaining conformity] even though it is usually invisible" (Scheff, 1988, p. 387). He argues that we are all constantly in a state either of pride or shame, but these experiences are profoundly taboo, accounting for the fact that shame is rarely referred to.

Lewis and her followers describe how such unacknowledged shame leads to other problematic emotions, typically, in Lewis's words, a "lightning-speed sequence from an evoked state of shame almost simultaneously into a humiliated fury and thence into guilt for what is processed by the person as forbidden anger— unjust, wrong, or inappropriate anger" (1990, p. 233). This kind of humiliated fury creates a "feeling trap" in which the person can oscillate between shame and anger, each state rekindling the other. Scheff (1987, 1988, 1995) and Retzinger, in her (1991) study of marital conflicts, have amplified Lewis's observations by applying them to interpersonal, as well as intrapersonal, dynamics. Thus each party's humiliated fury conveys disrespect to the other, evoking a similar experience of shame-rage, which in turn provokes more shame in the first, and so on. The result of this is that "denial of shame is both cause and effect of a continuing cycle of deception and self-deception about thoughts and feelings" (Scheff, 1995, p. 411).

Shame is therefore likely to be obscured by its proximity to other emotions, such as guilt or humiliated fury, making it harder for people to identify. The fact that even researchers and theorists of shame are not in agreement about whether shame is distinct from closely associated emotions such as guilt, embarrassment, and humiliation (Gilbert, 1997; Miller & Tangney, 1994; Wicker, Payne, & Morgan, 1983), adds weight to the notion that it may be difficult for people to identify their own shame.

The theories reviewed so far suggest, then, that the experience of shame and the source of shame are unlikely to be disclosed for a number of reasons. First, hiding and concealment are intrinsic parts of the emotion—its action tendency (Barrett, 1995; Lazarus, 1991) or instruction (Lindsay-Hartz et al., 1995). Second, as H. Lewis (1971) notes, there can be domains of unacknowledged, undifferentiated, and bypassed shame, where people are minimally aware of their own experience of shame at the time that they experience it. Third, as Lewis and Scheff suggest, talking about shame (which usually involves revealing feelings of inadequacy, inferiority, and possible badness) may be taboo. Shame can remain unacknowledged because people feel ashamed of their own shame. Fourth, shame may be hard for people to distinguish from other emotions it is closely associated with, especially, for example, embarrassment, humiliation, shyness, social anxiety, or guilt.

Shame and the Management of Identity

Lewis's ideas were derived from psychotherapy transcripts. A broader sociological perspective on the disclosure of shame is provided by Goffman's dramaturgical account of human interaction (Goffman, 1959). Goffman proposed that a fundamental human motive is the maintenance of a person's identity claims in particular interactions. In large part, Goffman's work involves subtle analyses of how this motive manifests itself in multifarious ways in a wide variety of social situations. Although not quite central in Goffman's writing, this fundamental process is seen as driven by the emotions of embarrassment and shame. These are both thought to occur when a person fails to uphold his or her identity claims in a particular situation. In Goffman's words:

> Given the fact that the individual effectively projects a definition of the situation when he enters the presence of others, we can assume that events may occur within the interaction which contradict, discredit, or otherwise throw doubt on this projection. When these disruptive events occur, the interaction itself may come to a confused and embarrassed halt. Some of the assumptions upon which the responses of the participants had been predicated become untenable, and the participants find themselves lodged in an interaction for which the situation has been wrongly defined and is now no longer defined. At such moments the individual whose presentation has been discredited may feel ashamed while the others present may feel hostile, and all the participants may come to feel ill at ease, nonplussed, out of countenance, embarrassed, experiencing the kind of anomaly that is generated when the minute social system of face-to-face interaction breaks down. (Goffman, 1959, p. 23)

Although Goffman did not formally separate shame and embarrassment as we might today (e.g. Miller, 1996), he did write extensively and insightfully on the manifold means employed by people to hide what he calls "destructive information"—information which would cause embarrassment or shame in an encounter were it known by the other interactants. Goffman talks of two core sets of practices which people use to maintain identity in interactions. The first of these is "corrective" and occurs when people act in such a way as to minimize or cover up identity slips that other people make. For example if someone has a stutter, other people would simply carry on the conversation as if nothing embarrassing has occurred. The second set of practices are "preventive"—they consist of our attempts to maintain our own identity claims. In this case, a person might nod sagely and remain silent in order to conceal the fact that they have a stutter. It is into this latter category that the importance of controlling destructive information about oneself belongs. Thus as Goffman put it: "A basic problem for many performances, then, is that of information control; the audience must not acquire destructive information about the situation that is being defined for them."   (1959, p. 26).

In his book, *Stigma: Notes on the management of a spoiled identity*, Goffman makes a distinction between those who have to manage the discomfort of having their shameful qualities exposed for all to see and those who harbor qualities which *if known* would cause them to suffer the shame of exposure:

> The term stigma and its synonyms conceal a double perspective: does the stigmatised individual assume his differentness is known about already or is evident on the spot, or does he assume it is neither known about by those present nor immediately perceivable by them? In the first case one deals with the plight of the *discredited*, in the second of the *discreditable*. (1963, p. 14; italics in original).

This important distinction suggests that shame may operate in different ways depending on whether it is an outcome that has currently been realized, so that the identity a person is projecting has actually been discredited, or whether such an outcome is simply feared (see Andrews, this volume, chapter 9). It is those who fear being discredited who are likely to be motivated to avoid disclosure of their shameful characteristics and to "pass" as normals. Thus much of Goffman's analysis concerns what could be termed "techniques of nondisclosure." Goffman's work gave rise to the study of *facework*, defined as the "artful process of diffusing and managing self-focused emotions and other-focused emotions," key among which are shame and pride (Ting-Toomey, 1994, p. 4). To date the affective underpinnings of facework have been largely neglected by researchers (Ting-Toomey & Cocroft, 1994).

Since Goffman's landmark work, self-presentation and image management have attracted much attention, with a large literature supporting the power of self-presentation (e.g., Leary, 1995). The evidence is now overwhelmingly in favor of humans as image managers, sensitive to the interests of their audience and striving to manage their self-presentations in order to maximize positive approval and minimize disapproval. Strangely, the research on self-presentation has become increasingly separated from the shame literature. There is much, however, that each could gain from the other.

Shame "Acting at a Distance"

For Goffman, it is the *anticipation* of shaming interactions that leads to various forms of hiding and nondisclosure. Goffman's approach contrasts with the focus of more emotion-based work on hiding and nondisclosure, where these reactions arise as a *consequence* of experiencing shame. Tomkins (1963) outlined a dynamic process that takes place between shame which is produced by negative social feedback—a response to the punishing responses of valued others—and shame which is anticipatory. Tomkins proposed that ideoaffective structures, which he called "theories" (in his later work he referred to similar structures as "scripts," Tomkins, 1995), are constructed by individuals around various core affects, and the function of these theories is to guide the interpretation, experience, and reaction to events in one's environment. In the case of negative affects, such as shame, the purpose of the theory is

> to guide action so that negative affect is not experienced. It is affect acting at a distance. Just as human beings can learn to avoid danger, to shun the flame before one is burnt, so also can they learn to avoid shame or fear before they are seared by the experience of such negative affect. (Tomkins, 1963, p. 320–321).

This warning function of the emotions develops in the context of how individuals learn to regard their own emotional experience. Thus, if shame is socialized in what Tomkins calls a "rewarding" fashion (e.g., parents are comforting when a child experiences shame), the affect of shame will not be feared and shunned, and therefore only a weak theory of shame will develop. On the other hand, if the affect of shame is itself punished (e.g., children are ridiculed or punished if they display shame), or if shame is taboo as Scheff (1988) argued, then a strong theory of shame will develop. As a consequence, more will be invested in the development of the emotion as an early warning signal (e.g., of social disapproval or rejection), prompting the person to take avoidant action.

One possible paradoxical effect of a "fear of shame" or "shame of shame" is that the stronger the theory of shame, the less shame may be manifested overtly in interpersonal situations. It is therefore possible that an incapacity to experience shame openly will deprive an individual of any interpersonal benefits that might be associated with the display of shame (see Keltner & Harker, this volume, chapter 4). Tomkins's ideas have been restated in the light of recent cognitive science and applied to the study of transference phenomena by Singer and Singer (1992, 1994). Their 1992 paper contains a useful case study of transference in psychotherapy, drawing on Tomkins's ideas, in which they highlight the fact that emotion scripts function automatically and unconsciously but may be identified in both transference enactments and childhood memories. The function of these scripts is to act as commentaries or cautionary tales (Singer & Salovey, 1993) about the likely consequences of pursuing particular goals. From this perspective, scripts involving shame could be seen as cautionary tales about the pursuit of the goal of being valued by others (see Singer & Singer, 1992). This kind of internalized anticipatory shame is compatible with the low-key and "invisible" experiences of shame that H. Lewis (1971) and Scheff (1988) write about, and it may need to be contrasted with more overt forms of shame (see Keltner & Harker, this volume, chapter 4). Lansky (1995), in a review of psychoanalytic approaches to shame, makes a similar distinction between shame "as a signal of danger to the sense of self among others (the superego anxiety)" and shame as the "searing anguish resulting from exposure as having failed or as being unlovable and deserving rejection or inferior status (the emotion)" (Lansky, 1995, p. 1080). People may generally only be able to articulate what Lansky calls the "emotion" of shame; however, the attempt to articulate and become conscious of scripts or superego states of shame, of which we are only minimally aware, may be one of the major goals of therapy, enabling the client to engage more freely in the pursuit of desired and valuing relationships (Singer & Singer, 1992).

In summary, Goffman (1959, 1963) and Tomkins (1963) have added a further dimension to the treatments of shame considered earlier in this chapter. They suggest that shame can have preemptive functions and, in this capacity, prompt a considerable range of behaviors designed to conceal and protect the self. Such a function has been alluded to by psychoanalytic writers on shame (Lansky, 1995) and may be compatible with the low-visibility unacknowledged shame alluded to by H. Lewis (1971) and Scheff (1988). Preemptive shame of this kind may play a major role in people's decision making. Later in this chapter it will be suggested that anticipatory shame of this kind plays a part in the nondisclosure of emotions more generally.

Empirical Studies of Disclosure and Shame

In the previous sections a robust link was found between shame and concealment at a theoretical level. It remains to be seen to what extent this position is supported empirically.

The Aversive Effects of Embarrassment and Shame

A number of social psychology experiments, which were not intended specifically to look at the inhibitory effects of shame on disclosure, nevertheless imply that the threat or experience of shame diminishes affiliative tendencies. In an early experiment by Sarnoff and Zimbardo, participants were led to believe that they would have to take part in an experiment where they would have "to suck on a number of objects commonly associated with infantile oral behavior" (1961, p. 360), a manipulation which was expected to lead to high anxiety because of the threat of being ridiculed and censured. Subjects in this high-anxiety condition showed a marked decrease in affiliation, as indexed by their desire to wait alone for the supposed investigation rather than in the company of others. In a study of coping, Folkman, Lazarus, Dunkel-Schetter, DeLongis, & Gruen (1986) found that:

> When threat to self-esteem was high, subjects used more confrontive coping, self-control coping, accepted more responsibility, and used more escape-avoidance compared to when threat to self-esteem was low; they also sought less social support.   (Folkman et al., 1986, p. 997)

Brewin, McCarthy, & Furnham (1989) studied the relationship between cognitive appraisals and individuals' self-reported attempts to seek social support. Social withdrawal following a stressful experience was associated with appraisals of low consensus of the negative outcome (i.e., the person felt that other people would not have had such a negative outcome), global self-attributions, and blame of personal inadequacy. As the authors point out, these appraisal dimensions have been linked to the experience of shame, suggesting that social withdrawal was associated with the degree to which the participants felt shame. In a review of self-defeating behavior patterns, Baumeister and Scher (1988) cite a number of studies which demonstrate that people are prepared to sacrifice tangible rewards in order to evade situations where they might lose face. In one such study, subjects were confronted with a trade-off between money and the expectation that they would be exposed to an emotional state in which core features of the self would become salient. As in other studies, subjects preferred to avoid exposure rather than maximize monetary profit (Baumeister & Cooper, 1981). Baumeister and Scher conclude that "the importance of high self-focus and negative affect in causing self-destructive behavior was . . . confirmed, although some further evidence is desirable." (1988, p. 12).

Shamelike or embarrassing predicaments are therefore strong motivators of socially avoidant behavior. In all but the Brewin et al. (1989) study, avoidance was associated with the *threat* of shame or embarrassment. Thus, these studies go some way toward supporting Goffman's view that people will be powerfully motivated to avoid situations in which they might experience shame. This focus, in every study except Brewin et al.'s (1989), on the anticipation of shame or embarrassment might be why the word *shame* is not used by these authors (although Baumeister and Scher, 1988, mention embarrassment). As suggested above, such anticipatory shame may be particularly invisible, occurring only momentarily in consciousness. Given this, and the fact that shame and embarrassment are distinct affective states (Edelmann, 1995; Miller & Tangney, 1994), it is obviously desirable to have more direct evidence on the role of shame in socially avoidant behavior.

Studies of Shame

Lindsay-Hartz (1984; Lindsay-Hartz et al., 1995) interviewed 19 people about their experiences of shame and guilt. She found that all of the interviewees who described an experience of shame "emphasised that they felt a desire to hide and 'get out' of the interpersonal situation in which they found themselves" (1984, p. 692). This desire to escape she relates to the fact that the negative self-image of the person who is ashamed "is experienced as a social reality" (1984, p. 698). As she puts it, "If others cannot see us, and if we can even hide from ourselves, then we have no social reality" (1984, p. 698). Lindsay-Hartz's findings are consistent with a study by Frijda, Kuipers, & ter Schure (1989) in which the authors attempted to predict the names of 16 different emotions recalled by 60 subjects from questions about the action tendencies of those emotions. Positive responses to a question about wishing to disappear from view distinguished shame from the other emotions. A pilot interview study of ten psychotherapy patients (Macdonald & Tantam, 1994) found some evidence of social avoidance in the wake of shamelike experiences (such as being in a social situation where one wanted to hide or disappear and feeling humiliated by other people). It was found that in 88% of cases participants expressed concern about the negative characteristics they revealed in the situations they described—suggesting that, at least according to the criteria adopted by H. Lewis (1971), they were experiencing shame. Seventy percent of the responses to a question about how they behaved afterward mentioned some form of social avoidance, and in 72% of the responses to the question "was there anything you wanted to hide or conceal?" the subject mentioned something they wanted to conceal. Given the fact that this collection of narratives included a number of experiences that did not appear to be experiences of shame, the data does suggest a high association between shame, or shamelike, experiences and socially avoidant and hiding behavior.

"Social Sharing" of Shame

The research considered so far has focused on the participants' experience of wanting to hide or conceal themselves at the time that they felt the shame. Both the theory and the research suggests that shame is unlikely to be disclosed voluntarily to others at the time that it is happening. However, an important secondary question concerns whether people are prepared to talk about their shame afterward. Goffman's (1963) theory suggests that people would on the whole be motivated to avoid the disclosure of potentially discrediting experiences. This assumption is apparently confirmed in a study by Shimanoff (1984), in which references to emotion words in conversations by college students and married couples were analyzed; it was found that shame was among the least frequently mentioned emotions (along with grief, loneliness, pride, and resentment). While fitting in with the theoretical perspectives reviewed earlier, for instance, Scheff's proposal that shame is profoundly taboo, this finding may of course simply reflect the fact that people do not talk about shame in an everyday conversational context or when they are being tape-recorded. However, nondisclosure carries with it the risk that one will be found out and in the process lose control of how negative information about the self is presented. Additionally, if we acknowledge our shame, we are signaling a susceptibility to social control, which may be appeasing (Keltner & Harker, this volume, chapter 4) and lead to increased acceptance.

Research by Rimé and his colleagues (Rimé, Mesquita, Philippot, & Boca, 1991; Rimé et al., 1996) has established that generally everyday emotional experiences are associated with "social sharing" after the event—people generally tell someone else about the emotional experiences they have had. Summarizing the results of a number of retrospective studies of social sharing, which included 913 participants whose age ranged between 12 and 60 years and covered 1384 emotional episodes, the "observed proportion of cases in which subjects reported having talked with people about the emotional episode varied from 90 to 96.3% of the sample, according to the study" (Rimé et al., 1996, p. 4). Shame was included in a number of these studies. Rimé et al. (1991) asked 87 participants to describe shame, anger, sadness, fear, or happiness experiences, after which they were asked to fill in a social-sharing questionnaire. Contrary to the authors' expectations, shame did not differ from the other emotions in either the proportion of social sharing or the manner in which they were shared. Thus it was found that for shame, as for the other emotions, the subjects reported, in more than 50% of cases, that their first sharing of the experience involved giving the other person a full account of what happened, telling the other persons what the event had meant, and telling the other person how the subject had felt. However, the study did reveal some differences between shame and the other emotions. First, shame was discussed less than other emotions with acquaintances, colleagues, and parents, so that the recipient of social sharing was more likely to be a partner, friend, or sibling. Second, the social sharing was less likely to take place with "the first person encountered right after the event" (Rimé et al., 1991, p. 448). Thus, evidence from this study suggests that while people *are* prepared to share their experiences of shame, they are also more cautious and selective about whom they do it with, generally choosing equal-status intimates. Shame was also included in the basic emotions investigated by Rimé et al. (1996) in two prospective diary investigations of social sharing. In the first of these studies, no differences in social sharing were found between shame and other emotions in a sample of 41 female students. However, in the second study, a replication and extension of the first, there was a nonsignificant trend for shame to be less socially shared *on the day the emotion happened* (25% compared with the overall average of 58%). There were only 8 instances of shame among the 459 emotions recalled overall, and unfortunately no data was presented about social sharing *after* the day that the emotion took place. It may well be that, in line with Rimé et al.'s (1991) finding, shame was simply shared later and more selectively. Overall, the evidence from Rimé and his colleagues suggests that, surprisingly in view of the association between shame and hiding, people do talk about their experiences of shame, but they take care about whom they tell.

Rimé and his colleagues studied social sharing in nondistressed populations, and their research paradigm was designed to elicit typical rather than extreme emotional experiences. However, there is some evidence that shame may be disclosed even when it is extremely distressing. An unpublished interview and questionnaire study by Terwijn (1993), in which 46 respondents were asked to describe the "worst shame" in their lives, included a number of questions about the disclosure of the experience to others. Terwijn found that 60% of her respondents had talked about their experience with one or more others; of these, 18% had talked to a therapist, although, in line with Lewis's (1971) findings, they had not all, apparently, used the word *shame*. The experience was generally not disclosed to the individuals who were most involved in the participants' shame, a factor which Terwijn linked with lack of resolution of the shame experience. Shame may also be disclosed to the same extent as other unpleasant emotions by psychologically distressed people. A diary study by Macdonald, Duncan, Morley, & Gladwell (1997) compared the disclosure of instances of shame, guilt, hatred, and disgust experienced by 38 psychotherapy patients in the week after their assessment interviews. Although overall social sharing was considerably less than in Rimé's samples—interestingly, only 32% of the emotions were disclosed—shame did not appear to be less shared than the other emotions. It was found that 29.4% of the instances of shame were shared, compared with 29.2% of the guilt, 45% of the hatred, and 21.4% of the disgust instances. Once again, when it comes to talking about the emotion after the event, shame does not appear to be less disclosed than other emotions. However, in this study, shame was rated as being more *difficult* to disclose.

Disclosure of Shame in Research Interviews

Parallel evidence relating to disclosure of shame after the event is provided by the extent to which participants in research interviews are willing to reveal their shame. Lindsay-Hartz (1984) found that, in contrast to describing experiences of guilt, her respondents had greater difficulty and more resistance to describing experiences of shame. Apparently, responses such as, "I know I've felt ashamed, but I can't think of any specific examples" (p. 691) and "Well, I can think of an example, but I don't think I want to tell you about it" (p. 691) were characteristic of this reticence. However, Lindsay-Hartz *was* able to obtain accounts of shame from her respondents. She concludes: "If one does not ask, one does not find out about such experiences (p. 693)."

Terwijn (1993) employed an ingenious procedure both for recruiting participants and for enabling them to talk about their shame. Terwijn initially asked people in an Amsterdam library if they would fill in an "Emotion Memories Questionnaire," which asked respondents if they had ever felt a particular range of emotions, and if they were prepared to talk in more detail about one emotional episode. One third of the people who filled in the questionnaire agreed to do this. Participants were then asked to come to the laboratory, where the true focus of the study was explained. Then, using a method developed by Pennebaker, Hughes, & O'Heeron (1987), they were left alone in a dimly lit room equipped with a tape recorder and asked to describe in detail their experience of shame. Following this, they filled in a questionnaire asking them specific questions about their experience. Terwijn reports that most participants found that this was a good experience (and indeed some of them apparently found that the experience helped them to come to terms with their shame).

Andrews and her colleagues (Andrews, 1995; Andrews & Hunter, 1997) asked both community and psychiatric samples whether they had ever felt ashamed of their bodies, character, or behavior, both at the time of the interview and at other times in their lives. If they responded positively to any of these questions, they were asked to describe their feelings in detail. These researchers found that people were apparently quite willing to answer questions of this nature.

Finally, in two interview studies conducted with a total of 32 psychotherapy patients, most participants were willing to talk about experiences of shame, although in two cases the patients refused to talk about particular incidents that had come to mind (Macdonald & Tantam, 1994). Three themes emerged from comments made by interviewees in this latter study, which may have been associated with patients' willingness to disclose. First, the disclosure was taking place in an environment which was effectively sealed off from their normal day-to-day lives. It was stressed that the interviews were confidential, and that, if any portions were quoted in a final report of research, care would be taken to remove any details which might identify the subjects. Second, a number of participants said that they were eager to assist in research that might benefit other people who suffered distress similar to their own. As one participant said, "I'm stuck the way I am, ah, so maybe anything I say might help a little bit in research, might be able to help somebody else." Third, some of the participants indicated that talking about their experiences of shame made them feel somewhat better. Indeed, one participant said that it didn't matter what he was asked; he had come to the interview intending to talk about a situation in his life which it turned out had caused him a considerable amount of shame. Another factor, which none of the participants referred to but which may well have been important in the participants' decision to disclose, was that it was made very clear that no pressure would be put on participants to reveal anything they chose not to. It seems likely that this element of control was useful in reducing their anxieties about being exposed.

Recent research on shame has therefore tended to demonstrate that people are willing to talk about shame, at least in a research setting, when they are asked directly. It may be that the interviewer has to provide the word *shame* before individuals volunteer their experience as such. Indeed, although many of the participants in Terwijn's study had spoken about the experiences where they had felt the worst shame in their lives, they generally had not actually used the word *shame*. Perhaps, in addition to offering the word *shame*, the researchers are conveying the message that the individuals can be understood and accepted in spite of their shame.

Anticipated Shame and Emotional Disclosure

Recent research has suggested that shame may play a role in the nondisclosure of negative emotional experiences generally. There has been a considerable body of research in recent years which has demonstrated that people benefit from disclosing disturbing emotional experiences to others (e.g. Pennebaker & Beall, 1986; Pennebaker, 1993). Explanations of this phenomenon have concentrated on two intrapsychic factors. First, it is assumed that undisclosed emotions require inhibition, which is effortful and therefore costly to the individual (e.g., Traue, 1995). Second, the benefits are thought to reflect the extent to which disclosure facilitates the assimilation of the disturbing emotion to the individual's knowledge structures prior to the disturbing experience (e.g., Pennebaker & Francis, 1996). This process of cognitive assimilation has also been invoked to explain the mechanism of emotional change in psychotherapy (Stiles et al., 1990). However, as Kelly and McKillop (1996) have pointed out, so far there has been little attempt to map out the social dimensions and implications of disclosure, perhaps because much of the research to date has involved written disclosure that takes place when the participant is alone (e.g., Pennebaker & Beall, 1986). Kelly and McKillop make the point that disclosure does not normally occur in a vacuum and that the qualities of the recipient of the disclosure are unavoidably central in evaluating the benefits of disclosure. Indeed, even written disclosure in psychological studies takes place within a context in which there is an implicit permissiveness, in addition to the trustworthiness conveyed in the emphasis on confidentiality. In their paper, Kelly and McKillop survey a range of studies which suggest that in a great many instances recipients of disclosures may respond in ways that are damaging to the confidant. For instance, they cite research that suggests that people who have experienced traumas are likely to receive unsatisfactory responses when they relate their experience to others; and they point out that because people construct their identities through interactions with others, in such cases disclosure could lead to the construction of a negative identity. This more social perspective on disclosure implies that social emotions such as shame and guilt may influence the decision to disclose or withhold confidences.

Work by Finkenauer and her colleagues (Finkenauer & Rimé, 1996; Finkenauer, Rimé, & Lerot, 1996) suggests that the social emotions of shame and guilt do indeed play an important role in the inhibition of emotional experiences that are not socially shared. Finkenauer and Rimé (1996) aimed to examine factors which might underlie the nondisclosure of the 10% or less of emotions which, according to the research on social sharing (Rimé et al., 1991; Rimé et al., 1996), are not disclosed to others. They asked participants to recall an important emotional episode that they had never told anyone and one which they had shared with another person. They found that while emotional secrecy was not associated with the intensity or traumatic nature of the emotional experience, it was associated with the degree to which secret episodes elicited shame, guilt, and perceptions of responsibility. On the basis of these results, the authors proposed a social model of secrecy, in which nondisclosure of emotional experiences was hypothesized to result largely from the projected personal and interpersonal consequences of disclosure. Finkenauer et al. (1996) explored this idea in a study in which participants were interviewed following an induction in which they were asked to imagine either an important negative event that they would have kept secret or one that they would have shared. Results indicated that compared with the shared emotional experience the secret one was associated with the perception of social threat. Furthermore, the anticipation of revealing the secret elicited significantly more shame, guilt, embarrassment, and unease than subjects in the sharing condition anticipated they would feel the first time they shared their emotional event. In these studies, nondisclosure is thus associated with shame evoked by the anticipation of disclosure.

In Macdonald et al.'s (1997) diary study, participants who had not disclosed an emotion were asked, "did the thought of telling anybody make you feel any shame?" A very high proportion, 90.9% (10 of 11 undisclosed episodes), of the responses to this question were positive when the emotion itself was shame. However, 72.7% (8 of 11) of the instances of undisclosed hatred, 66.7% (12 of 18) of the instances of undisclosed guilt, and 54.5% (6 of 11) of the instances of undisclosed disgust were also accompanied by shame of this nature. This suggests that anticipatory shame may have played a part in over half of the undisclosed instances of guilt, hatred, and disgust. Participants were also asked questions in follow-up interviews about why they had chosen not to disclose. Qualitative data from these interviews is consistent with Finkenauer's social model of secrecy. Thus, references to shame and embarrassment about the experience, such as "I felt ashamed of the way I felt" or "I feel as though there's something wrong with me, because I feel like that" were accompanied by many references to how the participants imagined disclosure of their emotions would have negative interpersonal consequences; for instance, "anybody else I may, or try to talk to that I know may end up telling me to stop being so stupid" or "it's depressing, and I really don't feel I ought to burden people with my depression" (Macdonald et al., 1997, p. 13).

These studies illustrate that shame associated with the projected interpersonal consequences of an action is also associated with inhibition of that action (in this case the disclosure of emotional experiences). This is highly congruent with both Goffman's (1959, 1963) analysis of dealing with destructive personal information and Tomkins's (1963) model of shame acting "at a distance" in order to preempt higher intensity experiences of shame. These studies also supplement the existing literature on the dynamics of disclosing negative emotional experiences by emphasizing the role of the projected interpersonal consequences of disclosure, including shame, in the decision to disclose. Indeed, it is possible that the increased cognitive organization and narrative coherence that has been associated with beneficial disclosure (Pennebaker, 1990; Pennebaker & Francis, 1996) is itself related to the degree to which the participants become able to account for their experience in a way that does justice both to the actual events and to the survival of an identity which is not strangulated by shame or guilt, as H. Lewis (1987) has suggested.

Conclusion

There is evidence to suggest that the action tendency of shame is one of hiding and concealment (Frijda et al., 1989; Lindsay-Hartz, 1984; Macdonald & Tantam, 1994). Further evidence suggests that the threat of being embarrassed or ashamed leads to socially avoidant behavior (Baumeister & Scher, 1988; Folkman et al., 1986; Sarnoff & Zimbardo, 1961;). However, it does not appear to be the case that people will automatically avoid talking about their experiences following a shaming event. Rimé and his colleagues (Rimé et al., 1991; Rimé et al., 1996) have shown that shame is regularly shared, though more selectively than other emotions. Even very severe experiences of shame were found to have been disclosed in Terwijn's (1993) study. Macdonald et al. (1997) found that experiences of shame were not disclosed to a lesser degree than other emotions in a psychologically distressed sample, although shame appeared to be harder to disclose. Participants in studies of shame have generally been willing to reveal their experiences of shame in a research setting (e.g., Andrews, 1995; Lindsay-Hartz, 1984; Macdonald & Tantam, 1994). It was suggested that many experiences of shame involve minimal awareness and that these forms of shame might function as warning signals that play an important role in decision making (cf. Goffman, 1959; Tomkins, 1963). A small number of studies provide preliminary evidence that shame of this kind may play an important part in the decision to disclose negative emotional experiences in general (Finkenauer & Rimé, 1996; Macdonald et al., 1997). So far, little research attention has been paid to the supposed therapeutic effects of disclosing experiences of shame (e.g., H. Lewis, 1971), and exploration of the possible benefit or harm associated with the disclosure of shame in therapeutic contexts awaits future research.

Acknowledgments   The author would like to thank P. Gilbert and B. Andrews for many helpful comments on earlier drafts of this chapter.

References

Andrews, B. (1995). Bodily shame as a mediator between abusive experiences and depression. *Journal of Abnormal Psychology, 104* (2), 277–285.

Andrews, B., & Hunter, E. (1997). Shame, early abuse and course of depression in a clinical sample: A preliminary study. *Cognition and Emotion, 11*, 373–381.

Barrett, K. C. (1995). A functionalist approach to shame and guilt. In J. P. Tangney & K. W. Fischer (Eds.), *Self-conscious emotions: The psychology of shame, guilt, embarrassment and pride* (pp. 25–63). New York: Guilford Press.

Baumeister, R. F., & Cooper, J. (1981). Can the public expectation of emotion cause that emotion? *Journal of Personality, 49, 49–59.*

Baumeister, R. F., & Scher, S. J. (1988). Self-defeating behavior patterns among normal individuals: Review and analysis of common self-destructive tendencies. *Psychological Bulletin, 104* (1), 3–22.

Brewin, C. R., MacCarthy, B., & Furnham, A. (1989). Social support in the face of adversity: The role of cognitive appraisal. *Journal of Research in Personality, 23*, 354–372.

Edelmann, R. (1995, April). *Embarrassment and shame: Related or discrete constructs?*

Paper presented at the annual conference of the British Psychological Society, Warwick, United Kingdom.

Finkenauer, C., & Rimé, B. (1996). Emotionelle Geheimnisse: Determinanten und konsequenzen (Emotional secrecy: Determinants and consequences). In A. Spitznagel (Ed.), *Geheimnis—Geheimhaltung*. Gottingen: Hogrefe. [English version available from first author.]

Finkenauer, C., Rimé, B., & Lerot, S. (1996, July). *A social model of secrecy*. Paper presented at the 11th general meeting of the European Association of Experimental Social Psychology, Gmunden, Austria.

Fischer, K. W., & Tangney, J. P. (1995). Self-conscious emotions and the affect revolution: Framework and overview. In J. P. Tangney & K. Fischer (Eds.), *Self-Conscious emotions: The psychology of shame, guilt, embarrassment and pride* (pp. 3–22). New York: Guilford Press.

Folkman, S., Lazarus, R. S., Dunkel-Schetter, C., DeLongis, A., & Gruen, R. (1986). Dynamics of a stressful encounter: Cognitive appraisal, coping, and encounter outcomes. *Journal of Personality and Social Psychology, 50*, 992–1003.

Frijda, N., Kuipers, P., & ter Schure, E. (1989). Relations among emotion, appraisal, and emotional action readiness. *Journal of Personality and Social Psychology, 57* (2), 212–228.

Gilbert, P. (1997). The evolution of social attractiveness and its role in shame, humiliation, guilt and therapy. *British Journal of Medical Psychology, 70*, 113–147.

Goffman, E. (1959). *The presentation of self in everyday life*. Harmondsworth: Penguin.

Goffman, E. (1963). *Stigma: Notes on the management of a spoiled identity*. London: Penguin.

Kelly, A. E., & McKillop, K. J. (1996). Consequences of revealing personal secrets. *Psychological Bulletin, 120* (3), 450–465.

Lansky, M. R. (1995). Shame and the scope of psychoanalytic understanding. *American Behavioral Scientist, 38* (8), 1076–1090.

Lazarus, R. S. (1991). *Emotion and adaptation*. New York: Oxford University Press.

Leary, M. R. (1995). *Self-Presentation: Impression management and interpersonal behavior*. Madison, WF: Brown & Benchmark.

Lewis, H. B. (1971). *Shame and guilt in neurosis*. New York: International Universities Press.

Lewis, H. B. (1987). Shame—the "sleeper" in psychopathology. In H. B. Lewis (Ed.), *The role of shame in symptom formation* (pp. 1–28). Hillsdale, NJ: Erlbaum.

Lewis, H. B. (1990). Shame, repression, field dependence, and psychopathology. In J. L. Singer (Ed.), *Repression and dissociation* (pp. 233–258). Chicago: University of Chicago Press.

Lewis, M. (1992). *Shame: The exposed self*. New York: The Free press.

Lindsay-Hartz, J. (1984). Contrasting experiences of shame and guilt. *American Behavioral Scientist, 27* (6), 689–704.

Lindsay-Hartz, J., de Rivera, J., & Mascolo, M. F. (1995). Differentiating guilt and shame and their effects on motivation. In J. P. Tangney & K. W. Fischer (Eds.), *Self-Conscious emotions: The psychology of shame, guilt, embarrassment and pride* (pp. 274–300). New York: Guilford Press.

Macdonald, J., Duncan, E., Morley, I., & Gladwell, S. (1997, March). A diary and interview study of the experience and disclosure of shame, guilt, hatred and disgust by psychotherapy patients. Paper presented at the annual conference of the Society for Psychotherapy Research, Ravenscar, United Kingdom.

Macdonald, J., & Tantam, D. (1994). Pilot interview study of shame experienced in the lives of psychotherapy patients. Unpublished study.

Miller, R. S. (1996). *Embarrassment: Poise and peril in everyday life*. New York: Guilford Press.

Miller, R. S., & Tangney, J. P. (1994). Differentiating embarrassment and shame. *Journal of Social and Clinical Psychology, 13* (3), 273–287.

Pennebaker, J. W. (1990). *Opening up: The healing power of confiding in others.* New York: Morrow.

Pennebaker, J. W. (1993). Overcoming inhibition: Rethinking the roles of personality, cognition, and social behavior. In H. C. Traue & J. W. Pennebaker (Eds.), *Emotion, inhibition and health* (pp. 100–115). Toronto: Hogrefe & Huber.

Pennebaker, J. W., & Beall, S. K. (1986). Confronting a traumatic event: Towards an understanding of inhibition and disease. *Journal of Abnormal Psychology, 95,* (3), 274–281.

Pennebaker, J. W., & Francis, M. E. (1996). Cognitive, emotional, and language processes in disclosure. *Cognition and Emotion, 10* (6), 601–626.

Pennebaker, J. W., Hughes, C. F., & O'Heeron, R. C. (1987). The psychophysiology of confession: Linking inhibitory and psychosomatic processes. *Journal of Personality and Social Psychology, 52,* 781–793.

Retzinger, S. (1991). *Violent emotions: Shame and rage in marital quarrels.* Newbury Park, CA: Sage.

Rimé, B., Mesquita, B., Philippot, P., & Boca, S. (1991). Beyond the emotional event: Six studies on the social sharing of emotion. *Cognition and Emotion, 5* (5/6), 435–465.

Rimé, B., Philippot, P., Finkenauer, C., Legast, S., Moorkens, P., & Tornqvist, J. (1996). *Mental rumination and social sharing in emotion.* Manuscript submitted for publication.

Sarnoff, I., & Zimbardo, P. G. (1961). Anxiety, fear, and social affiliation. *Journal of Abnormal and Social Psychology, 62* (2), 356–363.

Scheff, T. J. (1987). The shame-rage spiral: a case study of an interminable quarrel. In H. B. Lewis (Ed.), *The role of shame in symptom formation* (pp. 109–149). Hillsdale, NJ: Erlbaum.

Scheff, T. J. (1988). Shame and conformity: The deference-emotion system. *American Review of Sociology, 53,* 395–406.

Scheff, T. J. (1990). Socialization of emotions: Pride and shame as causal agents. In T. Kemper (Ed.), *Research agendas in the social emotions* (pp. 281–304). Albany, NY: State University of New York Press.

Scheff, T. J. (1995). Conflict in family systems: The role of shame. In J. P. Tangney & K. W. Fischer (Eds.), *Self-Conscious emotions: The psychology of shame, guilt, embarrassment and pride* (pp. 393–412). New York: Guilford Press.

Shimanoff, S. B. (1984). Commonly named emotions in everyday conversations. *Perceptual and Motor Skills, 58,* 514.

Singer, J. A., & Salovey, P. (1993). *The remembered self: emotion and memory in personality.* New York: Free Press.

Singer, J. A., & Singer, J. L. (1992). Transference in psychotherapy and daily life: Implications of current memory and social cognition research. In J. W. Barron, M. N. Eagle, & D. L. Wolitsky (Eds.), *Interface of psychoanalysis and psychology* (pp. 516–537). Washington, DC: American Psychological Association.

Singer, J. A., & Singer, J. L. (1994). Social-cognitive and narrative perspectives on transference. In J. Masling & R. Bornstein (Eds.), *Empirical perspectives on object relations theory* (pp. 157–193). Washington, DC: American Psychological Association.

Stiles, W. B., Elliott, R., Llewelyn, S. P., Firth-Cozens, J. A.. Margison, F. R., Shapiro, D. A., & Hardy, G. (1990). Assimilation of problematic experiences by clients in psychotherapy. *Psychotherapy, 27* (3), 411–420.

Terwijn, H. (1993). *An emotion theoretical approach to shame: A study of shame experiences.* Unpublished masters thesis, University of Amsterdam.

Ting-Toomey, S. (1994). Face and facework: An introduction. In S. Ting-Toomey (Ed.), *The challenge of facework: Cross-cultural and interpersonal Issues* (1–14). New York: State University of New York Press.

Ting-Toomey, S., & Cocroft, B. (1994). Face and facework: Theoretical and research issues. In S. Ting-Toomey (Ed.), *The challenge of facework: Cross-cultural and interpersonal issues* (307–340). New York: State University of New York Press.

Tomkins, S. S. (1963). *Affect, imagery, consciousness: Vol. 2. The negative affects.* New York: Springer.

Tomkins, S. S. (1995). Script theory. In E. Demos (Ed.), *Exploring affect: The selected writings of Silvan S. Tomkins.* (pp. 312–388) Cambridge: Cambridge University Press.

Traue, H. C. (1995). Inhibition and muscle tension in myogenic pain. In J. Pennebaker (Ed.), *Emotion, disclosure and health* (pp. 155–176). Washington, DC: American Psychological Association.

Wicker, F. W., Payne, G. C., & Morgan, R. D. (1983). Participant descriptions of guilt and shame. *Motivation and Emotion, 7,* 25–39.

PART III

PSYCHOPATHOLOGY

8

The Emotional Disorders
of Shame

Digby Tantam

Dick was a runner. He would set himself goals which shocked other runners, so demanding did they seem. He became something of a celebrity and even became an exemplar for others. He laughed about recreating a network of runners taking documents from place to place, and his friends took him seriously and pushed him into starting a business. It surprised him by being successful, and he felt increasingly resentful of the demands that it made of him. He felt obliged to these friends who had given him money to start it up, and he considered that, as he had played some sort of role all his life, he might as well carry on playing the role of businessman. But after a year of attending meetings, taking messages, issuing invoices, and occasionally running (he had, by now, taken on other people to do much of the actual running), he began to come in late and finally sold the business at much below its probable value, returning himself to live on welfare.

This was one in a series of fresh starts that Dick had made, all of them ending in him withdrawing or making himself unavailable despite other people's interest in him and what he had to offer. It was true of Dick's forays into competitive sport, into treatment, and into an intimate relationship with a female partner. All of these began successfully, but, once other people began to place their confidence in him, Dick dropped out. Dick felt himself to be two people: the social person that everyone else saw, and the self that only he knew. The social self was what other people wanted, and even admired, but Dick could get no satisfaction from this. He experienced himself putting on an act to avoid criticism by doing what other people expected of him. His true self had to be kept secret. Dick had become very good at keeping it so, and now he only showed himself in casual encounters with strangers. Even then, he agonized over the harm that he may have done, for he saw himself as inherently destructive.

Dick was referred to me because he suspected that he had Asperger syndrome, a type of autism. He avoided gaze, and took this to be a symptom of the disorder. He had previously seen a psychiatrist for his anxiety symptoms and had counseling for over a year. The first time that Dick came to see me he wanted to be seen in a different room, explaining that he had only at the last minute decided to come, was sure that nothing useful would be gained by coming, and was even more sure that nothing would be gained if we stayed in the room that I had chosen. He seemed cool, ironic, and very much together.

Dick had sufficient anxiety symptoms to make a diagnosis of anxiety disorder. An additional diagnosis might be self-defeating personality disorder (American Psychiatric Association, 1987), if the emphasis were placed on Dick's throwing away his chances. This diagnosis would also fit Dick's recklessness for his own personal safety: many of his running exploits stretched him to the limit and put him in danger of falls or accidents. Dick could also be diagnosed legitimately as having narcissistic personality disorder, if the emphasis were placed on Dick's need to control the interview and his perception of himself as uncontainably destructive. Schizoid personality disorder is another plausible diagnosis, based on Dick's social isolation and his preference for social withdrawal as a means of coping with anxiety.

A psychotherapeutic formulation might be that Dick, through repeated assumption of blame for situations that went wrong, had developed a schema of himself as both powerful and damaging. Some evidence for this was Dick's belief that he could see into other people, through their social selves, and into their secrets. Furthermore, Dick believed that when other people realized that he knew, they rejected him because of what he had done wrong by intruding into them.

An alternative psychotherapeutic formulation might be that, first, Dick was incapable of intimacy because the care that he had received as an infant had been wrong for him; and second, that he had overcome this by developing a false self capable of superficial closeness, which, however, proved insufficient to sustain a deeper relationship over a longer period. There was evidence for this formulation, too, in that Dick had never had a true friend. He had moved so as to put the greatest distance between himself and his parents and rarely contacted them. He was no closer to his sister and could not understand why she kept up relations with their parents herself. He attributed his lack of warm feelings toward them to the constant physical punishment that he had received at their hands and remembered occasions when his mother had struck him over and over again until he had not dared move. Knowing this, a psychoanalytically influenced therapist might refine the formulation to include unexpressed rage that had to be constantly repressed, but still leaked out and gave rise to anxiety symptoms.

Each of the accounts that I have given of Dick addresses many of his symptoms, and several provide a plausible explanation of them. None of them are couched in the terms that Dick himself might use of his own experience: they are all very much another person's view.[1] Dick's expressed concern was about the presence or absence of autism, a suspicion that Dick based on his inability to meet another person's gaze; but behind that was his experience that very often he wanted to be out of sight, particularly out of the sight of anyone that he knew.

The conjunction of a negative judgment of oneself by others, an acceptance that it is justified, and an urge to hide oneself and one's fault away constitutes "being ashamed." Dick's account of himself was chosen because it is more than usually expressive of these three elements. But Dick's account also express how shame can become the organizer of a person's narrative about him-or herself, their "script" (Nathanson, 1987), and that the narrative may conceal shame as well as reveal it. Dick constantly returned to the theme of the impossibility of therapy because he could not help but hide his true feelings, his true self, from the therapist. This has implications both for noncompliance with treatment, including resistance to self-understanding, and for the design of treatment methods that are specific for shame. These implications will be considered again in a final section in this chapter.

Shame and Guilt

Clinicians are familiar with guilt as an explanation for behavior and know that shame and guilt are both associated with wrongdoing, but they may be less familiar with the specifics of shame. Many clinical discussions about shame-based disorders begin with the question, "What is the difference between shame and guilt?" Many differences have been suggested—guilt applies to actions, shame to the self (Lewis, 1975); guilt accrues to voluntary action, shame may be conferred by one's status, one's body, or by another's actions if one is identified with them; guilt never has a positive connotation, but shame does (compare guiltless and shameless as epithets); and anxiety is less strongly associated with shame than with guilt (but see Andrews elsewhere in this volume). Despite these and other published distinctions, the two concepts continue to be conflated by practitioners and by patients/ clients. This suggests that the difficulties are more fundamental than it appears.

> Jean had married in haste and repented at leisure. Her husband was stingy with money, given to flying into a rage, and had difficulty in sustaining an erection. Adding some kink to their lovemaking often helped the latter problem, but doing so often left Jean feeling used. Jean eventually met another man but felt that she could not leave her husband because they had two young children. So she began an affair, saying later to her therapist that she had always felt guilty about this.

Jean had broken a commitment and caused other people grief, and she thought that there was a price set on this. Paying this back—expiation—required that she suffer herself and that she, too, experience loss. The divorce settlement was not favorable to her, and one of her daughters elected to live with her father. So Jean did have to make sacrifices. She also set herself to making as good a new home as she could so that her daughters would suffer as little as possible. After some years, she was able to conclude that she had done enough and suffered enough, that she no longer need feel guilty. However, she felt continued anxiety and became short-tempered. She became increasingly sensitive to what she saw as her mother's rejection of her, something which she realized had been long-standing but previously overlooked. She was distressed, too, that she could not get as close to her new partner as she had expected. As her conversations with her therapist developed, Jean spoke of continuing to keep it a secret from her daughters that she had had a relationship with their stepfather before her marriage ended. She also spoke of several incidents with her mother and her ex-husband in which she had been treated as not being of any account and felt unable to make herself matter to either of them. At times she felt enraged by this, but at other times she felt that she had been to blame because she had always tended to hide her feelings.

As in Dick, so in Jean: the elements of "being ashamed"—perceived negative judgments by others, acceptance by the self that these judgments are justified, and an urge to hide—were present for Jean, too, but coexisted with guilt. The movement of the therapy from guilt issues to shame issues represented, at least so far as the therapist was concerned, a refocusing of treatment on the issues which Jean had up to then been avoiding and which had therefore undermined her adaptation to the divorce. The beliefs that were associated with shame—about her value to others, about whether she would be "heard" by them—were more central to herself, more closely linked with other fundamental beliefs about herself, than were the beliefs about the marriage contract, which were associated with guilt (see Gardos & Cole, 1980; Niedenthal, Tangney, & Gavanski, 1994, for a similar conceptual analysis). Jean could get rid of the guilt by confessing it and then by reparative action. She felt that she could never overcome her rejection by her mother, and one might hypothesize that to get rid of the beliefs that maintained her shame would have required her to tear out beliefs that constituted the fabric of herself. Indeed, I shall argue later that this may be required.

Jean's case is consistent with most psychoanalytic accounts of shame and guilt which place the development of shame at the time of the development of self-consciousness and the development of guilt: at the onset of latency, when the child internalizes rules of social conduct. Weiss (O'Connor, Berry, Weiss, Bush, & Sampson, 1997) has extended the term *guilt* to include reactions to traumatic experience, such as separation or surviving a trauma that affects other family members. O'Connor et al., (1997) have developed an Interpersonal Guilt Questionnaire which includes these items, but field testing indicates that there is considerable correlation with shame scores on other scales, as well as with guilt scores.

Shame and Humiliation

Jean only referred to shame once, in connection with her concealment of her infidelity from her daughters. She talked about her humiliation by her husband and her mother's rejection of her, but not of being shamed by them. Humiliation (Gilbert, 1997) is associated with two of the three elements of the shame situation: negative judgment by others and the wish to hide humiliation or to hide from humiliation (see table 8.1). Unlike in shame, there is no acceptance that the negative judgment is justified, and so no reevaluation of oneself is necessary; indeed, there may be a strong motive to make the other give up their negative judgment. There need be a minimum of reappraisal, and the maximum attention can be given to solutions to the problem, which might range from avoidance to revenge. It is possible to look forward to a moment when one can stop hiding and be able to say,

Table 8.1 The Family of Self-Conscious Emotions and Their Relation to the
Three Responses to Shame

Self-Conscious Emotion	Perception that Others Find Fault with Self	Perception of Self as at Fault	Hiding to Cope with Fault
Shame	+	+	+
Guilt	+	+	
Depression		+	+
Embarrassment			+
Humiliation	+		+

A plus sign indicates the emotion is present.

"I'll show them." Shame offers no such simple solutions. To be shamed is to be stopped in one's tracks. There appears to be no end to the need to hide, because no reversal of the negative judgment seems possible.

Shame and Depression

There is a connection between shame and the occurrence of depressive disorder (Gilbert, 1992; see this volume, chapter 10), and there are links between being ashamed and being depressed. Social withdrawal is a sensitive indicator of depressive disorder, as is negative self-appraisal. What is different from shame is that others' judgments are less negative. This may not be true of chronic depression, when a person may be judged to have failed to make sufficient effort to improve.

Erica was in her 60s and had lost her husband some years before. He had left her a thriving business, and after a decent time she met someone else and married him. This marriage was less successful than her first, and the couple split up. Erica developed low mood, early morning waking, and loss of appetite. She was treated with antidepressants, but her condition failed to improve, and she took an overdose of tablets. In the hospital, she avoided contact with the other patients and did not want to see her children. She had to be persuaded to leave her bed, where she preferred to lie with the curtains around her. She talked of suicide often. She said that she had let her children down and that she had betrayed her first husband by marrying a man who had taken her money and would throw it away. Her daughters argued with her, as did most of the hospital staff, saying that her second husband had seemed a nice man and that it was quite appropriate that she wanted a companion for her old age. Erica appeared unable to listen to these points of view, saying—sometimes repeatedly in a kind of moan—that she had done wrong.

She failed to respond to high doses of antidepressants at first, but then spent a weekend with one of her daughters, who told her that her long illness was beginning to have a bad effect on the family and that the grandchildren were becoming very worried about her. It was time for Erica to make an effort, to put these silly ideas behind her, for the grandchildren as much as for anyone else.

Erica did improve and even, that weekend, ordered bulbs for the garden. Her daughter considered this to be enormously encouraging, because up to then Erica had spoken of suicide as the only option for the future. The medical staff were also reassured and agreed to Erica's leaving the hospital for a few days. When she failed to return, a search of her home was made, and she was found dead of an overdose of her antidepressants. The postmortem examination suggested that she had killed herself on the afternoon of the day that she was sent home.

Erica's negative self-appraisal was not at first matched by criticism from anyone else, and Erica could just tolerate the exposure that her stay in the hospital entailed. When her daughter echoed Erica's own self-criticism, her wish to hide from the situation became intolerable. Erica ordered the bulbs almost certainly to misdirect her family and the psychiatric staff so that she would be allowed home, there to efface herself completely.

Shame and Embarrassment

John was 22. He had been a nervous child who had mixed little with other children but had a few close friends. At school no one had thought him particularly different. His teachers had noticed that John was not very good at responding in class but had not thought this through enough to know that John became panicky whenever he was singled out in front of other people or that he had managed by devious means to miss ever having to make a class presentation. After school, life became very difficult for John. Every social situation seemed to be fraught with the possibility of being ridiculed. His fair skin showed every change of color, and he felt that his blushes, which seemed to begin whenever anyone so much as looked at him, made him stand out like a beacon.

John met diagnostic criteria for social phobia and, if his development was taken into account, for avoidant personality disorder, too. His parents would have said that he was abnormally shy, and his friends that he was too easily embarrassed. John felt that he could not stand being exposed to other people's scrutiny, but when pressed, he admitted that he did not feel that people judged him negatively or that they had reason to. He just found their gaze aversive.

I take John to be suffering from morbid embarrassment, or rather from morbid sensitivity to embarrassment. He exemplifies the distinction that I want to make between embarrassment and shame: embarrassment is the impulse to hide or conceal, without the justified self-blame which is associated with shame.

Shame and Disorders of Emotion and Sentiment

Emotional traits are normally considered to be dispositions to enter one particular emotional state rather than another. Such dispositions may also influence cognitive appraisal: anxiety traits may predispose a person to find their environment threatening, for example. Frijda, Mesquita, Sonnemans, and Van Goozen (1991) apply the term *sentiments* to dispositions to appraise objects according to particular emotions. They suggest that sentiments become evident as affects and as tendencies to approach or avoid objects and that they provide an alternative formulation to the phenomena that others describe as personality traits and disorders. *Trait shame* is therefore, in Frijda et al.'s terms, a sentiment of shame. The pervasiveness of the sentiment of shame, its effect on apparently unrelated life experiences, is described by Nathaniel Hawthorne in his study of shame, *The Scarlet Letter*. Other people's reactions to Hester Prynne, he wrote, "seemed to argue so wide a diffusion of her shame, that all nature knew of it; it could have caused her no deeper pang had the leaves of the trees whispered the dark story among themselves–had the summer breeze murmured about it–had the wintry blast shrieked it aloud! Another peculiar torture was felt in the gaze of a new eye. When strangers looked curiously at the scarlet letter–and none ever failed to do so–they branded it afresh in Hester's soul." (pp. 105–106).

Hester Prynne is not constantly reminded of her sentiments of shame because she constantly feels ashamed, but because she is constantly shamed. She is legally required to wear a scarlet "A," for "adulteress," sewn on all her clothing wherever she goes, and this constantly elicits from others reactions which are shaming. The impact of shaming–the social action whose purpose is to create shame in someone–is one reason why shame has such an important social control function. The other is that the impulse to hide when shame is experienced is so powerful that a person may withdraw from the society in whose eyes he or she has been shamed and may even withdraw from all human society altogether. Shaming may create shame even where a person had not believed themselves to have been at fault or where their fault may have been involuntary or vicarious. One may be shamed by the actions of one's brother, for instance, or by any person with whom one is identified.

Confusingly, the word *shame* applies to an action about which a right-thinking person would be ashamed–as in the newspaper headline "XX's night of shame"–as well as applying to the social action of shaming, the experience of shame, and the sentiment of shame. So far in this chapter, I have not distinguished between what is sometimes called *state*shame and trait shame. State shame, the experience of feeling ashamed, may be a transient emotion and is not indicative of any emotional disorder. Indeed, quite the opposite. The inability to experience shame is often taken to be an indication of a person being particularly immoral or unfeeling. The sentiment of shame, that is, trait shame, is what is associated with emotional disorder. When I refer to *shame* in this chapter, it will be to the sentiment of shame unless otherwise specified.

Shame (the sentiment of shame) may arise because of a constant awareness, perhaps through constant reminders, of a fault about which I am ashamed (this is, for example, the experience of Pastor Dimmesdale, the foil to Hester Prynne in *The Scarlet Letter*) or through the actions of others who shame me. Hester Prynne's situation is the latter, because the mark of her shame (the scarlet letter "A") is there for all to see, and everywhere she goes she has to endure other people's shaming reactions to it. Constant exposure of the source of shame is also the experience of a person who is ashamed of their body or some aspect of their manifest self, such as a scar, an accent, or simply a ready blush.

Sight is of particular importance in shame (Pines, 1987) and provides many metaphors for the processes surrounding it, including those of social rejection. Being "seen through" by others, being overlooked, being put out of sight, turning away are all rejecting experiences that predispose a person to drop their eyes, hang their head, or remove themselves, and so be already one step towards shame-proneness. Paradoxically, the same effect may be produced by staring, although this may be because prolonged staring at another person is considered intrusive in most social situations and in most cultures. To stare is therefore to overlook the other person's right to privacy.

Conditions associated with shame-proneness are those that repel attention or attract the kind of attention which seems to leave one naked. Gilbert and McGuire (this volume, chapter 5) have considered the personal capacities that bear on this, which they term *social attention holding power*. This concept emphasizes the significance of attracting attention—unwanted attention in the case of shame—but does not account for the equal shame of being ignored or deliberately shunned. In any case, although it is true that there is some degree of personal control over one's social presentation and that one may be criticized for one's failure to exercise this control, I do not think that this is a significant source of shame. Shame may be engendered by inadvertent incongruity as readily as by flaunting the rules. What matters is that one looks different. Skin pigmentation or its lack, obesity (Stunkard & Wadden, 1992), deformity, size and public behavior are just some features that may set people apart from others.

Hester Prynne's sentiment of shame, with its attendant impulse to hide, is at war with the social requirement that her shame be publicly revealed, and it is the shame sentiment which is eventually altered and changed into a sentiment of reconciliation and tolerance. Hester's lover in *The Scarlet Letter*, Pastor Dimmesdale, also undergoes a change in his sentiments, but this time it is the cancerous effect of a hidden shame. Interestingly, his is the more malignant sentiment ultimately, although the source of his shame remains hidden until the end and the shame remains anticipated rather than actual. Elsewhere I have described Hester's sentiment as *shamefacedness* and Dimmesdale's as *mortification* (Tantam, 1991).

The characters of living people are less clearly marked than are those of characters in books. Real people do not have single sentiments, and even if there appears to be one sentiment which dominates the others, as may often be the case of a person with a psychological disorder, this sentiment may not be easily pigeonholed. In fact, as I have argued elsewhere, naming an emotion or a sentiment may be more like naming a previously undiscovered plant rather than identifying one that is already in the flora. One and the same sentiment may therefore be named and renamed according to how it is appraised and reappraised.

Embarrassment and being ashamed are two of a family of related emotions (see table 8.1), which are all unpleasant. They all bear on a person's relationship with others and may have a common phylogeny (see Gilbert & McGuire, this volume chapter 5). Because they are predicated on an appraisal of others' judgments of oneself, they develop only after a child has started to acquire a theory of mind (Dasser, Ulbaek, & Premack, 1989); that is, from the age of two up. It seems likely that they become further articulated as the child learns explicit social rules and their link with social sanctions. This is also the developmental step that leads to the child's first self-awareness, for example, when children notice a spot on their nose when they see themselves in a mirror; it therefore seems an understandable misnomer that this family of emotions belongs to the class of "self-conscious" emotions. Emotions regularly experienced at this time of life may therefore be particularly likely to influence the development of beliefs about the self,[2] and these may, in turn, influence the readiness with which particular emotions are evoked in the future. What the newly self-conscious child is developing would thus, in Frijda et al.'s terms, be their first sentiments.[3]

Several clinical implications follow.

- Clinicians need to be alert not just to emotions but to sentiments, that is, heightened tendencies to experience certain emotions. A person who has the sentiment of shame may not be ashamed all the time.
- Any member of the family of emotions in table 8.1 may segue into any other, so that a person who apparently presents with a problem of embarrassment, guilt, or humiliation may reexperience this as shame ("get in touch with their shame" is what psychotherapists say) at some point during the treatment.
- Shame is defined by particular beliefs and by a particular tendency to social action, the tendency to conceal. The concealments that people use may become hypertrophied and lead to emotional disorders.
- Many different feelings may be associated with shame, including sadness, anxiety, disgust, and anger. The dominant feeling tone of an emotional disorder may not, therefore, be a clue to whether or not shame is involved.

Disorders Linked to Sentiments of Shame

In over 600 publications that link shame and disorders found in a recent search of the clinical psychology and psychiatry literature, only 13 were in key psychiatry journals. There are many more reports of disorders associated with shameful events, of which childhood sexual abuse (Lisak, 1994) has been the one to receive by far the most attention (van der Kolk, 1996). Child sexual abuse is not the only predisposing factor for later shame-proneness. Being physically abused as a child may predispose a person to later anger dyscontrol, and this may lead to perpetuation of the cycle of abuse by a parent, usually a father, who is unable to control anger. Being the child of a parent with alcoholism may be shaming, independently of any increased risk of abuse (Hibbard, 1993). Shaming experiences in adulthood may also lead to chronic concealment, with mental health consequences. Failure in a role expectation, such as reproduction (Shapiro, 1993), or having mental illness in the family (Fink & Tasman, 1992) are examples. Shame-proneness may itself become a trigger for further shame.

Childhood sexual abuse has attracted more attention than any other potential cause of shame and has been implicated in the following conditions: bulimia nervosa (Kearney-Cooke & Striegel-Moore, 1996; Thornton & DeBlassie, 1989); dissociative disorder, including multiple personality (Ross, 1989); borderline (Herman, 1989; Silk, Lee, Hill, & Lohr, 1995; and linked to shame by Lewis, 1987) and narcissistic personality disorders (Wright, O'Leary, & Balkin, 1989; also linked to shame by Moses-Hrushovski, 1994); male rage/domestic violence (Terr, 1991; and linked to shame by Dutton & Golant, 1995); depression, particularly occurring in adolescence (Boney-McCoy & Finkelhor, 1996; also linked to shame by Carey, Finch, & Carey, 1991) but also later in life (Mullen, Romans-Clarkson, Walton, & Herbison, 1988) when shame may also be the mediating factor (Andrews, 1995); substance abuse (Aaltonen & Makela, 1994; Lisak, 1994; also linked to shame by O'Connor & Weiss, 1993; posttraumatic stress disorder (Myers, 1989; also linked to shame by numerous authors, e.g., Stone, 1992); and love or sex addiction (Dubrow-Eichel, 1993, who names shame as the intervening link). A few disorders have been linked directly to shame, although not particularly linked to childhood sexual abuse. These include body dysmorphic syndrome (de Ridder, 1997); paranoid disorders (Lewis, 1987); and social phobia (Orsillo, Heimberg, Juster, & Garrett, 1996).

Cultural Factors

Family therapists' experience suggests that families are the most important determinant of what constitutes shame triggers. One way that this happens is by what is concealed and kept unspoken (Imber-Black, 1993). Family culture is itself influenced by the culture of the society of which it is a part. Some societies have cultures which are particularly likely to inculcate shame and thus have a higher prevalence of shame-related disorders. Shame-related syndromes, sometimes with specific names, have been described as being particularly prevalent in Papua New Guinea (Sharpe, 1987), Qatar (el-Islam, 1994), Japan (Miyake & Yamazaki, 1995; Okano, 1994), and New Zealand (Sachdev, 1990).

A common feature of these cultures is that they are highly integrated, with people being known not just for themselves but for their links with others. Shame can therefore be induced not just by the negative judgments of one's neighbors but by finding oneself hidden from them by the collective rejection of "shunning."

A Nigerian man took a serious overdose of aspirin because of his debts and his inability even to think of a plan to meet them. He survived, and when interviewed in the hospital said that he had not really been sure that he wanted to kill himself but he was sure now. When asked why, he said that his brother would, like other men in his culture, be shamed by his behavior and would have no more to do with him. He could see no reason to live under those circumstances.

Sometimes a strong-minded person is able to hang on to their own perspective and not to take on the fault that others attribute to them, but this requires exceptional confidence in the rightness of one's own conduct, and it cannot overcome the social isolation of being shunned.

A Leicester resident, originally born in Pakistan, described her life since she had divorced her husband because of his physical abuse of her. "No other Asian will have anything to do with me. I'm on my own, completely. They call me shameless behind my back, but I've done nothing to be ashamed of."

The Implications of Attributing a Disorder to a Sentiment of Shame

It is more realistic to consider that shame is the sentiment which binds these experiences, events, and reactions together, rather than considering shame to be an event in a chain of causality which leads finally to a disorder. One can suppose that a person may quite easily come to see themselves as a "love addict" who is suffering from the aftereffects of childhood shaming, but this is surely to oversimplify a situation in which shame is constantly being reinvoked. Addiction may be what a person considers problematic, but it is surely more appropriate to consider it just one aspect of the working out of the shame motif in a person's life. Conceiving of a person's problem as the existential one of overcoming shame may be more helpful to them than pathologizing the problem. This may not just be true of love addiction but also of other, more established diagnostic conditions, such as borderline personality disorder or bulimia.

A golfer who slices a drive off the tee may subsequently attribute this to a preoccupation with business worries that he or she has been unable to shake off. This is not to say that the worries were part of the casual chain involved in the swing but that the muscular tension which was a component of worrying was also casually involved in the swing. Despite the fact that the worries are not a neuromuscular cause, relieving the worries may be efficacious in improving the swing. The business worries are a label that can be attached to the golfer's different way of acting on and reacting to his or her world. I take Frijda et al.'s (1991) concept of sentiment to be also about ways of acting on and reacting to the world; the shame sentiment, like business worries, is not a casual but a moral explanation. The concept involves consideration of how people see themselves in relation to the social world and what they intend to do about it. This is a different kind of discussion, a different universe of discourse, from discussions about disorders or defensive mechanisms. It is the type of discussion that people pursue when talking nontechnically. It is about you, me, and them as agents.

- Understanding a problem as a manifestation of a shame sentiment may enable access to the patient's own way of looking at their life. Although few of us would deny the importance of other people's judgments of us, many of us would indignantly repudiate suggestions that we are the puppets of mental mechanisms about which we know little or nothing. The former perspective is much more acceptable than the latter.
- An understanding of a person's actions in terms of shame (or humiliation or embarrassment) may be relevant irrespective of disorder or putative mental mechanism. Understanding the humiliating experience of being compulsorily treated for a mental illness may, for example, be relevant to an understanding of the outcome of schizophrenia (Birchwood & Tarrier, 1994).

Shame is maintained by hiding and by secrecy (Imber-Black, 1993). Bringing attention to the shame sentiment may be the first step in reversing this and in weakening the hold that shame has over a person. However, the "flavor" of shame is so pungent that it transmits itself even to discussions about shame, which become shaming in themselves. The relationship with the patient needs to be sufficiently strong to counteract this flavor, and the therapist him-or herself needs to be sufficiently in touch with his or her own shame to avoid the twin perils of either exonerating the patients or blaming and humiliating them. Therapists also need to be familiar with the means by which a person can hide or seek to undo shame, a number of which have been considered in this chapter.

Conclusions

Shame is a powerful, inhibitory emotion which strongly inclines a person experiencing it to withdraw from others. Social institutions exist in most, perhaps all, societies to shame individuals. Shame therefore provides a powerful means of social control, arguably the most important social control mechanism in some and probably important in all societies, including those supposedly individualistic societies in which guilt is presumed to predominate.

The potency of shame in mediating relationships with others may be one reason that, when it goes wrong, it is often associated with severe psychological disturbance. It may go wrong because an experience of being shamed may linger and become a sentiment of shame, which subverts persons' beliefs about themselves and others and alters their capacity for emotional response to others. It may also go wrong because a person is shamed not for the protection of society but to serve the emotional needs or bolster the power of an individual or a small group of individuals. Sexual abuse is an example of such victimization, but for all the publicity it has received, it is not the most common and may not be the most significant source of enduring shame and shame-related disorder.

Shame is one of a family of self-conscious emotions. People may experience any one of these at different times, depending on whether they experience themselves as, or believe others to consider them to be, at fault. These emotions, with the exception of guilt, all include a powerful urge to hide—to hide the trigger of the emotion, to hide oneself during the experience of the emotion, to hide the existence of the emotion, and even to hide the fact that one has something hidden. Hiding has the effect of taking the emotion out of a person's preoccupations and dealing with others, but clinical experience suggests that the price for this is that the emotion remains unprocessed and may even undermine, or mortify, psychological functioning. The clinical challenge of shame is, first to be aware of its presence, and, second, to find means of coping with it other than hiding. If there is a common theme to psychotherapy and counseling in this century, from Freud's description of resistance to Beck's description of underlying cognitive schemata, it is the development of an antithesis to the social instincts to avoid shame and to shun the person who is shamed.

Acknowledgments   I am grateful to the many patients who have endured sharing their shame with me. I am also grateful to Emmy van Deurzen for her valuable comments on an earlier version of this chapter. I am also grateful for the opportunity to lurk on a discussion of shame and male violence on the group psychotherapy list on the Internet. The cases described in this chapter are amalgamated from a number of different patients and do not correspond to particular individuals.

Notes

1. I would argue that the most effective psychotherapy occurs when the therapist starts out from the way that their patient/client appraises their world, recognizes what the patient/ client is intending by their actions, and comes to an explicit understanding with the patient/client about the ends of the treatment. Deurzen (1997) makes a similar point, arguing that existential philosophy provides a suitable framework for this endeavor. Schafer (1976) proposes that psychoanalysts should reformulate in terms that their patients themselves use, that is, using verbal expressions rather than nominal ones. I have elsewhere argued (Tantam, 1993) that the language of feeling and emotion is another means of achieving this.

2. It may be that my understanding of this is overinfluenced by psychoanalytic teaching. It certainly arrives at the same conclusion. Freud's idea of the threat of castration by the father of the young boy, given a less sexist and more psychologically understandable revision by Lacan, is equivalent to the discovery of other minds and the discovery of the existence of minds, including one's own. Lacan (1977) spoke of the child learning the "name of the father," learning in fact a new way of understanding the world in the "symbolic order," because the child had to account for the father. Although Lacan envisaged the child's development within a family unit, his use of the word *father* is more encompassing than the biological individual with that title and corresponds much more closely to the "other mind" of the cognitive psychologist. Freud and Lacan both supposed that this Oedipal stage was particularly important in the formation of the child's self-esteem, with the development of a superego (Freud) or a self-description (Lacan) which would influence the self throughout later life by causing the concealment of wishes and desires that would otherwise be expressed. I (Tantam, 1996) have explicitly linked Fairbairn's version (Fairbairn, 1952) of this story, also derived from Freud, to shame as a reaction to the mother's failure to make sense of the child's emotions.

3. Clinicians whose approach to shame has been influenced more by Tomkins's emotion theory than psychoanalysis also emphasize the importance of parenting, but couch in the language of the theater rather than in the language of feelings. Kaufman (1996), for example, describes various organizing affects in which shame takes part (shame-humiliation or shame-contempt, for example) which are elicited by particular scenes drawn from early life. These scenes or variations on them are given potency by the organizing affects and continue to elicit the organizing affects whenever they reoccur, which they are likely to do, throughout life. Individuals deal with the threat that this poses by means of a script. If Frijda were to discuss terminology with Kaufman, it is likely that he would say that his concept of *sentiment* includes scripts, organizing affects, and scenes in which those affects are elicited.

References

Aaltonen, I., & Makela, K. (1994). Female and male life stories published in the Finnish Alcoholics Anonymous journal. *International Journal of Addiction, 29,* 485–495.

American Psychiatric Association. (1994). *Diagnostic and Statistical Manual* (4th ed.). Washington, DC: American Psychiatric Association.

Andrews, B. (1995). Bodily shame as a mediator between abusive experiences and depression. *Journal of Abnormal Psychology, 104,* 277–285.

Birchwood, M., & Tarrier, M. (Eds.). (1994). *Psychological management of schizophrenia*. Chichester, UK: Wiley.

Boney-McCoy, S., & Finkelhor, D. (1996). Is youth victimization related to trauma symptoms and depression after controlling for prior symptoms and family relationships? A longitudinal, prospective study. *Journal of Consulting & Clinical Psychology, 64*, 1406–1416.

Carey, T. C., Finch, A. J., & Carey, M. P. (1991). Relation between differential emotions and depression in emotionally disturbed children and adolescents. *Journal of Consulting & Clinical Psychology, 59*, 594–597.

Dasser, N. V., Ulbaek, I., & Premack, D. (1989). The perception of intention. *Science, 243*, 365–366.

de Ridder, A. J. (1997). I see, I see what you don't see (body dysmorphic syndrome). *Nederlands Tijdschrift voor Geneeskunde, 141*, 225–227.

Deurzen, E. van. (1997). *Everyday mysteries. Existential dimensions of psychotherapy*. London: Routledge.

Dubrow-Eichel, S. K. (1993). The cultural context of sex and love addiction recovery. In E. Griffin-Shelley (Ed.), *Outpatient treatment of sex and love addicts* (pp. 113–135). Westport, CT: Praeger/Greenwood.

Dutton, D. G., & Golant, S. K. (1995). *The batterer: A psychological profile*. New York: Basic Books.

el-Islam, M. F. (1994). Cultural aspects of morbid fears in Qatari women. *Social Psychiatry and Psychiatric Epidemiology, 29*, 137–140.

Fairbairn, W. (1952). *Psychoanalytic studies of the personality*. London: Tavistock.

Fink, P. J., & Tasman, A. (Eds.). (1992). *Stigma and mental illness*. Washington, DC: American Psychiatric Press.

Frijda, N., Mesquita, B., Sonnemans, J., & Van Goozen, S. (1991). The duration of affective phenomena or emotions, sentiments and passions. In K. Strongman (Ed.), *International review of studies on emotion* (Vol. 1, pp. 187–225). Chichester, UK: Wiley.

Gardos, G., & Cole, J. O. (1980). Overview: Public health issues in tardive dyskinesia. *American Journal of Psychiatry, 137*, 776–781.

Gilbert, P. (1992). *Depression:The evolution of powerlessness*. New York: Guilford Press.

Gilbert, P. (1997). The evolution of social attractiveness and its role in shame, humiliation, guilt and therapy. *British Journal of Medical Psychology, 70*, 113–147.

Hawthorne, N. (1850, 1906). *The Scarlet Letter*. London: JM Dent & Sons.

Herman, J. L. (1989). Childhood trauma in borderline personality disorder. *American Journal of Psychiatry, 146*, 490–495.

Hibbard, S. (1993). Adult children of alcoholics: Narcissism, shame, and the differential effects of paternal and maternal alcoholism. *Psychiatry, 56*, 153–162.

Imber-Black, E. (Ed.). (1993). *Secrets in families and family therapy*. New York: Norton.

Kaufman, G. (1996). *The psychology of shame: Theory and treatment of shame-based syndromes*. (2nd ed.). New York: Springer.

Kearney-Cooke, A., & Striegel-Moore, R. H. (1996). Treatment of childhood sexual abuse in anorexia nervosa and bulimia nervosa: A feminist psychodynamic approach. In M. F. Schwartz & L. Cohn (Eds.), *Sexual abuse and eating disorders* (pp. 155–175). New York: Brunner/Mazel.

Lacan, J. (1977). *The four fundamental concepts of psychoanalysis*. London: Hogarth Press.

Lewis, H. B. (1971). *Shame and guilt in neurosis*. New York: International Universities Press.

Lewis, H. B. (Ed.). (1987). *The role of shame in symptom formation*. Hillsdale, NJ: Erlbaum.

Lisak, D. (1994). The psychological impact of sexual abuse: Content analysis of interviews with male survivors. *Journal of Traumatic Stress., 7*, 525–548.

Miyake, K., & Yamazaki, K. (1995). Self-conscious emotions, child rearing, and child psychopathology in Japanese culture. In J. P. Tangney & K. W. Fischer (Eds.), *Self-conscious emotions: The psychology of shame, guilt, embarrassment and pride* (pp. 488–504). New York: Guilford Press.

Moses-Hrushovski, R. (1995). *Deployment: Hiding behind power struggles as a character defense.* (Psychoanalytic Therapy) (Northvale, NJ: Aronson.

Mullen, P. E., Romans-Clarkson, S. E., Walton, V. A., & Herbison, G. P. (1988). Impact of sexual and physical abuse on women's mental health. *Lancet, 8590*, 841–845.

Myers, M. F. (1989). Men sexually assaulted as adults and sexually abused as boys. *Archives of Sexual Behavior, 18*, 203–215.

Nathanson, D. L. (Ed.). (1987). *The many faces of shame.* New York: Guilford Press.

Niedenthal, P. M., Tangney, J. P., & Gavanski, I. (1994). "If only I weren't" versus "if only I hadn't": Distinguishing shame and guilt in counterfactual thinking. *Journal of Personality and Social Psychology, 67*, 585–595.

O'Connor, L., Berry, J., Weiss, J., Bush, M., & Sampson, H. (1997). Interpersonal guilt: the development of a new measure. *Journal of Clinical Psychology, 53*, 73–89.

O'Connor, L. E., & Weiss, J. (1993). Individual psychotherapy for addicted clients: An application of control mastery theory. *Journal of Psychoactive Drugs, 25*, 283–291.

Okano, K. (1994). Shame and social phobia: a transcultural viewpoint. *Bulletin of the Menninger Clinic, 58*, 323–338.

Orsillo, S. M., Heimberg, R. G., Juster, H. R., & Garrett, J. (1996). Social phobia and PTSD in Vietnam veterans. *Journal of Traumatic Stress, 9*, 235–252.

Pines, M. (1987). Shame—what psychoanalysis does and does not say. *Group Analysis, 20*, 16–31.

Ross, C. A. (1989). *Multiple personality disorder.* New York: Wiley.

Sachdev, P. S. (1990). Whakama: Culturally determined behavior in the New Zealand Maori. *Psychological Medicine, 20*, 433–444.

Schafer, R. (1976). *A new language for psycho-analysis.* New Haven, CT: Yale University Press.

Shapiro, C. H. (1993). *When part of the self is lost: Helping clients heal after sexual and reproductive losses.* San Francisco, CA: Jossey-Bass.

Sharpe, J. (1987). Shame in Papua New Guinea. *Group Analysis, 20*, 43–48.

Silk, K., Lee, S. Hill, E., & Lohr, N. (1995). Borderline personality disorder symptoms and severity of sexual abuse. *American Journal of Psychiatry, 152*, 1059–1064.

Stone, A. M. (1992). The role of shame in posttraumatic stress disorder. *American Journal of Orthopsychiatry., 62*, 131–136.

Stunkard, A. J., & Wadden, T. A. (1992). Psychological aspects of severe obesity. *American Journal of Clinical Nutrition, 55*, (Suppl 2), 524S–532S.

Tantam, D. (1991). Shame and groups. *Group Analysis, 23*, 31–44.

Tantam, D. (1993). The developmental psychopathology of emotional disorders. *Journal of the Royal Society of Medicine, 86*, 336–340.

Tantam, D. (1996). Fairbairn. In G. Berrios & H. Freeman (Eds.), *150 Years of British Psychiatry* (Vol. 2). London: Athlone Press.

Terr, L. C. (1991). Childhood traumas: An outline and overview [see comments]. *American Journal of Psychiatry, 148*, 10–20.

Thornton, L. P., & DeBlassie, R. R. (1989). Treating bulimia. *Adolescence, 24*, 631–637.

van der Kolk, B. A. (1996). The complexity of adaption to trauma: Self-regulation, stimulus discrimination, and characterological development. In B. A. van der Kolk, A. C. McFarlane, & L. Weisaeth (Eds.), *Traumatic stress: The effects of overwhelming experience on mind, body, and society* (pp. 182–213). New York: Guilford Press.

Wright, F., O'Leary, J., & Balkin, J. (1989). Shame, guilt, narcissism and depression: Correlates and sex differences. *Psychoanalytic Psychology, 6*, 217–230.

9

Shame and Childhood Abuse

Bernice Andrews

There is now an abundance of evidence that early experiences of sexual and physical abuse increase the risk of later mental health problems (e.g., Andrews, Valentine, & Valentine, 1995; Holmes & Robins, 1987; Mullen et al., 1993). Chronic, recurrent, and more severe psychiatric disorders have also been shown to be associated with a history of abuse in clinical samples (Bryer et al., 1987; Carmen, Reiker, & Mills, 1984). Not everyone who experiences abuse is affected to the same degree, and the individual meaning attached to events plays an important role in explaining variations in response (Andrews, 1997a; Brown, 1989). Within this perspective, meaning is a function of the interplay between the individual's external world (the actual features and context of events) and his or her internal world (personal attitudes and schema concerning self and others). External factors, such as the severity of the experience and social factors surrounding it, are likely to affect the way abusive experiences are construed and thus affect outcome (see Beitchman et al., 1992 for a review). But while clinical observation and theory have provided insights, it is only recently that researchers have begun to investigate factors associated with the internal strand in the abuse/disorder link; in particular, the role that cognitive-affective factors might play. A particular focus of my own research has been to investigate the mediating influences of cognitive-affective factors in relation to abuse and disorders such as depression and bulimia. An earlier interest in self-blame led to a later focus on guilt and shame.

In the course of describing this research, I shall discuss theories that have related self-blame to victimization. The ways in which self-blame might be differentially related to both guilt and shame are also considered within this context. Consideration is given to the common meaning that might underlie sexual and physical abuse and whether this can help explain the roles played by guilt and shame in the link between early abuse and disorder. Finally, in the light of the evidence

176

presented, I shall discuss some of the complex links that might exist between self-blame, guilt, and shame in individuals who have experienced childhood abuse.

The Relation of Self-blame to Abuse and Depression

Much theory and research in this area has focused on the relation of self-blame to abusive experiences in adulthood, such as marital violence and rape. Initial theoretical insights were provided by Peterson and Seligman (1983) and Janoff-Bulman (1979). Peterson and Seligman applied the learned helplessness model to understanding reactions to victimization. In the original learned helplessness experiments, in situations where a simple response will terminate shock, the usual reactions of dogs given prior inescapable shock was passive acceptance of the painful stimulation. It was speculated that in humans helplessness could be learned and would generalize to future stressful situations that can be controlled and that this could provide a model for at least certain forms of depression (Seligman, 1975). According to Peterson and Seligman, the parallels between learned helplessness and maladaptive responses to victimization are that both are preceded by uncontrollable aversive events. The helpless individual responds with the belief of future response-outcome independence; in the victim, the belief involves self-definition as a victim, which carries with it a sense of vulnerability.

The reformulated revision of the theory (Abramson, Seligman, & Teasdale, 1978) further strengthened the parallel between learned helplessness and passive reactions to victimization. According to the reformulation, when people face situations in which they have no control, they make causal attributions that will influence how they react. Attributions have three important dimensions that will significantly affect outcome: first, they may be either internal to the person or external, referring to something about the situation; second, they may be either stable and persistent over time or unstable and transient; and third, they may be either global, thereby affecting a variety of outcomes, or specific, being limited to the situation. The theory predicts that internal attributions that follow bad events will affect self-esteem; the extent to which the attribution is stable will affect the chronicity of any incipient helplessness or depression; and the extent to which the attribution is global will affect whether the reactions are generalized to other situations. Individuals who typically attribute bad events to global, stable, and internal factors should be most prone to depression. In similar fashion, Peterson and Seligman (1983) proposed that victims of crime who make such attributions will react with greater deficits.

Characterological and Behavioral Self-Blame

The reformulation of the learned-helplessness theory also prompted Janoff-Bulman to ponder the common response of self-blame to victimization. In a seminal paper devoted to a discussion of studies of both depression and rape, Janoff-Bulman (1979) suggested that the concept of self-blame, when it referred to victims of misfortune, was not enough to explain any association between the aversive experience and any subsequent disorder. This is because self-blame can often relate to a positive belief in personal control over one's outcomes. She therefore made the distinction between characterological and behavioral self-blame, where the former involves attributions to a nonmodifiable source (one's character) and is associated with personal deservingness of negative outcomes. The latter involves attributions to a modifiable source (one's behavior) and is associated with a belief in the avoidability of negative outcome. It is argued that most people operate within an "illusion of invulnerability" and that behavioral self-blame is an adaptive response to victimization because it protects individuals from feeling vulnerable after a violent attack (Janoff-Bulman & Frieze, 1983).

Self-Blame in Women

In our prospective community study of women, designed to explore in general the role of psychosocial factors in the onset and course of depression, women who reported maritally violent relationships, either currently or in the past, showed double the rate of depression over a three-year period than other women (Andrews & Brown, 1988). The highest rate by far, however, was among those who had experienced abuse (either physical or sexual) in both childhood and adulthood (Andrews, 1995). In the subsample of 70 women victims of marital violence, we investigated the reasons for this within an attributional framework (Andrews & Brewin, 1990). We distinguished behavioral from characterological self-blame, as there was evidence that the latter but not the former was involved in depression (Janoff-Bulman, 1979). In a study of rape victims, Janoff-Bulman had also demonstrated that on the whole the women involved did not see themselves as deserving or provoking the rape. Rather, they blamed the attack on some modifiable aspect of their behavior. For example, they judged that they could have been more careful or not have been out so late at night. This was seen as a healthy response, as survivors would have retained some feeling of control over the risk of future attacks. In contrast, it had been suggested that those who are repeatedly assaulted or mistreated may be more likely to blame their character; they may feel that there must be something wrong with them if such an event happens more than once (Silver & Wortman, 1980).

Abused children are often told by their parents that they are bad and unloveable (Herbruck, 1979), and we thought this would be an additional reason for those abused in childhood to be more likely than others to respond to later abuse by blaming their character. In fact, there was already evidence of greater characterological self-blame (CSB) for hypothetical bad events in people who have been sexually victimized in childhood (Gold, 1986). As expected, we found that self-blame for marital violence was common, but women who had experienced either physical or sexual childhood abuse were more likely to blame their character, whereas women with no such experiences were more likely to blame their behavior. We also found that women with CSB were more likely than the other women survivors to have suffered persistent depression after the violent relationship had ended.

These results suggest that attributions involving characterological self-blame might explain at least some of the variability in response to abusive experiences. Furthermore, these attributions are likely to be shaped by past experiences of the same kind. This is clearly illustrated in the following accounts. Both women experienced severe violence from their partners, and, although neither was still in the relationship, they had both experienced persistent depression in the years that followed. The first had been severely beaten by her father as a child. When talking about her past marriage she said:

> I thought it was all my fault because he told me it was. I believed everything he said—that I was bad, not fit to be a mother.

The other who had been sexually abused by her father as a child said of a former partner:

> I thought about it a lot then and if I make an honest assessment I can't say that he was one hundred per cent bad and that I was the innocent party. I'm sure that there's something in me that provokes a man like that. I'm sure in some way I was responsible, and I couldn't cope with whatever it is in me. I don't know what it is. I think probably my manner, or the way I speak, something made him react in that way.

Links between Self-blame, Shame, and Guilt

Blaming stable negative characteristics of the self for abuse is likely to evoke a sense of helplessness due to the perception that such characteristics are unmodifiable. Feelings of helplessness and an inherent sense of badness have been noted both in the empirical and theoretical literature as central features of the experience of shame (e.g., H. B. Lewis, 1987; Tangney et al., 1996; Wicker, Payne, & Morgan, 1983). From an alternative perspective, it has been suggested that rather than occurring concurrently, internal, stable, and global attributions (akin to CSB attributions) for negative events actually lead to shame (Weiner, 1986; M. Lewis, 1992). In the context of sexual abuse, according to one theoretical model, these characterological attributions mediate the relationship between childhood sexual abuse and shame, and shame in turn leads to mental health problems (Feiring, Taska, & Lewis, 1996).

The nature of any relationship (causal or concurrent) between similar kinds of cognitive and affective factors is difficult to establish. However, there is some evidence from correlational studies of an association between shame and internal, stable, and global attributions for negative events in student samples. Tangney et al. (1992a) showed separate relationships between internal, stable, and global attributions for hypothetical negative events and a measure of shame-proneness. These attributional dimensions were also related to guilt-proneness, but once shame was partialed out, any associations disappeared. In studies of students in exam situations, shame was more highly correlated with attributions of lack of ability concerning failure than was guilt, which was more highly correlated with attributions of lack of effort (Weiner, 1986).

The Relation of Shame and Guilt to Early Abusive Experiences and Psychopathology

The question of whether characterological self-blame is a precursor or an integral part of shame requires further investigation and may never be resolved. Nevertheless, the observed relationship between CSB and early abusive experiences and CSB and persistent depression prompted me to pursue the question of cognitive-affective mediators in the abuse/disorder link by investigating the roles of pathological guilt and shame. CSB was separately related to both early physical and sexual abuse. Before presenting the empirical findings, I describe two broad theoretical perspectives that might aid understanding of the impact of these different experiences in terms of their underlying similarities.

Sexual and Physical Abuse: Do They Share a Common Meaning?

From a social-cognitive perspective, early representations of self and others are the result of experiences with primary attachment figures. According to attachment theory, such representations are assimilated and form the basis of cognitive schema. Mental representations based on negative childhood experiences with primary caregivers lead to vulnerability in the face of subsequent adversity (Bowlby, 1977, 1980). It has been speculated that the representational model of self constructed by individuals who have been abused in childhood is of one who is responsible for and deserving of harsh treatment (Egeland, Jacobvitz, & Paptola, 1984; Egeland, Jacobvitz, & Sroufe, 1988). Child sexual abuse may not necessarily be perceived as involving harsh treatment. Nevertheless, one of the earliest theories to incorporate a social-cognitive perspective in relation to the impact of abuse was that of Ferenczi (1932/1949), one of Freud's closest colleagues. Based on clinical observations of both perpetrators and abuse victims, in a paper that was perceived as heretical by his psychodynamic peers, Ferenczi proposed that experiences of both physical and sexual abuse were damaging to subsequent adult functioning. The experiences were distinct, but the affect or motivation of the actor, which was seen to be so damaging to the recipient, was the same. Both "passionate loving" and "passionate punishment" were accompanied by feelings of hatred and guilt toward the recipient, and such feelings were internalized by the innocent child. Ferenczi argued that in the case of sexual abuse it was the guilt feelings of the adult that made the love object an object of both loving and hating.

A more recent model that involves social cognition that pertains to sexual abuse is that of Finkelhor and Browne (1986). According to these authors, common patterns of reactions seen among adult victims of childhood sexual abuse are connected with four factors related to the initial experiences: traumatic sexualization, stigmatization, betrayal, and powerlessness. The factor identified as pertaining to shame is stigmatization, which occurs when the perpetrator of the abuse and others blame the victim and enjoin her or him with the need for secrecy. The child grows up with feelings of guilt and shame, believing she or he is damaged goods. While this model is claimed to be specific to child sexual abuse, stigmatization, as described, can also be seen as pertinent to early physical abuse.

Theories of the impact of abuse that focus on fairly sophisticated social-cognitive processes emphasize deservedness and responsibility and are as likely to predict pathological guilt as shame. Gilbert, from a rather different biosocial perspective, specifically identified shame as an important factor in depression (Gilbert, 1989). Although Gilbert's recent ideas place more emphasis on the relation between shame and attacks on, and loss of, social attractiveness (see Gilbert, 1997), his earlier insights provide a compelling perspective on the common meaning behind different types of abusive experiences. Within a general biosocial framework, Gilbert argues that evolution gave rise to four primary social competencies: care-eliciting, caregiving, cooperating, and competing. In evolutionary terms, competitive behavior is seen as probably the most primitive, involving the defense of scarce resources such as food, sexual partners, and territory. Appraisal mechanisms linked to this competency meant that even the most primitive species were able to evaluate their potential for acquiring and holding on to scarce resources relative to their conspecifics. Among primitive species, loss of such resources to others has been shown to result in defeat that involves a major change in physical state and ultimately in death. It is suggested that such an evaluative competency underlies human self-esteem and that defeat or loss of status in humans relates to a change in functioning that involves loss of self-esteem and subordinate status and that ultimately results in depression if self-esteem is not recovered.

Gilbert describes how, with evolution, territorial breeding gave way to group living, but the structure of the social group at this phylogenetic stage consisted of a dominance hierarchy with no potential for cooperative behavior. Subordinates with little resource-holding potential conveyed through submissive and appeasement gestures that they recognized their status, thus inhibiting hostile reactions in other more dominant animals. Once a submissive act has been accepted by the dominant other in the interaction, arousal in both parties may fall. However, submissive acts can trigger defeat states where submission is evaluated as a mark of inferiority, as in the aftermath of the experience of rape. Or submissive acts may exert an effect over time, gradually leading to a state of defeat; so, for example, an autocratic, aggressive husband may gradually succeed in reducing his wife to acting like a subordinate through physical threats and acts. There is evidence from ethological studies that defeat and subordinate status are related to biochemical changes that are associated with depressive states (see Gilbert & Maguire, this volume, chapter 5). At a cognitive-affective level, Gilbert relates involuntary submissive behavior in humans to shame. Shame is related to individual concerns about how one is regarded by others and is concerned with issues of defeat, intrusion, and ultimately destruction of the self. The perception that one is viewed by the attacker and others as an inferior and submissive victim presumably involves anticipation of their disdain and rejection. The experience of abuse, either sexual or physical, particularly where it is prolonged and reduces the victim to subordinate status, is thus associated with psychiatric disorder, especially depression, through feelings of submissive and shame. Gilbert and colleagues have recently reported an association between questionnaire measures of submissive behavior and both depression and shame-proneness in a student sample (Gilbert, Pehl, & Allan, 1994).

In drawing together social-cognitive and biosocial explanations of the impact of abuse, a common theme is the victims' view of how they are regarded by the perpetrator of the abusive act. Ferenczi's (1932/1949) premise was that the feelings of guilt and hatred experienced by the perpetrator were introjected by the victim. These insights relate to a phenomenon noted by Finkelhor (1983) that perpetrators use their power to manipulate victims' perceptions of reality, making the victims believe that it is their own fault that the abuse is happening. A psychodynamic interpretation of these observations might be that perpetrators of both physical and sexual abuse project their own guilt and other bad feelings onto their victims, who, in turn, internalize it. In Gilbert's theory, behaviors related to submission (observed in both humans and other animal species), such as a strong desire to escape, gaze avoidance, crouch (a tendency to curl up the body and look down), being frozen to the spot, and so forth, are the same as those seen in severe states of shame in humans. Gilbert notes that "the central focus is on the negative image of the self that is created in the mind of the other" (1989, p. 268). In other words, it would appear that Gilbert, like Ferenczi but from a very different perspective, suggests that the common meaning of physical and sexual abuse arises from the perception of the (submissive) victim that he or she is subordinate or inferior in the eyes of the (dominant) perpetrator. However, unlike Ferenczi and others who espouse a broadly social-cognitive perspective, Gilbert does not suggest that the perpetrator's actual perceptions of the victim are in fact internalized by the victim. One consequence of this is that a broadly social-cognitive framework allows for both shame and guilt as outcomes of abusive experiences, whereas within a biosocial framework only shame would be predicted.

Early Abuse and Pathological Guilt

In recent discussions in the literature there has been some dispute over whether guilt is as intense and negative an emotion as shame (e.g., Harder, 1995; Tangney, Burggraf, & Wagner, 1995). One outcome has been some agreement that pathological guilt observed in clinical samples may be qualitatively different from the "normal" guilt commonly experienced in nonclinical populations (Tangney, 1996). Our community sample of inner-city, predominantly working-class mothers provided an opportunity to investigate pathological guilt in relation to early abuse, as they constituted a group at high risk of depression. In the first three years of the study, we gathered clinical and other information at yearly intervals. Over that time, around 83 of the 286 women had at least one episode of depression that reached recognized criteria for major depressive disorder (Andrews & Brown, 1988). Previous studies had shown that psychiatric patients with histories of physical and sexual abuse have more severe symptoms, and specifically more suicidal symptoms, than other patients who were not abused (Bryer et al., 1987; Carmen et al., 1984), although other specifically depressive symptoms such as guilt that might distinguish abused from nonabused patients have so far not been investigated.

In a further analysis of the data for the present chapter, I therefore examined differences in symptoms in the 83 women with depressive episodes between those who did and did not report physical or sexual abuse in childhood. Women had been administered a standardized clinical interview, the Present State Examination (PSE; Wing, Cooper, & Sartorius, 1974). Core symptoms of depression in the PSE (other than depressed mood) that are included in the criteria for major depressive disorder are hopelessness, suicidal plans and actions, weight loss, tiredness, early waking, delayed sleep, poor concentration or inefficient thinking, neglect due to brooding, loss of interest, loss of libido, social withdrawal, self-depreciation, guilt, and retardation. The mean number of symptoms, including depressed mood, for the two groups was 10.43 for those with childhood abuse and 8.76 for the other women ($t = 2.54$, $p < .01$). Adopting a probability level of $< .01$ because of the number of comparisons, women with and without early abuse on the 15 separate depression symptoms showed significant differences on only 2; suicidal plans and actions (reported by 42% with abuse and 8% without, $\chi^2 = 11.95$, $p < .001$), and guilt (29% with abuse and 6% without, $\chi^2 = 6.72$, $p < .01$). Further logistic regression analyses to determine the relative contributions of physical and sexual abuse to symptoms of guilt and suicidal behavior showed that, while suicidal tendencies were equally related to early repeated physical and sexual abuse, guilt had a stronger association with physical abuse. A third of those reporting physical abuse and 19% reporting sexual abuse had pathological guilt (compared with 6% with no abuse). As might be expected, suicidal behavior was more common among women reporting pathological guilt; it was reported by 50% of those who also reported guilt, compared with 15% without guilt, $\chi^2 = 5.53$, $p < .02$.

Criteria for rating pathological guilt on the PSE were stringent (it had to be severe, out of voluntary control, and out of proportion to any behavior connected with it), and guilt was the most rarely reported depressive symptom in this community sample. It was clear that the guilt described was pathological, and, although similar in many respects, there were features that distinguished it from theoretical and empirical descriptions of shame. Both shame and pathological guilt appear to involve high levels of self-blame, although in pathological guilt the focus is more firmly on behavior and an obsession with having done wrong. Many of those with such guilt believed they had committed a sin or a crime, a feature not associated with shame. For example, one women who had had an abortion 9 years previously said she felt she was a murderer, and although she recognized it was justified at the time, she felt it was a very grave sin for which she could never be forgiven. In addition, both shame and pathological guilt appear to involve the anticipation of an external response. However, whereas shame, according to the literature, involves the anticipation of others' rejection and scorn, added dimensions in pathological guilt are the anticipation and deservedness of retribution and punishment from others. Most of the descriptions involved comments concerning deservedness of blame and punishment. For example, one woman survivor of childhood sexual and physical abuse was carrying on an affair with a married man. She felt she had sinned and committed a crime deserving punishment. When she fell down the stairs and damaged her back, she said, "because of the accident, I honestly felt that I was being punished." Another woman who had been permanently physically scarred as a result of her father's beatings as a child said:

> I feel blamed all the time. When the kids start saying things I blame myself, and when they're having a hard time at school I blame myself. . . . I feel I deserve it when people are critical. Sometimes I feel I'm being punished if something happens to the kids. I felt she was being punished for something I'd done wrong when she had the accident at school.

This evidence of a relationship between specific symptoms of both guilt and suicidal behavior and early abuse in depressed women is in line with Ferenczi's (1932/1949) contention that the common meaning of early physical and sexual abuse in terms of its impact lies in the internalization of the perpetrator's projected hatred and guilt by the victim. However, this might be more apparent for those who experience physical abuse. From an attachment theory perspective, the findings are also in accord with Egeland et al.'s (1984, 1988) proposal that the internal representation of self of those abused in childhood is of one who is responsible for an deserving of harsh treatment. It should be remembered, however, that these pathological guilt feelings occurred within depressive episodes; further investigation is needed to clarify whether guilt is common in abused individuals when they are not depressed or whether it is only activated in depressed states.

The Role of Shame in Relation to Abuse and Disorder

Evidence for an association between pathological guilt and early abuse was stronger for physical abuse and does not rule out a further association with shame, particularly as there is evidence from questionnaire studies for a strong association between the two emotions (see Andrews, this volume, chapter 2). The insights gained from the study of self-blame in the marital violence survivors were applied in the design of a subsequent study of a subset of the whole community sample of women that was followed over a further period. Overall, these 100 women were investigated over an 8-year period with four contacts; at the last contact 75 of their daughters, aged between 15 and 25, were also interviewed.

The evidence for an association between CSB and early abusive experiences and between CSB and general shame-proneness (Tangney et al., 1992a; Weiner, 1986) prompted this study. Because shame has been consistently noted in the literature to involve self-conscious feelings about the body (e.g. Gilbert, 1989; Mollon, 1984; Sartre, 1956), and because I wanted a measure that would provide a common and salient real-life focus for all the women, I chose to measure feelings of bodily shame. Within a lengthy interview that covered self-attitudes and past and present life experiences, both the mothers and daughters were asked direct questions about whether they had ever felt ashamed of their body or any part of it and about the onset and duration of shame feelings where they existed. Bodily shame was associated with early experiences of both sexual and physical abuse in both the older women and their daughters. The relationship held when separate measures of low self-esteem and body dissatisfaction were taken into account, suggesting that it was the specific shame element that was important in the association (Andrews, 1995, 1997b).

In the daughters, early abuse was associated with disordered eating and bulimia (Andrews et al., 1995; Andrews, 1997b). Bodily shame was also strongly related to bulimia (Andrews, 1997b). However, it was not clear whether shame was a preceding or concurrent factor in bulimia, because the young women were not questioned in detail about the onset of disorders that occurred more than 12 months prior to the interview. Nevertheless, examination of the transcribed accounts suggested that, in all cases of bulimia, onset or exacerbation of symptoms followed abuse and was concurrent with bodily shame. One explanation for the concurrent occurrence of bodily shame with bulimic symptoms may be that the shame measure was tapping directly into a central component of the disorder, that is, undue preoccupation with body shape and dread of getting too fat. However, although much of the focus for shame was on body parts such as breasts, buttocks, stomach, and legs, shame of other bodily aspects not directly related to shape, such as body hair, complexion, and facial features, was also commonly reported. Furthermore, shame per se has not been described and defined as a central element of bulimia according to recognized diagnostic criteria. While bodily dissatisfaction is recognized as a bulimic symptom, it could not account for the strong relationship between bodily shame and bulimia.

In the older women, bodily shame mediated the relationship between early abuse and episodes of chronic or recurrent depression in the 8-year period of the study when current level of depression was controlled (Andrews, 1995). In the absence of bodily shame, the relationship between early abuse and chronic or recurrent depression was lost. It was surprising, given the humiliation involved in marital violence and rape, that neither of these abusive adult experiences was related to bodily shame in the absence of childhood experiences. However, it was found that adult abuse increased the rate of chronic and recurrent depression among those with earlier abuse, and this might be explained by its propensity to provoke intense shame among women already prone to such feelings. In similar manner, it seems possible that nonphysically abusive life events or chronic problems involving humiliating experiences, such as hostile reactions and rejection in intimate sexual relationships, are more likely than other stressors to provoke or exacerbate bodily shame in already vulnerable individuals.

Shame was not a fleeting experience for those women who reported it but a chronic state that pervaded their adult lives. The two main themes in the content of the accounts involved individual concerns about bodily appearance in the eyes of others and behavior that involved concealment of the body. One woman recalled that she would not get into the communal shower when she was at school unless she was wearing her underwear. Another reported how she would not go anywhere without a jacket to cover her arms, even in hot weather. Several women spontaneously reported feeling so ashamed of their bodies that they would not let their husbands see them undressed. The accounts illustrate how bodily shame may differ from bodily dissatisfaction and low self-esteem. Both these factors involve not living up to one's own standards (which may reflect societal and cultural values), but they do not necessarily involve concealment of supposed deficiencies and inordinate concern about how one appears to others.

The research on shame has continued with a pilot study of depressed patients (Andrews & Hunter, 1997). The findings confirm the relation between bodily shame and early abuse in both female and male patients and suggest that nonbodily forms of shame that involve character but not behavior may also be related to early abusive experiences. In this small depressed sample, shame feelings were also related to a chronic and recurrent course of the disorder.

Discussion and Conclusions

Links between Guilt, Shame, and Self-blame Revisited

These results on characterological self-blame, guilt, and shame suggest that women (and perhaps men) who have suffered severe and humiliating abusive experiences in childhood are at an increased risk of feeling bad about themselves at the very core of their being. It seems likely from the evidence that, when faced with events involving subsequent humiliation in adulthood, these feelings would be reactivated or exacerbated. But before discussing these findings, I further consider the relationship between self-blame, shame, and guilt in the light of existing evidence and theory.

Blaming one's character for bad events was theoretically linked to shame by Helen Lewis (1987). She also equated blaming one's behavior for bad events with guilt. From her observations of patients in therapy, she described a pattern of behavior seen in shame-prone individuals where expressions of shame and behavior related to it were commonly followed by feelings and expressions of humiliated fury toward the person who had evoked feelings of shame. There is some support for this contention from a study showing an association between questionnaire measures of shame and anger (Tangney et al., 1992b). Lewis observed that humiliated fury was then followed by guilty feelings for real or imagined harm done to the other person—the guilt being connected with fear of abandonment or retaliation by the other person, led back to feelings of shame.

It is possible that feelings of humiliated fury are more common and more easily evoked among those who have been abused in childhood than among others. The extent to which such feelings are acted upon may depend on one's status and power in society in general and in one's immediate social milieu. For example, one study has shown male perpetrators of marital violence to be more likely than their wives to have experienced abuse in childhood (Rosenbaum & O'Leary, 1981), and most studies have found a link between current marital violence and abuse in childhood for the perpetrator (see Hotaling & Sugarman, 1984, for a review). Those who act upon feelings of humiliated fury may be more likely to feel remorse for their actions than to blame their character. An example of how this might work is evident in a study carried out by Walker (1983). From the descriptions provided by marital violence victims, Walker described a cycle of violence that occurs within violent marriages. She described how tension mounts, leading to the violent act. But following such acts, men often feel deep remorse, apologizing to spouses and trying to make up for their outbursts by proffering gifts and other expressions of commitment and support. Inevitably, though, once this honeymoon period is over, tension once more builds up and violence follows. In Walker's study, there was evidence that the period of contrition decreased as the relationship progressed, and there is also evidence that abuse perpetrators justify their actions and project blame onto others. A recent study of male attributions for perpetrating marital violence shows the most common response to be blame of the partner (Holtzworth-Munroe, 1991).

H. Lewis (1987) proposed that women's second-class status in the world of power increases their propensity to shame, although she did not make the connection between submissiveness and shame in the way outlined by Gilbert (1989). Those who have been made to feel inferior and subordinate as a result of past experiences may feel humiliated fury rather than righteous indignation when they are abused or maltreated in adulthood. This raises questions for future enquiries about the extent to which women in general, and abused women in particular, feel humiliated fury, the extent to which they express or suppress such feelings, and the extent to which this anger is related to subsequent characterological self-blame and shame and behavioral self-blame and guilt.

Further Speculation on the Mediating Role of Shame, Guilt, and Self-blame in Light of the Current Evidence

It appears that shame-proneness (at least in relation to the body) as a result of early abuse has different consequences, depending on the age and life-stage of the women in the research I have described. In younger women, feelings of shame about the body that result from abuse may lead to the avoidance of others' scorn through an unrealistic striving for perfection, manifested by restricted intake of food. Research has shown that, psychologically, dieters feel deprived of favorite foods and, when off the diet, are likely to overeat (Polivy & Herman, 1985). In this way, a disturbed eating pattern of bingeing and dieting ensues. It is possible that on account of her childhood experiences, especially when there has been maternal deprivation, the abused girl feels particularly deprived when she diets and therefore compensates even more than others. She may judge herself more harshly than others when she "lets herself down" by eating too much. This may lead her to take more severe and punitive action against herself, in the form of self-induced vomiting and laxative purging, than others might take in order to rid herself of unwanted food.

The persistence and severity of depression in the older woman who has been abused in childhood might be the result of a readily evoked shame/rage cycle. Feelings of shame may be elicited in response to real or imagined maltreatment by, or scorn of, others, and the ensuing humiliated fury may lead to feelings of guilty self-blame and self-hatred. In such situations, the self is seen as unworthy and deserving of misfortune. Unlike the majority of young men who move toward independence as they mature, the majority of women who have children find that their emotional and physical resources are bound up with ensuring the best care for them, and there is a greater need for both emotional and material dependence on the man. It is possible that as young women reach the stage of marrying or cohabiting and having children, they become less able to avoid potentially shame-provoking situations because of this dependency and loss of power in the outside world. Women without histories of childhood abuse may cope better in these circumstances than those with such histories. Because of a stronger sense of self-worth, they may feel subjectively equal to their partners, even when this is not the reality in terms of control over objective resources. In situations involving conflict with partners and others, feelings of subordination and submissiveness that lead to shame may not be so readily evoked.

While these speculations appear plausible in terms of the evidence described, it is important to keep in mind that the samples were limited to working-class mothers and their daughters who live in a somewhat deprived inner-city area. In the first 2 years of the study, around one fourth of the women were living on social security or unemployment benefits and two thirds of the women had a severe event or a major life difficulty. Such stressors involved interpersonal relationships and the wider environment, including problems with employment, finances, and housing. The study of a more heterogeneous group of women or a group with different demographic characteristics might have produced different results. For example, it is possible that in other less deprived samples of women with more objective autonomy, feelings of bodily shame may be less apparent or more readily concealed, because greater material resources may compensate for or mask submissive and subordinate feelings. It is possible that, in samples of women and men with more objective autonomy in the world, feelings of shame or characterological self-blame that result from early abuse may be more likely to be repressed and projected onto others—manifested as feelings of scorn and the need to humiliate others (see Miller, 1987). It may be, of course, that both shame and scorn are more easily elicited in those who have been abused and that humiliation of others occurs concurrently with unrepressed shame. The manifestation of feelings and behaviors that involve hostility toward others needs further investigation in this context.

Concluding Comments

It would appear that early abusive experiences may lead to a propensity to feel both shame and pathological guilt in adulthood. Although the two factors are likely to be highly related, unlike current conceptions of shame, pathological guilt seems to be tied up with the anticipation of punishment and with self-punitive behavior and may well influence the severity of any ensuing disorder. The evidence so far suggests that shame, which involves the anticipation of rejection and scorn for supposed deficiencies, plays a mediating role in the link between early abuse and disorder. It may act as a vulnerability factor for onset of disorder in abused individuals, as well as being related to a more persistent and chronic course.

Regarding the role of attributional style, unlike behavioral self-blame, characterological self-blame was related to both early abuse and chronic course of disorder in marital violence victims. Both theory and research point to behavioral self-blame as a "healthy" response to adversity, as it allows the possibility for behavioral change on future occasions. It can therefore be seen as being related to "healthy" guilt, rather than to guilt in its more pathological forms. On the other hand, CSB has been linked to shame and has been described in the literature both as a component part of shame and as a precursor of it. If it is viewed as a component, then the findings might simply be reflecting a more general feeling of shame for the violence in the marital violence victims. What is clear is that further investigation is needed to tease out the undoubtedly complex relationships between attributional style and both shame and pathological guilt.

Finally, the focus of this chapter has been on early physical and sexual abuse, two very severely threatening experiences. But there are also likely to be other early adverse experiences involved in the development of maladaptive cognitive-affective styles (see Andrews, 1997a; Gilbert, Allan, & Goss, 1995). Further research in this area in different populations that controls for other early adversity is likely to reap rewards.

References

Abramson, L. Y., Seligman, M. E. P., & Teasdale, J. D. (1978). Learned helplessness in humans:Critique and reformulation. *Journal of Abnormal Psychology, 87*, 49–74.

Andrews, B. (1995). Bodily shame as a mediator between abusive experiences and depression. *Journal of Abnormal Psychology, 104* (2), 277–285.

Andrews, B. (1997a). Early adversity and the creation of personal meaning. In M. Power & C. R. Brewin (Eds.), *The transformation of meaning in psychological therapies* (pp. 75–89). Chichester, UK: Wiley.

Andrews, B. (1997b). Bodily shame in relation to abuse in childhood and bulimia. *British Journal of Clinical Psychology, 36*, 41–50.

Andrews, B., & Brewin, C. R. (1990). Attributions of blame for marital violence: A study of antecedents and consequences. *Journal of Marriage and the Family, 52,*757–767.

Andrews, B., & Brown, G. W. (1988). Marital violence in the community: A biographical approach. *British Journal of Psychiatry, 153,* 305–312.

Andrews, B., & Hunter, E. (1997). Shame, early abuse and course of depression in a clinical sample: A preliminary study. *Cognition and Emotion, 11,* 373–381.

Andrews, B., Valentine, E. R., & Valentine, J. D. (1995). Depression and eating disorders following abuse in childhood in two generations of women. *British Journal of Clinical Psychology, 34*, 37–52.

Beitchman, J. H., Zucker, K. J., Hood, J. E., DaCosta, G. A., Akman, D., & Cassavia, E. (1992). A review of the long-term effects of child sexual abuse. *Child Abuse & Neglect, 16*, 101–118.

Bowlby, J. (1977). The making and breaking of affectional bonds: 1. Aetiology and psychopathology in the light of attachment theory. *British Journal of Psychiatry, 130*, 201–210.

Bowlby, J. (1980). *Attachment and loss: Vol. 3. Loss: Sadness and depression.* London: Hogarth Press.

Brown, G. W. (1989). Life events and measurement. In G. W. Brown & T. O. Harris (Eds.), *Life events and illness* (pp. 3–48). New York: Guilford Press.

Bryer, J. B., Nelson, B. A., Baker Miller, J., & Krol, P. A. (1987). Childhood sexual and physical abuse as factors in adult psychiatric illness. *American Journal of Psychiatry, 144*, 1426–1430.

Carmen, E. (Hilberman), Reiker, P. P., & Mills, T. (1984). Victims of violence and psychiatric illness. *American Journal of Psychiatry, 141*, 378–383.

Egeland, B., Jacobvitz. D., & Paptola, K. (1984). Intergenerational continuity of abuse. Paper presented at the Conference on Child Abuse and Neglect, Maine.

Egeland, B., Jacobvitz, D., & Sroufe, L. A. (1988). Breaking the cycle of abuse. *Child Development, 59*, 1080–1088.

Feiring, C., Taska, L., & Lewis, M. (1996). A process model for understanding adaptation to sexual abuse: The role of shame in defining stigmatization. *Child Abuse and Neglect, 20* (8), 767–792.

Ferenczi, S. (1949). Confusion of tongues between the adult and the child. *International Journal of Psycho-Analysis, 30*, 225–230. (Original work published 1932)

Finkelhor, D. (1983). Common features of family abuse. In D. Finkelhor, R. Gelles, G. Hotaling, & M. Straus (Eds.), *The dark side of families: Current family violence research* (pp. 17–28). London: Sage.

Finkelhor, D., & Browne, A. (1986). Initial and long-term effects: A conceptual framework. In D. Finkelhor (Ed.), *A sourcebook on child sexual abuse* (pp. 180–198). Newbury Park, CA: Sage.

Gilbert, P. (1989). *Human nature and suffering.* Hove, UK:Erlbaum.

Gilbert, P. (1997). The evolution of social attractiveness and its role in shame, humiliation, guilt and therapy. *British Journal of Medical Psychology, 70*, 113–147.

Gilbert, P., Allan, S., & Goss, K. (1995). Parental representations, shame, interpersonal problems, and vulnerability to psychopathology. *Clinical Psychology and Psychotherapy, 2*, 1–12.

Gilbert, P., Pehl, J., & Allan, S. (1994). The phenomenology of shame and guilt: An empirical investigation. *British Journal of Medical Psychology, 67*, 23–36.

Gold, E. R. (1986). Long-term effects of sexual victimization in childhood: An attributional approach. *Journal of Consulting and Clinical Psychology, 54*, 471–475.

Harder, D. W. (1995). Shame and guilt assessment, and relationships of shame-and guilt-proneness to psychopathology. In J. P. Tangney & K. W. Fischer (Eds.), *Self-conscious emotions: The psychology of shame, guilt, embarrassment and pride* (pp. 368–392). New York: Guilford Press.

Herbruck, C. (1979). *Breaking the cycle of child abuse.* Minneapolis, MN: Winston Press.

Holmes, S. J., & Robins, L. N. (1987). The influence of childhood disciplinary experience on the development of alcoholism and depression. *Journal of Child Psychology and Psychiatry, 28*, 399–415.

Holtzworth-Munroe, A. (1991). Attributions and maritally violent men: The role of cognitions in marital violence. In J. H. Harvey, T. L. Orbuch, & A. L. Weber (Eds.), *Attributions, accounts and close relationships* (pp. 165–175). New York: Springer-Verlag.

Hotaling, G. T., & Sugarman, D. B. (1984). An identification of risk factors. In G. L. Bowen, M. A. Straus, A. J. Sedlack, G. T. Hotaling, & D. B. Sugarman (Eds.), *Domestic violence surveillance system feasibility study Phase 1 Report: Identification of outcomes and risk factors* (pp. 3–66). Rockville MD: Westat.

Janoff-Bulman, R. (1979). Characterological versus behavioral self-blame: Inquiries into depression and rape. *Journal of Personality and Social Psychology, 37*, 1798–1809.

Janoff-Bulman, R., & Frieze, I. H. (1983). A theoretical perspective for understanding reactions to victimization. *Journal of Social Issues, 39*, 1–17.

Lewis, H. B. (1987). Shame and depression. In H. B. Lewis (Ed.), *The role of shame in symptom formation* (pp. 29–50). London: Erlbaum.

Lewis, M. (1992). *Shame: The exposed self.* New York: The Free Press.

Miller, A. (1987). *For your own good. The roots of violence in childrearing,* London: Virago.

Mollon, P. (1984). Shame in relation to narcissistic disturbance. *British Journal of Medical Psychology, 57*, 207–214.

Mullen, P. E., Martin, J. L., Anderson, J. C., Romans, S. E., & Herbison, G. P. (1993). Childhood sexual abuse and mental health in adult life. *British Journal of Psychiatry, 163*, 721–733.

Peterson, C., & Seligman, M. E. P. (1983). Learned helplessness and victimization. *Journal of Social Issues, 39*, 105–118.

Polivy, J., & Herman, C. P. (1985). Dieting and binging: A causal analysis. *American Psychologist, 40*, 193–201.

Rosenbaum, A., & O'Leary, K. D. (1981). Marital violence: Characteristics of abusive couples. *Journal of Consulting and Clinical Psychology, 49*, 63–71.

Sartre, J. P. (1956). *Being and nothingness.* New York: Philosophical Library.

Seligman, M. E. P. (1975). *Helplessness: On depression, development and death.* San Francisco: Freeman.

Silver, R. L., & Wortman, C. B. (1980). Coping with undesirable life events. In J. Garber & M. E. P. Seligman (Eds.), *Human helplessness: Theory and applications* (pp. 279–340). New York: Academic Press.

Tangney, J. P. (1996). Conceptual and methodological issues in the assessment of shame and guilt. *Behavior Research and Therapy, 34*, 741–754.

Tangney, J. P., Burggraf, S. A., & Wagner, P. E. (1995). Shame-proneness, guilt-proneness, and psychological symptoms. In J. P. Tangney & K. W. Fischer (Eds.), *Self-conscious emotions: The psychology of shame, guilt, embarrassment and pride* (pp. 343–367). New York: Guilford Press.

Tangney, J. P., Miller, R. S., Flicker, L., & Barlow, D. H. (1996). Are shame, guilt, and embarrassment distinct emotions? *Journal of Personality and Social Psychology, 70*, 1256–1269.

Tangney, J. P., Wagner, P., Fletcher, C., & Gramzow, R. (1992b). Shamed into anger? The relation of shame and guilt to anger and self-reported aggression. *Journal of Personality and Social Psychology, 62*, 669–675.

Tangney, J. P., Wagner, P., & Gramzow, R. (1992a). Proneness to shame, proneness to guilt, and psychopathology. *Journal of Abnormal Psychology, 101*, 469–478.

Walker, L. E. (1983). The battered woman syndrome. In D. Finkelhor, R. Gelles, G. Hotaling, & M. Straus (Eds.), *The dark side of families: Current family violence research* (pp. 31–48). London: Sage.

Weiner, B. (1986). *An attributional theory of motivation and emotion.* New York: Springer.

Wicker, F. W., Payne, G. C., & Morgan, R. D. (1983). Participant descriptions of guilt and shame. *Motivation and Emotion, 7*, 25–39.

Wing, J. K., Cooper, J. E., & Sartorius, N. (1974). *The measurement and classification of psychiatric symptoms.* Cambridge: Cambridge University Press.

10

Shame in the Labeling
of Mental Illness

Thomas J. Scheff

This study shows how a new level can be added to an existing theory. By analyzing the details of the dialogue in a single therapy session, I propose that my earlier labeling theory of mental illness can be enriched by including discourse analysis at a microlevel. The session that I use is between an anorexic woman and her therapist. The same session was analyzed in an earlier study (Labov & Fanshel, 1977). I show how discourse analysis complements earlier work on labeling of mental illness. Unacknowledged shame is seen as a cause of both primary and secondary deviance. In family systems, it causes primary deviance, and in the interaction between the family and the community, it causes secondary deviance.

Labov and Fanshel's (1977) case, "Rhoda," provides an extended example. It suggests that the family labeling process is subtle and outside of awareness. In the anorexic patient's family, stigmatization is a two-way street; through innuendo, all the family members—including the patient—surreptitiously attack each other. But only the patient's violence has an overt component. Like the family members, she attacks others through innuendo, but she also starves herself. All the others use only emotional violence. Since the violence of the family is hidden, it is the patient who was formally labeled. The labeling appears to be extremely subtle and complex, inadvertently reaffirming the status quo in the family. To the extent that the mental health professions side with the family, they too reaffirm and maintain the status quo.

Labeling Theory

I consider myself lucky to be able to criticize my own original formulation of labeling theory (Scheff, 1984a, b), because when I criticize the work of others, sometimes they take it personally. When I criticize my own work, I am free to view the criticism in its most favorable light, perhaps as a sign of intellectual growth, rather than showing how inadequate the original formulation was. Like most other theories of human behavior, the original theory was highly specialized, yet insufficiently detailed. It was specialized since it dealt behaviorally with social structure/process. It omitted most inner events, both those concerning mental illness and those concerning the societal reaction.

The original theory was also insufficiently detailed. First, it was formulated in terms of abstract concepts, "black boxes," that were not clearly defined. Second, the causal links between these concepts were not specified. The theory described the societal reaction as a system without defining the major subsystems or the links between them.

My final criticism is substantive, pointing toward a major deficit at the core of labeling theory: its omission of emotions. Although Goffman (1963) and others discussed stigma, they paid too little attention to emotions, particularly the emotion of shame.[1]

The original labeling theory was also oriented toward the formal labeling process, as it takes place in hearings and psychiatric examinations. Labeling (and non-labeling) in these contexts was crude and overt. But in the family, as we argue here, labeling is covert. It depends upon innuendo, manner, unstated implications, and especially emotion. To detect it, one must interpret words and actions *in context*.

At this stage of theory development, reliable methods may be premature, since they strip away context. The next step in developing a theory may be to understand a single case very well. Part/whole analysis allows one to show the relationship between the smallest parts of discourse and the very largest social system (Scheff, 1990, 1997). When one can demonstrate an understanding of the relation between parts and wholes in a series of cases, the stage is then set for a research mode oriented toward testing hypotheses. Since mental illness at this point is still a mystery and a labyrinth, we need to generate models that are interesting enough to warrant testing—ones that have face validity.

This chapter outlines a theory and method that specify the role of unacknowledged shame in mental illness and in the societal reaction. The theory involves a model of feeling traps, recursive loops of shame and anger. The method involves the systematic interpretation of sequences of events in discourse. Discourse from a psychotherapy session is used to illustrate the theory, to allow us to envision the hypothesized moment-by-moment causal sequence.

Pride, Shame, and the Social Bond

Cooley (1922) implied that pride and shame serve as intense and automatic bodily signs of the state of a system that is otherwise difficult to observe. Pride is the sign of an intact social bond; shame is the sign of a threatened one. The clearest outer marker of pride is holding up one's head in public and looking others in the eye, but indicating respect by alternately looking at and looking away. In *overt* shame, one shrinks, averting or lowering one's gaze, casting only furtive glances at the other. In *bypassed* shame, one stares, outfacing the other.

Pride and shame thus serve as instinctive signals, both to the self and to the other, that communicate the state of the bond. We react automatically to affirmations of and threats to bonds. But in early childhood most of us learn to disguise and ignore these signals. The idea of the social bond is repressed in modern societies, masked by the ideology of individualism. The emotions that express the bond—pride and shame—are also deeply repressed (Lewis, 1971; Scheff, 1990).

Lewis's (1971) work is particularly relevant to the conjecture under discussion. She found that in contexts high in potential for shame (as when a patient appears to suspect that the therapist is critical or judgmental), nonverbal indications of shame are plentiful. These include long or filled pauses ("well," "you know," "uh-uh-uh," and the like), repetition or self-interruption, and, particularly, a lowering of the voice, often to the point of inaudibility. These markers are all suggestive of hiding behavior.

In these contexts, however, the painful affect of overt shame was virtually never acknowledged by name. Instead, other words were used, which Lewis interpreted to be a code language. *Insecure, awkward, and uncomfortable* are several examples from a long list. This language is analogous to the code language for designating other unmentionables, such as sexual or "toilet" terms. Like baby talk about body functions used with children, the denial of shame is institutionalized in the adult language of modern societies. Lewis's findings, like the approaches of Cooley (1922), Goffman (1963), and especially Elias (1978–1983), suggest that shame is repressed in our civilization.

Although Goffman's, Elias's, and Lewis's treatments of shame are an advance over Cooley's in one way, in another way they are retrograde. Their treatment is much more specialized and detailed than Cooley's, whose discussion of the "self-regarding sentiments" is casual and brief. But Cooley had a vision of the whole system that is lacking in the more recent discussions. His treatment construes pride and shame to be polar opposites. It therefore lays the basis for our construct of the social bond; pride and shame are continuous signals of the state of the bond, an instant readout of the "temperature" of the relationship.

The emotion of pride is absent from Goffman's and (1967) and Lewis's (1971) formulations. Goffman's omission of pride is particularly disastrous. Since Lewis dealt only with psychotherapy discourse, we are free to imagine from her work that in normal conversation there is more pride than shame. But Goffman's treatments of "impression management," "face," and embarrassment concern normal discourse, leaving the reader with the impression that all human activity is awash in a sea of shame. He nowhere envisioned a secure social bond, much less a well-ordered society built upon secure bonds. Goffman's omission of pride and secure bonds is particularly misleading for the study of deviance; it undercuts a crucial distinction between "normal" persons and labeled persons. Social situations usually generate pride for the former and shame for the latter. This difference has extraordinary consequences for the social system.

Goffman's (1963) treatment of stigma, although perceptive and useful, is not complete. Like other labeling theorists, his discussion is specialized, focusing on the behavioral aspects of stigma. He acknowledges the emotional component of the societal reaction only in passing. In particular, he mentions shame only twice, once early in the essay: "[for the deviant] shame becomes a central possibility," (p. 7), and again at the end: "Once the dynamics of shameful differences are seen as a general feature of social life. . . ." (p. 140).

Goffman frequently refers to shame or shame-related affects, but only indirectly ("self-hate and self-derogation" [1963, p. 7]). Without a working concept of the relationship between emotion and behavior, Goffman and the other stigma theorists were unable to show its central role in mental illness and the societal reaction. As a step toward this end, it is first necessary to review once more how emotions may cause protracted conflict.

An earlier report (Scheff, 1987) described emotional bases of interminable conflicts. Like Watzlawick, Beavin, & Jackson (1967), I argue that some conflicts are unending; any particular quarrel within such conflicts is only a link in a continuing chain. Both primary and secondary deviance arise out of interminable conflicts. What is the cause of this type of conflict?

Lewis (1971, 1976, 1981, 1983) proposed that when shame is evoked but not acknowledged, an impasse occurs that has both social and psychological components. Here I sketch a model of impasse, a *triple spiral* of shame and rage *between* and *within* interactants. When a person has emotional reactions to their own emotions and to those of the other party, both become caught in a "feeling trap" (Lewis, 1971) from which they cannot extricate themselves. The idea that emotions are contagious *between* individuals is familiar; the concept of spirals subsumes contagion both between and within parties to a conflict.

A New Labeling Theory

My model follows from Lewis's (1971) analysis of therapy transcripts: shame is pervasive in clinical interaction, but it is invisible to interactants (and to researchers) unless Lewis's approach is used. (For methods that parallel Lewis's, see Gottschalk's [1995] "shame-anxiety scale.")

Lewis (1971) referred to the internal shame-rage process as a "feeling trap," as "anger bound by shame" or "humiliated fury." Kohut's (1971) concept, "narcissistic rage," appears to be the same affect, since he viewed it as a compound of shame and rage. When one is angry that one is ashamed, or ashamed that one is angry, then one might be ashamed to be so upset over something so "trivial." Such anger and shame are rarely acknowledged and are difficult to detect and to dispel. Shame-rage spirals may be brief, lasting a matter of minutes, or they can last for hours, days, or a lifetime, as bitter hatred or resentment.

Brief sequences of shame-rage may be quite common. Escalation is avoided through withdrawal, conciliation, or some other tactic. In this chapter, a less common type of conflict is described. Watzlawick et al. (1967, pp. 107–108) called it "symmetrical escalation." Since such conflicts have no limits, they may be lethal. I describe the cognitive and emotional components of symmetrical escalation, as far as they are evidenced in the transcript.

Labeling in the Family: A Case Study

Labov and Fanshel (1977) conducted an exhaustive microanalysis of a large segment of a psychotherapy session. They analyzed not only what was said but also *how* it was said, interpreting both words and manner (the paralanguage). They based their interpretations upon microscopic details of paralanguage, such as pitch and loudness contours. Words and paralanguage are used to infer inner states: intentions, feelings, and meanings.[2]

With such attention to detail, Labov and Fanshel were able to convey unstated *implications*. Their report is evocative; one forms vivid pictures of patient and therapist and of their relationship. One can also infer aspects of the relationship between Rhoda and her family, since Rhoda reports family dialogues. Labov and Fanshel showed that the dispute style in Rhoda's family is indirect: conflict is generated by nonverbal means and by implication.

Indirect inferences, from a dialogue that is only reported, are made in order to construct a causal model. Obviously, in future research they will need to be validated by observations of actual family dialogue. It is reassuring, however, to find that many aspects of her own behavior that Rhoda reports as occurring in the dialogues with her family are directly observable in her dialogue with the therapist. For example, the absence of greeting and Rhoda's covert aggression in the dialogue she reports with her aunt can be observed directly in the session itself (not included in this chapter, but discussed in Scheff, 1989).

The Feud between Rhoda and Her Family

Rhoda was a 19-year-old college student who had a prior diagnosis of anorexia. She had been hospitalized because of her rapid weight loss, from 140 to 70 pounds. When her therapy began, she weighed 90 pounds. At 5 feet 5 inches in height, she was dangerously underweight.

Her therapy sessions took place in New York City in the 1960s. Rhoda lived with her mother and her aunt, Editha; her married sister also figures in the dialogue. The session that was analyzed by Labov and Fanshel was the 25th in a longer series, which appeared to end successfully. The therapist reported improvement at termination. At a 5-year follow-up, Rhoda was of normal weight, married, and raising her own children.

Labov and Fanshel focused on the web of conflict in Rhoda's life, mainly with her family and, to a lesser extent, with her therapist. The conflict was not open but hidden. The authors showed that Rhoda's statements (and those she attributed to the members of her family) were packed with innuendo. They inferred that the style of dispute in Rhoda's family was indirect: although the family members were aggressive toward each other and hurt by each other, both their aggression and their hurt were denied.

Labov and Fanshel's method was to state explicitly as verbal propositions what was only implied in the actual dialogue. This method proposed a cognitive structure for the conflict in Rhoda's family: it translated utterances, words, and paralanguage into purely verbal statements. The set of verbal statements served as a compact, clarifying blueprint for a dense tissue of complex maneuvers that were otherwise difficult to detect and understand.

In addition to this type of analysis, Labov and Fanshel also used another. Following the lead of the therapist, they pointed out cues that were indicative of unacknowledged anger. To reveal this emotion, they used verbal and nonverbal signs: words and paralanguage (such as pitch and loudness). Hidden challenges in

Rhoda's family were made in anger and resulted in anger. Rhoda's therapist made explicit reference to this matter: "So there's a lot of anger passing back and forth" (5.27[c]). There were also myriad indications of unacknowledged anger and other emotions in the session itself.

Emotions were not central to Labov and Fanshel's study, but they are to mine. Building upon their assessment of cognitive conflict and their (and the therapist's) analysis of anger, I show shame sequences in the session that were apparently unnoticed by both patient and therapist. Labov and Fanshel frequently noted the presence of embarrassment and of the combined affect they called "helpless anger," but they made little use of these events.

My study leads me to conclude that labeling occurs at two different levels—the informal and the formal. At the informal level, labeling is quite symmetrical: Rhoda labeled and blamed Aunt Editha and her mother just as much as they labeled and blamed her. The family members casually insulted each other almost constantly. In some sentences, several different insults were implied at once. As Labov and Fanshel pointed out, conflict seemed to be endemic in this family.

At the formal level of labeling, however, there was no symmetry whatsoever. Although the mother and the aunt were just as violent with their insults, threats, and rejections as Rhoda, it was only Rhoda who was physically violent; she tried to starve herself. In contrast to the constant verbal violence, Rhoda's overt violence was highly visible; her dangerously low body weight bore ostensible witness to her self-assault. Although the verbal violence seemed to be visible to the therapist and was documented by Labov and Fanshel, it was invisible in Rhoda's community. If labeling theory is going to lead to further understanding of mental illness, it will need to take a new direction, to make visible what has hitherto been invisible: violence in the microworld of moment-to-moment social interaction.

I use two excerpts (Labov & Fanshel, 1977, pp. 364, 365). The first involves Rhoda's relationship with her mother; the second, with her Aunt Editha. The first excerpt occurred early in the session—it deals with a telephone conversation that Rhoda reported. The mother was temporarily staying at the house of Rhoda's sister, Phyllis. (Since pauses were significant in their analysis, Labov and Fanshel signified their length: each period equals .3 second.)

Excerpt 1

1.8   R.: An-nd so—when—I called her t'day, I said, "Well, when do you plan t'come **home?**"
1.9   R.: So she said, "Oh, why!"
1.10 R.: An-nd I said, "Well, things are getting just a little too **much!** [laugh] This is—i's jis' getting too hard, and. . . .I—"
1.11 R.: She s'd t'me, "Well, why don't you tell **Phyllis** that!"
1.12 R.: So I said, "Well, I haven't talked to her lately."

Rhoda, a full-time student, argues that she can't keep house without help. Her mother puts her off by referring her to Phyllis. The implication—that the mother is there at Phyllis's behest—is not explored by the therapist. Rather, she asks Rhoda about getting help from Aunt Editha. Rhoda's response:

Excerpt 2

2.6 [a] R.: I said t'her (breath) w-one time—I asked her—I said t'her.
    [b]   "Wellyouknow, wdy'mind takin' thedustrag an'justdust around?"
2.7   R.: Sh's's, "Oh-I-I—it looks **clean** to me," . . .
2.8 [a] R.: An' then I went like **this**.
    [b]   an' I said to her, "**That** looks **clean** t'you?"
              (It appears that at this point, Rhoda had drawn her finger across a dusty
              surface and thrust her dusty finger into Editha's face.)
2.9 [a] R.: And she sort of . . . I d'no-sh' sort of gave me a funny look as if I—hurt
              her in some way,
    [b]   and I mean I didn't **mean** to, I didn't **yell** and **scream**.
    [c]   All I did to her was that "**That** looks clean to you?". . . .

The therapist persists that Rhoda may be able to obtain help from Editha. In a later
segment (not shown), Rhoda denies this possibility.

Rhoda's Helpless Anger toward Her Aunt

I will begin analysis with the least complex segment, the dialogue that Rhoda
reports between herself and her aunt (2.5–2.9). Labov and Fanshel showed a thread
of underlying anger, anger that is denied by both parties.

Rhoda has explained prior to this excerpt that dust "bothers" her—that is,
makes her angry. The authors argue that the request that Editha "dust around"
(2.6[b]) involves an angry challenge to Editha's authority, a challenge that neither
side acknowledges. It assumes that the house is dusty, that Editha knows it, that
she has ignored her obligation to do something about it, and that Rhoda has the
right to remind her of it.

Although Rhoda uses "mitigating" devices, speaking rapidly and casually, she
ignores the etiquette that would have avoided challenge.

(Labov and Fanshel wrote, "The making of requests is a delicate business and
requires a great deal of supporting ritual to avoid damaging personal relations
surrounding it" [p. 96].) To avoid challenge, Rhoda might have begun with an
apology and explanation:* "You know, Aunt Editha, this is a busy time for me, I
need your help so I can keep up with my schoolwork." Rhoda's actual request is
abrupt. (As is customary in linguistics, an asterisk (*) is used to denote a counterfactual, a hypothetical statement not made in the actual dialogue.)

Editha's response is also abrupt: "Oh-I-I—it looks clean to me. . . ." She has
refused Rhoda's request, intimating inaccuracy in Rhoda's appraisal. The ritual
necessary to refuse a request without challenge is at least as elaborate as that of
making one. Editha could have shown Rhoda deference:* "I'm sorry Rhoda, but
. . . ," followed by an explanation of why she was not going to honor the request.

Rhoda's response to what she appears to have taken as an insult is brief and
emphatic: she contemptuously dismisses Editha's contention. She wipes her finger
across a dusty surface and thrusts it close to Editha's face: "*That* looks *clean* to
you?" Labov and Fanshel noted the aggressive manner in Rhoda's rebuttal: she
stresses the words *that* and *clean*, as if Editha were a child or hard of hearing. They
identified the pattern of pitch and loudness as the "Yiddish rise-fall intonation":

*"By *you* that's a *monkey* wrench?" implying repudiation of the other's point of view. "If you think this is clean, you're crazy" (p. 202). Rhoda's response escalates the level of conflict: she has openly challenged Editha's competence.

Finally, Rhoda describes Editha's response, which is not verbal but gestural: she gives Rhoda a "funny look as if I—hurt her in some way." Rhoda denies any intention of hurting Editha and that Editha has any grounds for being hurt: "I didn't yell and scream," implying that Editha is unreasonable.

Labov and Fanshel noted the presence of anger not only in the original interchange but in Rhoda's retelling of it. The nonverbal signs, they said—choking, hesitation, glottalization, and whine—are indications of *helpless anger*. Rhoda "is so choked with emotion at the unreasonableness of Editha's behavior that she can not begin to describe it accurately" (p. 191). Helpless anger, the authors wrote, characterizes Rhoda's statements throughout the whole session: "she finds herself unable to cope with behavior of others that injures her and seems to her unreasonable" (p. 191).

Labov and Fanshel further noted that her expressions of helpless anger were "mitigated":

> All of these expressions of emotion are counterbalanced with mitigating expressions indicating that Rhoda's anger is not extreme and that she is actually taking a moderate, adult position on the question of cleanliness. Thus she is not angered by the situation, it only "bothers" her. Even this is too strong; Rhoda further mitigates the expression to "sort of bothers me." (p. 191)

Mitigation in this instance means denial: Rhoda denies her anger by disguising it with euphemisms.

What is the source of all the anger and denial? Let us start with Rhoda's helpless anger during her report of the dialogue. Helpless anger, according to Lewis (1971), is a variant of shame-anger: we are ashamed of our helplessness. In retelling the story, Rhoda is caught up in in a shame-anger sequence: shame that she feels rejected by Editha, anger at Editha, shame at her anger, and so on.

Helpless anger has been noted by others besides Lewis and Kohut (1971). Nietzsche (1887/1967) referred to a similar affect ("impotent rage") as the basis for resentment. Scheler (1912/1961) used Nietzsche's idea in his study of *ressentiment*—pathological resentment. Horowitz (1981), finally, dealt with a facet of helpless anger under the heading "self-righteous anger."

Rhoda and her family are caught in a web of *ressentiment*, to use Scheler's term. Each side attributes the entire blame to the other; neither side sees their own contribution. As Labov and Fanshel showed, one of Rhoda's premises is that *she* is reasonable and the members of her family are unreasonable. The reported dialogues with her family imply that the family holds the opposite premise: that *they* are reasonable, but she is unreasonable.

My theory suggests that the dialogue between Rhoda and Editha is only a segment of a continuous quarrel. Since it is ongoing, it may not be possible to locate a particular beginning; any event recovered is only a link in a chain (Watzlawick et al., 1967). Starting at an arbitrary point, suppose that Rhoda is "hurt" by Editha's failure to help. That is, she feels rejected, shamed by Editha's indifference, and angry at Editha for this reason. She is also ashamed of being angry, however. Her anger is bound by shame. For this reason it cannot be acknowledged, let alone discharged.

Editha may be in a similar trap. Rhoda is irritable and disrespectful, which could cause Editha shame and anger. She could experience Rhoda's hostility as rejecting, arousing her own feelings of helpless anger. Reciprocating chains of shame and anger on both sides cause symmetrical escalation.

The Impasse between Rhoda and Her Mother

Excerpt 1, as reported by Rhoda, may point to the core conflict. It is brief—only three complete exchanges—but as Labov and Fanshel (1977) showed, it is packed with innuendo. My analysis follows theirs, but expands it to include emotion dynamics.

Rhoda's first line, as she reports the conversation, is seemingly innocuous: "Well, when do you plan t'come home?" To reveal the unstated implications, Labov and Fanshel analyzed understandings about role obligations in Rhoda's family. Rhoda's statement is a demand for action, disguised as a question. They pointed out affective elements: it contains sarcasm (p. 156), criticism (p. 161), challenge (pp. 157, 159), and rudeness (p. 157). The challenge and criticism are inherent in a demand from a child that implies that the mother is neglecting her obligations.

Implicit in their comments is the point I made about Rhoda's approach to her aunt. It was possible for Rhoda to have requested action without insult, by showing deference, reaffirming the mother's status, and providing an explanation and apology. Rhoda's request is rude because it contains none of these elements.

Rhoda's habitual rudeness is also indicated by the absence of two ceremonial forms from all her dialogues, not only with her family, but also with her therapist: any form of greeting and the use of the other's name and title. Does Rhoda merely forget these elements in her report of the dialogues? Not likely, since they are also missing in the session itself. Labov and Fanshel tell us that the transcript begins "with the very first words spoken in the session; there is no small talk or preliminary settling down . . . Instead the patient herself immediately begins the discussion." Rhoda neglects to greet the therapist or call her by name. Since Rhoda is junior to the therapist, her aunt, and her mother, the absence of greeting, name, and title is a mark of inadequate deference toward persons of higher status. Rhoda's casual manner is rude.

The mother's response is just as rude and just as indirect. According to Rhoda's report, her mother also neglects greetings and the use of names. Like Rhoda's aunt, she neither honors the request nor employs the forms necessary to avoid giving offense. Rather than answering Rhoda's question, she asks another question—a delay that is the first step in rejecting the request.

Labov and Fanshel stated that the intonation contour of the mother's response ("Oh, *why'* ") suggests "heavy implication." They inferred: *"I told you so; many, many, times I have told you so." (When Rhoda gives a second account of this dialogue [4.12–4.15], she reports that the mother actually said, "See, I told you so.") What is it that the mother, and presumably others, has told Rhoda many times? The answer to this question may be at the core of the quarrel between Rhoda and her family.

Whether it is only an implication or an actual statement, the mother's I-told-you-so escalates the conflict from the specific issue at hand—whether she is going to come home—to a more general level: Rhoda's status. Rhoda's offensiveness in her opening question involves her mother's status only at this moment. The mother's response involves a general issue. Is Rhoda a responsible and therefore a worthwhile person, or is she sick, mad, or irresponsible?

Labeling, Shame, and Insecure Bonds

At a superficial level, the mother's I-told-you-so statement involves only Rhoda's ability to function on her own. As can be seen from Rhoda's complaints at the end of the session, however, this implication is symbolic of a larger set of accusations that Rhoda sees her mother and sister as leveling at her: she is either willfully or crazily not taking care of herself, starving herself, and she doesn't care about the effect of her behavior on her family. Her family's basic accusation, Rhoda feels, is that she is upsetting them, but she doesn't care. Rhoda formulates this accusation at the end of the transcript.

Excerpt 3

T. What are they feeling?
5.26R. . . . that I'm doing it on purp—like, I w's-like they . . . well-they s-came out an'tol' me in so many words that they worry and worry an' I seem to take this very lightly.

To Rhoda, the mother's I-told-you-so epitomizes a host of infuriating, shaming charges about her sanity, responsibility, and lack of consideration. Note particularly that the labeling process to which Rhoda refers here is not explicit; it occurs through innuendo.

The labeling of Rhoda by the other family members and its emotional consequences underlie the whole family conflict. Yet it can be detected only by a subtle process of inference, understanding the meaning of words and gestures *in context*, in actual discourse. Both the theory and the method of the original labeling theory were too abstract to detect this basic process.

Rhoda responds (in 1.10) not to the underlying implication of her mother's evasion but to the surface question, "Why do you want to know?" Because, she answers, "things are getting just a little too much." The key element in Rhoda's response is the *affect*. Labov and Fanshel stated that the paralanguage (choked laughter, hesitation, glottalization, and long silence [p. 170]) is an indication of embarrassment (p. 171). Rhoda responds to her mother's accusations by becoming *ashamed*. The shame sequence that is described is a marker for stigmatization that is otherwise hidden behind polite words.

Rhoda's shame may indicate that she feels that her family's charges have some basis or that the implied rejection leads her to feel worthless or both. Since no anger is visible at this instant, it is either absent or bypassed. The verbal text, however, suggests that Rhoda is feeling shame and guilt. She is acknowledging that she needs her mother—a need she has repeatedly denied in the past. She may feel that she is at fault for this reason.

Labov and Fanshel contrasted the force of the mother's response with the weakness of Rhoda's comment (at 1.10). The mother says, "Why don't you tell Phyllis that?" Labov and Fanshel stated that the hesitation and embarrassment that characterize 1.10 are absent from this response. It is a forceful rejection of Rhoda's claims and, by implication, a criticism of Rhoda for even making the request. The mother's emotional response to Rhoda's embarrassment is not simply unsympathetic; it is aggressively rejecting. From the emotional standpoint, Rhoda's back is to the wall. She is trapped in the helpless role of the blamed, with her mother as the aggressive blamer.

The analysis of shame in this dialogue points to an otherwise hidden issue. At this moment we can see that in her family, Rhoda has literally no one to whom she can turn. She is at odds with her aunt. We know from her reports of her sister's comments that Rhoda and she are also in a tangle. No father is mentioned. Rhoda and her family are in a perpetual war, a war hidden beneath the surface of conventional discourse. All of Rhoda's bonds are threatened, yet she has no way of understanding her complete alienation.

The stage is set for violent emotion and/or violent behavior; for mental illness (Rhoda appears to be delusional about her eating and body weight), murder, or suicide (in this case, self-starvation). That the potential for suicide arises when individuals have no one to whom they can turn was conjectured by Sacks (1966) on the basis of his analysis of calls to a suicide prevention center. The repression of shame and the bondlessness that is its cause and effect can give rise to primary deviance in the form of mental illness, murder, or suicide.

In Rhoda's response (1.12), she continues in the role of the one at fault: "Well, I haven't talked to her lately." Her mother has defeated her on all counts. She has refused Rhoda's request without the ritual that would protect Rhoda's "face"; she has implied a victory over Rhoda ("I told you so") that undercuts Rhoda's status; and she has criticized her for making an inappropriate request to the wrong person.

Rhoda appears to feel too baffled, upset, and helpless for an angry counterattack. Her anger at her mother may feel too shameful to countenance. It is reserved for lesser targets: her aunt, her sister, and the therapist. Her mother's rejection, with the implied threat of abandonment, could be the basic source of Rhoda's shame.

Even to the casual reader, the mother's tactics are transparent. Why is Rhoda so baffled by them? Why didn't she use a response like the one suggested by the authors: *"Oh, come off it, Ma! You know it's really up to you when you come home, not Phyllis. Get off my case!"

Rhoda's ineptness may be due to her intense shame, evoked beginning with the first question, at asking her mother for help. In this instance, the massiveness of the unacknowledged shame is befuddling almost to the point of paralysis.

In the overt form of shame, one is so flustered that speech is disrupted, with inaudibility, repetition, stuttering, and fragmentation. Even though she is only reporting the dialogue, Rhoda's speech shows many of these markers. Bypassed shame, on the other hand, may disrupt one's ability to think clearly, forcing one into a holding pattern, repeating set responses not particularly appropriate to the moment (Scheff, 1987). This dialogue suggests that Rhoda is overwhelmed with both kinds of shame.

At the heart of the quarrel is a series of threats between Rhoda and her mother. As in all interminable quarrels, it is not possible to identify the first link. I begin with Rhoda's basic threat, without signifying that it came first: *"If you don't stop shaming me, I will starve myself!" Her mother's basic threat: *"If you don't stop shaming me, I'll abandon you!"

The abandonment threat in this case is literal: the mother has left Rhoda to stay with her other daughter. Normally, the threat of abandonment would be largely symbolic; carrying out a threat of abandonment is probably rare. But whether it is real or symbolic, threats of abandonment may be the key link in the causal chain.

This chain has potentially lethal force because none of it is visible to both participants. There are four links: (1) Rhoda's shame in response to her mother's behavior toward her; (2) her threat to starve; (3) the mother's shame in response to Rhoda's behavior; (4) her threat to abandon Rhoda. Rhoda is aware of none of these links. Nearest to her awareness is the mother's threat to abandon her; next, the shaming by her mother. Rhoda is unaware that her mother is shamed by Rhoda's aggressive and self-destructive behavior, and she denies that she is starving herself. The mother is aware of only one link: Rhoda's threat to starve herself. Because of this awareness, she talks to and about Rhoda in code, not daring to mention Rhoda's threat. Her shame over Rhoda's behavior, her own shaming of Rhoda, and her threat to abandon Rhoda apparently are not experienced by her.

The driving force in the quarrel is not the anger that was interpreted by the therapist but the shame in the field between Rhoda and her family. The anger in this family is both generated and bound by shame. Rhoda experiences her mother's threat of abandonment and her mother's anger as shaming. The mother experiences Rhoda's threat of self-starvation and Rhoda's anger as shaming. The symmetry is complete: each side is threatened and shamed by the other, and each side can see only the other's threat.

The system of threats and hidden emotions is comparable to that which precedes conflict between nations (Scheff, 1994). Each side feels its credibility would be diminished by backing down in the face of threat. Each side therefore escalates the level of threat. The resulting emotions have no limit, unless outside mediation occurs or shame is dispelled. "War fever" may be code language for collective shame-rage spirals.

The theory advanced here attempts to explain the emotional sources of mental illness and the excessive force of the societal reaction to mental illness, the roots of primary and secondary deviance. Rhoda and her family are caught in an interminable conflict that is driven by triple spirals of shame and anger within and between the disputants. For brevity, I have not included my (1989) analysis of the transaction between Rhoda and her therapist, but because of its relevance to the argument, I provide a brief summary.

Although Rhoda attacks the therapist surreptitiously, using the same tactics she uses against the authority figures in her family—her mother and her aunt—the therapist is too wily to become enmeshed in them. She gets angry, but she doesn't attack Rhoda back, as Rhoda's mother and aunt do. By avoiding enmeshment in the family conflict, the therapist is able to form a secure bond with Rhoda, leading ultimately to a successful course of therapy.

Research in the labeling tradition suggests that therapists like this one are probably rare. Therapists and other agents outside the family often become entangled in family conflicts, usually siding with the family against the patient. Bowen's

(1978) seminal analysis of family systems implies this course. Several of our earlier case studies illustrate the enmeshment of the outside agents on the side of the family (Retzinger, 1989; Scheff, 1984a, 1987).

Retzinger's (1989) study of a psychiatric interview goes further; she shows how the psychiatrist is entangled with the family position and how this enmeshment leads to renewed psychiatric symptoms, as predicted by Lewis's theory (1981). The theory proposed here explains the extraordinary forces that underlie mental illness and the reaction to it, chain reactions of shame and anger, feeling traps both in patients and in those reacting to them.

Bonds, Communication, and Conflict

A recent study of mental illness using a strictly biographical method has produced findings parallel to ours. Porter (1990) provides an even-handed assessment of endogenous and environmental contributions to mental illness in a large number of well-documented cases. His summary of the findings for one case—the nineteenth-century patient John Perceval—can be taken to represent his conclusions for the majority of his cases:

> Perceval believed that religious terror had brought on his insanity, and that the behaviour of his family had exacerbated it. But *the real cause of the appalling severity and prolongation of his condition was the medico-psychiatric treatment* he had received. Perceval unambiguously condemned as intrinsically counter-productive the very philosophy of placing mad people in lunatic asylums. It set the lunatic amongst "strangers" precisely when he *needed to be with his fellows* in familiar surroundings. It estranged him from his family. It put him in the charge of an unknown doctor, rather than those members of the caring professions he knew well, his regular physician or his clergy man. It set him in the midst of fellow lunatics, who, if truly mad, must surely be those people least capable of sustaining the mind of one who had just been crushed under a terrible blow. Precisely at the moment when a person needed his morale to be boosted, he was thrown into a situation that must "*degrade him in his own estimation.*" (Porter, 1990, pp. 180–81, emphasis added)

This statement clearly supports labeling theory and points particularly to the two elements in labeling that are emphasized by the new theory: the weakening of social bonds and the accompanying unacknowledged shame. That the psychiatric treatments of the composer Robert Schumann and the dancer Nijinsky resulted in the complete severing of their social bonds is particularly shocking (Porter, 1990).

The position that Porter, a historian, takes toward his findings seems equivocal. He cites none of the labeling theory literature; he states that he sides neither with the patients nor with the psychiatrists. Yet his closing message acknowledges some strain. The first line of his conclusion reads, "This book has not pleaded a cause" (p. 231). He goes on to say that his aim has been merely to focus attention on a body of forgotten writings, the memoirs of the mad. Yet at the end of the conclusion, he states, "clearly, no reader will have taken the opening statement of this

Conclusion at face value" (p. 232). For reasons that are never stated, Porter is reluctant to acknowledge the implications of his findings. He seems to make the error of equating taking a stand on his own findings with "pleading a cause."

The case in this chapter contains the three elements fundamental to my theory: inadequate bonds, dysfunctional communication, and destructive conflict. Before her contact with the therapist, Rhoda appears to have been alienated from everyone in her family. No father is mentioned, and she seems to have the barest cognitive attunement with her mother and aunt and virtually no understanding at the emotional level.

The dialogues with her mother and aunt that Rhoda reports clearly indicate dysfunctional patterns of communication. She and her mother are extremely indirect, evasive, and withholding with each other, and she and her aunt are violently disrespectful, although in underhanded ways. It is of great interest that although she tries the same tactics she uses in her family on the therapist, the therapist is able to sidestep them, giving Rhoda what turns out to be important lessons in how to communicate directly but respectfully.

The theme of violence is present in these dialogues only in the form of Rhoda's attempts at self-starvation. Like virtually all the other important issues in Rhoda's family, these attempts are disguised and denied: Rhoda claims that she is only dieting and that she is not underweight. As in most important issues in social communication, contextual, prospective, and retrospective knowledge beyond the discourse itself is needed to interpret the meanings of statements and events.

Support for the theory is also found in the cues for hidden emotion that both the therapist and Labov and Fanshel (1977) point out in their interpretations. Although the therapist only interprets Rhoda's and her family's anger, Labov and Fanshel's careful analysis of microscopic cues in verbal and nonverbal behavior provides support for our theory of shame-rage spirals. Their analysis frequently pointed to instances of "embarrassment" (shame) and "helpless anger" (shame-anger), suggesting the sequences required by the theory. The theory of shame-rage spirals fills in the wiring diagram of the black boxes in labeling theory: unacknowledged alienation and shame drive the labeling machine.

As in its earlier formulation, our extended labeling theory implies a critique of conventional psychiatry, which is individualistic and affirms the status quo. In focusing exclusively on Rhoda's pathology, it denies the pathology in the family system of which she is a part and, by implication, in the larger social system, our current civilization.

Notes

1. Peggy Thoits and John Braithwaite are exceptions. Thoits (1985) published a study that connects emotions and labeling, and Braithwaite (1989) a theory of stigmatization that explicitly links stigma and shame. Braithwaite's framework links low crime rates with "reintegrative," or what we would call normal, shame and high crime rates with stigmatization (or recursive shame). He also makes a connection between normal shame and community. His work implies the fundamental link between shame and the social bond described in this paper, but it is limited by his omission of the role of pride.

2. This section is based on Scheff 1989.

References

Bowen, M. (1978). *Family therapy in clinical practice*. New York: Aronson.

Braithwaite, J. (1989). *Crime, shame, and reintegration*. Cambridge: Cambridge University Press.

Cooley, C. H. (1922). *Human nature and the social order*. New York: Scribner's.

Elias, N. (1978–1983). *The civilizing process* (Vols. 1–3). New York: Vintage.

Goffman. E. (1963). *Stigma*: Notes on the management of a spoiled identity. Englewood Cliffs: Prentice-Hall.

Goffman, E. (1967). *Interaction ritual: Essays on face-to-face behavior*. Garden City, NY: Anchor.

Gottschalk, L., 1995, *Content analysis of verbal behavior*. Hillsdale, N.J.: Erlbaum.

Horowitz, M. (1981). Self-righteous rage. *Archives of General Psychiatry, 38* (Nov.), 1233–1238.

Kohut, H. E. (1971). Thoughts on narcissism and narcissistic rage. In P. Ornstein (Ed.), *The search for the self*. New York: International Universities Press.

Labov, W., & Fanshel, D. (1977). *Therapeutic discourse*. New York: Academic Press.

Lewis, H. (1971). *Shame and guilt in neurosis*. New York: International Universities Press.

Lewis, H. (1976). *Psychic war in men and women*. New York: New York University Press.

Lewis, H. (1981). *Freud and modern psychology: Vol. 1. The emotional basis of mental illness behavior*. New York: Plenum.

Lewis, H. (1983). *Freud and modern psychology: Vol. 2. The emotional basis of human behavior*. New York: Plenum.

Nietzsche, F. (1967). *On the genealogy of morals*. New York: Vintage. (Original work published 1887)

Porter, R. (1990). *A social history of madness*. New York: Dutton.

Retzinger, S. (1989). A theory of mental illness: Integrating social and emotional aspects. *Psychiatry, 52* (3), 325–335.

Sacks, H. (1966). *The search for help: No one to turn to*. Unpublished doctoral dissertation, University of California, Berkeley. University Microfilms. DAI: 27 (1967) 11, p. 3953.

Scheff, T. (1984a). *Being mentally ill* (2nd Ed.). Chicago: Aldine.

Scheff, T. (1984b). The taboo on coarse emotions. *Review of Personality and Social Psychology, 5*, 146–169.

Scheff, T. (1987). The shame-rage spiral: Case study of an interminable quarrel. In H. Lewis (Ed.), *The role of shame in symptom formation* (pp. 109–149). Hillsdale, NJ: Erlbaum.

Scheff, T. (1989). Cognitive and emotional components in anorexia: Reanalysis of a classic case. *Psychiatry, 52*, 148–160.

Scheff, T. (1990). *Microsociology: Discourse, emotion and social structure*. Chicago: University of Chicago Press.

Scheff, T. (1994). *Bloody revenge: Emotions, nationalism and war*. Boulder, CO: Westview.

Scheff, T. (1997). *Emotions, social bonds, and human reality: Part/whole analysis*. Cambridge: Cambridge University Press.

Scheler, M. (1961). *Ressentiment*. Glencoe, IL.: The Free Press. (Original work published 1912)

Thoits, P. (1985). Self-labeling processes in mental illness: The role of emotional deviance. *American Journal of Sociology, 91*, 221–248.

Watzlawick, P., Beavin, J. H., & Jackson, D. (1967). *The pragmatics of human communication*. New York: Norton.

11

Shame in the Therapeutic Relationship

Suzanne M. Retzinger

This chapter deals with countertransference and its relationship to emotions and the social bond. The nature of psychotherapy involves intense relationships and reciprocal bonds, with all the accompanying emotions. Shame, particularly, seems to play an important role in therapeutic relationships. The psychoanalytic literature has not provided a detailed account of the role of emotion between therapist and patient. My formulation puts emotion at the center. The identification of shame cues may provide a tool for psychotherapists.

Countertransference Conceptualized

Since 1910, when Freud invented the term *countertransference*, there has been vast outpouring of writing about it. Although it is a psychoanalytically derived term, it has been used with all forms of therapy. The general consensus suggests that countertransference refers to the feelings aroused in the therapist in response to the therapeutic relationship (Racker, 1968). Historically, these feelings have been thought to be negative.

The concept of countertransference was at first thought to be a source of disturbance in the analyst (such as feelings of ineptness in the therapist; Reich, 1951) and an impediment which must be kept out of the sessions. Because it has been viewed in a negative light, there is stigma connected with countertransference. But currently, countertransference is being reconsidered as a potential therapeutic tool. Indications of countertransference can help the therapist maneuver toward a therapeutic outcome. It becomes destructive only when the therapist either ignores the signals or acts on them.

Those who view countertransference as a tool also conceptualize it as part of the relationship matrix: transference and countertransference go hand in hand (Greenberg & Mitchell, 1983; Hedges, 1992; Kohut, 1971; Levenson, 1983; Marshall & Marshall, 1988; Racker, 1968; Sandler, 1976; Stolorow, Brandschaft & Atwood, 1987). For instance, Kohut (1971) called his relationship matrix "self-object" relations.

Stolorow et al. (1987) considered the rhythm of relationships as they ebb and flow between *contact* and *breaks in contact*. Stolorow and colleagues (1987) viewed the therapist-patient relationship as a unit in itself and thought the negative therapeutic reaction cannot be considered apart from the context in which it occurs.

Balint and Balint saw the therapeutic situation as the "result of the interplay between the patient's transference and the analyst's countertransference, complicated by the reactions released in each other by the other's transference onto him" (1939, p. 228). Like the others, Marshall and Marshall also see inherent relatedness: "the definition of transference involves the countertransference" (1988, p. 103).

In this chapter, countertransference is considered in a relatedness framework: therapist and patient mutually affect one other, eliciting feelings in each other. The countertransference reaction will be dealt with as part of a complex pattern of relatedness within and between both interactants as they mutually affect each other.

In this framework, countertransference does not lie only in the past but is about signaling during the present functioning, especially in the capacity to make a secure attachment and to be aware of how and when contact is broken. Emotion cues can provide clues to the state of the bond at any given moment and may be an effective tool for monitoring countertransference.

What countertransference seems to entail, in part, is a transgression of social-emotional boundaries between closeness and distance. Much of the empirical work identifying countertransference includes over-and underfunctioning, which concerns social-emotional distance. What makes distancing difficult is that different people require different levels of closeness and distance for comfort.

Ideological Countertransference

The analyst, like any person, has an array of ideological beliefs. These can involve theoretical perspectives and worldviews; belief systems, such as that the therapist must always be supercompetent; and other abstract concepts that are projected onto the therapeutic situation. In this way, ideological countertransference is a form of triangling (Bowen, 1978). It involves a third party, belief, ideology, and so forth, rather than a direct reciprocal relationship with the patient.

Ideological countertransference can disrupt therapeutic relationships and lead to isolation, breakdown in the therapist-patient relationship, and iatrogenic effects. Kernberg (1965) used the word *countertransference* for the therapist's reaction to the patient's transference, which makes it not the therapist's problem but simply part of the data. In ideological countertransference, the data is construed in such a way that it becomes the patient's problem.

One important belief involves a therapist's theoretical training or clinical ideology (Gartner et al., 1990; Hedges, 1992; Scheff, 1984; Stein, 1986). By placing the problem, as defined by the belief system, within the patient, the therapist's own reactions to the patient can be ignored, thereby freeing him or her of personal or social responsibility. Denying countertransference reactions and the ideology from which they spring produces a healthy-therapist–sick-patient polarization. There ceases to be an opportunity to connect with the patient on a human level.

When two persons have very different perspectives, it may be difficult for them to connect. To see a patient out of control or acting bizarrely can be frightening; presenting an unusual perspective may stimulate a primitive part of the self that resembles this "craziness." Inviting connection is scary—we may reach out for a link to the patient and be met with no response. The immediate emotional reaction can be one of fear, anger, or embarrassment, which leads to discrimination or projection. When this response is ignored, the ideology of healthy therapist–sick patient is created, leading to social isolation for the patient. The impact of this isolation can produce iatrogenic effects, exacerbating the patient's symptoms.

Ideological countertransference involves a closed system, one that does not lend itself to connecting with a patient. An open system allows variation and growth; it is effective in connecting with patients where they are.

The Role of Shame in Countertransference

The study of the social bond and shame can be used to demystify the concept of countertransference and provide a tool for treatment. If one is alert to shame and embarrassment cues, they can reveal the state of the therapeutic relationship at any given moment. Shame in the therapeutic session may indicate that the bond is in need of repair—it is either too close or too distant. If the therapist can tolerate his or her own shame, as well as the patient's, impasse can be avoided or broken.

Messner (1979) gives a list of observable cues to therapeutic impasse. These include unreasoning distaste for the patient, criticism, feelings of inadequacy in the therapist, rejection, irritation, indifference, discomfort, withdrawal, and so on. Many of his items include elements of being engulfed or isolated from the patient, as well as indications of anger or shame. Neither he, nor anyone else, has spelled these reactions out explicitly as they pertain to the therapist's emotional and relational states.

Shame is used here to include all its derivatives: embarrassment, humiliation, mortification, social discomfort, and so on. Shame is often viewed from an individual and internal perspective. I will describe it more broadly in its social context. Shame is different from other emotions in that it is about the self in relationship to others.

Shame symbolizes mutual social involvement and at the same time reminds us of our separateness. Shame tells us that we are both separate and social beings and guards the boundaries of privacy and intimacy (Lynd, 1958). For shame to occur, we must care in some way about the other. To neglect to acknowledge damaged or threatened bonds or the shame that is evoked leaves relationships open to disruption. Shame occurs when persons are not connected—either too close or too distant. Being too close is engulfment, being too distant is isolation; both can involve violation of boundaries. Shame is about alienation. In Buber's words, there is no "I-thou" relationship.

Alienation involves either too much togetherness (engulfment) or too much separateness (isolation). Each human being constantly monitors his or her own closeness to and distance from others. Shame is like a thermostat; it helps regulate relationships; if it fails to function (e.g., is repressed, unconscious, ignored, projected, etc.), regulation becomes impossible.

Lewis's (1971) work on shame was a profound attempt to understand treatment failure by systematically analyzing hundreds of transcribed psychotherapy sessions. In part, her interest in shame "stemmed from the discomforts of the analyst in the patient-therapist relationship" (p. 14). Her method was to trace sequences of the patients' emotions from neurotic symptoms (often the patient's hostility) back to their source, in unanalyzed shame. She discovered that "shame in the patient-therapist relationship was a special contributor to the negative therapeutic reaction" (p. 11). Lewis showed that one unresolved aspect of transference is bypassed, or unconscious, shame, which was easily overlooked.

Lewis (1971) described shame in its two main variants: overt undifferentiated shame and bypassed shame. Whereas overt shame is analogous to being ashamed, bypassed shame is a state of shame that is largely unconscious. Bypassed shame is a low-visibility state which is difficult to detect. Bypassed shame cannot be detected in bodily arousal; it is primarily observed in thought processes and relationships between persons. Sometimes it is confused with guilt. The concept of bypassed shame is critical for understanding the therapeutic process; it can have a dramatic effect on outcomes.

Although Lewis began her work with the therapeutic relationship and was interested in the analyst's discomfort, in her written work she neglected to explore the unanalyzed feelings of the therapist and how they affect the patient. She did not provide an equal analysis of the therapist's feelings—the effect of the patient on the therapist. One unresolved aspect of countertransference may be the therapist's bypassed shame, which is overlooked. This is an important omission, since the therapist's reactions can be directly related to countertransference and a source of further shame for the patient. When we begin to look at behavior in terms of relatedness, shame takes on a new meaning.

In all interactions, bonds are either being built, maintained, repaired, or damaged. There are intense emotional reactions to lapses in the bond. Reactions can include feelings of helplessness, frustration and hatred, or discomfort. Other responses include anger, grief, fear, or shame. Shame, particularly, plays an important role in therapeutic relationships. If a therapist is in a state of shame which is not acknowledged, it may be difficult to navigate within the relationship and may disrupt behavior; at best one can go into a holding pattern, repeating routine responses rather than finding new responses to a unique situation.

The detection of shame can be used for understanding countertransference and treatment failure. If we understand shame as an important part of countertransference, denial of shame by the therapist constitutes a major obstacle which is likely to lead to treatment failure.

Understanding the Nature of Shame

Emotions have common roots that comprise discrete families. For example, although the various forms of anger (resentment, rage, annoyance, irritation, etc.) arise in different circumstances and have varying intensities, their common characteristics (active, forward-moving, specific facial expressions, voice tones, and physiological changes) place each in a family called *anger*. This is the case with each major emotion: anger, fear, grief, shame, joy, and pride.

Social emotions are distinguished by the fact that they are about maintenance of relationships. Unlike other families of emotion, a major characteristic of shame is the self in its relationship to others. Shame is not concerned with the organism as an isolated entity but with relationship between persons, the regard of others— with preservation of the relationship. Shame guards the boundaries of privacy and intimacy (Lynd, 1958; Schneider, 1977; Wurmser, 1981). Shame always occurs in response to other human beings, if only in the imagination.

When social-emotional boundaries are violated (unrequited love, exposure, etc.), the self feels like the object of injury, while the other is experienced as the source of the injury. The self feels helpless, while the other seems powerful. The self may or may not be flooded with unpleasant feelings, while the other appears intact. Even if not flooded with feelings, both people are focal in awareness. *Shame can remain out of conscious awareness and still be present.*

Frequent and intense unacknowledged shame arises from and generates failure of social connection. Under this condition, distortion can take place, making it difficult to function. With intense sequences of emotion generated by shame, it may become excessively difficult to regulate self in relation to other. Lewis's main theme is: when shame is evoked and remains unanalyzed, symptoms will either be maintained or increase.

Identifying Shame

Identification of shame states includes: variants and vocabulary, stimulus or source of shame, conscious content and experience, position of self in the field, and defenses against shame. The variations range from mild forms, such as social discomfort, to intense forms, such as mortification, and include such emotional states as embarrassment, dishonor, disgrace, humiliation, and chagrin.

There are hundreds of ways of disguising the shame experience. Lewis (1971) noticed that certain words continually reoccurred in contexts of shame and were accompanied by the use of certain gestures. Some vernacular terms include feeling *uncomfortable, insecure, uneasy, confused, worthless, inadequate, stupid, foolish, silly, weird, helpless, unable, impotent,* and so on.

Each of these words, and many others, belongs to the common experience of the self in its relation to another. If the shame vocabulary is compared with the much smaller vernacular language used to describe anger, guilt, fear, or grief, the extent of the shame lexicon is larger than those describing any other emotional experiences. This is a clue to the ubiquity of shame.

The source of shame involves an other-to-self message that is experienced as involving an injury to self: self is the object of disappointment, rejection or fear of rejection, betrayal, judgment, exposure, unrequited love, ridicule, intrusion, and so on. The injury can be real or imagined.

The message can be very subtle, involving only a slight gesture (e.g., nose wrinkle, speech cadence slightly off) or blatant, overt forms (Goffman, 1967). The other in these situations can be perceived as alienated, separate, or unlike oneself—the bond is not intact; there is no reciprocal connection. The other could be viewed as caring less about the relationship than you do. In therapy it could be that the patient sees the therapist as "just doing it for the money": "it's not a real relationship because I have to pay for it. Anyway, I'm not as important to the therapist as she is to me; she has many patients, I have only one therapist." The self can feel as though it is being observed by the other. The other is focal in awareness and may appear laughing, ridiculing, watching, powerful, active, in control, unjust, hostile, unresponsive, and so on; the other's self appears intact.

Lewis (1971) identified the forms of unidentified shame. On the overt side, during shame one might feel paralyzed, helpless, passive, childish, out of control of the situation. There may be blushing, tearing, or other unpleasant bodily arousal. Overt shame is relatively easy to detect but can be given a label which disguises its nature, for example, "I felt really *weird*." The experience may be removed from the person altogether, for example, "the *situation* was uncomfortable"; "It is not I who am embarrassed, the situation was weird." Feeling is denied and projected onto an external source.

Bypassed shame is more difficult to detect. It is seen mainly in ideation, which includes varieties of thought such as how one is deficient; the self is focal in awareness, the other may be viewing the self. Thoughts may take the form of what *should* have been said or *might* have been said or may include mentally replaying earlier scenes over and over. Bypassed shame could be manifest in rapid speech, thought, or behavior. Comparisons between self and other are frequent, where the self appears inferior in some way: less beautiful, intelligent, strong, and so on; or one might simply wonder what the other person thinks of him or her or wonder about sufficiency of self (the impostor syndrome may be an example). Persons in a state of shame might function poorly as agents or perceivers; thoughts, speech, or perception is obsessive. Thoughts might be divided between imaging the self and imaging the other or may be absorbed with self-identity and whether the self has been discredited.

Although shame often appears trivial in the outer world, because of the importance the experience has to the self, the feelings refuse to subside. A characteristic defense against shame is to turn away from the experience, to hide from the pain of rejection by using various tactics, one of which is anger. The turning away makes shame difficult to recognize or communicate (Lynd, 1958), and it often remains unacknowledged. When shame is unacknowledged, it can play havoc in relationships. (For a more complete list of identifying markers for shame and anger, see Retzinger, 1991, 1995).

Shame–Anger Affinity

When shame is evoked, but not acknowledged, anger may be aroused by indications that the other does not value the self or imputes injurious thoughts toward the self. Anger can be directed toward self or other. Shame and anger seem to have an affinity. Many researchers and theorists have observed the co-occurrence of anger with other emotions such as shame, guilt, fear, or anxiety (see Retzinger, 1991). Shame seems to play a particularly important role in anger and hostility.

Shame and anger get joined because of the social nature of shame: it is often experienced as an attack coming from the other (whether real or imagined). The special quality of emotional communication in shame-rage is a message about how enraged the self feels at its inferior place in the eyes of the other. When shame is not acknowledged, the other may be seen as the source of hostility, creating a type of entrapment that can easily lead to escalation.

In my own earlier studies of resentment (Retzinger, 1985, 1987, 1991), I observed that whenever persons described a situation that caused them to feel angry, shame was also prominent. In fact, the anger was preceded by ideation of separation, an indicator of shame. Rapidly alternating sequences from shame to rage were recorded using videotapes and printed photographs. Moreover, I showed that when shame is prominent, anger subsides very slowly, asymptotically, leaving a residue of anger. Anger is a particularly good place to begin to trace sequences back into shame because anger is usually more visible than shame (see Retzinger, 1991, 1995 for verbal and nonverbal cues to anger.)

Unacknowledged shame serves both as an inhibitor and as a generator of anger, rendering the person impotent to express anger directly toward the other (withholding behavior), while simultaneously generating further anger, which may eventually emerge as demeaning or hostile criticism, blame, insult, withdrawal, or physical attack. The same dynamics are seen in passive-aggressive behavior.

A characteristic response of shame is to hide from the painful experience. All kinds of hiding behaviors indicate the presence of shame. "Denial is . . . a characteristic defense against shame" (Lewis, 1971, p. 89).

A summary of the main ingredients in shame-rage is:

1. The bond is violated or is perceived to be violated.
2. Shame signals disruption in the bonding system.
3. Shame is denied (not acknowledged). The self feels alienated and experiences the other as the source of attack; that is, one may feel misunderstood.
4. Anger follows as a defense or protest against the threat. When the bond is ignored, anger can serve as a mechanism for saving one's own face.

Shame-rage has a cyclic character: because it is usually regarded as an inappropriate state, the defense is to turn away from the stimulus situation and often to project it onto the other.

In the cases which follow, I treat the patient-therapist as a unit. I analyze three cases in terms of shame and countertransference: the case of Freud and Dora is analyzed in terms of ideological countertransference; a case I call "Paul and Dr. L.," taken from a case study by London (1989) of her personal experience with countertransference, is reanalyzed using the concept of shame; and the third, an interview from Gill, Newman, and Redlich (1954), which I call "Roberta and Dr. B," is analyzed in terms of both personal and ideological countertransference. In the text I use **boldfaced** print to indicate anger, *italics* to indicate shame, and ***bold italics*** to indicate shame–rage simultaneously.

The Case of Dora and Freud

One of the clearest examples of ideological countertransference is seen in the case of Freud and Dora. Although we don't know Freud's emotional state, we do know Dora's. There seem to be some similarities with the case of Roberta and Dr. B, which follows. I compare an early case—the case of Lucy R—with Freud's later case, that of Dora. Freud's treatment of Lucy (Freud & Breuer, 1896/1961) was successful in that she became aware of the source of her conflict and her symptoms were reduced. After Freud wrote *The Interpretation of Dreams* (1905/1953), many treatments, as in the case of Dora, were unsuccessful—Dora left analysis in a state of humiliation.

In the earlier case, Lucy was a governess who was in love with her employer and hoped to marry him; her love was painfully unrequited. She had symptoms of depression, chronic rhinitis, and hallucinatory experiences of smelling cigar smoke.

At the time of *Studies in Hysteria* (Freud & Breuer, 1896/1961), Freud was making new discoveries and was open to what was occurring with his patients; he was empathic and intuitive in treating Lucy. He focused on Lucy's humiliation over unrequited love for her employer and for having been severely scolded by him. After she discovered the unconscious source of her conflict, the symptoms disappeared; her spirits were high. Freud's theory of hysteria was born out of his practice and careful observation of his patients. Freud's theory matched his practice. At the time he treated Lucy, Freud was working within an open system.

After Freud wrote *The Interpretation of Dreams* (1905/1953), he became wedded to the theory of unconscious sexual wishes from childhood as the source of neurotic symptoms. Since his identity was tied to his theory, he was no longer free to explore. Dora was a young woman of 16 who told her father that his closest friend, Herr K, had made sexual advances toward her; Dora's father did not believe her. Dora became depressed, had headaches, and left a suicide note, among other symptoms.

Because Freud tried to fit Dora into his theory, the case was a fiasco. Herr K actually had been making passes at Dora. Her father was having an affair with Frau K, and he looked away from his friend's advances toward his daughter to distract attention away from the affair with his friend's wife. Freud did not focus on Dora's humiliation over the betrayal but pressured her to admit her guilt over forbidden sexual excitement about Herr K, which he interpreted in her dreams. Freud tried to persuade Dora that she had feelings for Herr K and welcomed his advances— that she was unconsciously in love with him, as well as with her father.

Freud was not empathic in his analysis with Dora; he was unable to understand Dora's dilemma or to help her understand her emotional responses, as he did with Lucy. By forcing Dora to conform to his theory, he may have been defending against his own shame of being wrong. Because he did not acknowledge his shame, Freud humiliated Dora further. The four principal people in Dora's life had betrayed her; Freud joined in the betrayal. He followed his theory at her expense: his theory and practice diverged; he tried to force Dora to fit his theory.

The ability to be sensitive to the particular case keeps a system open: getting at unconscious conflict was appropriate in Lucy's case, but not in Dora's. Lucy *was* in love with her employer; Dora was disgusted and felt betrayed by Herr K's advances and by her father and Freud's collusion. In Dora's case it was not helpful to fit the patient into the idea that she had forbidden sexual longings; the theory needed to be modified but was not. The immediate shame and humiliation in Dora's case were far more important for therapeutic intervention than the more distant issues of sexuality. Ideological countertransference involved a closed system that was insensitive to the patient's suffering and led to treatment failure with Dora.

The Case of Paul and Dr. L

This case is taken from London (1989), where she analyzes her own countertransference.

Paul is in therapy with Dr. L, a female analyst, for problems in love and work. According to Dr. L, Paul views himself "as a helpless victim of the manipulations of women who have all the power. . . ." Dr. L goes on to say that eventually she found herself "feeling *exasperated*, even *tortured*, by Paul's constant talk of women—all of whom he saw as pathological, defective, and rejecting" (p. 200) When he did allow himself to think of Dr. L, his awareness of her existence was limited to her "*competence*" to meet his needs (London, 1989).

In her analysis of her own countertransference with Paul, Dr. L refers to anger but does not refer directly to shame, although she does use what I call code words to describe this experience; both emotions are evident in her case material.

Paul begins his acquaintance with Dr. L by explaining that she will be under the scrutiny of his watchful eye:

P: I want to know if you are good. . . . Something comes through no matter what, in tone of voice, the words. I will know if you are competent.
T: What thing will you be looking for?
P: What I will be looking for is your feeling of confidence, I want you to be fully confident in yourself. I need a person who is very confident or I will not feel confident. I will be watching you closely for the least little sign or slip.
T: *Should I watch my step?*
P: (laughing) Oh no. Be yourself, you can't help it or pretend, but I'll be watching for it. . . . (London, 1989, pp. 201–202)

During the course of treatment, the patient's asthmatic symptoms disappeared, but Dr. L's asthma reoccurred and became chronic. She found herself becoming increasingly insensitive to the patient's troubles and began to see him as "deficient, thick-headed and possibly even malevolent." She had thoughts that *she was a failure* and that something was the matter with her, which turned into thoughts that the supervisor was a failure and that something was the matter with him (p. 205). She goes on to say, "By now I was so **enraged** myself that I was glad of Paul's suffering, and decided he deserved it. He was hopeless and helpless, but then, *so was I*. Sometimes his words felt like blows, battering, beating me to death. Perhaps *I deserved* it, perhaps hopelessness and suffering were all there was on earth" (p. 206).

Dr. L's countertransference is evident: she is in an impasse with Paul. Dr. L feels "too *uncomfortable*" in therapy with Paul. The bond between them is damaged, painful emotions are rampant. The interaction between therapist and patient is marked by shame and anger. Anger is obvious, shame less so; shame appears as self-doubt and uncertainty. Shame is being denied by both parties and is being displaced onto the other in the form of hostility.

Let us take a closer look at the shame: Paul is the careful observer, Dr. L the observed. He sets the tone for how he'll be viewing her from his vantage point— she must be an ideal person in order for him to be helped. He avoids the role of the one being observed and analyzed by emphasizing his role as the observer. He sets the context for humiliating Dr. L as a way of avoiding his own shame.

As a prelude, he describes himself as "*helpless victim of the manipulations of women who have all the power*" (p. 201; my italics). He not only feels *powerless* in the eyes of the women in his life, he is **angry** with them. Paul sees all women as "**pathological, defective and rejecting** . . . When he allowed himself to think of [Dr. L] his awareness of [her] existence was **limited to [her] competence to meet his needs**" (pp. 200–201).

Paul's shame is apparent in his feelings of helplessness and powerlessness. In order to avoid feeling his own shame, he creates an enactment of the position he feels with the women in his life with Dr. L, putting her in the position of the observed. Paul recreates his own experience with women in his life in the session on an analogic, as well as verbal, level. He was apparently using her as he had felt used.

Dr. L was unable to steer clear of Paul's reenactment. She found herself feeling "**exasperated**," "*tortured*," and "**insensitive**" to Paul's troubles. Anger was evident in her perception that he was "**deficient, thick-headed and possibly even malev-olent**." Anger also appeared in that she was **glad of his suffering, and thought he deserved it**. Her own feelings of shame become evident when Dr. L begins to have thoughts that *she is a "failure."* The shame seems to be outside her conscious awareness and is short-lived and quickly disguised by anger in the thought that her "**supervisor was a failure and that something was the matter with him**" (p. 205). She also becomes *obsessed* with the thought that she had made a *mistake* in choosing to become an analyst. Dr. L was *split* between feeling **Paul deserved to suffer** and thinking *she deserved to suffer*. A characteristic of shame is to hide from the pain through splitting, as well as through anger. She oscillates between shame and anger. *Hopelessness* became a theme of her thoughts. Cues for shame in her description of the situation are evident.

Tracing back in time and looking at the context, we find clues to the origin of Dr. L's shame. The context is ripe for shame. Dr. L is the *object* of Paul's scorn by reason that she is a *woman*. Paul places himself in a powerful position vis-à-vis Dr. L; he is ridiculing, not specifically of her but of women in general, and demands perfection from her. Paul's view of Dr. L is *focal* in her awareness; she gets caught in viewing herself through his eyes in a negative light. Dr. L soon becomes over-wrought by painful emotion; she feels *deficient*, which has an avalanche effect. She is split between imaging herself and imaging him and begins to function poorly. Under Paul's scrutiny, Dr. L becomes self-conscious. She is caught between his scrutinizing eye and her own idealized image of herself.

To summarize, Dr. L is caught in a countertransference reaction. In the moment she is unaware of the countertransference or her shame; instead she focuses on her hate for Paul. Under these conditions, Dr. L had great difficulty forming a therapeutic alliance with the patient. The bond between them is damaged. It appears that her self-boundaries were permeable to the extent that she was unable to maintain self in relationship to her patient. Only when she begins to look at her countertransference does this relationship begin to change. Dr. L's shame reaction may have been a signal of qualities in herself which were not unlike those of Paul.

Had she acknowledged her own feelings of shame initially (or was at least aware of the signals that indicate shame), Dr. L may not have gotten caught in the web Paul spun—his demand that she be totally confident. Her own idealized image of having to be perfect may also have interfered. She did not take the viewpoint that no one is perfectly confident at all times and it is all right not to be or that this was Paul's need and it was not her job to fulfill it. She could have said: *"I know you would like me to be fully confident, so you will feel so also. What would happen if you felt not confident?" In denying shame, the bond between them deteriorated, spiraling into rage. Therapy took a turn for the worse. By focusing on the current relationship and the feelings exchanged she might have escaped entrapment. In this case we find the context for shame:

1. Dr. L is the object of scorn, contempt, ridicule; Paul is the source.
2. Dr. L feels paralyzed, helpless, passive; Paul is ridiculing, powerful, active.
3. Dr. L is flooded with shame and rage; although Paul is also in a state of shame and rage, he appears intact. It was Dr. L's asthma which worsened; Paul's improved.
4. Both patient and therapist are focal in awareness for Dr. L. She is being closely observed.
5. Dr. L begins to function poorly, as she is divided between imaging her self and Paul. The boundaries are permeable.
6. Even in the vignette, there are many markers for shame in Dr. L's description of her experience.
7. The reaction to shame by Dr. L was anger toward Paul.

Anger is not always the response—it could be infatuation or withdrawal, under different circumstances.

I suggest that it was shame rather than anger which played a major role in Dr. L's resistance to acknowledging and dealing effectively with her countertransference. Lewis (1987) thought resistance was a misnomer for shame. Being aware of her own anger, as well as the patient's, was an important step. But focusing on the bond between them and the shame that existed could have saved the situation from disaster.

The Case of Roberta and Dr. B

The case of Roberta and Dr. B is taken from Gill, Newman, and Redlich 1954; this discussion is based in part on my earlier article (Retzinger, 1989). Roberta had already been admitted to a mental hospital before the initial interview. Virtually no background is given on this patient. Gill et al. say that she is a young schizophrenic woman with complaints of being nervous and feeling molested and not herself. During the course of the interview, Roberta's symptoms seem to be exacerbated by Dr. B's treatment of her; there are increases in symptomatic behavior at several points during the actual interview. (The complete transcript and audio recording of this interview is available at university libraries along with the book; Gill, Neman, & Redlich, 1954.)

During the interview, Dr. B demonstrates that he has the capacity to connect with Roberta, but he fails to do so for much of the session. When he does empathize with Roberta, her shame seems to be reduced—or at least does not increase. She seems to appreciate it when Dr. B gives her a genuine human response and is quite responsive in return. Instead of continuing in this vein, he gets caught in countertransference, both personal and ideological.

The course of events takes a sharp turn with a sudden shift in Dr. B's approach 10 seconds after he makes an error and gets caught; in the process, he identifies closely with Roberta. He reacts to the error with shame markers and personal countertransference. He retreats into the security of technique, leaving behind the possibility of connection—ideological countertransference. Dr. B now has an agenda: to see if Roberta knows that she is mentally ill, which is implicit in his questioning and testing of Roberta's sanity. He never makes his agenda explicit. Roberta is unaware of Dr. B's agenda. The hidden agenda helps to maintain the distance between therapist and patient.

Besides an ideological issue, there also seems to be a personal issue going on with Dr. B in his relationship with Roberta. In excerpt 1 below, Roberta notices Dr. B looking at the clock and confronts him:

Excerpt 1

P. 286: . . . Am I boring you?
T. 287: Boring? Why?
P. 287: You keep looking at the clock.
T. 288: *Did I? Yes. You didn't* . . . you don't bore me at all. No.
P. 288: Mmm. I mean I just don't know what to do about it. And I don't see why . . . what a sischiatry . . . a psychiatrist would have to do with that. I . . .

Roberta drops the incident in 288 and goes back to telling her story. But instead of acknowledging his part in the exchange and providing a brief explanation, Dr. B denies that he was bored; he seems embarrassed. He perseveres in 289 and reverts to patronizing Roberta:

Excerpt 2

T. 289: **You are a very perceptive person too. You know? How you noticed that I . . .**
P. 289: You think I'm keen.
T. 290: **Oh yes.**
P. 290: **And I don't. I think I'm very stupid. And I can't** (Uses very broad "a.") **understand.**
T. 291: **Simultaneously with P. 290.) I hardly knew myself I was looking at the clock.**

P. 291: You don't realize it. I don't either.

T. 292: Mmmhnn.

P. 292: I can see people and I . . . I'll stare right at them and I don't realize it. And . . .

Roberta does not respond favorably to Dr. B's condescension and appears angry; her tone is harsh. She then empathizes with his dilemma (291 and 292) and mitigates his feelings by explaining that she has done the same thing herself. They switch roles at this point.

There is evidence that Dr. B is in a state of shame:

1. The editorial commentary states:

"He was obviously feeling *uneasy* about this," and "[it] is a good example of how a therapist's preoccupation with his own *anxious feelings* can be disturbing in an interview." (T. 289–291; Gill et al., 1954, p. 379)

2. Dr. B perseveres. That his feeling refuses to subside suggests shame. He continues on the topic for eight exchanges.
3. His speech is somewhat fragmented and halting: "Did I? Yes. *You didn't . . . you don't* bore me at all. No."
4. The context is that he is under the watchful eye of the patient.
5. He begins to function poorly.

Identification with a mental patient may have caused Dr. B shame, as suggested in the commentary (T. 295–297, p. 381):

The patient has told the therapist that he is right when he says his mind wanders and he is not aware of what he does—that he and she are alike. *This may be felt by the therapist as an attack.* To the patient it was a friendly identification.

Excerpt 3

P. 297: . . . Are you confused?

T. 298: I'm a little confused now. Yes.

P. 298: Th-That's what I wanted to know. (Very softly.)

T. 299: But I can see how you must feel.

P. 299: *(Softly.)* Its awful.

T. 300: *(10)* **You said before you don't think this is anything mental.**

P. 300: No.

Ten seconds after P. 299, where they connect, there is an abrupt shift. T. 300 is the beginning of a series of exchanges in which Dr. B investigates P.'s "insight" into her illness; it continues for 29 exchanges. Dr. B reverts to rigid use of technique and to his hidden agenda—to see if Roberta knows that she is crazy. Because his feelings remain unacknowledged, Dr. B compromises connection for his ideological beliefs and diagnostic task.

The editors' commentary on T. 300 notes that Dr. B grasps at the psychiatric framework: "You are mentally disturbed—that is why I did not understand you."

Dr. B shuns a relatedness framework. Perhaps his momentary closeness to a mental patient was threatening to him—a countertransference reaction. He reverts to rigid use of technique. His ideological countertransference serves as a defense. Human connection is lost.

The following excerpts occur just before Roberta's symptoms increase. Dr. B tries to get Roberta to admit she is crazy in 25 instances between 300 and 332; Roberta makes 21 attempts at protesting and rejecting his explanations. The level of conflict increases between them; the bond is increasingly damaged. Exchanges 324–331 illustrate the dynamics leading to iatrogenic effects in a 50-second timespan. Excerpt 4 occurs after Roberta complains about being sick of life.

Excerpt 4

T. 324: **So there IS something which is not right**
P. 324/5: Yes *I-thing-it it jis isn't* my head and my BO::dy
T. 325/6: [**But you call it amNE::SIA**]
P. 326: . . . (volume softens) (2.5) There are scientific explanations besides (1) *other explanations for it (over soft) ()* I-don't-see-why-I-should-go-back-tu-living-with-a-family **I don't wanna be with**() . . . *He doesn't seem to want me:/: () An that-in itself HURTS me very much.*
T. 327: **Who is he.**
P. 327: *I don't know.*
T. 328: **You'd like-you have no idea.**
P. 328: [*I see-im (inaud)] clearly in my mi::nd sometimes*
T. *329:* **But you don't know who he is.**
P. 329: *Mmm no (very soft> I'm not gonna say if I <do>*
T. 330: Mmm.
P. 330: *I-I be-I'd feel SILLY if-f-found out the o::pposite*

Excerpt 4 exemplifies an ideological belief as a countertransference response and dynamics of countertransference; Dr. B's tone (T. 324) is "AHA! so you do have a problem." His statement shows little respect for Roberta's perception and appears hostile; it damages the relationship further. Even if Roberta is wrong, he could have presented in a way which would build or maintain the bond between them, rather than damage it. Dr. B is in a state of shame which is not acknowledged. He makes no further attempts in this interview to connect or to empathize with Roberta. He continues to use technique and theory in a rigid way.

Commentary for T. 324–326 states that the therapist is

trying to convince her it is something he knows about and that she is psychotic. We are trained to do this: to see if a patient is crazy, not to see what a patient thinks about it. We are trained to think that if a patient sometimes admits he is crazy it is insight and that the possibilities of therapy are better. (Gill et al., 1954, p. 391)

In P. 326 Roberta concludes with a very strong emotional expression of being "hurt." Dr. B does not respond to the feeling but questions her further. "Who is he" is not a real question, but a test of her reality. Roberta withdraws by denying that she knows anything. The quarrel continues, with Dr. B pressing further. Dr. B rephrases and repeats his question twice, again challenging Roberta's competence. She *interrupts* Dr. B, reciprocating the disrespect. The third time he asks the same question in 329, she refuses to answer.

By exchange 329 Roberta is also in a state of both shame and rage. Roberta's shame seems to increase in the fragmented speech and in the use of the code word "SILLY". There is also the possibility of being misunderstood further, a shame context. Roberta tells Dr. B about a vital part of herself. Dr. B misses the point.

Roberta reverts to symptomatic behavior as social connection fails and the conflict intensifies. Roberta suddenly shifts topics, her tone changes, and emotion markers disappear. Instead there are words of temporal expansion: "everything," "nothing," and "all." She withdraws into a hidden world. The editors say, "the patient escapes to her fantasy."

The increase in symptomatic behavior seems to be directly linked to the patient's unacknowledged shame. Her shame was exacerbated by the continued damage to the bond, resulting from the therapist's own unacknowledged shame and countertransference.

In summary, Dr. B seems to be caught in countertransference. I suggest that Dr. B was in a state of bypassed shame over the clock incident, as well as *discomfort* about being too close with a psychotic patient. When Roberta confronts him, Dr. B triangles onto a third thing—the use of his techniques—and questions her more intensely: ideological countertransference. Rather than a corrective relational experience, there are tragic interpersonal consequences. As the bond between them deteriorates, Roberta relapses into her "fantasy" world.

Conclusion

Shame is not simply a painful feeling but involves a dynamic social process which occurs in interaction within, as well as between, persons. Shame serves as a distance regulator by signaling to self and other a threat to the bond. Having a sense of shame is crucial in the ability to regulate internal and social distance (Schneider, 1977).

Shame states can be either overt or bypassed. Although shame often occurs outside conscious awareness, there are signals which indicate its presence and which I have described at length (Retzinger, 1991, 1995).

The three cases illustrate the use of shame as a tool for detecting countertransference. If not identified, countertransference can disrupt therapeutic relationships, including gaps in power positions, isolation, breakdown in the therapist-patient relationship, and iatrogenic effects. Ideological countertransference basically involves a closed system of ideology, as well as denial of shame, which prevents connection with a patient. When shame remains unacknowledged, there can be no mutual connection. An open system allows variation and growth; it is effective in connecting with a patient.

By placing the problem completely within the patient, a therapist's own reactions to the patient can be ignored. Denying countertransference reactions produces a healthy-therapist–sick-patient polarization. The opportunity to connect with the patient on a human level may be sabotaged. While the therapeutic relationship is a professional relationship, it is also a human relationship, with all the emotions which occur between two people. Shame plays an important role in regulating the therapist-patient relationship and can provide a tool for navigating one's way in the labyrinth of complex issues.

References

Balint, A., & Balint, M. (1939). On transference and countertransference. *International Journal of Psychoanalysis, 20,* 223–230.

Beck, A. (1976). *Cognitive therapy and the emotional disorders.* New York: International Universities Press.

Bowen, M. (1978). *Family therapy in clinical practice.* New York: Jason Aronson.

Freud, S. (1953). *Interpretation of dreams.* In *The Standard Edition of the complete psychological works of Sigmund Freud* (vols 4 & 5, pp.). London: Hogarth Press. (Original work published 1905).

Freud, S., & Breuer, J. (1961). *Studies on hysteria.* New York: Avon Books. (Original work published 1896)

Gartner, J., Harmatz, M., Hohmann, A., & Larson, D. (1990). The effect of patient and clinician ideology on clinical judgment: A study of ideological countertransference. *Psychotherapy, 27,* 98–104.

Gill, M., Newman, R., & Redlich, F. C. (1954). *The initial interview in psychiatric practice.* New York: International Universities Press.

Goffman, E. (1967). *Interaction ritual: Essays on face-to-face behavior.* Garden City, NY: Anchor.

Greenberg, J. R., & Mitchell, S. (1983). *Object relations in psychoanalytic theory.* Cambridge, MA: Harvard University Press.

Hedges, L. E. (1992). *Interpreting the countertransference.* Northvale, NJ: Aronson.

Horowitz, M. J. (1981). Self-righteous rage and the attribution of blame. *Archives of General Psychiatry, 38,* 1233–1238.

Izard, C. (1971). *The face of emotion.* New York: Appleton-Century-Crofts.

Kernberg, O. (1965). Notes on countertransference. *Journal of the American Psychoanalytic Association, 13,* 38–56.

Kohut, H. (1971). *The analysis of the self.* New York: International Universities Press.

Levenson, E. (1983). *The ambiguity of change.* New York: Basic Books.

Lewis, H. B. (1971). *Shame and guilt in neurosis.* New York: International Universities Press.

Lewis, H. B. (1987). Resistance: A misnomer for shame and guilt. In D. Milman & G. Goldman (Eds.), *Techniques of working with resistance* (pp. 209–225). Northvale, NJ: Aronson.

London, A. (1989). Unconscious hatred of the analyst and its displacement to a patient and supervisor. *Modern Psychoanalysis, 14* (2), 197–220.

Lynd, H. (1958). *On shame and the search for identity.* New York: Harcourt.

Marshall, R., & Marshall, S. (1988). *The transference-countertransference matrix: The emotional-cognitive dialogue in psychotherapy, psychoanalysis and supervision.* New York: Columbia University Press.

Messner, E. (1979). Autognosis: Diagnosis by the use of the self. In A. Lazare (Ed.), *Outpatient psychiatry* (pp. 230–237). Baltimore: Williams & Wilkins.

Racker, H. (1968). *Transference and countertransference.* New York: International Universities Press.

Reich, A. (1951). On countertransference. *International Journal of Psychoanalysis, 32,* 25–31.

Retzinger, S. M. (1985). The resentment process: Videotape studies. *Psychoanalytic Psychology, 2,* 129–151.

Retzinger, S. M. (1987). Resentment and laughter: Video studies of the shame-rage spiral. In H. B. Lewis (Ed.), *The role of shame in symptom formation* (pp. 151–181). Hillsdale, NJ: Erlbaum.

Retzinger, S. M. (1989). A theory of mental illness: Integrating social and emotional aspects. *Psychiatry, 52* (3), 325–335.

Retzinger, S. M. (1991). *Violent emotions: Shame and rage in marital quarrels.* Newbury Park, CA: Sage.

Retzinger, S. M. (1995). Identifying shame and anger in discourse. *American Behavioral Scientist, 38* (8), 1104–1113.

Sandler, J. (1976). Countertransference and role-responsiveness. *International Review of Psycho-Analysis, 3,* 43–47.

Scheff, T. J. (1984). *Being mentally ill* (2nd ed.). Chicago: Aldine.

Scheff, T. J. (1987). The shame-rage spiral: A case study of an interminable quarrel. In H. B. Lewis (Ed.), *The role of shame in symptom formation* (pp. 109–149). Hillsdale, NJ: Erlbaum.

Scheff, T. J. (1990). *Microsociology: Discourse, emotion and social structure.* Chicago: University of Chicago Press.

Scheff, T. J., & Retzinger, S. M. (1991). *Emotions and violence: Shame and rage in destructive conflict.* New York: Lexington.

Schneider, C. (1977). *Shame, exposure and privacy.* Boston: Beacon.

Stein, H. F. (1986). Sick people and trolls: A contribution to the understanding of the dynamics of physician explanatory models. *Culture, Medicine and Psychiatry, 10,* 221–229.

Stolorow, R. D., Brandschaft, B., & Atwood, G. E. (1987). *Psychoanalytic treatment: An intersubjective approach.* Hillsdale, NJ: Analytic Press.

Tangney, J., Wagner, P., Fletcher, C., & Gramzow, R. (1992). Shamed into anger? The relation of shame and guilt to anger and self-reported aggression. *Journal of Personality and Social Psychology, 62,* 669–675.

Tangney, J., Wagner, P., Hill-Barlow, D., Marschall. D., & Gramzow, R. (1996). Relation of shame and guilt to constructive versus destructive responses to anger across the lifespan. *Journal of Personality and Social Psychology, 70,* 797–809.

Tomkins, S. (1963). *Affect, imagery, consciousness: Vol. 2 The negative affects.* New York: Springer.

Wurmser, I.. (1981). *The mask of shame.* Baltimore: Johns Hopkins University Press.

PART IV

CULTURE

12

Domains of Shame

Evolutionary, Cultural, and Psychotherapeutic Aspects

Deborah F. Greenwald & David W. Harder

The single imperative that best explains physical characteristics of organisms and enduring patterns of behavior is the advantage conferred upon an individual in the successful transmission of genes to the next generation (e.g., Cosmides, Tooby, & Barkow, 1992). Such transmission occurs through direct reproductive success (linear descendants) and also through inclusive fitness (all individuals who share common genes, including kin such as siblings, cousins, and their offspring; Wenegrat, 1990). These evolutionary principles have resulted, via natural selection acting over many millennia, in characteristics that promote fitness, such as size, intelligence, physical configuration, coordination, and so on. In addition, characteristic patterns of behavior with regard to mating and preferences for situations that offer favorable reproductive conditions, such as specific habitats, relative absence of predators, and nutritional foods, are also seen as evolutionarily determined. Recently, this perspective on fitness has been extended (e.g., de Waal, 1996; Gilbert, 1997; Wright, 1994) to consider the value of emotions.

This chapter will focus on the role of shame, which is most frequently presented in the psychological literature as a powerful pathological negative affect that involves a sense of insufficiency or inadequacy (e.g., Harder, 1995; Tangney, Burgraff, & Wagner, 1995) that can accompany, and perhaps cause, maladaptive psychological functioning. Undeniably, such severe and extreme emotional shame states occur; however, we argue here that shame is typically experienced in milder forms that serve to facilitate, rather than impede, socially and personally adaptive behavior. Shame is discussed here in its role as a signal that orients one to potential, but usually avoidable, negative social consequences, which can hinder successful reproduction and psychological well-being alike. As such, shame plays an essential part in promoting fitness through the regulation of behavior in the areas of group identity, social bonding, and competitive mating success.

Historically, psychologists have tended to focus on the psychopathological aspects of dysphoric affects such as shame, perhaps because they are more concerned with reducing psychic discomfort than with the usefulness of such feelings in the promotion of fitness. More recently, some psychologists (e.g., Clark & Watson, 1994; Damasio, 1994; Ekman & Davidson, 1994; Frijda, 1994; Izard, 1993) have discussed the "adaptive" functions of negative as well as positive affects for individual physical survival, social decision making, and psychological well-being, but they have not yet begun a detailed examination of the role of shame (with the notable exception of Gilbert, 1997).

Fear, for example, is an obvious spur to survival through the activation of behaviors to avoid danger. The ability to sense pain is also a signal to avert far worse outcomes, such as the loss of bodily integrity. Even emotions of sadness, grief, and depression have been seen as beneficial, either because they limit a damaging loss of status in the face of social failures and facilitate acceptance of such defeats (Gilbert, 1992b, 1995; Price & Gardner, 1995) or because they offer ways to conserve energy and relinquish futilely pursued goals (Beck, 1987; Clark & Watson, 1994). Similarly, dysphoric emotions such as guilt and shame should, in most situations, lead the individual to more adaptive functioning.

Human beings must manage a complex array of emotions and behaviors in order to maintain themselves in their social network so as to maximize fitness. Affects such as shame and guilt play a useful, even essential, role in guiding individuals' behavior to match well with the values of their particular group. These values are themselves based on a number of factors, some or all of which are related to inclusive fitness within that social setting. For example, hunting and gathering societies have different values than pastoral societies, based in part on differences in what behaviors are necessary in order to thrive in these environments (Barry, Child, & Bacon, 1959; Berry, 1967). These values are communicated via social norms, including those regarding what behavior will be seen as shameful. Individuals, in following these guidelines, are likely to act in a way that enhances their fitness.

From the evolutionary perspective, then, the capacity, or potential, to experience the universal emotions of shame and guilt (Ekman, 1994; Fridlund, Ekman, & Oster, 1986; Wallbott & Scherer, 1995) are hardwired into the brain's neural circuitry by natural selection. The particular triggers for these emotions, that is, what makes an individual feel guilty or ashamed, as well as the form in which these affects are expressed, may well differ widely from culture to culture (Tooby & Cosmides, 1992; Wallbott & Scherer, 1995). The capacities to experience these two types of dysphoria and to use them in the modification of behavior (according to the norms of an individual's culture) improve fitness, though the mechanism of their operation might not, at first, be obvious. Close analysis suggests that both shame and guilt can aid in the control of behaviors that would be destructive to fitness through disruptive effects upon social cohesion and resultant social rejections (Gilbert & McGuire, this volume, chapter 5, Guisinger & Blatt, 1994). In the case of shame, for example, were an individual unable to experience the feeling as an internal warning signal, he or she might behave shamelessly with no sense of discomfort and thereby incur serious exclusions by social companions (Gilbert & McGuire, this volume, chapter 5, describing an example from Miller, 1993). The protection of the group and access to mates might well be lost.

Phenomenologically, shame has been described (Ferguson, Stegge, & Damhuis, 1991; Harder, 1995; Lazarus, 1991; H. Lewis, 1971; Lindsay-Hartz, de Rivera, & Mascolo, 1995; Tangney, 1992; Wicker, Payne, & Morgan, 1983) as a self-conscious awareness that one is being viewed, or might be viewed, by others with an unflattering gaze. Experiences of embarrassment, inadequacy, ridicule, and humiliation are variants of shame. In contrast, the related but distinct affect of guilt (Ferguson, Stegge, & Damhuis, 1991; Harder, 1995; H. Lewis, 1971; Tangney, 1992; Tomkins, 1987) involves a feeling of remorse for what was done, or not done, that could harm another. Shame is a more public experience of exposure or possible exposure, whereas guilt is more an internal affair. Shame implies a reduction in one's standing vis-à-vis others because of conduct disapproved of by them. We submissively lower our eyes, aware that we have lost face, that others might find us ridiculous. In contrast to guilt, where condemnation comes only from the self, shame makes the sufferer want to shrink away from others.

Because guilt functions independently of potential observation by others, it can exert control where shame cannot. This characteristic of guilt proves particularly advantageous when people are away from the scrutiny of the social group and when strong impulses, such as the wish to hurt a family member, could seriously weaken the fitness of the individual. The capacity for guilt, which can check such tendencies, enables individuals to enhance the likelihood of having their genes survive into the next generation by "warning" them not to damage those who share their genes and/or constitute important personal resources.

In a different way, the capacity for shame serves these same evolutionary goals of fitness by providing an additional source of control on behavior. Indeed, shame would seem to have a broader restraining influence upon behavior than guilt, because the inhibiting presence of others often has force even when an internal conscience does not. For example, a man who would rather spend all his earnings on himself rather than give any to his wife and children can still be shamed into supporting his family. Or, when someone will not contribute privately to a church collection or other charity, a contribution may still be elicited when the appeal is made in public and others in the group are already making gifts. Thus, public shaming can enforce prosocial behavior (de Waal, 1996; H. Lewis, 1971; Pines, 1995) even in situations where guilt cannot. Prohibitions made by parents to children (and owners to canine pets, for that matter) can be quite effective and can elicit shamelike reactions of face-lowering, gaze aversion, submissiveness, and shrinking away. Guilt can work more independently but often fails to control problematic behavior, which might still be transformed into socially acceptable conduct through fear of public shaming.

Therefore, although shame and guilt work differently, both affects constrain behavior into channels that are socially approved of and/or culturally appropriate. The two emotions are associated with distinct, if at times overlapping, areas of behavior and facilitate the maintenance of social relationships, which in turn enhance fitness (Gilbert, 1997). These affects often work together, interlaced (Carroll, 1985; Harder, 1995; H. Lewis, 1971), and are not easily separable in the descriptions of those who experience them (Binder, 1970; Shaver, Schwartz, Kirson, & O'Connor, 1987; Tangney, 1992; Wicker, Payne, & Morgan, 1983); and both are needed to regulate conduct.

Guilt

The adaptationist perspective adopted here regarding guilt is relatively new (Baumeister, 1996; Baumeister, Stillwell, & Heatherton, 1995; Pines, 1995). Since the work of Freud (1905/1953, 1920/1966) brought guilt under intense scrutiny as the primary pathogen of psychopathology, the predominant perspective on guilt has undergone several reversals, only recently swinging toward a more favorable view of its usefulness to our well-being. Early on, guilt was regarded as an unfortunate side effect of civilization, a crippling emotion instilled by society through the agency of parents to hobble impulses. As a product of an overly powerful superego, guilt prevented the full and satisfactory expression of feelings and desires. Neurotics, guilt's victims, could repair to a therapist, so that the demons of excessive conscience could be exorcised and the capacity to enjoy life's pleasures no longer inhibited.

Eventually, however, a backlash occurred. Freud was by no means as antiguilt as psychologists' focus on psychopathology had first led them to believe—a fact that has been rediscovered in recent years (e.g., Pines, 1995). Freud (1930) saw guilt as the main force that leads the individual to be a viable social being, countering internal (id) pressures to be blindly self-centered. Guilt serves a signal function by way of mild and often unconscious anxiety. To avoid feeling continued and increasing anxiety and/or crushing guilt, the individual is alerted to change behaviors and thoughts that might bring harm to others and often to attempt some form of reparation (Barrett, 1995; H. Lewis, 1971) toward an injured party. Such alterations can successfully reduce anxiety and guilt to a minimum.

This and similar rehabilitated perspectives on guilt have lately lent support to Freud's original notion that guilt was generally useful and necessary (e.g., Baumeister, 1996; Baumeister, Stillwell, & Heatherton, 1995; Tangney et al., 1995; Tangney, 1996). This trend has most emphasized the function of guilt in the maintenance of interpersonal relationships (Baumeister & Tice, 1990; H. Lewis, 1971). Baumeister and Tice (1990), for example, claim that the purpose of guilt, once it is felt, is to induce the individual to repair relationships that have been damaged by disproportionate self-gratification and neglect of the other's needs. The impulse to do penance, often associated with guilt, serves to motivate reparations.

The present authors agree that guilt is generally a beneficial governor of behavior. It functions as a signal, as a cognitive-emotional expectation, to regulate or prevent actions that would violate obligations to family, the larger social group, and deities. Only excessive or inappropriately chronic guilt that cannot be set to rest by discontinuance of undesirable behavior and/or reparation to an injured party (Bybee & Quiles, in press; Harder, 1996; Jones & Kugler, 1993) need be regarded as harmful.

Shame

We maintain that shame, invariably linked of late by some theorists (e.g., Kaufman, 1989; M. Lewis, 1992; Tangney et al., 1995) to psychopathology and to socially maladaptive behaviors, should also be thought of as having adaptive functions that parallel those of guilt. Like guilt, shame can be severe and extreme and can lead to catastrophic emotional reactions. However, shame is usually experienced in milder forms that also serve to facilitate reparative behavior. As guilt leads to attempts to repair the effects of the behavior that led to the guilt feeling, shame motivates behavior that aims to ameliorate the perceived damage to one's status or good name (Lansky, 1995). These less severe shame experiences typically prompt exertions to repair the harm: the loser of the competition wants a rematch, the person who behaves shamefully tries to behave in a more socially approved fashion, and the individual who is insulted demands an apology. Viewed in this way, mild to moderate shame and the anticipation of shame direct behavior along paths that increase fitness by supporting social bonds (English, 1994) and the maintenance of status.

Shame can also, like guilt, signal the possibility or expectation of severe negative consequences: social rejection, greater shame, or crippling anxiety. This, in turn, motivates the individual to cease the behavior which gave rise to the signal, which can help avoid both further shame and still more devastating consequences to the self. For example, with twinges of anticipatory shame, a teenager might carefully select an acceptable wardrobe, avoiding the possible ostracism or ridicule that might follow the wearing of clothing that differs too greatly from the peer group norm. As a result, this young person may, in fact, feel no further sense of shame with regard to clothing, so carefully and successfully have the choices been monitored. The teenager is not free of the capacity for shame but rather avoids a strong sense of shame by adaptively using the signal that a mild internal experience of the affect provides. Thus, in our view, both guilt and shame can be either global, paralyzing, and intense affects or, more typically, mild signals alerting one to avoid behavioral pitfalls so that life can be relatively guilt-and shame-free. Such an adaptive, relatively successful avoidance of the more extreme experiences of guilt and shame would promote acceptance by, and both reproductive success and fitness within, the social group.

Domains of Shame

We propose that there are at least four types of shame experiences, related to distinct areas of human functioning and vitally related to fitness: conformity, prosocial behavior, sex, and status/competition. The first two types largely affect inclusion in a group as a member in good standing, while the second two areas regulate the individual's mating success. Shame from these various sources, while conceptually distinct, can arise in intermixed and overlapping ways, such that the same behavior or setting might well engender shame from more than one domain. As one example, rejection of one's sexual advances can produce shame from the sexual sphere and an accompanying sense of lowered status in relation to same-sex rivals. Although we are proposing a broad taxonomy of shame categories that we consider the most important for fitness, there is no assumption made here that this list of shame domains is complete.

It can be assumed that both genetic and acquired individual variability are involved in the capacity to feel shame. While the inborn aspect of variability can only be inferred at this point, the acquired differences are evident in the large cultural variations (de Rivera, 1989; Kitayama, Markus, & Matsumoto, 1995; Scherer & Wallbott, 1994; Wallbott & Scherer, 1995) in proneness to various types of shame. We can also assume that, within limits, benefits can accrue to those with both higher and lower degrees of this trait under differing cultural and personal circumstances. Someone who is relatively immune to a particular domain of shame might freely engage in behaviors that would leave others wincing with anticipated discomfort. Such risky behavior might often lead to personal loss or rejection but also may result in individual gain, as will be discussed below. On the other hand, a very high degree of shame-proneness may produce carefully monitored behaviors, reducing risk and thus ensuring a safe, shame-free existence but one without the possible benefits of a greater degree of risk-taking.

Conformity

Human beings demonstrate strong tendencies to conform to group standards (Asch, 1955/1988). A degree of conformity is a requirement for acceptance by the group (Sherif, Harvey, White, Hood, & Sherif, 1988; Sherif & Sherif, 1964) and for the protective and reproductive benefits that result from membership in the social unit. The capacity to experience shame over lack of conformity is useful in regulating behavior that identifies members of a group. Individuals who obviously violate these social norms may well be marginalized or ostracized, so that they are impeded in their drive for fitness.

Conformity shame regulates many behaviors related to dress, language, food consumption, rituals, deportment, and so on. The regulations may sometimes be arbitrary, with little or no inherent survival value. However, they determine what is appropriate for the social self in a variety of roles, according to class, status, ethnic group, age, gender, profession, and so forth. Adherence to these standards is a major mechanism by which group members identify with each other (Hogg & Abrams, 1988). The continuance of group membership depends, to a considerable extent, on learning what the rules of behavior are for various roles one fills and insuring that one's behavior conforms in order to continue enjoying the benefits of belonging.

A group will attempt to ensure that there are easily recognizable traits and features for its members, to distinguish itself from close neighbors (Tajfel, 1978). Group members need to know and to recognize rapidly who belongs, much as members of a team or an army can take in each others' uniforms to avoid making potentially serious errors. Those within the group are to be trusted and protected (Crocker, Thompson, McGraw, & Ingerman, 1987; Sherif & Sherif, 1964; Tajfel, 1982), since generally they can also be counted on to reciprocate. These are the individuals who can be allowed within the walls of the city, the boundaries of the compound, the country club, the gang turf, or, indeed, one's home. For most of human history, the group's members, with their identifying similarities, were probably kinship connected. Under such circumstances, identification of similar individuals would insure acceptance by the genetically linked group most committed to aiding one's own survival and rejection of those who do not belong. Those who act too differently will be seen as nonmembers or strangers to be regarded with wary suspicion. This explanation would account for the enormous importance of identification with an in-group, a community, tribe, ethnic group, or nation, to the psychological well-being of an individual (Hogg & Abrams, 1988). To feel or to actually be excluded is to suffer, in lesser or greater degree, from a sense of stigma (Goffman, 1963). A member who anticipates feeling shame upon the violation of group norms will take precautions to avoid such behavior. The capacity for shame experience, then, and its avoidance through conformity, can prevent the social rejection or ostracism (Scheff, 1988) that could result from noncompliance.

Changes at puberty provide an illustrative example, and perhaps a special case, of the importance of shame in following group expectations. As children physically become adults, they are for the first time regarded as fully subject to social norms. Prepubescent juveniles are allowed more freedom in the eyes of the community, just as they are in other social mammalian species (e.g., de Waal, 1996). During puberty, pressure is put on individuals to conform to society more firmly, with initiation ceremonies generally commemorating this change in status (J. Brown, 1975; Turner, 1964). In many cultures adolescents show a very strong need to identify with their peers, their future bonding and mating group, and to distinguish themselves from those both younger and older than themselves (Berndt, 1979; B. Brown, 1990; Clasen & Brown, 1985; Steinberg & Silverberg, 1986). This need to join strongly with an age-mate cohort may account for the extreme embarrassment found in Western cultures among adolescents who are seen in public with their parents or who have younger siblings trailing behind them. Being recognized as part of the peer group may be sensed as a necessary precondition for the formation of socially advantageous alliances and for eventual mating success. The adolescent wish to be "cool" and the shame over being different are likely to be connected to the same need to establish fitness as is the wish to be financially successful or to be physically attractive. Possessing such qualities increases access to high-status mates and supportive allies within the primary social group.

Cultures differ in their emphases on conformity and on the shame that attaches to a lack of it. We hypothesize that a greater emphasis upon shame associated with nonconformity will occur in societies with collectivist (versus individualistic) values (Bierbrauer, 1992; Rabkin, 1975) or where a strong need for social cohesion exists, particularly when cohesion is threatened or difficult to establish. Such an emphasis could also reflect heightened danger or perceived danger from neighboring groups, so that any deviation from the norms is regarded with suspicion.

For those who are especially sensitive to conformity shame and manage to avoid such shame experiences, the advantages are a solid sense of group membership and a sense of well-being in that they "do things right." On the other hand, there are also potential losses: diminished freedom to follow their own inclinations; excessive worry over monitoring their behavior; and vulnerability to painful experiences of shame as they concern themselves with minor infractions of social rules.

Such individuals may lose, also, in that, by their very rule-abiding behavior, they indicate that they are group followers rather than leaders. While leaders are not without the capacity for shame and are often careful not to stray too far from what is acceptable, they often have greater latitude with regard to normative performance and, almost by definition, are able to alter the norms through their example. A leader does not face the same obligation to demonstrate membership in the group on the basis of conformity because everyone knows who they are. Those who are too worried about shame and show excessive conformity reveal themselves to be followers and of lower status.

Those relatively unconcerned with conformity shame have more freedom to follow their own dictates. As a result, they can be more spontaneous and creative and may, on a personal level, feel more at ease and comfortable with themselves. At the social level, they might make significant contributions out of patterns of perception, thought, and behavior that are innovatively different from the norm. Thus, lowered shame-proneness in this area can lead to more risk-taking practices, which may turn out to be very valuable economically or otherwise and enhance reproductive success. The person who creates changes may at first be regarded as foolish, eccentric, or a threat, but if the new trend becomes standard, then the originator can reap fame, status, and entitlements, all of which serve to enhance fitness. On the other hand, those who take such risks may experience social isolation instead, which can cause pain and reduce fitness. In sum, there are potential gains and losses with both conservative and risky strategies.

Prosocial Behavior

In addition to the powerful positive emotions that promote behaviors helpful to others, shame is also an essential motivator. Prosocial behavior, which connects individuals to each other and to social groups, increases fitness because it strengthens kinship and support networks and because others are likely to return favors to those perceived as helpful or cooperative (Axelrod & Hamilton, 1981; Cosmides & Tooby, 1992). Experimental evidence (Axelrod, 1984; Dawkins, 1989) suggests that when people fail to aid others in order to obtain an immediate self-advantage, their long-term fate is more negative than if they cooperate even at some cost to themselves.

Shame appears to be a far-reaching and potent means of enforcing social obligations (de Waal, 1996), which often include cooperative endeavors, and may well be also an important regulator of illegal behavior (Grasmick & Bursick, 1990). Individuals may not always wish to contribute to others' welfare, especially to those not close in genetic similarity, because a personal sacrifice is required, but concern with being shamed helps to modify these tendencies. Thus, when called upon to give charity in public settings, many are shamed into donations they would not make in private. Similarly, in realms as disparate as the elaborate rituals of the potlatch ceremony or the time and energy required for civic duties, shame, or the wish to be free of shame, can be a powerful motivator. Individuals benefit by maintaining their image as trustworthy contributors of their fair share and worthy of a reciprocal investment by others (Cosmides & Tooby, 1992; Fiske, 1992). Such prosocial displays, particularly of an altruistic sort, can often inspire respect and concrete support and, additionally, raise status within the social group (Hill, 1984). Prosocial shame, then, helps to maintain mutually supportive relationships.

Excessively strong sensitivity to such shame, however, might lead someone to give away too many resources, with or without accruing a compensatory gain from the benefits of high group regard. In contrast, insufficient prosocial shame, exemplified by the Scrooge-like character who will not do his share for humanity, can lead to isolation. However, such a disposition can also result in a great increase in personal wealth because all efforts are directed towards one's own needs, which can also produce a consequent rise in social status. Thus, extremes of prosocial shame ordinarily cause difficulties for fitness but can occasionally engender social respect—for example, through generosity or wealth acquisition—that might counteract the usual effects.

Sexual Shame

Shame about sexual behavior outside of socially approved norms, such as those regarding bodily exposure, choice of partner, and specific sexual practices, appears to be universal, albeit with large differences regarding what is shameful among cultures and, sometimes, between generations and genders. Unacceptable behavior can evoke derisive amusement or even disgust on the part of beholders and provoke shame on the part of the deviant individual. Fear of such shaming and the reduced status and mating possibilities that it can lead to is a potent agent for the control of sexual behavior.

While there are some universal values regarding sexual behavior—the incest taboo, for instance—for the most part, sexual values (Caplan, 1987) and the specifics that trigger sexual shame are very plastic. Differences in social expectations regarding sexual behavior and, therefore, in what individuals regard as shameful are presumably related to the conditions that affect fitness in a particular group. Fitness, in turn, may well relate to economic and health conditions, as the individual's behavioral strategies would need to adjust to different environments in order to maximize fitness. Abiding by social guidelines and avoiding shameful behavior facilitates the attraction and retention of mates and the maintenance of the status necessary for successful rearing of offspring.

Some cultures strongly restrict sexual activities and may reward sexual restraint. Individuals who violate these cultural norms may be publicly shamed and lose status if their behavior becomes known. Although their sexual behavior may temporarily increase their reproductive success, it can reduce their long-term fitness. As a result of the loss of status, there may be more limited access to the resources necessary for rearing children, a reduced desirability as a spouse (or even loss of a mate, if already married), and reduced inclusive fitness, too, as other members of the community shy away from marrying into the family. In cultures that encourage sexual activity, individuals will be motivated to show unmistakable evidence of sexual availability and involvement to avoid social devaluation that could reduce access to mates and status. The shame attached to violations of cultural sexual norms will spur members of a society to abide by these rules, which will, in turn, tend to increase their fitness.

The economic environment is likely to be one important constituent of the forces that shape cultural values and expectations, including those in the sexual realm. For example, during the years of the extreme poverty in Ireland, sexual restraint, even to the point of joining a celibate religious order, was encouraged. It can be assumed that each additional child reduced the chances of survival for the genetically related group, so that inclusive fitness might have been best served by having a portion of the offspring in any family go childless, allowing nieces and nephews more chances for survival. Other environmental factors that have a strong impact on fitness, such as health and disease, may also influence sexual values.

Increases in sexually transmitted diseases, for example, may tilt modern sexual values back toward restraint.

In short, shame in the sexual realm helps individuals to channel their sexual actions into patterns that tend to increase genetic fitness. Occasionally, however, a relative lack of sexual shame can also be associated with a biological advantage. In a humorous poem by Thomas Hardy, a young woman's complacent acceptance of her socially compromised status is linked to her greatly improved economic position:

—"You left us in tatters, without shoes or socks,
Tired of digging potatoes, and spudding up docks;
And now you've gay bracelets and bright feathers three!"
"Yes: that's how we dress when we're ruined," said she. (Hardy, "The Ruined Maid," p. 781).

In this contrarian fitness strategy, the young woman improves the survivability of her genes, because her children will be better fed and cared for than they would have been had she remained unruined and married a potato farmer.

Status/Competition Shame

Social status rankings are complex, vary considerably according to differing values across cultures, and show diverse behavioral bases within any particular culture. For most societies, there are multiple ways in which to acquire status, but in evolutionary terms all status hierarchies relate to fitness, directly or indirectly.

Some status hierarchies concern attractiveness to potential mating partners, while others raise one's position in other ways, thus increasing access to alliances and resources. These avenues to status are not mutually exclusive, and, in fact, often complement each other. Those who are high on one type of status are likely to benefit by a heightened position in other status hierarchies as well.

Individuals strive for status in intrasexual hierarchies to enhance their access and attractiveness to potential sexual partners. The wish to avoid shame associated with lower status can motivate efforts to maintain or increase one's attractiveness and may lead to intense exertions to do so. Such efforts might include physical exercise for weight control and/or a desirable body shape, the allocation of significant personal resources to dressing in culturally determined attractive fashions, and behaving in culturally approved patterns associated with masculine and feminine ideals of conduct. The potential rewards include a greater chance to acquire a desirable mate (who presumably increases one's fitness), which can also add prestige to one's social position.

Other status hierarchies are less directly related to mate attraction and may be based on a large number of different qualities valued by a society, including personal attributes (bravery, intelligence, good character, altruism, Hill, 1984), talents (in music, the military, or sports), possessions (money, land, livestock), influential political positions, or family connections. Status within these hierarchies often means greater control over resources (though not universally; Fiske, 1992), and, hence, increased ability to provide for one's kin and offspring, which can enhance mating opportunities for the latter.

Status competition, however, is usually costly, so that the wish to avoid the sting of shame from low or lowered status, whether from losing a battle or an election or not selling enough cars, can motivate the continued consumption of extensive resources. For high-status seekers in competitive societies, constant struggles with others to retain one's rank, continuous demonstrations of importance with expensive displays, repeated assertion of desirable qualities, or attempts to influence others through patronage might be required. In addition, high status can excite the envy and revenge of rivals, necessitating further efforts to defend a favorable position. Thus, heightened concern with the avoidance of shame from low status and the achievement of ambitious goals, can, even if successful, be excessively stressful and costly and lead to the neglect of other needs. If this competitive cast of mind becomes compulsive, at least as expressed in the Type A personality, it may carry disadvantages for health (Booth-Kewley & Friedman, 1987; Matthews, 1988) and for quality of relationships (Sanders, Smith, & Alexander, 1991).

In competitive societies, a strong sense of shame can attach to the individual who does not make such efforts and either gives up on achieving status or submissively allows another to win. In more cooperative societies (e.g., the Zuni and some monastic orders; Wright, 1994), the reverse can occur, and individuals who are viewed as overly competitive may feel shamed, thus avoiding self-promotion to maintain or advance social position.

When loss of status cannot be avoided, submissive shrinking away and the corresponding inner experience can lead one to accept lower social rank and to refrain from further risky, painful contests. Keltner (1995) provides empirical evidence that nonverbal appeasement and avoidance are concomitants of shame. In primates it has been observed (de Waal, 1996; Gilbert, 1992a; Wright, 1994) that the submissiveness of a defeated combatant in a male dominance struggle can stave off additional conflict. In humans submission in status competitions can be presumed to serve the same purpose; the shame associated with status loss (Gilbert, 1997) can facilitate the damage-limiting submissive behavior.

Those relatively unconcerned with the shame issuing from struggles for status can benefit from their less competitive strategy, which may compensate them for a lower position in the hierarchy. They are less likely to incite jealousy and challenges from others and may avoid the consequences of confrontations or conflicts, preserving health and resources. Knowing when to submit or avoid struggles for supremacy can increase fitness as well.

Summary

It is argued here that shame is associated with several distinct domains of behavior. A premonition of shame, rather than an intense experience of the affect, can serve as a signal to avoid those behaviors in each domain that might give rise to a full-blown shame state. If the signals are unheeded or one becomes the target of shaming by others, dysphoria will result that can range from a mild to a powerful intensity. Such signals of potential shame serve to guide individuals toward behavior that is culturally acceptable and which, by and large, is likely to increase fitness.

Whatever its domain of origin and whatever its intensity, shame has similar phenomenological elements, including embarrassment, a wish to be invisible, a sense of inadequacy, mortification, and anger. There may be distinct differences, however, in the quality of the shame experienced, depending upon the domain with which it is associated. For example, the shame felt upon competitive defeat is probably most commonly associated with mortification, and perhaps, simultaneously, an urge to placate the victor, while shame deriving from unconventionality seems to evoke more a wish to be invisible in front of those who conform more acceptably. Rageful anger may be particularly aroused when the winners of status confrontations humiliate or degrade their opponents (Gilbert, 1997; Scheff, 1987). These differences may well constitute an area of further fruitful exploration.

Individual Differences

There are considerable differences among individuals in what types of shame they are most responsive to and how intensely they experience the emotion. Genetic predispositions and personal histories might well lead to these differing shame sensitivities.

Cultural differences also exist that heighten responsiveness to particular behavioral domains. Societies differ extensively with regard to the relative emphasis placed on the different shame components according to the values of the culture. Some stress the importance of individual achievement and competition (American culture, for example) and thus produce numerous aggressive, status-seeking individuals. Other cultures, which espouse an ethos of cooperation and uniformity (such as Japan and some Native American tribes like the Zuni), exhibit more prosocial behavior and conformity, with fewer overt struggles for individual rank. As Wright (1994) points out, however, the status competition in the latter kind of society never really disappears and will often manifest itself indirectly in how noncompetitive individuals can appear. Hence, while some cultures shame the excessively competitive individual, other cultures shame those who are insufficiently competitive. Presumably, such differences are linked to geographic, historical, economic, and health conditions that favor particular forms of social relationship for maximum fitness.

It seems likely that there may be inverse relationships between the different types of shame described here. The conformity and prosocial forms that serve group ends necessarily entail some compromise of the individual's strivings. In contrast, the sexual and competitive types of shame serve primarily to control individual strivings that might harm group interests. As such, it is not surprising that conforming and competitive cultures should show different emphases in the patterns of characteristic shame domains.

As with cultures, individuals who feel strong conformity shame are probably less prone to shame connected with competition and vice-versa. On the level of the individual, for example, this opposition seems clear in those who single-mindedly seek or have already achieved high status through their competitive behavior. Such individuals appear afraid of status loss but are far less concerned with shame from social disapproval, a characteristic that makes their competitive efforts that much more effective. They do not appear to pay for their nonconforming or asocial behavior with shame, despite expressions of social censure around them. Observation suggests that others are often intimidated by, or even ambivalently admiring of, their boldness. Because it is clear that they are not particularly concerned with disapproval, others frequently become less critical of them. They do not exhibit the postures and gestures of submissiveness, so that others are less likely to attempt to shame them. Such an interactive pattern of behavior may well mark the competitive individual as someone with higher status, an impression that inhibits others further from trying to shame them and makes that individual still less prone to conformity shame.

The focus and effects of the feminist movement also illustrate these opposed tendencies in shame vulnerability. Women have been viewed as upholders of the prosocial aspects of a culture, representing what is moral and well-behaved. In the past, women were criticized for not behaving according to conventional norms and for being too assertive or competitive. As women have been encouraged (in Western societies, at least) to achieve status through individual initiative and employment rank, they appear to be somewhat less vulnerable to conformity and prosocial shame and increasingly vulnerable to shame over lack of occupational attainments.

Psychotherapeutic Implications

Thinking of shame primarily as a signal with adaptive functions can provide a new perspective for the therapist. Instead of viewing shame only as an extreme and pathological emotion (Tangney et al., 1995) and unwittingly causing shame in the client for possessing such a defect (Harder, 1990; H. Lewis, 1971), therapists can remember that shame is a necessary and even desirable human attribute that can sometimes go awry. Rather than attempting to eradicate shame, therapist and client can work together to modify its maladaptive or excessive manifestations.

Beyond the general effect of viewing shame in a new adaptive light, therapeutic implications may vary according to which domain or domains of shame are most characteristic of a person, whether the individual is overly concerned or underconcerned with the avoidance of shame (that is, whether the signal function is operating too readily or not readily enough), and, finally, whether shame has become a chronic dysphoric experience.

It is likely that the behavior of someone who is overconcerned with a particular domain of shame will be constrained or misguided because of the undue emphasis. Someone who is hypervigilant with regard to conformity shame, for example, will be less spontaneous, more conventional, less free to try new or different behaviors. Therapy could help such persons evaluate more objectively what they win and lose by their shame-avoidant lifestyle and whether even a slight alteration in favor of more risk-taking with regard to conformity might, indeed, improve their overall sense of well-being. Perhaps they overestimate how much they would actually be shamed by risky behavior or underestimate how pleasing to them more freedom in their behavioral repertoire would be.

Conversely, those who are underconcerned with conformity and feel little worry about the ensuing shame often disregard social convention and may be quite unaware of the negative consequences they incur. For example, someone who dresses too casually for a job interview because he or she does not place much importance on proper codes of behavior or perhaps is even somewhat resentful of such expectation may be largely unconscious of the potential loss of employment. In this kind of case, the absence of a shame signal may need to be remedied, to increase awareness of the self-defeating effects of ignoring social convention.

In contrast, another individual may be most highly responsive to signal shame related to status, not conformity, because of an exaggerated responsiveness to any situation that might be construed as competitive. While such behavior may, indeed, increase the individual's status over time, there may also be a cost in terms of affectionate or intimate relationships or in relaxation that the individual will unwittingly pay. Therapy can help such clients be more aware of the unintended effects of their intense attunement to shame over any potential loss of status, so that they might achieve, should they wish to, a greater balance in their lives, permitting them to form more gratifying relationships and/or to be more relaxed despite the continuing salience of status issues.

Someone with the opposite inclination might be ill attuned to competitive struggles for status, ignore numerous opportunities for material success and influential position, and behave in unconvincing ways when engaged in status conflicts. Heightening awareness of these options in treatment and assessing their importance for the subjective well-being of the client can compensate for low motivation from status/competition shame signals. Assertiveness training could also make the client more effective. It could literally, as well as figuratively, help the client to avoid the submissive, lowered-head posture typical of the shamed person (Barrett, 1995; M. Lewis, 1992).

In summary, signal shame constitutes the means by which human beings are alerted to behave in ways that have been, over evolutionary time, important for their genetic fitness. When one or more of the shame-governed behavioral domains is either overly or insufficiently important in a client's life, a problem in signal shame is inferred from related self-defeating attitudes (e.g., "I don't care what anyone thinks") and an unbalanced preoccupation with one domain of behavior. The therapist can evaluate the extent to which problems of signal shame are a source of difficulty or discomfort and facilitate balance.

The foregoing suggestions for dealing with signal shame, whether it is inhibitively high or insufficiently effective in one or more shame domains, derive from a cognitive-behavioral perspective (Beck, 1976). The behavioral homework suggested by such practitioners (Beck, 1976) can also help to demonstrate to the client the improvement that changes in accustomed patterns might bring. However, it should be noted that working from this shame framework does not at all exclude therapists with a more psychodynamic approach. Influences from early life that have created psychic structures that undervalue or overemphasize signals regarding shame can be explored and altered, so that these clients do not unduly continue in maladaptive paths.

A therapist faces a different kind of problem with clients who present with excessive feelings of shame, whether this state is primarily self-inflicted or the result of being shamed by others. When shame has developed into this type of chronic problem, so that the individual is constantly burdened by it, therapeutic inquiry into the domain most responsible for the shame experience might well point the way toward helpful interventions.

Empirical studies (Gilbert, Allan, Ball, & Bradshaw, 1996; Harder, 1996; Harder,

Cutler, & Rockart, 1992; Harder & Lewis, 1987; Harder & Zalma, 1990; Tangney, et al., 1995) and clinical/theoretical descriptions (Harder & Lewis, 1987; Levin, 1967, 1971; H. Lewis, 1971, 1986; Mayman, 1974) of the modal individual who suffers from excessive and chronic shame is a portrait of someone who exhibits social anxiety and phobic fearfulness, lacks self-confidence, experiences extreme shyness, worries about personal inadequacies, holds self-derogatory attitudes, feels frequent depression, and shrinks away from any risk-taking, assertiveness, or public exposure that might bring on critical confrontation with or ridicule from others. Such a prototypical shame-prone person would seem to have excessive and chronic problems with the conformity and status/competition areas of behavior. Generally, he or she would be too conventional in the former domain and insufficiently assertive in the latter. However, in addition to feeling constrained, typical of the person with too much conformity shame of the signal sort, such an individual usually also shows self-blaming accusations that he or she has already committed shameful acts. Here, the therapist's task is not only to reduce the concern with conformity but also to change the dysphoric affect and its source. Whether the source is a set of overlearned prior experiences of shame or current experiences, the therapist can help transform the shame feelings into emotions that are more useful, such as pride, confident optimism, and/or anger at maltreatment.

Because of the extensive overlap in the foregoing description of chronic shame sufferers and the clinical presentation of many depressive patients, therapy approaches that have already been found helpful with depression might prove useful with enduring shame problems as well.

However, this characterization of the usual shame-burdened individual may not adequately typify all of those with frequently painful shame feelings. Empirically replicated findings (Harder, 1996; Harder, Cutler, & Rockart, 1992; Harder & Lewis, 1987; Harder & Zalma, 1990; Tangney, et al., 1995) that link shame with symptoms of hostility and anger, paranoid ideation, and psychoticism (measured by the Symptom Checklist-90; Derogatis, 1983) suggest that many problems shown by the overly shame-prone may involve externalizing, as well as internalizing, tendencies. These associations match well with clinical accounts of shame centrality in numerous types of pathology not known for their depressive or shy and retiring natures—that is, narcissistic personality disorders (Harder, 1984; Kaufman, 1989; Kernberg, 1970; Kohut, 1971; Morrison, 1989), borderline personality disorders (Fischer, 1985; Kaufman, 1989; Lansky, 1987b), conduct disorders and delinquencies (Cassorla, 1986), alcoholism and drug abuse (Cook, 1993; Evans, 1987; Gomberg, 1987), paranoia (Kaufman, 1989), and domestic violence (Lansky, 1987a, 1992). Clinical accounts suggest that the problematic behaviors in such cases serve as drastic, avoidant defenses against chronic feelings of shame (Kaufman, 1989; Tomkins, 1987).

From the perspective put forth here, these individuals suffer from severe deficiencies in the signal aspects of conformity and prosocial shame, so that they often violate social norms and expectations. Clinical observation further suggests that, simultaneously, they are hypersensitive to the possibility of status loss and unfavorable (competitive) comparisons to others, which leads them to overreact and act out because of shame and anger (H. Lewis, 1971; Scheff, 1987) whenever the least hint of such comparisons occur. For example, someone with a borderline or narcissistic personality may find it intolerable to receive help, such as psycho-therapy, since it would suggest a "one-down," and therefore shameful, position (Harder, 1990; H. Lewis, 1971).

In cases where the chronic shame experience derives in major part from membership in a group that is marginalized by, and suffers discrimination from, the larger society—for example, ethnic minorities and those with physical disabilities or alternative lifestyles—therapy might also encourage client participation in actions that build group pride. Many in these groups have developed a strong sense of militant solidarity with others to overcome the shameful attitudes of earlier eras when they would often avoid public display of their "stigma" (Goffman, 1963). Participation in such groups can mitigate the sense of marginality. In addition, concentrating on one's achievements despite the handicap of membership in a devalued group can also be very helpful, as in the case of a paraplegic who has become a wheelchair marathon athlete.

Retrospect

In accord with an evolutionary perspective, this chapter assumed the primacy of fitness in the functioning of emotions. Shame, an affect usually regarded only as pathological, was presented here as a predominantly adaptive signal that orients one to potential but usually avoidable negative consequences for successful reproduction and psychological well-being. Four types of shame-producing behavioral domains that are particularly important for fitness were described: conformity, prosocial behavior, sex, and status/competition. The first two domains solidify an individual's membership in a cohesive, protective, and supportive social group, while the second two areas primarily regulate the individual's mating success. Advantages and disadvantages of individual variations in shame sensitivity in these four areas were considered. Finally, implications of this evolutionary perspective on shame for the conduct of psychotherapy were discussed.

References

Asch, S. E. (1988). Opinions and social pressure. In E. Aronson (Ed.), *Readings about the social animal* (5th ed., pp. 13–22). New York: Freeman. (Reprinted from *Scientific American, 193* (5), 1955 [Scientific American Offprint 450])

Axelrod, R. (1984). *The evolution of cooperation*. New York: Basic Books.

Axelrod, R., & Hamilton, W. D. (1981). The evolution of cooperation. *Science, 211,* 1390–1396.

Barrett, K. C. (1995). A functionalist approach to shame and guilt. In J. P. Tangney & K. W. Fischer (Eds.), *Self-Conscious emotions: The psychology of shame, guilt, embarrassment and pride* (pp. 25–63). New York: Guilford press.

Barry, H., Child, I., & Bacon, M. (1959). Relation of child training to subsistence economy. *American Anthropologist, 61,* 57–63.

Baumeister, R. F. (1996, August). Guilt is good: Prosocial and relationship-enhancing effects. In J. A. Bybee & J. Tangney (Cochairs), *Is guilt adaptive? Functions in interpersonal relationships and mental health.* Symposium conducted at the 104th annual convention of the American Psychological Association, Toronto, Canada.

Baumeister, R. F., Stillwell, A. M., & Heatherton, T. F. (1995). Interpersonal aspects of guilt: Evidence from narrative studies. In J. P. Tangney & K. W. Fischer (Eds.), *Self-Conscious emotions: The psychology of shame, guilt, embarrassment, and pride* (pp. 255–273). New York: Guilford Press.

Baumeister, R. F., & Tice, D. M. (1990). Anxiety and social exclusion. *Journal of Social and Clinical Psychology, 9*, 165–195.

Beck, A. T. (1976). *Cognitive therapy and the emotional disorders.* New York: International Universities Press.

Beck, A. T. (1987). Cognitive models of depression. *Journal of Cognitive Psychotherapy, An International Quarterly, 1*, 5–37.

Berndt, T. J. (1979). Developmental changes in conformity to peers and parents. *Developmental Psychology, 15*, 606–616.

Berry, J. W. (1967). Independence and conformity in subsistence-level societies. *Journal of Personality and Social Psychology, 7*, 415–418.

Bierbrauer, G. (1992). Reactions to violation of normative standards: A cross-cultural analysis of responsibility and justice: The view across cultures. *International Journal of Psychology, 27*, 181–193.

Binder, J. (1970). The relative proneness to shame or guilt as a dimension of character style. Unpublished doctoral dissertation, University of Michigan, Ann Arbor.

Booth-Kewley, S., & Friedman, H. S. (1987). Psychological predictors of heart disease: A quantitative review. *Psychological Bulletin, 101*, 343–362.

Brown, B. B. (1990). Peer groups and peer cultures. In S. S. Feldman & G. R. Elliot (Eds.), *At the threshold: The developing adolescent* (pp. 171–196). Cambridge, MA: Harvard University Press.

Brown, J. K. (1975). Adolescent initiation rites: Recent interpretations. In R. E. Grinder (Ed.), *Studies in adolescence* (3rd ed., pp. 40–51). New York: Macmillan.

Bybee, J. A., & Quiles, Z. N. (in press). Guilt and mental illness. In J. A. Bybee (Ed.), *Guilt and children.* New York: Academic Press.

Caplan, P. (Ed.). (1987). *The cultural construction of sexuality.* London: Tavistock/Routledge.

Carroll, J. (1985). *Guilt: The grey eminence behind character, history, and culture.* London: Routledge & Kegan Paul.

Cassorla, A. A. (1986). A preliminary investigation of the experience of shame in psychiatrically hospitalized, conduct disordered adolescents. *Dissertation Abstracts International, 47*, 1715B. (University Microfilms No. DA 8614664).

Clark, L. A., & Watson, D. (1994). Distinguishing functional from dysfunctional affective responses. In P. Ekman & R. J. Davidson (Eds.), *The nature of emotion* (pp. 131–136). New York: Oxford University Press.

Clasen, D. R., & Brown, B. B. (1985). The multidimensionality of peer pressure in adolescence. *Journal of Youth and Adolescence, 14*, 451–468.

Cook, D. R. (1993). *The Internalized Shame Scale manual.* Menomonie, WI: Channel Press. (Available from the author, Rt. 7, Box 270A, Menomonie, WI 54751)

Cosmides, L., & Tooby, J. (1992). Cognitive adaptations for social exchange. In J. H. Barkow, L. Cosmides, & J. Tooby (Eds.), *The adapted mind: Evolutionary psychology and the generation of culture* (pp. 163–228). New York: Oxford University Press.

Cosmides, L., Tooby, J., & Barkow, J. H. (1992). Introduction: Evolutionary psychology and conceptual integration. In J. H. Barkow, L. Cosmides, & J. Tooby (Eds.), *The adapted mind: Evolutionary psychology and the generation of culture* (pp. 3–15). New York and Oxford: Oxford University Press.

Crocker, J., Thompson, L. L., McGraw, K. M., & Ingerman, C. (1987). Downward comparison, prejudice, and evaluation of others: Effects of self-esteem and threat. *Journal of Personality and Social Psychology, 52*, 907–916.

Damasio, A. R. (1994). *Descartes' error.* New York: Putnam.

Dawkins, R. (1989). *The selfish gene* (3rd ed.). Oxford and New York: Oxford University Press.

de Rivera, J. (1989). Comparing experiences across cultures: Shame and guilt in Americans and Japanese. *Hiroshima Forum for Psychology, 14,* 13–20.

Derogatis, L. (1983). *SCL-90-R manual.* St. Petersburg, FL: Clinical Psychometrics.

de Waal, F. M. B. (1996). *Good natured: The origins of right and wrong in humans and other animals.* Cambridge, MA: Harvard University Press.

Ekman, P. (1994). All emotions are basic. In P. Ekman & R. J. Davidson (Eds.), *The nature of emotion: Fundamental questions* (pp. 15–19). New York: Oxford University Press.

Ekman, P., & Davidson, R. J. (1994). Afterword: What is the function of emotions? In P. Ekman & R. J. Davidson (Eds.), *The nature of emotion* (pp. 137–139). New York: Oxford University Press.

English, F. (1994). Shame and social control revisited. *Transactional Analysis Journal, 24,* 109–120.

Evans, S. (1987). Shame, boundaries and dissociation in chemically dependent, abusive and incestuous families. *Alcoholism Treatment Quarterly, 4,* 25–38.

Ferguson, T. J., Stegge, H., & Damhuis, I. (1991). Children's understanding of guilt and shame. *Child Development, 62,* 827–839.

Fischer, S. F. (1985). Identity of two: The phenomenology of shame in borderline development and treatment. *Psychotherapy, 22,* 101–109.

Fiske, A. P. (1992). The four elementary forms of sociality: Framework for a unified theory of social relations. *Psychological Review, 99,* 689–723.

Freud, S. (1930). *Civilization and its discontents* (Trans., Joan Riviere). London: Hogarth Press and Institute of Psycho-Analysis.

Freud, S. (1953). Three essays on the theory of sexuality. In J. Strachey (Ed.), *The standard edition of the complete psychological works of Sigmund Freud* (Vol. 7, pp. 135–243). London: Hogarth Press. (Original work published 1905)

Freud, S. (1966). *Introductory lectures on psychoanalysis.* New York: Norton. (Original work published 1920)

Fridlund, A. J., Ekman, P., & Oster, H. (1986). Facial expressions of emotion: Review of literature, 1970–1983. In A. Seligman & S. Feldstein (Eds.), *Nonverbal behavior and communication* (pp. 143–223). Hillsdale, NJ: Erlbaum.

Frijda, N. H. (1994). Emotions are functional, most of the time. In P. Ekman & R. J. Davidson (Eds.), *The nature of emotion* (pp. 112–122). New York: Oxford University Press.

Gilbert, P. (1992a). *Human nature and suffering.* New York: Guilford Press.

Gilbert, P. (1992b). *Depression: The evolution of powerlessness.* New York: Guilford Press.

Gilbert, P. (1995). Power, social rank, and depression: Comments on Price and Gardner. *British Journal of Medical Psychology, 68,* 211–215.

Gilbert, P. (1997). The evolution of social attractiveness and its role in shame, humiliation, guilt and therapy. *British Journal of Medical Psychology, 70,* 113–147.

Gilbert, P., Allan, S., Ball, L., & Bradshaw, Z. (1996). Overconfidence and personal evaluations of social rank. *British Journal of Medical Psychology, 69,* 59–68.

Goffman, E. (1963) *Stigma: Notes on the management of spoiled identity.* Englewood Cliffs, NJ: Prentice-Hall.

Gomberg, E. L. (1987). Shame and guilt issues among women alcoholics. *Alcoholism Treatment Quarterly, 4,* 139–155.

Grasmick, H. G., & Bursick, R. J. (1990). Conscience, significant others, and rational choice: Extending the deterrence model. *Law and Society Review, 24,* 837–861.

Guisinger, S., & Blatt, S. J. (1994). Individuality and relatedness: Evolution of a fundamental dialectic. *American Psychologist, 49,* 104–111.

Harder, D. W. (1984). Character style of the defensively high self-esteem man. *Journal of Clinical Psychology, 40,* 26–35.

Harder, D. W. (1990). Comment on Wright, et al., "Shame, guilt, narcissism, and depression: Correlates and sex differences." *Psychoanalytic Psychology, 7,* 285–289.

Harder, D. W. (1995). Shame and guilt assessment, and relationships of shame-and guilt-proneness to psychopathology. In J. P. Tangney & K. W. Fischer (Eds.), *Self-Conscious emotions: The psychology of shame, guilt, embarrassment and pride* (pp. 368–392). New York: Guilford Press.

Harder, D. W. (1996, August). Guilt and symptoms of psychopathology: Chronic versus moral standards guilt. In J. A. Bybee & J. Tangney (Cochairs), *Is guilt adaptive? Functions in interpersonal relationships and mental health*. Symposium conducted at the 104th annual convention of the American Psychological Association, Toronto, Canada.

Harder, D. W., Cutler, L., & Rockart, L. (1992). Assessment of shame and guilt and their relationships to psychopathology. *Journal of Personality Assessment, 59,* 584–604.

Harder, D. W., & Lewis, S. J. (1987). The assessment of shame and guilt. In J. N. Butcher & C. D. Spielberger (Eds.), *Advances in personality assessment* (Vol. 6, pp. 89–114). Hillsdale, NJ: Erlbaum.

Harder, D. W., & Zalma, A. (1990). Two promising shame and guilt scales: A construct validity comparison. *Journal of Personality Assessment, 55,* 729–745.

Hardy, T. (1992). The Ruined Maid. In W. Harmon (Ed.), *The Top 500 Poems* (p. 781). New York: Columbia University Press.

Hill, J. (1984). Human altruism and sociocultural fitness. *Journal of Social and Biological Structures, 7,* 17–35.

Hogg, M. A., & Abrams, D. (1988). *Social identifications*. London and New York: Routledge.

Izard, C. E. (1993). Organizational and motivational functions of discrete emotions. In M. Lewis & J. M. Haviland (Eds.), *Handbook of emotions*. New York: Guilford Press.

Jones, W. H., & Kugler, K. (1993). Interpersonal correlates of the Guilt Inventory. *Journal of Personality Assessment, 61,* 246–258.

Kaufman, G. (1989). *The psychology of shame: Theory and treatment of shame-based syndromes*. New York: Springer.

Keltner, D. (1995). Signs of appeasement: Evidence for the distinct displays of embarrassment, amusement and shame. *Journal of Personality and Social Psychology, 68,* 441–454.

Kernberg, O. F. (1970). Factors in the psychoanalytic treatment of narcissistic personalities. *Journal of the American Psychoanalytic Association, 18,* 51–85.

Kitayama, S., Markus, H. R., & Matsumoto, H. (1995). In J. P. Tangney & K. W. Fischer (Eds.), *Self-Conscious emotions: The psychology of shame, guilt, embarrassment and pride* (pp. 439–464). New York: Guilford Press.

Kohut, H. (1971). *The analysis of the self*. New York: International Universities Press.

Lansky, M. R. (1987a). Shame and domestic violence. In D. L. Nathanson (Ed.), *The many faces of shame* (pp. 335–362). New York: Guilford Press.

Lansky, M. R. (1987b). Shame in the family relationships of borderline patients. In J. S. Grotstein, M. F. Solomon, & J. A. Lang (Eds.), *The borderline patient* (pp. 187–199). Hillsdale, NJ: Analytic Press.

Lansky, M. R. (1992). *Fathers who fail: Shame and psychopathology in the family system*. New York: Analytic Press.

Lansky, M. R. (1995). Shame and the scope of psychoanalytic understanding. *American Behavioral Scientist, 38* (8), 1076–1090.

Lazarus, R. S. (1991). *Emotion and adaptation*. New York: Oxford University Press.

Levin, S. (1967). Some metapsychological considerations on the differentiation between shame and guilt. *International Journal of Psycho-Analysis, 48,* 267–276.

Levin, S. (1971). The psychoanalysis of shame. *International Journal of Psycho-Analysis, 52,* 355–362.

Lewis, H. B. (1971). *Shame and guilt in neurosis*. New York: International Universities Press.

Lewis, H. B. (1986). The role of shame in depression. In M. Rutter, C. E. Izard, & P. B.

Read (Eds.), *Depression in young people: Developmental and clinical perspectives* (pp. 325–339). New York: Guilford Press.

Lewis, M. (1992). *Shame: The exposed self.* New York: Free Press.

Lindsay-Hartz, J., de Rivera, J., & Mascolo, M. F. (1995). Differentiating guilt and shame and their effects on motivation. In J. P. Tangney & K. W. Fischer (Eds.), *Self-Conscious emotions: The psychology of shame, guilt, embarrassment and pride* (pp. 274–300). New York: Guilford Press.

Matthews, K. A. (1988). Coronary heart disease and Type A behaviors: Update on and alternative to the Booth-Kewley and Friedman (1987) quantitative review. *Psychological Bulletin, 104,* 373–380.

Mayman, M. (1974, August). The shame experience, the shame dynamic, and shame personalities in psychotherapy. Paper presented at the annual meeting of the American Psychological Association, New Orleans. (Available from the author, 1027 E. Huron St., Ann Arbor, MI 48109)

Miller, W. I. (1993). *Humiliation.* New York: Cornell University Press.

Morrison, A. P. (1989). *Shame: The underside of narcissism.* Hillsdale, NJ: Analytic Press.

Pines, M. (1995). The universality of shame: A psychoanalytic approach. *British Journal of Psychotherapy, 11,* 346–357.

Price, J., & Gardner, R. (1995). The paradoxical power of the depressed patient: A problem for the ranking theory of depression. *British Journal of Medical Psychology, 68,* 193–206.

Rabkin, L. Y. (1975). Superego processes in a collective society: The Israeli kibbutz. *International Journal of Social Psychiatry, 21,* 79–86.

Sanders, J. D., Smith, T. W., & Alexander, F. (1991). Type A behavior and marital interaction: Hostile-dominant responses during conflict. *Journal of Behavioral Medicine, 14,* 567–580.

Scheff, T. J. (1987). The shame-rage spiral: A case study of an interminable quarrel. In H. B. Lewis (Ed.), *The role of shame in symptom formation* (pp. 109–149). Hillsdale, NJ: Erlbaum.

Scheff, T. J. (1988). Shame and conformity: The deference-emotion system. *American Review of Sociology, 53,* 395–406.

Scherer, K. R., & Wallbott, H. G. (1994). Evidence for universality and cultural variation of differential emotion response patterning. *Journal of Personality and Social Psychology, 66,* 310–328.

Shaver, P., Schwartz, J., Kirson, D., & O'Connor, C. (1987). Emotion knowledge: Further exploration of a prototype approach. *Journal of Personality and Social Psychology, 52,* 1061–1086.

Sherif, M., Harvey, O. J., White, B. J., Hood, W. R., & Sherif, C. W. (1988). *Intergroup conflict and cooperation: The Robber's Cave experiment.* Middletown, CT: Wesleyan University Press.

Sherif, M., & Sherif, C. W. (1964). *Reference groups: Exploration into conformity and deviation of adolescents.* New York: Harper & Row.

Steinberg, L., & Silverberg, S. B. (1986). The vicissitudes of autonomy in early adolescence. *Child Development, 57,* 841–851.

Tajfel, H. (1978). *Differentiation between social groups: Studies in the psychology of inter-group relations.* San Diego, CA: Academic Press.

Tajfel, H. (1982). Social psychology of intergroup relations. *Annual Review of Psychology, 33,* 1–39.

Tangney, J. P. (1992). Situational determinants of shame and guilt in young adulthood. *Personality and Social Psychology Bulletin, 18,* 199–206.

Tangney, J. P. (1996, August). Functional and dysfunctional guilt. In J. A. Bybee & J. Tangney (Cochairs), *Is guilt adaptive? Functions in interpersonal relationships and mental health.* Symposium conducted at the 104th annual convention of the American Psychological Association, Toronto, Canada.

Tangney, J. P., Burggraf, S. A., & Wagner, P. E. (1995). Shame-proneness, guilt-proneness, and psychological symptoms. In J. P. Tangney & K. W. Fischer (Eds.), *Self-Conscious emotions: The psychology of shame, guilt, embarrassment and pride* (pp. 343–367). New York: Guilford Press.

Tomkins, S. S. (1987). Shame. In D. L. Nathanson (Ed.), *The many faces of shame* (pp. 133–161). New York: Guilford Press.

Tooby, J., & Cosmides, L. (1992). The psychological foundations of culture. In J. H. Barkow, L. Cosmides, & J. Tooby (Eds.), *The adapted mind: Evolutionary psychology and the generation of culture* (pp. 19–136). New York and Oxford: Oxford University Press.

Turner, V. (1964). Betwixt and between: The liminal period in *Rites de Passage*. In J. Helm (Ed.), *Symposium on new approaches to the study of religion* (pp. 4–20). Seattle, WA: University of Washington Press.

Wallbott, H. G., & Scherer, K. R. (1995). Cultural determinants in experiencing shame and guilt. In J. P. Tangney & K. W. Fischer (Eds.), *Self-Conscious emotions: The psychology of shame, guilt, embarrassment and pride* (pp. 465–487). New York: Guilford Press.

Wenegrat, B. (1990). *Sociobiological psychiatry*. Lexington, MA: Lexington Books/Heath.

Wicker, F. W., Payne, G. C., & Morgan, R. D. (1983). Participant descriptions of guilt and shame. *Motivation and Emotion, 7,* 25–39.

Wright, R. (1994). *The moral animal: Evolutionary psychology and everyday life*. New York: Pantheon.

13

Gender, Shame, and Culture

An Anthropological Perspective

Nancy Lindisfarne

In this chapter I argue that notions of honor and shame are socially defined. That is, words and behaviors which may be translated into English as *honorable* or *shaming* must be understood ethnographically in terms of who, locally, controls definitions of *honor* and *shame* and for what purpose.

Anthropological descriptions of honor and shame in the Mediterranean and Middle East have often emphasized idealized, hegemonic versions of social identities and ignored the shifting reality of people's experience of social beings. Thus, an ideal of female virginity and versions of hegemonic masculinity have been much discussed: the radical differentiation of men and women has been taken for granted, and there has been a focus on local idioms which naturalize the privileges of socially dominant men. Yet not all men are equally honorable; many behave in ways which are believed to be weak or shameful. Nor is honor an attribute that pertains only to men; women too may also behave honorably, just as they may, on other occasions, be said to act shamefully.[1]

When such evaluations are cast as problems, it becomes possible to ask how people become, or are made, aware of their shame, or of having been shamed. We may then also ask how such an evaluation may be reified to express apparently absolute gendered differences between individuals—between men and women, and between those who are honorable and those who feel themselves to have been shamed—while simultaneously defining inequalities *within* these categories.

The ethnographic literature on the notions of honor and shame in the Mediterranean and Middle East is extensive and contains, in particular, much on the vocabularies and behaviors which have been translated as *honor*, particularly as it relates to hegemonic masculinities.[2] Today, however, the biases in this literature are very clear. They include, first, an emphasis on *masculinized honor* and an emphasis on uncontextualized rhetorical statements (rather than how particular

246

judgments are expressed through social interaction). There is, third, an emphasis on the points of view of those who claim social superiority over others.

This reanalysis seeks to get beyond these biases by asking new questions. How, for instance, do certain behaviors come to be known as honorable or shaming in any particular setting? To what extent are the labels *honor* and *shame* mutually constructed? And who makes such judgments about honorable or dishonorable behavior of whom, in what settings, and with what measure of agreement and disagreement?

The ethnographic examples I offer have been chosen deliberately to challenge simplistic analytic uses of the notions of honor and shame. Rather, I argue that meaning is always context-related and derives from the whole range of evaluative notions employed in a particular setting. I suggest too that the range of local evaluations translated by social analysts as honor or shame are, like the analysts' own use of these terms, part of a rhetoric of social control which both creates and sustains differences between people and that these differences may construe gendered, sexual, class, ethnic, and other identities.

The ethnography I present is a deliberate collage; my focus is the emphasis on gendered difference in anthropological literature on honor and shame. My aims are twofold: first, to explore the extent to which abstract notions of female virginity and chastity (i.e., feminized honor) construct idealized, hegemonic versions of masculinity and femininity, or honor and shame. Second, to ask how a plurality of gendered, or honorable or shame, identities emerges in practice.

Anthropological Understandings of Honor and Shame

Pitt-Rivers (1977), though he wrote of honor and shame in essentialized terms, was interested in the ways these labels, and the social evaluations they imply, are contested. Thus, in English and Spanish usage particularly, *honor* and *shame* construe an ideology of control based on two quite opposed notions. One is honor (and thus also shame) in a competitive sense; in the other, altruism and generosity are central. In any particular social setting, no relationship is ever seen exclusively in one sense or the other; the same linguistic idioms and conceptual framework are used for both aspects of every relationship. Both passivity and competitiveness, both equality and inequality, can be explained and justified. The fascinating sleight of mind this involves has been documented by a number of authors (cf. Peristiany, 1965; Gilsenan, 1976, 1996). Thus, the mechanisms which allow honor in a competitive sense (as on the field of battle or in terms of worldly success) to be translated into honor in an absolute, naturalized, and literally religious sense (when social inequality is created by a monarch in God's name) are transparent in the British "Honors" system: the House of Lords is full of people with bellicose or rich merchant ancestors.

The absence of social honor, recognition, or prestige may sometimes be labeled and even experienced as shame; yet rhetorical pronouncements rely not only on semantic ambiguity but also on a graduated scale of more or less honorable or shameful deeds. Implicit in such usage and, indeed, mutually construed are a range of alternative, subordinate, and often subversive points of view.

Gender, Honor, and Shame

As suggested above, in the anthropological literature, honor and shame has been treated as a loose category around which comparative descriptions can be organized. As Davis has written:

> Among systems of prestige and control . . . honour systems are distinct [in that] they generally have as one of their components the control by men of women's sexuality, and the resulting combination of sex and self importance makes a unique contribution to the human comedy in life (1969, p. 69).

Descriptions of systems of honor and shame are disarmingly consistent in their focus on competition between dominant men and the passive subordination of women. The flavor of conventional analyses is well conveyed in David Gilmore's account:

> Sexuality is a form of social power. . . . Women themselves are often non-productive materially—ideally they are 'excluded' from nondomestic work. . . . Rather, they carry an immaterial or conceptual resource, their chastity, arbitrarily elevated to central position as an exchange value. . . . Female modesty is metamorphosed, almost in the manner of a fetish, into a pseudocommodity, or more accurately, a capital good. . . . The masculine experience of sexuality becomes broadened conceptually to encompass a triad involving two men or groups of men and a woman, who is reduced to an intermediating object. Female sexuality becomes objectified, not only a libidinal goal in itself, but a contentious and arbitrating social index for masculine reputation (1987, pp. 4–5).

In a related passage, Gilmore writes that "the correlative emphasis on female chastity and the desirability of premarital virginity remain strong throughout the region despite modernization" (1987, p. 3), yet the considerable variation in practice throughout the Mediterranean region throws doubt on the status of his generalization.

Gilmore has described a dominant folk model which couples a rhetoric of gender with what, following Scott (1990), may be called the euphemism of power. In this way Gilmore illustrates how both local idioms of honor and shame and anthropological analyses can underwrite forms of patriarchy. His focus is on men's activities and on ideals expressed by dominant men. Yet, by his own account, the dynamics of the system *create differences between more and less honorable men and women* and *depend on the relation between men and women*. Moreover, Gilmore's description is at a level of abstraction which simplifies and lends a spurious coherence to a more complex social reality. One consequence of this descriptive tidying is the way men and women are presented as radically different; there is the implication that these gendered identities are biologically given and remain constant throughout the life of an individual. Moreover, because gender is presented as unitary, it seems unproblematic that gendered difference, honor and shame, are located in a quasi-physical attribute—female chastity or modesty, the virgin's unbroken hymen—which is then treated as a thing and ranked and valued along with other commodities.[3]

Attributes and Things: A Virgin's Hymen

Malti-Douglas (1991), in her excellent book on gendered discourse in Arabo-Islamic writing, illustrates how a gendered attribute (such as a virgin's hymen) can be used to define and evaluate all dimensions of personhood. Malti-Douglas examines the rich medieval corpus of anecdotal prose, the *adab* literature, in which *woman* becomes a character type whose voice, wit, and survival depend on her duplicity, her physicality, and the manipulation of her body.

Thus in one oft-told story, a slave girl, on being offered for sale to a caliph, is asked, "Are you a virgin or what?" She replied, "Or what, O caliph." He laughs and buys her (Malti-Douglas, 1991, p. 36). In a second story:

> two slave girls were shown to a man, one a virgin and one who had been deflowered. He inclined to the virgin, so the deflowered one said, "Why do you desire her since there is only one day between her and me?" But the virgin replied, "And surely a day with thy Lord is as a thousand years of your counting." The two pleased him so he bought them. In a variant ending, the man buys only the virgin (1991, p. 36).

Many ethnographies of the Mediterranean and Middle East report on an obsession with female virginity which amounts to the kind of fetishism, a fixation with dismembered body parts, which Strathern (1988) suggests may be intimately related to ideologies of private property. Certainly, virginity is often commoditized: the hymen is a store of value which may be disposed of, exchanged, and used as the measure of both men and women. For instance, in Zakariyya Tamir's short story, "The Eastern Wedding," "the price of the young girl is agreed on, so much per kilo, and she is taken to the marketplace and weighed in" (Tamir, 1978, quoted in Malti-Douglas, 1991, p. 142). Yet it is the men involved in the bargain who ultimately will be judged more or less honorable or shamed. Such calculations are by no means only fictional exaggerations: marriage payments may be calculated both in terms of the cost of a woman's upbringing and her purported virginity (cf. Tapper, 1991), and the relative standing of different families (men and women) will be evaluated by others in terms of their honor or shame in the light of the bargain struck.

Treated from this perspective, there are many questions to be asked about parts or aspects of human beings that can be objectified, owned, and alienated, sold, or exchanged. What are the sources of value and how do they produce gendered difference, and how are the differences in social evaluation connected with notions of honor and shame (Tapper, 1991)? What is the commodity logic which allows men to see women as other men's property and renders women part-objects through bride prices? Thus, in the stories retold by Malti-Douglas, how are buyers and sellers, as well as the women who are for sale, gendered by such transactions: how are "manly honour" or "dishonour" and shame construed through such deals? Or if, as I will argue, protection and predation, responsible and competitive behavior, are intimately related aspects of dominant versions of masculinity, then how do men protect women and themselves from accusations of shame or dishonor? How is male agency understood and how does it impinge on various parts of those who are being "protected"? In short, how are the metaphors of property and protection constituted, experienced, and sustained in everyday life? Put more generally, how do fetishism and commoditization intersect to construe masculinity and femininity in systems that make use of idioms of honour and shame?

The categorical images of competitive men and passive women we are presented with in the summary accounts of honor and shame are often contradicted in more extented ethnographic descriptions. Other indigenous notions of honor associate men with conciliatory, cooperative behavior and allow women agency in certain contexts as wives and mothers on the one hand and as devilish creatures of voracious sexuality on the other (cf. Pitt-Rivers, 1965, 1977). In short, when attention is paid to everyday negotiations involving both men and women, a range of variant identities emerges: many nuances of masculinity and femininity and many degrees and kinds of honorable or shameful behavior.

Competitions and the Control of People

In any setting, notions of honor and shame are not separate from the political economy. Rather, they are a mode of interpretation through which inequalities are created and sustained. Thus, the rhetoric of hegemonic masculinity depends heavily on stereotypes of women as weak and emotional, both needing support and potentially treacherous. Female virginity and chastity are both prized and precarious. In practice, the protection of and predation on men, as well as women, can be justified in terms of values derived from the ideology of honor and shame.

Take, for example, the Durrani Pashtuns of Afghanistan. Many Durrani versions of hegemonic masculinity are expressed through idioms that may be translated in terms of a notion of honor. These idioms celebrate maleness in terms of both physical strength and moral strength of character, rationality, and responsibility. Honorable men are those who are physically attractive, "far sighted," "mature," and "deep" (Tapper, 1991, pp. 208 ff.). Such men are likely to be those who most effectively monitor virginity and control the sexual behavior of "their own" women; they are also likely to act as oppressors of other men and usurpers of "other men's" women (Tapper, 1991, p. 239).

Men prey on other men, most often using the idiom of a woman's reputed behavior to explain and justify their actions. Men who demonstrate weakness by failing to control either women's behavior or their own independence in the arrangement and completion of marriages lose credibility and find themselves on a downward spiral. They become extremely vulnerable to further exploitation. Thus, a man may be labeled "dishonorable," or femininized as "soft" or "weak," when a daughter elopes, "stolen" by another man; when he is forced to arrange a marriage for a daughter against his wishes; when he is cuckolded; and even when others, acting on gossip about women's behavior, take advantage of his precarious control of household resources in sheep or land.

In effect, women's actions, the choices they make with respect to their sexuality, and the consequences of those choices are treated as an index of a man's success ("honor") or failure ("shame") to provide economically and compete politically. Moreover, in spite of the severe sanctions associated with women's sexual misbehavior, these sanctions are not uniformly applied. Not only does female prostitution exist within the community (Tapper, 1991), but also men are sometimes judged foolish or shameful when, in conformity with idealized notions of honor, they overreact by killing a woman in circumstances when they can literally ill afford to do so (Tapper, 1991; cf. Gilsenan, 1976). Among men, degrees of affluence, political credibility, and control of other people coincide. Conversely, women often have more personal autonomy (but little else) when the men of the household with which they are associated are poor and vulnerable to the machinations of other men.

Some men are more able or willing than others to conform to the ideals of honor and hegemonic masculinity. Subordinate variants (i.e., degrees of shame) also form a continuum which depends on interpretation. No one will act without a cogent explanation of their motives and an account of their expectations and various gains. However, they will be believed only if there is no doubt that they are operating from strength, not weakness.

There is a considerable discrepancy between, on the one hand, men's and women's public agreement with the dominant idioms of honor and shame and the ideology of gender and, on the other, the great range of their actions. In competitions for honor, many nuanced masculinities are created; yet because the interpretations of dominant men often frame discourses on gender, an illusion of masculinized honor and thus hegemonic masculinity, the related ideal of female chastity and the gender hierarchy between men and women remain intact. It is arguable that this is a measure of the fiercely competitive environment in which the Durrani live. Men's everyday lives are riven politically. Their commonality (and privileges) as men depends almost entirely on the rhetoric of honor and shame and the collective disparagement of women. In short, the ideal of male domination is sustained in reiterated statements which put rhetorical gloss on the cumulative, but diverse and often ambiguous, episodes during which individual men and women interact unequally. A patriarchal ideology may be embodied in the lives of socially dominant men, but this does not mean that all men are honorable or successful patriarchs, nor are all women passive, virginal, or chaste.

Subversive Women, Subordinate Masculinities, Shame Identities

The idioms of honor and shame construct various masculinities in terms of the control of women's sexual behavior. Yusuf Idris' short story, "The Shame" (1978), illustrates how the abstract value of a woman's chastity may be interpreted in practice and how various masculinities (of the brother, husband, putative lover, and others) are created through such interpretations. The story is written from the point of view of male protagonists whose perceptions are fused with those of their male author.

"The Shame" explores the masculinities revealed in the relationship between a woman's guardian and the man accused of seducing her. Farag, the brother, uses bravado to hide his fear of responsibility for his vivacious sister Fatma, who "even aroused the dormant virility in little boys" (p. 158).

Fatma's imputed lover Gharib, a rake and bully, is secretly intimidated by Fatma's beauty, propriety, and fear of being compromised by sexual innuendo, the "shame" of the story's title. Nonetheless, the villagers fabricate a relationship between them. Farag's duty is to kill his sister and her lover: "but before he made himself guilty of their blood, their own guilt must be proved" (p. 165). In this, the village women were bolder than the men, forcing a physical examination of Fatma's hymen, while simultaneously heaping curses on her putative lover Gharib (pp. 166, 167). Two women examine the girl, an experienced "dresser of brides," whose home is said to be the site of clandestine meetings of men and women and who villagers fear might lie about what she discovers, and a much respected Christian woman whose honesty is not in question. Meanwhile, the brother, Farag, "were he not a man, . . . could have been taken for a grief-stricken widow bemoaning a dead husband" (p. 168).

Fatma's innocence is proved, yet Farag beats her mercilessly: "he felt bound to perform some spectacular act by which to reply to the people's gossip. . . ." In his turn, Gharib's father abuses his son and threatens to drown him, yet the father is "secretly proud to have sired a seducer no woman could resist, and that his son was accused of rape" (p. 174). Both Fatma and Gharib are severely chastened by the episode, and well-meaning friends suggest they should marry to save face all around. In the end Fatma, who had, in spite of her innocence, lost "that thing that gave her purity" (p. 176), returns to her ravishing ways with newfound defiance, while Gharib remains the unreconstructed rake.

The story derives its narrative impetus from notions of hegemonic masculinity, but it describes various and nuanced interpretations of honor and shame. Thus, the cause of men's violence toward women (and men) is twofold: a man's commitment to ideals of honor as judged by neighbors and others; and his own dishonor or shame, which lies not only in the actions of women but also in those of men who have challenged his authority as a surrogate father, brother, and neighbor and rendered him socially impotent. Local attributions of dishonor suggest ways in which the rhetoric of honor also inscribes ideas of the unique, bounded, and coherent person. The notion of shame or dishonor is one way of describing the discrepancies between presentations of masculinity before different audiences, while violence may be a means through which the illusion of wholeness is reasserted.

In this story and others (cf., e.g., Tamer, 1985), it is the voices of superiors, men who control resources, that are most audible. But they are not the only ones. Definitions are not fixed but are repeatedly negotiated in everyday interactions. It is through such negotiations that subordinates can modify and transform dominant idioms and structures.

A Virgin, or What?

Contextualized interpretations of female virginity and chastity can be compared cross-culturally and historically and would ideally also include a consideration of related themes: among them, notions of male virginity and chastity, as well as the ways in which myths of seduction and betrayal construct a Don Juan archetype of masculinity.

To return specifically to female virginity: in upper Egypt and the Sudan people explain pharaonic circumcision and the infibulation of girls seven and eight years old as preventing "any suspicion on the bridegroom's part that the bride is not a virgin" (Eickelman, 1989). However, as Boddy's work attests, virgins are made, not born. Divorced or widowed women "may undergo reinfibulation in anticipation of remarriage, thus renewing, like the recently delivered mother, her virginal status" (1982; p. 687). Boddy argues that both operations are less about the control of female sexuality than about its socialization. She writes:

> Through occlusion of the vaginal orifice, her womb, both literally and figuratively, becomes a social space: enclosed, impervious, virtually impenetrable. Her social virginity . . . must periodically be reestablished at those points in her life (after childbirth and before remarriage) when her fertility once again is rendered potent (1982, p. 696).

Though a man's increased sexual pleasure is sometimes offered as an explanation for the operation, Boddy dismisses this argument as implausible:

> it may take as long as two years of continuous effort before penetration can occur. For a man it is a point of honor to have a child born within a year of his marriage, and often, the midwife is summoned in secret, under cover of darkness, to assist the young couple by surgically enlarging the bride's genital orifice . . . (1982, p. 686; cf. Boddy, 1989).

Virginity in this case is in no sense natural but is created by an elaborate operation insisted upon and performed by women. Nor is sexual intercourse necessarily an unmediated act between bride and groom. Moreover, virility is reckoned less in terms of male sexuality than of fertility (Boddy, 1982); that is, what men share is the right to allocate and benefit from a woman's reproductive potential, but it is women, whose femininity is enhanced by infibulation, who carry the burden of producing a masculinity focused on fatherhood (Boddy, 1982).[4]

Boddy's ethnography is exceptionally rich. It raises an important question—how are images of an "infinitely renewable virgin" (Carter, 1991, p. 153) related to particular versions of an idealized male sexuality? Not only is the seduction of a virgin a widespread idiom which conveys a notion of essentialized, almost heroic, virility, but also the repetition of such an act sometimes defines the very essence of maleness and masculinized honor. For instance, Bouhdiba (1985) writes of visions of paradise as an "infinite orgasm" where men experience eternal erections and have repeated intercourse with *houris* who, after each penetration, become virginal again (Bouhdiba, 1985, cited in Delaney, 1991, pp. 319–320). The practice of hymen repair, like that of reinfibulation, raises questions about the relation between notions of virginity and the masculinities they construct.

Writing of lower-class Neapolitans, Goddard (1987) begs the question which should be asked wherever there is a sexual double standard: why bother with virginity, particularly when it is often a charade? Goddard criticizes the literature on honor and shame for its functionalist circularity, male bias, and focus on normative aspects of the honor code in small-scale communities (Goddard, 1987). She argues that the honor code must be understood in terms of its implications for women and the extent to which they are "consenting and active participants in [the] manipulation of honour" (1987, p. 179).

However, it is not enough to explain the double standard in terms of women being "seen as the boundary markers and the carriers of group identity" (Goddard, 1987, p. 180). Rather, it seems likely that more basic processes of gendering are at stake.

Goddard writes that virginity "is a crucial element in the relationships of men and women" (1987, p. 175): "men want or even expect to marry virgins"; a woman's sullied reputation diminishes her chances of marriage, while after marriage a woman's fidelity is assumed (pp. 176–177). Meanwhile, "it is expected of a 'normal,' 'healthy' man that he will take every opportunity for sex that presents itself and his self-image will be thereby enhanced," while women who "themselves control their sexuality and decide whether or not to dispose of their virginity" (p. 176) realize their "potential corruption" if they transgress (p. 177). Nonetheless, sexual experimentation both within and outside the institution of "a house engagement" is not uncommon, and women, who themselves dream of white weddings, are often pregnant when they marry the man who was their first lover (pp. 175–176). Failing such a marriage, women have only two options: the streets or hymen repair, which, in a large city like Naples, is a relatively anonymous, inexpensive, and simple operation. (pp. 175–177).

Hymen repair is by no means unique to Naples, nor without historical precedents. In the central Middle East, young, unmarried women may now even have the operation performed before they go out with each new boyfriend! And, when the state of a woman's hymen may be investigated by either her own or a prospective groom's family, some Middle Eastern women, during premarital sexual encounters, will insist on anal, rather than vaginal, intercourse to avoid trouble and shame.

Herzfeld has also pointed to the puzzles surrounding virginity. He notes that among Cretans, "sex before marriage is tolerated for women, and reference to chastity has a rhetorical value" (cited in Loizos & Papataxiarchis, 1991, p. 230, n. 22). Herzfeld's explanation of the apparent paradox of the idealized virginal woman and everyday sexual license is that "women *creatively deform* their submission [to male dominance]" (1991, pp. 80–81). Herzfeld is probably right, but he does not go far enough. His argument does not explain why demonstrations that a bride is *virgo intacta* are widespread, nor does it allow for a discussion of the ways in which stereotypes of women structure inequalities between men. Surely, the unasked questions are: Why is female virginity an important ideal in the first place? And why must it be sustained by hypocrisy and practiced by subversion? A Spanish saying runs, "If all Spanish women are virtuous and chaste and all Spanish men are great seducers and lovers, someone has to be lying." Or, as an Iranian friend put it, why does every middle-class marriage begin with a lie to which both bride and groom subscribe: that the bride is a virgin on her wedding night?

The Rhetoric and Practice of Wedding-night Defloration

The celebrations which follow the bloodied proof of a bride's virginity are extensively documented in the ethnographic literature. Yet, as we have seen, female virginity cannot be treated as a uniform cultural trait. However, within any one setting, the rituals associated with a bride's defloration radically differentiate men from women (as part of a dominant discourse on gender and honor) and also define a range of other gendered or shame identities (which are normally muted by local and anthropological emphases on hegemonic masculinity).

The ethnography of wedding-night defloration provides a striking example of the force of Strathern's argument about "dividual" persons whose identities depend on exchanging parts of themselves with other persons (see cf. Cornwall & Lindisfarne, 1994b; Strathern, 1988, pp. 14 ff., 348 ff.) Thus, the unambigiously female and male identities of bride and groom depend on intercourse and the exchange and transformation of essences and separable bits: semen, the penetrated hymen, and hymenal blood among them. Momentarily, an archetypal masculinity and femininity are created and revealed through interaction. Through the sex act, gendered identities, masculinized honor, and male domination are temporarily, but literally, embodied. And the marital state also anticipates further exchanges and transformations: among them, marital intercourse and the creation of the un-gendered child in the female womb. However, in the return to everyday life, new ambiguous identities emerge. Clichés of femininized masculinities and masculin-ized femininities abound: among them henpecked husbands, cuckolds whose wives have given them "horns," termagant matrons, and "big balled women" (Brandes, 1981, pp. 229, 231; cf. Blok, 1981).

Following Strathern, we can begin to ask questions about the ways in which ideas of gender difference, honor, and shame are produced by "dividual" persons (cf. Hollway, 1984). Just as the bride and groom acquire fleeting but unambiguous gender identities through consummation, so too do the generic categories *men* and *women* receive confirmation through the defloration of a bride. Consider how the Algerian men whom Ali Ghalem (1984) describes are, *qua* men, united through the orgasmic quality of the public rituals associated with consummation:

> The excitement of the group grew; the women were waiting impatiently for the consummation of the deflowering ritual. On the men's side of the house the anticipation was less visible, but it stirred up the desires and imagination, and their memories of pleasure of the heart and body . . . [The groom] drank his tea gravely, hoping to overcome his anxiety. He was intimidated by this very young girl; she did not appeal to him; her body was not open to life, but he had to make a woman of her and quickly, since they were waiting outside. . . . The ears glued to the door outside heard the young woman's cries. . . . On the men's side a few good riflemen fired the wedding volley. The joy was at its zenith, the party reached paroxysm. [The groom], hugged and congratuated by the friends around him, had only one desire, to get out, to get out quickly. [His friends'] bodies stiffened with desire, and then, re-lieved by that strange and secret complicity of men, proud of their virility and in that moment deeply bound together (1984, pp. 34–35).

Ghalem's description of the wedding night raises questions about desire which have hardly been addressed in the literature on honor and shame. How is it con-stituted—as an emotion, a force, or a need in terms of satisfaction—and how are those moments when desire is allowed licit expression related to attributions of honor, not shame?

Westermarck's extended description of ceremonies of the "bride's drawers" (1914, pp. 228 ff., 266 ff.) in Morocco offers ethnographic examples of the variant masculinities and femininities which are a product of an idealized notion of bridal virginity. Thus, he notes, the groom does not necessarily manage intercourse on the wedding night and the ceremony takes place only after hymenal blood has appeared (Westermarck, 1914, 1914). A masculinity, or masculinized honor which trades on images of male potency, must be altered by such a delay, and, in turn, must define subordinate masculinities and masculinized shame. Westermarck does not discuss such delays further, yet his account of consummations treated as *le droit de seigneur* or performed by a paid proxy (Westermarck, 1914; cf. Giovannini, 1987) suggests the range of possibilities which may be practiced.

The absence of social honor, recognition, or prestige may sometimes be labeled and even experienced as shame. In some places, manual defloration rather than *lege artis* relieves the groom of worries about his potency, but in general impotence seems to be hedged with taboos. Some of these are local: thus, popular accounts of "wedding night murders" in Turkey suggest that brides may be killed merely for being the inadvertent witnesses of their husbands' impotence and thus "shame."[5] In the ethnographic literature, impotence is a topic often mentioned only in passing:[6] thus, we learn little of the consequences for a groom who fails to deflower his bride because he is too old, fat, or terrified. How is his "shame" expressed, experienced, and perceived by others? And what of those who are helped by a friend or proxy, a midwife, their mothers, and sometimes by even their mothers-in-law? One poignant image is of a young boy who cries out in an Afghan ballad:

Je ne suis qu'un petit garcon, pere;
Pourquoi me maries tu?
Ma femme ne me connaît pas;
Elle se fait des rêves d'une mari.
Hai! Hai! Le matin j'ai si froid,[7]

while a striking and terrible image comes from Michel Khleifi's superb feature film, *A Wedding in Galilee*. The groom's impotence is a metaphor for the helplessness and shame of the Palestinians in the face of their Israeli oppressors; as the wedding guests pound obscenely on the door, the young bride deflowers herself with a knife and defiantly displays her own hymenal blood.

Clearly, public recognition of a man's capacity for penetrative sex with his virgin bride often defines an adult masculinity and masculinized honor and associates this kind of sexuality with economic privilege and control over others. However, in spite of the importance of this moment, it is interesting that Westermarck, like most other ethnographers, jumps from the specter of impotence to the problem of the nonvirgin bride. Both bride and groom may have a vested interest in covering up not only male impotence but also the bride's prior unchastity. As Westermarck notes in passing, a man will hesitate to accuse his bride of unchasteness because he thus admits that he himself has slept with a "bitch" (1914; pp. 236, 254, 270). Unfortunately, he does not explore further the perception of interests which may lead to a cover-up, but he does offer some clues to the fear of shame in such cases and thus the fabrication of hegemonic masculinity. Westermarck writes:

it may also happen that the bride's parents, in order to avoid a scandal, bribe the bridegroom to conceal the fact . . . in which case the blood of a fowl or pigeon is used as a substitute for the lacking signs of virginity (1914, pp. 229, 240, 243, 246).

It is worth considering not only the sheer logistics of the chicken-blood solution, but also the subordinate (or shame) masculinities which it constructs. In what ways does the groom's ignorance of, or acquiescence to, such a strategem qualify his relations with his new in-laws and his bride? And are they all implicated in a cover-up vis-à-vis their neighbors? And there may be quite other dynamics when virginity is irrelevant or faked in wedding-night encounters. Thus, Loizos tells of a Cypriot couple who took great glee in telling him how, in the 1940s, they had conspired together to empty a bladder of chicken blood on the marriage bed and avoid parental knowledge and disapproval of their premarital encounters. Then it was shameful for a bride to be pregnant at her wedding, while her groom would be mocked as a donkey because of his uncontrolled sexuality.[8] Or the trickery may only concern the bride and groom: Rifaat's short story, "Honour" (1990), tells of a nonvirgin bride who deeply dislikes her new husband. The woman pays a midwife to help her put ground glass up her vagina to make herself bleed and to shame her groom by causing him excruciating pain and social mortification.

Indeed, virginity as it is revealed by, and reveals, virility may be ritually marked in circumstances which completely belie it or make its proof impossible. Jamous (1981) and Combs-Schilling (1989), both writing of Morocco, argue that the use of henna in wedding ceremonies actually precludes the need for dissimulation. They argue that henna symbolizes blood and

> blood spilling rather than sexual intercourse consummates . . . first marriage ceremonies. . . . sexual intercourse may or may not have happened before that night and may or may not happen on that night. Yet as long as the male spills blood and it is publicly exhibited . . . the young man becomes a man and the young woman a woman, each acquiring the rights and duties associated with the new status (Combs-Schilling, 1989, p. 194).

While such an argument mistakenly renders all young men and men the same, there can be no doubt that such circularities protect masculinized versions of honor and hegemonic ideals.

Rhetorically, the virgin's unbroken hymen is an attribute which stands for a unitary individual, and, at that moment when chastity is proven, it defines that individual's gender as entirely and unambiguously female. Hymenal penetration also creates an unambiguously gendered and honorable male: it is the means by which a man makes known his virility to himself and others. Finally, hymenal penetration effects a radical transformation: the womb thus acted upon is transformed and can be made to realize its fertile potential and, by extension, that of the man.

Gendered Identities: The Rhetoric of Honor and Shame

Where there is such a focus on virginity, impotence, and delayed consummation, as well as drugged brides (Dorsky, 1986), wedding night rape (Hegland, 1992; Westermarck, 1914), and the absence of proof of a bride's virginity, all become pressing, if censored, concerns. In short, we will greatly mislead ourselves if we consider that the display of bloodied linen, the cries of joy (by all but the bride), the gunshots and waving flags have only to do with the abstractions we translate as *honor* and *shame*.

There can be no doubt that the rhetoric of honor is politically effective because it operates at a level of abstraction which hides classificatory ambiguities and alternative points of view, while empowering some fortunate men and women. A bride's defloration by penetrative sex is a ritual moment when, ideally, a "real," "honorable" man is potent and a "real," "honorable" woman is chaste, when gendered difference and hierarchy can be experienced as quintessentially real. Undoubtedly, this is one aspect of what the rhetoric of honor is for (cf. Davis, 1969). However, even the quintessential moment of defloration defines other, subordinate or shame identities. And, of course, everyday interactions produce an even wider range of ambiguous and ever-changing masculinities and femininities.

Notes

1. An earlier version of this paper, entitled "Variant Masculinities, Variant Virginities: Rethinking Honour and Shame," appeared in Cornwall and Lindisfarne (1994a). Fieldwork in Afghanistan was funded by the SSRC (Project No. HR 1141/1).
2. See especially Pitt-Rivers (1965) and (1977); for more recent examples, see Wikan (1984) or Herzfeld (1985).
3. Models which emphasize an extreme dichotomization of gender reinforce heterosexual biases; other sexualities are often ignored or inadequately described. For instance, Wikan's suggestion that male homosexual prostitutes in Oman constitute a third sex does not do justice to her own more complex ethnography (1977; Shepherd, 1978, 1987). However, there are some exceptions: cf. Delaney's (1991) discussion of the relation between body morphology and gendered identities in the case of male homosexuality and sex change operations in Turkey.
4. We know little of how subordinate and variant masculinities are refracted through hegemonic notions of fatherhood. Certainly men who have not fathered children are often deemed less than "real men," and the stigma may be such that sterile men connive with their wives to gain heirs (cf. Peters, 1980, Tapper, 1991). But what of the masculine identity of those men who never marry or those whose children do not survive infancy or prove defective in some way?
5. Deniz Kandiyoti, personal communication.
6. There are, of course, some exceptions: see, e.g., Wikan (1977).
7. My thanks to Pierre Centlivres for bringing this to my attention. The ballad was translated by Darmesteter (1888–90).
8. Peter Loizos, personal communication.

References

Blok, A. (1981). Rams and billy goats: A key to the Mediterranean code of honour. *Man, 16* (3), 427–440.
Boddy, J. (1982). Womb as oasis: The symbolic context of Pharaonic circumcision in rural northern Sudan. *American Ethnologist, 9* (4), 682–698.
Boddy, J. (1989). *Wombs and alien spirits*. Madison, WI: University of Wisconsin Press.
Boudhiba, A. (1985). *Sexuality in Islam*. London: Routledge & Kegan Paul.
Brandes, S. (1981). Like wounded stags: Male sexual ideology in an Andalusian town. In S. B. Ortner & H. Whitehead (Eds.), *Sexual meanings: The cultural construction of gender and sexuality* (pp. 216–239). Cambridge: Cambridge University Press.
Carter, A. (1991). *Wise children*. London: Vintage.
Combs-Schilling, M. (1989). *Sacred performances: Islam, sexuality and sacrifice*. New York: Columbia University Press.
Cornwall, A., & Lindisfarne, N. (Eds.). (1994a). *Dislocating masculinity: Comparative ethnographies*. London: Routledge.
Cornwall, A., & Lindisfarne, N. (1994b). Dislocating masculinity: Gender, power and

anthropology. In A. Cornwall & N. Lindisfarne (Eds.), *Dislocating masculinity: Comparative ethnographies* (pp. 11–47). London: Routledge.

Darmesteter, J. (1888–1890). *Chants populaires des Afghans*. Paris: Ernest Leroux.

Davis, J. (1969). Honour and Politics in Pisticci, *Proceedings of the Royal Anthropological Institute*, 69–81.

Delaney, C. (1991). *The seed and the soil*. Berkeley, CA: University of California Press.

Dorsky, S. (1986). *Women of 'Amran*. Salt Lake City, UT: University of Utah Press.

Eickelman, D. (1989). *The Middle East: An anthropological approach*. Englewood Cliffs, NJ.: Prentice-Hall.

Ghalem, A. (1984). *A wife for my son*. London: Zed.

Gilmore, D. (1987). Introduction: The shame of dishonour. In D. Gilmore (Ed.), *Honour and shame and the unity of the Mediterranean* (pp. 2–21). Washington, DC: American Anthropological Association.

Gilsenan, M. (1976). Lying, honor, and contradiction. In B. Kapferer (Ed.), *Transaction and Meaning*, (pp. 191–219). Philadelphia: Institute for the Study of Human Issues.

Gilsenan, M. (1996). *Lords of the Lebanese marches: Violence and narrative in an Arab society*. London: Tauris.

Giovannini, M. (1987). Female chastity codes in the circum Mediterranean: Comparative perspectives. In D. Gilmore (Ed.), *Honour and shame and the unity of the Mediterranean* (pp. 61–74). Washington, DC: American Anthropological Association.

Goddard, V. (1987). Honour and shame: The control of women's sexuality and group identity in Naples. In P. Caplan (Ed.), *The cultural construction of sexuality* (pp. 166–192). London: Tavistock.

Hegland, M. (1992). Wife abuse and the political system: A Middle Eastern case study. In D. A. Counts, J. K. Brown, & J. C. Campbell (Eds.), *Sanctions and sanctuary* (pp. 210–235). Boulder CO: Westview.

Herzfeld, M. (1985). *The poetics of manhood: Contest and identity in a Cretan mountain village*. Princeton, NJ: Princeton University Press.

Idris, Y. (1978) *The Cheapest Nights*, London: Heineman.

Herzfeld, M. (1991). Silence, submission, and subversion: Towards a poetics of womanhood. In P. Loizos & E. Papataxiarchis (Eds.), *Contested identities. Gender and Kinship in modern Greece* (pp. 79–97). Princeton, NJ: Princeton University Press.

Hollway, Wendy (1984). Gender difference and the production of subjectivity. In J. Henriques, W. Hollway, C. Urwin, and V. Walkerdine, (Eds.), *Changing the subject: psychology, social regulation and subjectivity*. London: Methuen.

Jamous, R. (1981). *Honneur et 'Baraka'*. Cambridge: Cambridge University Press.

Loizos, P., & Papataxiarchis, E. (Eds.). (1991), *Contested Identities: Gender and kinship in modern Greece*. Princeton, NJ: Princeton University Press.

Malti-Douglas, F. (1991). *Woman's body, woman's word*. Princeton, NJ: Princeton University Press.

Peristiany, J. (Ed.). (1965). *Honour and shame*. London: Weidenfeld & Nicolson.

Peters, E. (1980). Aspects of bedouin bridewealth among camel herders in Cyrenaica. In J. Comaroff (Ed.), *The meaning of marriage payments* (pp. 125–160). London: Academic Press.

Pitt-Rivers, J. (1965). Honour and social status. In J. Peristiany (Ed.), *Honour and Shame* (pp. 19–77). London: Weidenfeld & Nicolson.

Pitt-Rivers, J. (1977). *The fate of schechem or the politics of sex*. Cambridge: Cambridge University Press.

Rifaat, A. (1990). Honour. In M. Badran & M. Cooke (Eds.), *Opening the Gates* (pp. 78–83). London: Virago.

Scott, J. (1990). *Domination and the arts of resistance: Hidden transcripts*. New Haven, CT: Yale University Press.

Shepherd, G. (1978). Transsexualism in Oman? *Man*, *13* (1), 133–134.

Shepherd, G. (1987). Rank, gender and homosexuality: Mombasa as a key to understanding sexual options. In P. Caplan (Ed.), *The cultural construction of sexuality* (pp. 240–270). London: Tavistock.

Strathern, M. (1988). *The gender of the gift*. Berkeley, CA: University of California Press.

Tamer, Z. (1985). *Tigers on the Tenth Day* London: Quartet.

Tapper, N. (1991). *Bartered brides*. Cambridge: Cambridge University Press.

Westermarck, E. (1914). *Marriage ceremonies in Morocco*. London: Curzon.

Wikan, U. (1977). Man becomes woman: Transsexualism in Oman as a key to gender roles. *Man, 12* (2), 304–319.

Wikan, U. (1984). Shame and honour: A contestable pair. *Man, 19* (4), 635–652.

14

The Sacred and the Social

Cultures of Honor and Violence

Dov Cohen, Joseph Vandello, & Adrian K. Rantilla

I t is a ritual for those who complain about the decline of our culture to point out all the trivial things that people have been killing their acquaintances, friends, and family members over recently. It's almost never hard to find these examples. Open the newspaper and in a week one can pretty easily find an extensive list of things that one party deemed important enough to kill the other party over. Somewhere near the top of the list is going to be sexual jealousy, and in terms of male-on-male violence, you can add things like spilled beer, suspicious glances, escalated name-calling contests, and stepped-on shoes. That's the American list. Certainly, the lists of offenses that must be punished by death are going to vary from culture to culture, but they will have one thing in common. That is, many of the acts that led to a killing will probably seem quite trivial to outsiders.

The question is: What's going on here? And to answer that, one has to get over astonishment at the facts of the case and understand that these incidents are about something of profound and fundamental importance to many people the world over. These cases are about social status. They are about position in a hierarchy. They are about making it known that one is not someone to be messed with. In short, they are about honor and its opposite, shame. These are fundamentally social constructs, and, far from representing a breakdown of our civilization and culture, they represent an outgrowth of our social organization and our social nature. As later parts of this chapter will argue, honor, and specifically honor-related violence, are strong not where our society is falling apart but where it is strongest and exerts most control over its members.

The Importance of Honor

It is necessary to clarify something here. Honor—defined as virtuous conduct or social status—is important in cultures the world over (Daly & Wilson, 1988; Pitt-

261

Rivers, 1968; Sandel, 1996; Triandis, 1996). But when anthropologists talk about cultures of honor and when we talk about a culture of honor here, we mean a culture in which male strength and power are highly valued and in which men are prepared to kill to defend their status as honorable men. This is the manliness whose essence is "fearlessness, readiness to defend one's own pride and that of one's family" (Pitt-Rivers, 1961, cited in Gilmore, 1990, p. 45). It is the manliness embodied in the taunt that Truk Islanders commonly use when they want to instigate a fight. "Come, are you a man?! I will take your life now" (Gilmore, 1990, p. 67).

Creating the Culture of Honor

Why would this type of "manly" honor be important? In many societies without adequate law enforcement or state mechanisms to redress grievances, the answer is relatively clear. Honor—your reputation—is what you have to protect yourself. It is what deters people from threatening you and yours. People use violence to make it clear that they are not to be trifled with, on big matters or on small ones. As Daly and Wilson wrote:

> A seemingly minor affront is not merely a "stimulus" to action, isolated in time and space. It must be understood within a larger social context of reputations, face, relative social status, and enduring relationships. Men are known by their fellows as "the sort who can be pushed around" or "the sort who won't take any shit," as people whose word means action and people who are full of hot air, as guys whose girlfriends you can chat up with impunity or guys you don't want to mess with. In most social milieus, a man's reputation depends in part upon the maintenance of a credible threat of violence (1988, p. 128).

Consistent with this, cultures of honor have sprung up where individuals had to rely on only themselves for protection. As anthropologist Julian Pitt-Rivers has written:

> whenever the authority of law is questioned or ignored, the code of honor re-emerges to allocate the right to precedence and dictate the principles of conduct . . . (as) among aristocracies and criminal underworlds, school boy and street-corner societies, open frontiers and the closed communities where reigns "The Honorable Society," as the Mafia calls itself

(quoted in Ayers, 1984, p. 275; see also Conrad, 1954, pp. 108–110, for a fictional depiction).

Sustaining the Culture of Honor

One can see then how the forces of social disorganization—loose social ties, no law enforcement, a lack of order—create the conditions for a culture of honor to develop. But perhaps, more interestingly, once such a system that values honor is in place, it is the forces of culture and patterned social interaction that keep the system going. Socialization, peer enforcement of norms, laws, customs, and so on, keep such practices strong. It is culture that can buttress norms for honor past the point where it is functional for individuals to uphold such norms.

Perhaps, then, we can learn most about the social nature of honor and shame and the way violence is tied up with these two concepts by studying a society where behaving in a culture-of-honor way is not just a consequence of behaving rationally in a potentially threatening environment. That is, perhaps we can learn most about the way social norms reinforce a culture of honor by examining a culture of honor where people are not in danger of having their herds rustled away, their wealth or their lives taken by competitors, their families attacked, or the women of their village kidnapped. This is why the study of honor in the southern United States of the twentieth century can be so informative.

Southern Culture of Honor as a Case Study

Historically, the cultures of honor of the southern and western United States were quite adaptive responses to economic and ecological circumstances. Because these regions were frontiers without adequate law enforcement and because, in many places, residents of the region made a precarious living by herding animals (an easily stolen commodity), it made sense for residents to adopt a tough, "don't-mess-with-me" stance to scare off potential rivals or thieves (Fischer, 1989; McWhiney, 1988). Herdsmen the world over are likely to adopt a stance of sensitivity to affronts as a way of warning others that any encroachments—big or small—on their land, their animals, or their persons will not be tolerated (Campbell, 1965; Edgerton, 1971; Nisbett & Cohen, 1996; Schneider, 1971). And such a stance was all the more functional in regions of the eighteenth-and nineteenth-century South and West, where the law was quite weak (Courtwright, 1996; Fischer, 1989; Frantz, 1969; Gastil, 1971; McWhiney, 1988).

In the present day, however, most southerners and westerners are no longer herders, and most places in these regions can hardly be characterized as frontiers. Yet, the culture of honor remains quite strong and is linked to high rates of violence there even today.

Our recent research on U.S. southern and western culture has helped outline the contours of at least one type of culture of honor and has looked at a number of mechanisms by which this culture has been kept in place. In studying the South, we can see the relevance of social and cultural factors that perpetuate hypermasculine gender roles and the violence created by them. The cultures of honor of the South and West are by no means prototypical cultures of honor (for more classical descriptions, see Gilmore, 1990; Jacquemet, 1996; or Pitt-Rivers, 1965, on cultures of honor in the Mediterranean). But it is interesting to examine them because they constitute at least one manifestation of what a subculture of honor looks like when it is embedded in an American, industrialized context.

Culture of Honor in the U. S. South

History

From descriptions of historians and cultural observers, there can be little doubt that the Old South possessed some version of a culture of honor. As Fischer has written:

In the absence of any strong sense of order as unity, hierarchy, or social peace, backsettlers shared an idea of order as a system of retributive justice. The prevailing principle was lex talionis, the rule of retaliation. It held that a good man must seek to do right in the world, but when wrong was done to him, he must punish the wrongdoer himself by an act of retribution that restored order and justice in the world (1989, p. 765).

As with many cultures of honor, a wrong was not just something done to one's physical person but also to one's reputation. Insults or affronts were the probes by which people tested each other to see how much they could get away with. A man who allowed himself to be affronted was a man who could be walked over with impunity. Thus, "a man who absorbs insults is not a man at all" (Gilmore, 1990, p. 67).

Seemingly "trivial" insults took on important meanings as men had to prove themselves ready to retaliate against slights to their honor. One eighteenth-century observer of the South noted that fights occur when one party

has in a merry hour called (the other) a Lubber or a thick-Skull or a Buckskin, or a Scotsman, or perhaps one has mislaid the other's hat, or knocked a peach out of his Hand, or offered him a dram without wiping the mouth of the Bottle; all these, and ten thousand more quite as trifling and ridiculous are thought and accepted as just Causes of immediate Quarrels. (Fithian, 1774, cited in Gorn, 1985, p. 19)

But these affronts paled in comparison to the importance of insults and attacks against members, particularly female members, of one's family. So, as in many cultures of honor, insults or attacks were considered particularly heinous when they were directed against women whom men were in charge of protecting (Fiske, Markus, Kitayama, & Nisbett, 1997; Jacquemet, 1996; Schneider, 1971).

In the Old South, as in the ancient world, "son of a bitch" or any similar epithet was a most damaging blow to male pride. . . . To attack his wife, mother, or sister was to assault the man himself. Outsider violence against family dependents, particularly females, was a breach not to be ignored without risk of ignominy. An impotence to deal with such wrongs carried all the weight of shame that archaic society could muster. (Wyatt-Brown, 1982, p. 53)

In the Old South, "a crime of passion in response to a family wrong was often greeted with acquittal. If the law intervened at all, the penalty was often slight" (Wyatt-Brown, 1982, p. 43). And even into the early twentieth century, the legal system took a bit of a hands-off, settle-it-yourself approach. Brearley (1934) has written that in much of the South, it was impossible to convict someone of murder if (1) the perpetrator had been insulted and (2) he had warned the victim of his intent to kill if the insult was not withdrawn or somehow compensated for. In the present day, we can see the influence of the culture of honor on the behaviors, attitudes, institutional practices, social policies, and crime rates of the U. S. South and West.

Honor in the Present-day South and West

When one examines homicide rates of the present-day U. S. South and West, there can be little doubt that these regions retain at least some of the original culture-of-honor character described by historians. The U.S. South and West are the most violent regions of the country, but they are violent only when it comes to honor-related infractions. The South and West are comparable to the rest of the country in their rates of felony-homicides, that is, homicides committed in the context of another crime such as robbery or burglary. But the South and West have significantly higher rates of honor-related violence. The rates for brawl-related, lovers'-triangle, and argument-related homicides—thus, homicides where self-protection and defense of honor are of central importance—are far higher in the South and West than in other regions (Nisbett & Cohen, 1996; Reaves & Nisbett, 1997; Rice & Goldman, 1994). Reed, in reviewing similar data, also concluded that "lovers' quarrels and family disputes are a dangerous business in the South. . . . The southerner who can avoid both arguments and adultery is as safe as any other American, and probably safer" (1981, p. 13). Importantly, such homicide rate differences get bigger as one looks at smaller and smaller cities, suggesting that where the modern forces of homogenization have been kept at bay, cultural differences between the North and South are strongest (Nisbett & Cohen, 1996).

In attitude surveys, southerners also express opinions consistent with a culture-of-honor stance that makes violence an acceptable redress for an insult. Southerners do not endorse violence in the abstract, nor do they do so when asked about specific incidents of violence not related to personal honor. However, when it comes to issues of protection of self, personal honor, and the socialization of children, southerners (and to a lesser extent westerners) respond with greater approval than do their northern counterparts (Cohen & Nisbett, 1994; Ellison, 1991; Ellison & Sherkat, 1993; Nisbett & Cohen, 1996). For example, twice as many southerners as northerners would approve of a man punching a drunk stranger who bumped into the man and his wife on the street (15% vs. 8%), and almost twice as many southerners as northerners think it would be "extremely justified" for a man to shoot another person because that person sexually assaulted his 16-year-old daughter (47% vs. 26%). Such acts of violence become incorporated into the southern definition of what it means to be a man. In the above example, almost one in four southern respondents would criticize someone as being "not much of a man" if he did not shoot the person who sexually assaulted his daughter. The comparable figure for the North was 1 in 10 (Cohen & Nisbett, 1994).

Such values are implicit in expectations of children. When asked questions about what a 10-year-old boy would be expected to do when he was either challenged or repeatedly bullied, more southerners than northerners said the boy would be expected to "take a stand and fight" (Cohen & Nisbett, 1994). As Reed notes, "southerners learn, as they grow up, that some disputes are supposed to be settled privately, violently sometimes, without calling in 'the authorities'. . . . If you were called out for some offense, you fought. I guess you could have appealed to the teacher, but that just—wasn't done. And that phrase speaks volumes" (1981, p. 13; see also Miller & Sperry, 1987).

Southerners do not just give lip service to such values; they act them out in some very striking ways. In a series of laboratory experiments, southern and northern male students showed qualitatively different responses to being insulted. In a typical experiment, students who had been invited to the lab were given a brief cover story and then were told to fill out a short form and drop it off at a table at the end of a hallway. As the subject did this, a confederate, who was seemingly unconnected with the experiment, bumped into the subject with his shoulder and rudely called him an "asshole." While northerners tended to regard this more as an occasion for amusement than for anger, the results were strikingly different for southerners, according to covert observer ratings. The modal southern response was to show more anger than amusement (true of 85% of southerners, compared to only 35% of northerners) (Cohen, Nisbett, Bowdle, & Schwarz, 1996).

Further, the insult seemed to affect southerners on a visceral level. We took saliva samples from subjects before and after they were insulted, and then later assayed these samples for cortisol (a hormone associated with stress) and testosterone (a hormone associated with aggression, competition, and dominance). Southerners who had been insulted were substantially more likely than any other group (uninsulted southerners, insulted northerners, and uninsulted northerners) to show increases in both hormones (Cohen, Nisbett, Bowdle, & Schwarz, 1996).

Insulted southerners also tended to be more cognitively primed for aggression, as shown by their more violent completion of short vignettes that began with one person affronting another. And they also acted out these aggressive tendencies in subsequent behaviors with other people. Whereas uninsulted southerners were our most polite and deferential group, southerners who had previously been insulted were the most likely to (1) become domineering in an interpersonal encounter with another confederate and (2) respond aggressively to a different confederate, who played "chicken" with the subject while walking down a long, narrow hallway. In the latter case, this was not a trivial act. The confederate that the subject was playing chicken with was 6'3", 250 pounds, played college football, and was walking rapidly down a hallway that was blocked off so that only one person could comfortably pass (Cohen, Nisbett et al., 1996).

Finally, we also found that southerners who had been insulted believed that their masculine reputation was greatly diminished in the eyes of someone who witnessed the insult. Northerners, however, did not feel their reputation was harmed (Cohen, Nisbett, et al., 1996).[1]

Perhaps it is this last finding that is most significant when we consider the question of cultural maintenance. If southerners think they will be considered "wimps" for not responding to an insult, whereas northerners do not, they may respond aggressively simply because it is expected of them and because not behaving that way leads to social stigmatization. Such social norms increase in power when they are tied, as they are in the South and many other cultures of honor, to ideas about masculinity. Responding with toughness and strength becomes embedded in the definition of being a man. The ultimate rationale for why it is important to be tough gets lost, and being tough becomes something a man just does (see discussions by Cohen, 1997b; Cohen & Vandello, 1997a; Gilmore, 1990; Nisbett & Cohen, 1996; Roebuck & Murty, 1996).

What also makes these norms so powerful is that they are *collectively* held, so that everyone knows what is expected of them, as well as of everyone else in the culture. Thus, when conflicts escalate, both parties know that the other party may be contemplating violence to save face. This knowledge can force the parties to strike first because each person knows that violence is possible and, what's more, each person knows that the other person knows this. (To make it complicated, suppose A and B are in a conflict. A knows, first, that B may feel affronted and may feel compelled to respond with violence; second, that B knows that A is aware of the potential for violence; and third, that B knows that A knows both these basic social facts. A similar calculus can be going on in B's head. Expectations for both parties get knotted together and tangled as they consider what each party knows, what each party knows about the other party knowing, and finally what each party knows about the other party knowing about they themselves knowing.)

In less complicated terms, "Violence may breed violence . . . simply by raising the risks of perceived nonviolence. A rational man in a violent milieu will be quicker on the trigger than the same man in a more pacific setting" (Daly & Wilson, 1988, p. 286). Or, "as one observer in the [Old] South noted, enemies would meet, exchange insults, and one would shoot the other down, professing that he had acted in self-defense because he believed the victim was armed" (McWhiney, 1988, p. 163). And this phenomena illustrates the importance of a cultural-level, as opposed to a purely individual-level, explanation of behavior. What is important is not necessarily the concepts about honor and shame that individuals carry around in their heads but cultural-level variables that define the shared expectations, rules, and scripts for a given situation.

The Role of Women

It is important to note that males are not the only ones with such shared scripts and expectations. Given the important role women play in socialization, it would be surprising if women did not somehow contribute to the perpetuation of the culture of honor. Violence in all cultures is predominately committed by men, but one might expect to see women in cultures of honor either participating in violence themselves or at the very least supporting it in their men. This seems to be true in many traditional cultures of honor, and there is some evidence that it is also true in the South as well (Chadwick, 1970; Daly & Wilson, 1988; Fischer, 1989; McWhiney, 1988; Pitt-Rivers, 1968; Wyatt-Brown, 1982). Thus:

1. In attitude surveys, southern women, like southern men, are more likely to support culture-of-honor type violence than are their northern counterparts. And indeed, the gap between southern and northern women is at least as big as the gap between southern and northern men (Nisbett & Cohen, 1996; see also Ellison, 1991).

2. Southern women kill at a far greater rate than their northern counterparts. While southern men account for a disproportionate 41% of all white-male-perpetrated homicides in the United States, southern women account for an even more disproportionate 48% of white-female-perpetrated homicides. However, because the overwhelming majority of female-perpetrated homicides are in response to violence by a partner, it is unclear whether this higher rate of homicide is merely a reaction to more violent southern men or reflects a lower threshold for what southern women will "tolerate" from their partners before becoming violent themselves. One might suspect that both could be true (Nisbett & Cohen, 1996).

3. Finally, we did not run any female subjects in our lab experiments. How-

ever, in one of the studies we did ask about the regional background of the subjects' parents. It appeared that having a mother from the South was important for producing the "southern" response to the affront—and further, having a southern mother seemed to be even more important for producing the southern response than having a southern father. Caution is warranted, however, because cell sizes were small (Nisbett & Cohen, 1996).

Thus, from the indications we have, women do play an important role in fostering culture-of-honor values (see also Cohen & Vandello, 1997a). Undoubtedly, it is important to give more study to the role of women in nurturing or curbing violence in children, as well as supporting or restraining its use by adults (see also Miller & Sperry, 1987). Next, however, we briefly turn to more macrolevel factors that perpetuate the culture of honor.

Honor and Institutions

Notions about honor are recognized in the organizational arrangements, laws, and social policies of the South and West. The media and other institutions reinforce the idea that violence can be an acceptable response to affronts and personal violations. In one study, newspapers across the country were sent facts for a story involving an incident in which one person stabbed another after being insulted in various ways (Cohen & Nisbett, 1997). Reporters knew the facts were hypothetical but were instructed to turn them into a news story as if it would run in their paper. As they turned the facts into an article, southern and western reporters wrote the stories in a way that made the stabbing seem more provoked, less aggravated, and much more sympathetic than did northern reporters. A control condition showed that southern and western papers were not more sympathetic to violence of all sorts, but only to violence relating to defense of honor (Cohen & Nisbett, 1997).

In another study, employers were sent letters from job applicants who were inquiring about work. In a bogus letter (which employers thought was real), the job applicant described his qualifications and also mentioned that he had a criminal record after killing someone who had taunted and attacked him in a bar fight. Again, southern and western employers responded in a more cooperative and understanding way than did northern employers (Cohen & Nisbett, 1997). And again, a control condition showed that this greater sympathy was not shown to just any crime, but only to violence in defense of honor. In one (extreme) case, a southern employer provided particularly empathic feedback to the man who killed after being provoked:

As for your problem of the past, anyone could probably be in the situation you were in. It was just an unfortunate incident that shouldn't be held against you. Your honesty shows that you are sincere. . . .
I wish you the best of luck for your future. You have a positive attitude and a willingness to work. Those are the qualities that businesses look for in an employee. Once you get settled, if you are near here, please stop in and see us.

No letter from a northern employer was nearly so sympathetic to a man who had killed in defense of his honor.

Honor and the Law

The acceptability of using violence to preserve honor has been codified in formal laws and social policies of the region (Cohen, 1996). Thus, with respect to condoning violence in self-defense and in national defense, southern and western legislators are far more permissive. Southern and western lawmakers are more hawkish on foreign policy and support a stronger national defense than do their northern counterparts. Southern and western laws and lawmakers are more libertarian when it comes to controlling citizens' access to guns. And southern and western states are also more likely to allow citizens to use deadly force to defend themselves, instead of requiring them to retreat or "act in a cowardly and humiliating role" (LaFave & Scott, 1986, p. 659). That is, they are more likely to reject the "retreat rule" in favor of the "true man" rule, allowing a man to stand his ground and fight in his own defense (Cohen, 1996). As one Oklahoma court explained the issue.

> Under the old common law, no man could defend himself until he had retreated and until his back was to the wall; but this is not the law in free America. Here the wall is to every man's back. It is the wall of his rights; and when he is [assailed] at a place where he has a right to be . . . he may stand and defend himself (*Fowler v. State*, 1912, 126 Pacific 831, cited in Mischke, 1981, p. 1007).

Such present-day differences are actually quite surprising and may be a hint of even greater differences that occurred before state laws across the country modernized. As one example, while many states had implicit versions of the "unwritten rule" (allowing a man to kill his wife's lover if caught in flagrante delicto), the rule was actually explicit in four southern and western states (Georgia, New Mexico, Texas, and Utah) and was on the books there until the 1960s and 1970s (Taylor, 1986). Again, such collective representations—laws, policies, media, institutional behaviors, and so on—may reinforce, as well as reflect, the culture-of-honor stance (Cohen & Nisbett, 1997; Cohen & Vandello, in press; Kuran, 1995; Sunstein, 1995).

Social Organization, Honor, and Violence

As notions about honor suffuse southern and western culture, one might actually make a counterintuitive prediction about the level of social organization and the level of violence in a society. It is a strong current of Western thought that aggressive impulses are a part of human nature and need to be restrained by the "civilizing" forces of family, community, and religion. In political science, this idea is associated with thinkers such as Hobbes (1651/1957). And in psychology, one of its most notable proponents was Freud, particularly in his *Civilization and its Discontents* (1930/1961). The idea permeates a major school of thought in sociology (Lee, 1996; Pfohl, 1985; Sampson, 1993; Wrong, 1961), present-day political discourse (Elshtain 1996a, 1996b), and lay theories of society and crime (Herbert & Daniel, 1996; Kaminer, 1996). Cohesive communities, strong families, and religious adherence are believed to tame our naturally aggressive impulses.

However, from a cultural psychology perspective, this explanation may be too simple and perhaps even incorrect. In cultures of honor, the stronger and more cohesive the family and community, the more culturally approved violence it may breed. Thus, in the South and West, the tighter the social organization, the more honor-related violence there seems to be. For example, both residential stability (defined by the percentage of citizens who have lived in the same place for 5 years) and family stability (defined by the presence of traditional, nuclear family structures) are associated with opposite patterns of violence in the West and South as opposed to the North. That is, while family and residential stability are associated with *less* violence in northern counties, they are associated with *more* violence in southern and western counties.

For the years around 1980, in stable residential communities of the North, the argument-related homicide rate for white males aged 15 to 39 was 47 per million. For less stable communities, it was 67 per million. In the South and West, the opposite pattern held. Homicide rates in more stable communities in the South and West were 228 per million, compared to 183 per million in less stable communities (interaction $p < .01$) (Cohen, 1997a). Importantly, this interaction held only for argument-and brawl-related violence, not for felony-related violence, suggesting that tighter social organization is associated only with culturally appropriate honor-related violence, not violence in general (Cohen, 1997a).

In addition, tighter social organization in northern states tends to be associated with less consumption of violence (less viewing of violent television, reading violent magazines, producing college football players, obtaining hunting licenses, and spending on state national guard units), as standard social theory would predict. But tighter social organization is actually associated with more such violence consumption in the South and West. Using the above indicators of "Legitimate Violence" (Baron & Straus, 1988, 1989), we found that the less socially organized northern states had an average "legitimate violence" score of .31 (a standardized average of the indicators above), whereas the more organized ones had an average score of −. 39. In contrast, southern and western disorganized states had an average score of .10, and southern and western organized states had an average score of .20 (interaction $p < .03$) (Cohen, 1997a).

There is also evidence that the above patterns hold on an individual level. General Social Survey (GSS) respondents who came from more traditional, nuclear-family households in the North tended to be relatively less endorsing of violence. In the South and West, they tended to be relatively more endorsing of it (Cohen, 1997a).

Additionally, GSS respondents from the North who were closer to their families (that is, visited or talked to members of their family more often) were less approving of violence than their more distant counterparts (mean for respondents close to the family = .43; mean for respondents distant from the family = .44). For respondents from the South and West, however, those who were closer to their families were *more* approving of violence than those who were more distant (mean for close respondents = .47, mean for distant respondents = .44; interaction $p < .04$). Importantly, these patterns of results were true only for gun ownership data and for attitudes about *honor*-related violence (that is, violence in response to an affront or threat to protection). Results did not hold for violence that was not related to personal honor (Cohen, 1997a). The pattern once again suggests the importance of looking at culture—and how tight social organization can actually feed certain forms of violence—when examining the honor and violence connection.

Interpersonal Behavior in a Culture of Honor:
The Paradox of Politeness

Concerns about honor guide many aspects of interpersonal behavior in cultures such as the one described above. If one has been shamed, some redress must be given. And in many (but not all) such cultures, it is thus extremely important not to offend another's honor in the first place. Since one cannot back down from a conflict without losing face, the safest course is to avoid conflict before it starts. Indeed, in many societies with very high rates of violence, there is a considerable emphasis on congeniality, politeness, and "good company" (Knauft, 1985).[2] As the anthropologist Elizabeth Colson has noted, "it should . . . be no surprise to us if some people live in what appears to be a Rousseauian paradise because they take a Hobbesian view of their situation: they walk softly because they believe it necessary not to offend others whom they regard as dangerous" (1975, p. 37).

Strong codes for etiquette and politeness develop and regulate social behavior in these cultures. The practice of dueling was sometimes defended on the grounds that it encouraged such civility. As the historian McWhiney has written about the Old South,

> Southerners and other Celts believed that (dueling) also promoted courtesy and the careful weighing of words before speaking. . . . "When a man knows that he is to be held accountable for his want of courtesy, he is not so apt to indulge in abuse. In this way, dueling produces a greater courtesy in society and a higher refinement." (Kibler, 1946, cited in McWhiney, 1988, p. 170)

In the present day, similar reasoning is still advanced. Jeffrey Snyder, a writer and activist for a more armed populace, notes

> Robert Heinlein's famous dictum that "An armed society is a polite society." Knowing that one's fellow citizens are armed, greater care is naturally taken not to give offense. The proposition is, of course, difficult to prove, but you can find some support for it in English literature. Observe the polite formality with which strangers address each other in inns in, for example, Fielding's *Tom Jones* or (with comedic exaggeration) in Dickens's *Pickwick Papers*. (Cited in Will, 1993, p. 93; see also Snyder, 1993)

"Or as is famously said in American literature, by the hero of Owen Wister's *The Virginian*, 'When you call me that, smile!' Such was politeness in the armed society of nineteenth-century Wyoming" (Will, 1993, p. 93).

And this may help explain one of the South's essential contradictions. The South is widely known for its hospitality and chivalry. Even in our lab experiments, southerners who have not been insulted are the most polite and deferential group when playing the "chicken" game or meeting a stranger (Cohen, Nisbett et al., 1996; Nisbett & Cohen, 1996). However, all this politeness masks an explosive potential for aggression. Thus, while the South leads the rest of the nation in homicide, "the southerner is proverbially gentle in manner. It has been said that until he is angered enough to kill you, he will treat you politely" (Carter, 1963, p. 59; see also De Lisser, 1996; Nethaway, 1996; Reed, 1986; C. Wilson, 1989, for ethnographic evidence about southern politeness).

The problem, in terms of a cultural maintenance perspective, is that all this politeness may come at a cost. Most people will agree that—all other things being equal—it is better to have a more polite society than a less polite society. However, the problem is that this emphasis on politeness and suppression of confrontation may deprive southerners of the behavioral repertoire needed to regulate conflict before it spirals out of control.

As the economist Thomas Schelling (1963) has pointed out, many conflicts amount to coordination games. If two opposing parties are ever to arrive at a solution, they must be able to signal to each other where they are willing to compromise. To avoid a full-blown conflict, A and B must come to an understanding of what will be tolerated and what exceeds the bounds of toleration and constitutes an act of aggression. Such resolution can be arrived at through an understanding of what the "natural" boundaries are and through communication (subtle or overt) about where the "line in the sand" lies. The problem is that when disputants cannot communicate, there is likely to be misunderstanding, and, after a period of relative calm, a full-blown destructive conflict is likely to erupt.

Such conditions are present in cultures of honor that strongly encourage politeness and suppression of anger. To spell the logic out, because anger means violence in many cultures of honor, it becomes a very dangerous thing to express. In expressing anger, one might be inviting violence, because the shared expectation is that anger is a prelude to battle. Thus, it becomes reasonable to hide one's anger and one's aggressive intentions until one is actually ready to enter into a full-blown conflict. For this reason, expressions of anger are driven underground, and disputants may be unable to provide warnings or checks on behavior to keep the other party from treading over the line—*until it is too late*. In many cultures, there are very rich methods of checking another person's behavior and regulating a conflict before it erupts—overt declarations of anger, biting humor, veiled threats, calculated bluffs, and so on (see, for example, Downe, 1996; Lewis, 1989; Schelling, 1963). But in the southern culture of honor, because anger is so dangerous and one must keep up a facade of politeness, these tools for controlling conflict may be unavailable to people.

Our own research suggests this may be true. In one laboratory experiment, we had a confederate of ours provoke a subject with a series of mild annoyances. The provocations were not intensely personal but were meant to irritate the subject. In this experiment, subjects were supposedly participating in a simulated "art therapy" session in which they were to draw pictures of childhood memories. As they did so, the confederate would repeatedly hit the subject with paper wads as he attempted to throw his paper in the trash, or he would call the subject "Slick," or he would write on the subject's drawings, or he would make annoying comments about the subject's artwork.

In response to this irritating confederate, northern subjects tended to be more confrontational and express their anger to the confederate immediately, eventually leveling off in their expressions of anger when they realized that these expressions were doing no good. Southern subjects, on the other hand, showed little affect during the first part of the experiment. But, of course, the annoyances kept coming, and at some crucial point, the southerners let go—becoming far more angry and confrontational toward the confederate than northern subjects ever were and showing much greater volatility in the hostile emotions they expressed. Whereas northerners tended to show their anger right away, southerners tended to hold it in at the beginning, only to end the experiment by becoming much more threatening to our confederate. Initial politeness and final explosion seem to be part of the etiquette prescribed by the southern culture of honor (Cohen, Vandello et al., 1997).

Some correlational evidence suggests it also works this way outside the lab. We obtained data from Levine and colleagues (1993, 1994), who examined how helpful or friendly various cities were. Levine's measures included data about United Way contributions per capita, percentage of "lost letters" returned, and the amount of help bystanders offered as confederates dropped pens, asked for change, or otherwise enlisted the aid of passersby. Not surprisingly, the South was the most helpful and friendly region of the United States (Levine, Martinez, Brase, & Sorensen, 1994). But perhaps more interesting than this main effect was what politeness was associated with in southern as opposed to nonsouthern parts of the country. Consistent with what one would expect, the more helpful cities in the non-south were, the less violence occurred there. However, in the South, the more friendly cities were, the *more* argument and brawl-related violence there tended to be. Thus, in the South, unlike the North, the most polite cities were also the ones with the most honor-related violence. Again, politeness, congeniality, and the underlying threat of force seem to work together in guiding people's everyday social interactions in the South (Cohen, Vandello et al., 1997; see also Nethaway, 1996).

The Social and Personal Nature of Honor—When the Outside Becomes the Inside

Honor and dignity

It should not be surprising that manners are so important in the southern culture of honor, because manners are how people indicate the amount of respect another deserves. And here again, the social nature of honor is evident. "To possess honor requires acknowledgment from others; it cannot exist in solitary conscience" (Gorn, 1985, p. 39). Accordingly, historians and sociologists have drawn a contrast between the culture of *honor* in the South and the culture of *dignity* in the North. Dignity carried "the conviction that each individual at birth possessed an intrinsic value at least theoretically equal to that of every other person" (Ayers, 1984, p. 19). Thus:

> In a culture of dignity, people were expected to remain deaf to the same insults that southern men were expected to resent. "Call a man a liar in Mississippi," an old saying went, "and he will knock you down; in Kentucky, he will shoot you; in Indiana, he will say, 'You are another.' " Dignity might be likened to an internal skeleton, to a hard structure at the center of the self; honor, on the other hand, resembles a cumbersome and vulnerable suit of armor that, once pierced, leaves the self no protection and no alternative except to strike back in desperation. Honor in the southern United States cannot be understood without reference to dignity, its antithesis and adversary in the North. (Ayers, 1984, p. 20)

This distinction between external esteem and internal self-respect is undoubtedly important. But it also misses something of crucial importance—especially when one considers questions of cultural maintenance. That is, human beings are fundamentally social, and we internalize the values of our culture. Our external suits of armor occasionally become our internal skeletons, as we construct ourselves according to our social roles and know ourselves as others know us. Thus, it should not be surprising that southerners internalize the norms of honor to the extent that their own self-respect depends at least in part on their willingness to answer an insult. Accordingly, in the lab experiments reported earlier, it is important to note that insulted southerners become more aggressive, show increases in their cortisol, and elevate their testosterone levels—even when no one else is around to see them get insulted (Cohen, Nisbett et al., 1996). The code of honor may get internalized as part of the self, and perhaps this is another reason why it is such a hearty and persistent force, both within people and over generations.

Honor and Hierarchy

Something else must be said about the social nature of honor, however. Competition is always most intense between equals or near equals (see Daly & Wilson, 1988; Pitt-Rivers, 1968). And in the southern culture of honor—as in cultures of honor generally—there were groups of people who were defined as inferior, especially those who were not white males; and even among white males, there was hierarchy according to factors such as social class.

Generally, in cultures of honor, deference must be paid to a person higher on the social ladder. Not receiving this deference may cause the superior to react with violence. However, the superior's honor is not technically at stake, because one's honor is "impregnable from below" (Pitt-Rivers, 1968, p. 508). Thus, "the honor of a man could not be impugned by someone who was not a social equal. . . . The impudence or the infidelity of an inferior could be punished, but honor was not attained by reacting to the action of an inferior" (Pitt-Rivers, 1968, p. 508). Indeed, in some cases, a superior might even show magnanimity by ignoring an affront from someone "lower" than himself (Pitt-Rivers, 1968, p. 509).

These rules seemed to hold in the Old South, particularly among elites. Regarding dueling, for example, "it was not considered proper for a true gentleman to accept a challenge from a social inferior" (Finkelman, 1989, p. 1503).

> In the eyes of the gentry, poor whites as well as blacks were outside the circle of honor, so both groups were subordinate. Thus, a herdsman's insult failed to shame a planter since the two men were not on the same social level. Without a threat to the gentleman's honor, there was no need for a duel. (Gorn, 1985, p. 41)

This did not mean that there would be no punishment, however. In reacting to those lower on the social ladder, it just might mean that "horsewhipping the insolent fellow sufficed" (Gorn, 1985, p. 41; see also C. Wilson, 1989).

Considerations of class, caste, and status bring us to one of today's extremely important concerns. That is, they bring us to consideration of a group that has been habitually cut off and excluded from participation in the mainstream of a culture; that has been denied status and the economic opportunities to attain it; and that has been virtually abandoned by a larger society that oppressed the group, then turned its back on it and looked away from the results. It brings us to consideration of the inner cities, which, cut off from the larger society, have developed their own cultures of honor.

Honor and American Inner Cities

As noted, cultures of honor characterize many societies the world over (Fiske et al., 1997; Gilmore, 1990). This is not just true in the unindustrialized regions of the world or regions like the U.S. South and West that are now industrialized but have a culture-of-honor legacy. The culture of honor is a living adaptation that has been reinvented today in many very modern communities. For the industrialized Western countries, perhaps the most salient example of this is our inner cities (see, for example, Phillips, 1996). Again, in the United States, honor and status are quite important for residents of the inner city, where—in the words of a famous rap song—"911 is a joke," and people have to rely on themselves for protection.[3]

People who talk about violence often propose this experiment: Call for a pizza. Call for an ambulance. Call for the police. See which gets there first. In environments where the pizza beats the police, the culture of honor may be a very rational adaptation. In terms of individuals having to rely on themselves for protection and to bring about justice, the frontiers of the eighteenth and nineteenth centuries may have been the rural areas of the South and West, but the frontier of today may be in pockets of our inner cities (see also Courtwright, 1996).

As sociologist Elijah Anderson has written, "the code of the streets is actually a cultural adaptation to a profound lack of faith in the police and the judicial system . . . the street code emerges where the influence of the police ends and personal responsibility for one's safety is felt to begin" (1994, p. 82).

> At the heart of the code is the issue of respect—loosely defined as being treated "right" or granted the deference one deserves. . . . In the street culture, especially among young people, respect is viewed as almost an external entity that is hard-won but easily lost, and so must constantly be guarded. The rules of the code in fact provide a framework for negotiating respect. The person whose very appearance—including his clothing, demeanor, and way of moving—deters transgressions feels that he possesses, and may be considered by others to possess, a measure of respect. With the right amount of respect, for instance, he can avoid "being bothered" in public. If he is bothered, not only may he be in physical danger but he has been disgraced or "dissed" (disrespected). Many of the forms that dissing can take might seem petty to middle-class people (maintaining eye contact for too long, for example), but to those invested in the street code, these actions become serious indications of the other person's intentions. Consequently, such people become very sensitive to advances and slights, which could well serve as warnings of imminent physical confrontation. (Anderson, 1994, p. 82)

Even those who do not subscribe to the "street code" are forced to play by its rules when they are in the public arena.

The operating assumption is that a man, especially a real man, knows what other men know—the code of the streets. . . . Implicit in this is that everybody is held responsible for being familiar with the code. . . . So when a person ventures outside, he must adopt the code—a kind of shield, really—to prevent others from "messing with" him. In these circumstances, it is easy for people to think they are being tried or tested by others even when this is not the case. For it is sensed that something extremely valuable is at stake in every interaction, and people are encouraged to rise to the occasion, particularly with strangers. (Anderson, 1994, pp. 89–92)

Thus, the culture of honor has been reinvented in our urban communities; and here again one sees the importance of a cultural-level analysis that considers how collective, shared expectations contribute to violence, perpetuate these norms, and force everyone to play by the culture of honor's rules.

In Defense of Honor

Honor's Inspiration

In general, cultures of honor get well-deserved attention because they are often associated with epidemics of violence. But as we have seen, such cultures tend to have a profound, pervasive impact on many aspects of interpersonal relations. And while such cultures may give rise to violence, they may also emphasize a sense of "manliness" that inspires men. The results of this "manly" inspiration are often desirable.

It is not a coincidence that more than a few proposals for revitalizing our inner cities revolve around the idea of using honor, respect, discipline, and the masculine ideal to inspire men to work and be productive. These ideals are most explicit in proposals to instill "masculine" virtues of discipline and chivalry through institutions such as all-male academies, the military, boot-camp type training programs, and even religious schooling. But these ideals also subtly underlie proposals to revitalize our inner cities through job creation, which—aside from its economic benefits—is often viewed as a way of providing men legitimate avenues for gaining respect through self-reliance and through being the breadwinners of their families (Anderson, 1994; Klein, 1996; W. Wilson, 1987, 1996).

There is no question then that manly honor can be a very useful resource in inspiring prosocial behavior. The question, though, is what type of honor and what avenues for achieving it we should have. This is where the hypermasculine culture of honor that emphasizes physical toughness, bravado, and macho might look like it is doing more harm than good.

However, even this issue is not so simple. Or, at least, it is not so simple for many societies across the world. Strutting machismo may look like an anachronism for some people in our modern world, where technical knowledge and smooth social skills are more advantageous than physical courage or prowess. But for people in many cultures, the living is not so "easy." Neighboring tribes threaten. They steal a tribe's resources and kidnap their women (Chagnon, 1966, 1968, 1974, 1992; Gilmore, 1990; see also Patton, 1996). They conduct raids and kill. And providing for one's family is also not an easy undertaking. For example, big-game hunting and deep-sea fishing can be very dangerous tasks (Gilmore, 1990). As the anthropologist David Gilmore (1990) points out in his book *Manhood in the Making*, cults of manhood tend to be found in places where the living is hard. He writes: "The harsher the environment and the scarcer the resources, the more manhood is stressed as inspiration and goal. This correlation could not be more clear, concrete, or compelling" (Gilmore, 1990, p. 224). In such places, the 3 P's of manhood are stressed: protecting, providing (for family and community), and procreating. All are necessary for the perpetuation of a culture that is threatened by both nature and human forces.

The concepts of honor, shame, and manhood become entwined and are what inspire men in such societies to do what is risky and courageous, as well as that which just appears belligerent and violent:

> To be men, most of all, they must accept the fact that they are expendable. This acceptance of expendability constitutes the basis of the manly pose everywhere it is encountered; yet simple acquiescence will not do. To be socially meaningful, the decision for manhood must be characterized by enthusiasm combined with stoic resolve or perhaps "grace." It must show a public demonstration of positive choice, of jubilation even in pain, for it represents a moral commitment to defend the society and its core values against all odds. (Gilmore, 1990, pp. 223–224)

It is doubtful that individuals consciously understand such principles as they apply to their own lives (Cohen, 1997b; Cohen & Vandello, 1997a). But that is where manhood, honor, and shame come in. This positive choice is something that a man "just does." Honor is the reward that societies give to those who have made this positive choice. Shame is the punishment it offers to those who do not make it.

In essence, honor is a man's claim on the world. It is what he demands and receives for doing what society deems is worthy of respect. As Pitt-Rivers notes, "honor is not only the internalization of the values of society in the individual but the externalization of his self-image in the world" (1968, p. 504).

In many societies, honor becomes the ultimate explanation for a man's actions. David Mandelbaum writes about the Arabic and Persian word for honor (*izzat*):

> It is a word often heard in men's talk, particularly when the talk is about conflict, rivalry, and struggle. It crops up as a kind of final explanation for motivation, whether for acts of aggression or beneficence. (1988, p. 20)

Honor and shame are fundamentally social and cannot occur in a vacuum. Honor "claimed" means little if it does not become honor "paid" (Gorn, 1985; Pitt-Rivers, 1968; see also Dostoyevsky, 1862/1966; Sandel, 1996). That is what all the manly posturing, all the violence, and all the fighting are about. Far from being the product of a world where social pressures are not felt intensely, violence in cultures of honor results from social pressures felt too intensely.

Honor and the U.S. South

Given what has just been said about the usefulness of honor as a prosocial force, readers may wonder why we have focused our research on the U. S. South, a region where the culture of honor might appear outdated. One reason was obviously convenience. But there is another reason that runs deeper. By studying a region where the concept of manly, macho honor no longer seems useful to survival in economic or material ways, we can see more clearly how it is a social and cultural construct. We can see that such a culture persists long after it may be an economically functional adaptation, and we can examine the social mechanisms that carry the culture and continue to perpetuate it. The U. S. South represents one example of a culture that continues to uphold such a tradition past the point where it seems to be a purely ecological or material adaptation.

But there is another point to consider. Whether the southern culture of honor is indeed "outdated" is an open question. If, as we have contended, southern aggression and southern politeness go hand in hand, then it may be perfectly reasonable for people to want to preserve the culture of honor. That is, it might be perfectly reasonable for people to trade off a slightly elevated risk of violence for the sake of more civility and friendliness in everyday life. And, in addition, possession of a sense of honor may be a "good" in itself that, for many people, justifies facing a slightly higher risk of violence. Honor is a virtue, ideal, and psychic reward for southerners in the same way "dignity" is for northerners (see Ayers, 1984). Whether this is a reasonable stance is obviously a political or philosophical matter open to debate. But at the very least, one must admit it is not an open-and-shut case (see also Cohen & Vandello, 1997b).

In general, there are many ways human societies solve the problems of order, survival, and living "the good life" (Coleman, 1990; Colson, 1975; Huntington, 1993, 1996; Schneider, 1971; Shweder, 1993; Will, 1983). And whether having honor as an "organizing principle" (Fiske et al., 1997) is, on the whole, beneficial or costly is a deeply philosophical and probably unanswerable question. However, it is clear that acts of both profound heroism and generosity, as well as nasty, vicious violence over "trivial" things, are inspired by the principles of honor and shame. Perhaps it is safest to say that one cannot understand these acts and the behavioral rituals that surround them until one understands the cultures and social meaning systems that these principles and behaviors spring from.

Acknowledgments   Work on this chapter was supported in part by grants from the Russell Sage Foundation and the University of Illinois Research Board.

Notes

1. It is worth noting that we can rule out many other factors as confounds, because the northerners and southerners from our experiments were strikingly similar on many dimensions, including: family income, father's or mother's occupations, father's or mother's level of education, father's or mother's level of military service, marital status of parents now and as participants were growing up, number of brothers, number of sisters, college entrance exam scores, high school grade point average, whether subjects were now or had even been in a fraternity, religious preference, and church attendance (Cohen, Nisbett, et al., 1996; see also Cohen, Vandello, Puente, & Rantilla, 1997). Similarly, regarding the survey data and homicide rate data, we can rule out many confounds regarding education, income, and other demographic variables, because results

hold both when these variables are and are not controlled for (Cohen & Nisbett, 1994; Nisbett & Cohen, 1996).

2. Interestingly, there seem to be multiple solutions to the problem of how one should behave in a culture of honor. One strategy is the one discussed here: that is, be polite, deferential, and avoid conflict. But there are also other possible strategies, one of them being to strut, brag, seek out conflict, or try to be the meanest, fiercest person around. And there are many cultures of honor where people also adopt some version of this strategy (Anderson, 1994; Campbell, 1965; Daly & Wilson, 1988; Gorn, 1985). Thus, there may be multiple equilibria (for example, excessive politeness or excessive belligerence) that are possible for a given society. The reasons for one solution or another emerging are matters for future speculation and examination. For more discussion of the politeness issue, see Cohen, Vandello et al. (1997) or Cohen & Vandello (1997b); and for more discussion of multiple equilibria, see Schelling (1978) or Kuran (1995).

3. 911 is the emergency number for police in the United States.

References

Anderson, E. (1994, May). The code of the streets. *Atlantic Monthly, 5*, 81–94.

Ayers, E. L. (1984). *Vengeance and justice*. New York: Oxford University Press.

Baron, L., & Straus, M. A. (1988). Cultural and economic sources of homicide in the United States. *Sociological Quarterly, 29*, 371–392.

Baron, L., & Straus, M. A. (1989). *Four theories of rape in American society: A state-level analysis*. New Haven, CT: Yale University Press.

Brearley, H. C. (1934). The pattern of violence. In W. T. Couch (Ed.), *Culture in the South* (pp. 678–692). Chapel Hill, NC: University of North Carolina Press.

Campbell, J. K. (1965). Honour and the devil. In J. G. Peristiany (Ed.), *Honour and shame: The values of Mediterranean society* (pp. 112–175). London: Weidenfeld & Nicolson.

Carter, H. (1963). *First person rural*. Garden City, NY: Doubleday.

Chadwick, N. (1970). *The Celts*. Harmondsworth, UK: Penguin Books.

Chagnon, N. A. (1966). *Yanomamo warfare, social organization, and marriage alliances*. Unpublished doctoral dissertation, University of Michigan, Ann Arbor.

Chagnon, N. A. (1968). *Yanomamo, the fierce people*. New York: Holt, Rinehart & Winston.

Chagnon, N. A. (1974). *Studying the Yanomamo*. New York: Holt, Rinehart & Winston.

Chagnon, N. A. (1992). *Yanomamo: The last days of Eden*. San Diego, CA: Harcourt Brace Jovanovich.

Cohen, D. (1996). Law, social policy, and violence: The impact of regional cultures. *Journal of Personality and Social Psychology, 70*, 961–978.

Cohen, D. (1997a). *Anomie and the culture of honor: When more social organization leads to more violence*. Unpublished manuscript, University of Illinois, Urbana.

Cohen, D. (1997b). Ifs and thens in cultural psychology. In R. S. Wyer, Jr. (Ed.), *Advances in social cognition*. Mahwah, NJ: Erlbaum.

Cohen, D., & Nisbett, R. E. (1994). Self-protection and the culture of honor: Explaining southern violence. *Personality and Social Psychology Bulletin, 20*, 551–567.

Cohen, D., & Nisbett, R. E. (1997). Field experiments examining the culture of honor: The role of institutions in perpetuating norms about violence. *Personality and Social Psychology Bulletin, 23*, 1188–1199.

Cohen, D., Nisbett, R. E., Bowdle, B. F., & Schwarz, N. (1996). Insult, aggression, and the southern culture of honor: An "experimental ethnography." *Journal of Personality and Social Psychology, 70*, 945–960.

Cohen, D., & Vandello, J. (1997a). *Enforcement of the norms of a culture of honor*. Unpublished manuscript, University of Illinois, Urbana.

Cohen, D., & Vandello, J. (1997b). *The paradox of politeness.* Unpublished manuscript, University of Illinois, Urbana.

Cohen, D., & Vandello, J. (in press). Meanings of violence. *Journal of Legal Studies.*

Cohen, D., Vandello, J., Puente, S., & Rantilla, A. (1996). "When you call me that, smile!": How norms for politeness and aggression interact in the southern culture of honor. Unpublished manuscript, University of Illinois, Urbana.

Coleman, J. S. (1990). *Foundations of social theory.* Cambridge, MA: Harvard University Press.

Colson, E. (1975). *Tradition and contract: The problem of order.* Chicago: Aldine.

Conrad, J. (1954). An outpost of progress. In R. P. Warren & A. Erskine (Eds.), *Short story masterpieces* (pp. 88–114). New York: Dell.

Courtwright, D. T. (1996). *Violent land: Single men and social disorder from the frontier to the inner city.* Cambridge, MA: Harvard University Press.

Daly, M., & Wilson, M. (1988). *Homicide.* Hawthorne, NY: Aldine De Gruyter.

De Lisser, E. (1996, October 29). Culture clash: Northern charm and southern efficiency. *The Wall Street Journal,* pp. A1, A14.

Dostoyevsky, F. (1966). A nasty story. In F. Dostoyevsky, *The gambler/Bobok/A nasty story* (pp. 185–238). Baltimore: Penguin. (Original work published 1862)

Downe, P. J. (1996, November). *Laughing because it hurts: Costa Rican women's use of humor in violent context.* Paper presented at the American Anthropological Association annual meeting, San Francisco.

Edgerton, R. (1971). *The individual in cultural adaptation.* Berkeley, CA: University of California Press.

Ellison, C. G. (1991). An eye for an eye? A note on the southern subculture of violence thesis. *Social Forces, 69,* 1223–1239.

Ellison, C. G., & Sherkat, D. E. (1993). Conservative protestantism and support for corporal punishment. *American Sociological Review, 58,* 131–144.

Elshtain, J. B. (1996a, October 21). The lost children. *The New Republic,* 30–36.

Elshtain, J. B. (1996b, November 4). Lost city. *The New Republic,* 25.

Finkelman, P. (1989). Dueling. In C. R. Wilson & W. Ferris (Eds.), *Encyclopedia of southern culture* (pp. 1503–1504). Chapel Hill, NC: University of North Carolina Press.

Fischer, D. H. (1989). *Albion's seed: Four British folkways in America.* New York: Oxford University Press.

Fiske, A. P., Markus, H., Kitayama, S., & Nisbett, R. E. (1997). *The cultural matrix of social psychology.* Unpublished manuscript, University of Michigan, Ann Arbor.

Frantz, J. B. (1969). The frontier tradition: An invitation to violence. In H. D. Graham & T. R. Gurr (Eds.), *The history of violence in America* (pp. 127–154). New York: Bantam Books.

Freud, S. (1961). *Civilization and its discontents.* New York: Norton. (Original work published 1930).

Gastil, R. D. (1971). Homicide and a regional culture of violence. *American Sociological Review, 36,* 412–427.

Gilmore, D. D. (1990). *Manhood in the making: Cultural concepts of masculinity.* New Haven, CT: Yale University Press.

Gorn, E. J. (1985). "Gouge and bite, pull hair and scratch:" The social significance of fighting in the southern backcountry. *American Historical Review, 90,* 18–43.

Herbert, W., & Daniel, D. (1996, June 3). The moral child. *U.S. News and World Report,* 52–59.

Hobbes, T. (1957). *Leviathan* (M. Oakeshott, Ed.). Oxford: Oxford University Press. (Original work published 1651.)

Huntington, S. P. (1993, Summer). The clash of civilizations? *Foreign Affairs, 72,* 22–49.

Huntington, S. P. (1996, November/December). The West: Unique, not universal. *Foreign Affairs, 75,* 28–46.

Jacquemet, M. (1996, November). *Men of honor, men of anger: Affective posturings in*

Italian criminal trials. Paper presented at the American Anthropological Association annual meeting, San Francisco.

Kaminer, W. (1996, October 14). The last taboo. *The New Republic,* 24–32.

Klein, J. (1996, October 28). The true disadvantage. *The New Republic,* 32–36.

Knauft, B. (1985). *Good company and violence: Sorcery in a lowland New Guinea society.* Berkeley, CA: University of California Press.

Kuran, T. (1995). *Private truths, public lies: The social consequences of preference falsification.* Cambridge, MA: Harvard University Press.

LaFave, W. R., & Scott, A. W. (1986). *Substantive criminal law.* St. Paul, MN: West.

Lee, R. S. (1996). The ecology of violence in the United States. *International Journal of Group Tensions, 26,* 3–19.

Levine, R. V. (1993, October). Cities with heart. *American Demographics,* 46–54.

Levine, R. V., Martinez, T. S., Brase, G., & Sorensen, K. (1994). Helping in 36 U.S. cities. *Journal of Personality and Social Psychology, 67,* 69–82.

Lewis, M. (1989). *Liar's poker.* New York: Norton.

Mandelbaum, D. G. (1988). *Women's seclusion and men's honor: Sex roles in North India.* Tucson, AZ: University of Arizona Press.

McWhiney, G. (1988). *Cracker culture: Celtic ways in the Old South.* Tuscaloosa: University of Alabama Press.

Miller, P., & Sperry, L. L. (1987). The socialization of anger and aggression. *Merrill-Palmer Quarterly, 33,* 1–31.

Mischke, P. E. (1981). Criminal law-homicide-self-defense-duty to retreat. *Tennessee Law Review, 48,* 1000–1023.

Nethaway, R. (1996, July 28). Southern white men on honor. *The Orlando Sentinel,* p. G5.

Nisbett, R. E., & Cohen, D. (1996). *Culture of honor: The psychology of violence in the South.* Boulder, CO: Westview.

Patton, J. Q. (1996, November). *Thoughtful warriors: The sociobiology of status and alliance in a small-scale Amazonian society.* Paper presented at the American Anthropological Association annual meeting, San Francisco.

Pfohl, S. (1985). *Images of deviance and social control: A sociological history.* New York: McGraw-Hill.

Phillips, S. A. (1996, November). *Enmity and alliance among Los Angeles Bloods and Crips.* Paper presented at the American Anthropological Association annual meeting, San Francisco.

Pitt-Rivers, J. (1965). Honour and social status. In J. G. Peristiany (Ed.), *Honour and shame: The values of Mediterranean society* (pp. 21–77). London: Weidenfeld & Nicolson.

Pitt-Rivers, J. (1968). Honor. In D. Sills (Ed.), *International encyclopedia of the social sciences* (pp. 503–511). New York: Macmillan.

Reaves, A. L., & Nisbett, R. E. (1997). *The cultural ecology of rural white homicide in the southern United States.* Unpublished manuscript, University of Michigan, Ann Arbor.

Reed, J. S. (1981). Below the Smith and Wesson line: Reflections on southern violence. In M. Black & J. S. Reed (Eds.), *Perspectives on the American South: An annual review of society, politics, and culture* (pp. 9–22). New York: Gordon & Breach.

Reed, J. S. (1986). *Southern folk plain and fancy: Native white social types.* Athens, GA: University of Georgia Press.

Rice, T. W., & Goldman, C. R. (1994). Another look at the subculture of violence thesis: Who murders whom and under what circumstances. *Sociological Spectrum, 14,* 371–384.

Roebuck, J. B., & Murty, K. S. (1996). *The southern subculture of drinking and driving: A generalized deviance model for the southern white male.* New York: Garland.

Sampson, R. J. (1993). Family and community-level influences on crime: A contextual theory and strategies for research testing. In D. Farrington, R. J. Sampson, & P. H.

Wilkstrom, (Eds.), *Integrating individual and ecological aspects of crime* (pp. 152–168). Stockholm, Sweden: National Council for Crime Prevention.

Sandel, M. J. (1996, December 23). Honor and resentment. *The New Republic*, 27.

Schelling, T. C. (1963). *The strategy of conflict.* New York: Oxford University Press.

Schelling, T. C. (1978). *Micromotives and macrobehavior.* New York: Norton.

Schneider, J. (1971). Of vigilance and virgins: Honor, shame and access to resources in Mediterranean societies. *Ethnology, 10*, 1–24.

Shweder, R. (1993, Winter). "Why do men barbeque?" and other postmodern ironies of growing up in the decade of ethnicity. *Daedalus, 122*, 279–308.

Snyder, J. R. (1993). A nation of cowards. *Public Interest, 113*, 40–55.

Sunstein, C. R. (1995, December 25). True lies. *The New Republic*, 37–41.

Taylor, L. J. (1986). Provoked reason in men and women: Heat-of-passion manslaughter and imperfect self-defense. *UCLA Law Review, 33*, 1679–1735.

Triandis, H. C. (1996). The psychological measurement of cultural syndromes. *American Psychologist, 51*, 407–415.

Will, G. F. (1983). *Statecraft as soulcraft: What government does.* New York: Simon & Schuster.

Will, G. F. (1993, November 15). Are we "a nation of cowards"? *Newsweek*, 93–94.

Wilson, C. R. (1989). Manners. In C. R. Wilson & W. Ferris (Eds.), *Encyclopedia of southern culture* (pp. 634–637). Chapel Hill, NC: University of North Carolina Press.

Wilson, W. J. (1987). *The truly disadvantaged.* Chicago: University of Chicago Press.

Wilson, W. J. (1996). *When work disappears: The world of the new urban poor.* New York: Knopf.

Wrong, D. (1961). The oversocialized conception of man in modern sociology. *American Sociological Review, 26*, 183–193.

Wyatt-Brown, B. (1982). *Southern honor: Ethics and behavior in the Old South.* New York: Oxford University Press.

Index

Printed in the United States
135353LV00005B/143/A

9 780195 114805

14339064R00163

Made in the USA
Lexington, KY
22 March 2012